THE LAW OF ELECTRONIC COMMERCE AND THE INTERNET IN THE UK AND IRELAND

THE LAW OF ELECTRONIC COMMERCE AND THE INTERNET IN THE UK AND IRELAND

Steve Hedley, MA, LLB, BSc
Professor of Law
University College Cork

Cavendish
Publishing
Limited

Sydney • London

First edition published in 2006 by
Cavendish Publishing Limited, The Glass House,
Wharton Street, London WC1X 9PX, United Kingdom
Email: info@cavendishpublishing.com
Website: www.cavendishpublishing.com

Published in the United States by Cavendish Publishing
c/o International Specialized Book Services,
5824 NE Hassalo Street, Portland,
Oregon 97213-3644, USA

Published in Australia by Cavendish Publishing (Australia) Pty Ltd
45 Beach Street, Coogee, NSW 2034, Australia

© 2006 Steve Hedley, MA, LLB, BSc

British Library Cataloguing in Publication Data
Hedley, Steve
The law of electronic commerce in the UK and Ireland
1. Electronic commerce – Law and legislation – Great Britain
2. Electronic commerce – Law and legislation – Ireland
I. Title
343.4'109944

Library of Congress Cataloguing in Publication Data
Data available

ISBN 10: 1-85941-973-9
ISBN 13: 978-1-85941-973-1

1 3 5 7 9 10 8 6 4 2

Printed and bound in Great Britain

CONTENTS LIST

TABLE OF CASES

TABLE OF PRIMARY LEGISLATION

Ireland

United Kingdom

United States of America

TABLE OF SECONDARY LEGISLATION

TABLE OF JOURNALS REFERRED TO

Col JL & Soc Prob	Columbia Journal of Law and Social Problems
Col LR	Columbia Law Review
COLR	Cork Online Law Review (http://colr.ucc.ie)
Comm LP	Commercial Law Practitioner
Comms L	Communications Law
Comp Week	Computer Weekly (http://www.computerweekly.com)
Con LR	Construction Law Reports
Conv (NS)	Conveyancer
Corn ILJ	Cornell International Law Journal
Corn LR	Cornell Law Review
Crim LR	Criminal Law Review
CSTLR	Columbia Science and Technology Law Review (http://www.stlr.org/)
CTLR	Communications Technology Law Review
Currents	Currents: International Trade Law Journal
CW	Copyright World
CWLR	California Western Law Review
CWRJIL	Case Western Reserve Journal of International Law
CWRULR	Case Western Reserve University Law Review
Dayt LR	Dayton Law Review
DDRM	Due Diligence and Risk Management
DLTR	Duke Law and Technology Review (http://www.law.duke.edu/journals/dltr/)
Duke LJ	Duke Law Journal
E-Law	E-Law (http://www.murdoch.edu.au/elaw/)
E-Week	E-Week (http://www.eweek.com)
EBL	Electronic Business Law
ECLR	E-Commerce Law Reports
ECT	E-Commerce Times (http://www.ecommercetimes.com)
Edin LR	Edinburgh Law Review
EIPR	European Intellectual Property Review
EJ	Economic Journal
ELR	European Law Review
Emory ILJ	Emory International Law Review
Emory LJ	Emory Law Journal
Ent LR	Entertainment Law Review
FCLJ	Federal Communications Law Journal (http://law.indiana.edu/fclj)

FIPMELJ	Fordham Intellectual Property Media and Entertainment Law Journal
Fla LR	Florida Law Review
German LJ	German Law Journal (http://www.germanlawjournal.com)
GLJ	Georgetown Law Journal
GSULR	Georgia State University Law Review
Harv LR	Harvard Law Review
HCELJ	Hastings Communications and Entertainment Law Journal
heise online	heise online (http://www.heise.de)
HICLR	Hastings International and Comparative Law Review
HJOLT	Harvard Journal of Law and Technology
HLJ	Hibernian Law Journal
Hof LR	Hofstra Law Review
Houston LR	Houston Law Review
HWLJ	Harvard Women's Law Journal
ICLJ	Irish Criminal Law Journal
ICLQ	International and Comparative Law Quarterly
ICTL	Information and Communication Technology Law
IDEA	IDEA (http://www.idea.piercelaw.edu)
IJCLP	International Journal of Communications Law and Policy (http://www.digital-law.net/IJCLP/)
IJECLP	International Journal of Electronic Commerce Law and Practice
IJEP	International Journal of Evidence and Proof
IJLIT	International Journal of Law and Information Technology
ILJ	Industrial Law Journal
ILT	Irish Law Times
Ind LJ	Indiana Law Journal
InfoWorld	InfoWorld (http://www.infoworld.com)
Internet News	Internet News (http://www.internetnews.com)
Iowa LR	Iowa Law Review
IPD	Intellectual Property Decisions
IPQ	Intellectual Property Quarterly
IPTF	Intellectual Property and Technology Forum (http://www.bc.edu/bc_org/avp/law/st_org/iptf/)
IRIPCL	International Review of Industrial Property and Copyright Law
IRLCT	International Review of Law Computers and Technology
ISLR	Irish Student Law Review (http://www.islr.ie/)
ITLT	IT Law Today

JBL	Journal of Business Law
J Contract L	Journal of Contract Law
J Cr L	Journal of Criminal Law
JHTL	Journal of High Technology Law (http://www.jhtl.org)
JIBFL	Journal of International Banking and Financial Law
JIBL	Journal of International Banking Law
JIBLR	Journal of International Banking Law and Regulation
JILT	Journal of Information, Law and Technology (http://www2.warwick.ac.uk/fac/soc/law/elj/jilt/)
JLS	Journal of Law and Society
JMJCIL	John Marshall Journal of Computer and Information Law
JOL	Journal of Online Law (http://www.wm.edu/law/publications/jol/)
JSEBL	Journal of Small and Emerging Business Law
JSIJ	Judicial Studies Institute Journal
JSWFL	Journal of Social Welfare and Family Law
JTLP	Journal of Technology Law and Policy (http://grove.ufl.edu/~techlaw)
JWIL	Journal of World Intellectual Property
L&P	Law and Policy
Law Teach	Law Teacher
LCLR	Lewis and Clark Law Review
LLAELR	Loyola of Los Angeles Entertainment Law Review
LLR	Louisiana Law Review
Lloyd's MCLQ	Lloyd's Maritime and Commercial Law Quarterly
Loy LR	Loyola Law Review
LPP	Legislation and Public Policy
LSGI	Law Society Gazette (Ireland)
LUCLJ	Loyola University Chicago Law Journal
MacNewsWorld	MacNewsWorld (http://www.macnewsworld.com)
Maine LR	Maine Law Review
Md LR	Maryland Law Review
Med LR	Medical Law Review
Mercer LR	Mercer Law Review
Minn LR	Minnesota Law Review
MIPLP	Marquette Intellectual Property Law Review
MJIL	Melbourne Journal of International Law
MLI	Medical Law International

MLSRP	Minnesota Legal Studies Research Papers
Monash ULR	Monash University Law Review
Motley Fool	The Motley Fool (http://www.fool.com)
MTTLR	Michigan Telecommunications and Technology Law Review (http://www.mttlr.org)
MSLR	Michigan State Law Review
NCLR	North Carolina Law Review
NCJOLT	North Carolina Journal of Law and Technology (http://www.jolt.unc.edu)
NDLR	Notre Dame Law Review
News.Com	News.Com (http://news.com.com)
Nexus	Nexus, A Journal of Opinion
NILQ	Northern Ireland Legal Quarterly
NLJ	New Law Journal
Notts LJ	Nottingham Law Journal
NS	New Scientist
Nw ULR	Northwestern University Law Review
NYT	New York Times
NYULR	New York University Law Review
OJ	Official Journal of the European Union
OSLJ	Ohio State Law Journal
OUT-LAW	OUT-LAW (http://www.out-law.com/)
PDP	Privacy and Data Protection
Pepp LR	Pepperdine Law Review
PLC	Practical Law for Companies
PLPR	Privacy Law and Policy Reporter (http://www.austlii.edu.au/au/journals/PLPR)
PPL	Psychiatry Psychology and the Law
Prospect	Prospect
PSILR	Penn State International Law Review
QUT LJJ	QUT Law and Justice Journal (http://www.law.qut.edu.au/about/ljj/editions/)
RCTLJ	Rutgers Computer and Technology Law Journal
Register	The Register (http://www.theregister.co.uk)
RFC	Request For Comments series (http://www.faqs.org/rfcs/)
RJOLT	Richmond Journal of Law and Technology (http://law.richmond.edu/jolt)

RJT	La Revue Juridique Thémis (http://www.themis.umontreal.ca)
RULR	Regent University Law Review
SCCHTLJ	Santa Clara Computer and High Technology Law Journal
Science	Science
SCLR	Santa Clara Law Review
SCRIPT-ed	SCRIPT-ed (http://www.law.ed.ac.uk/ahrb/script-ed)
SHJSL	Seton Hall Journal of Sports Law
SJLR	St John's Law Review
SJLS	Singapore Journal of Legal Studies
SJLTA	Southwestern Journal of Law and Trade in the Americas
SLT	Scots Law Times
So Calif LR	Southern California Law Review
Sol Jo	Solicitors Journal
SSRN	Social Science Research Network (http://ssrn.com)
Stan LR	Stanford Law Review
STLR	Stanford Technology Law Review (http://stlr.stanford.edu)
Suff ULR	Suffolk University Law Review
SULR	Seattle University Law Review
Syr LR	Syracuse Law Review
Syr ULTJ	Syracuse University Law and Technology Journal
TELJ	Technology and Entertainment Law Journal
TELTJ	Temple Environmental Law and Technology Journal
TICLJ	Temple International and Comparative Law Journal
TTLR	Texas Tech Law Review
Tx LR	Texas Law Review
U Chi LF	University of Chicago Legal Forum
U Cinn LR	University of Cincinnati Law Review
UC Davis LR	University of California at Davis Law Review
UCDLR	University College Dublin Law Review
UCLA JLT	UCLA Journal of Law and Technology (http://www.lawtechjournal.com)
ULLR	University of Limerick Law Review
U Penn LR	University of Pennsylvania Law Review
UPJIEL	University of Pennsylvania Journal of International Economic Law
URLR	University of Richmond Law Review
USFLR	University of San Francisco Law Review
UTLR	University of Toledo Law Review

Va JIL	Virginia Journal of International Law
Va LR	Virginia Law Review
Vand JTL	Vanderbilt Journal of Transnational Law
Vand LR	Vanderbilt Law Review
Vill LR	Villanova Law Review
VJOLT	Virginia Journal of Law and Technology (http://www.vjolt.net)
VNUNet	VNUNet (http://www.vnunet.com)
WDPR	World Data Protection Report
Will LR	Willamette Law Review
WILR	World Internet Law Report
Wired	Wired (http://www.wired.com)
WJCLI	Web Journal of Current Legal Issues (http://webjcli.ncl.ac.uk)
WLJ	Washburn Law Journal
WMBRJ	William and Mary Bill of Rights Journal
WMLR	William Mitchell Law Review
WULQ	Washington University Law Quarterly
WVJOLT	West Virginia Journal of Law and Technology (http://www.wvu.edu/~law/wvjolt)
Yale LJ	Yale Law Journal
YJIL	Yale Journal of International Law
YJLT	Yale Journal of Law and Technology
ZDNet	ZDNet (http://www.zdnet.com)
ZDNet UK	ZDNet UK (http://www.zdnet.co.uk)

PREFACE

'Electronic commerce law' and 'Internet law' are very new entities. Text writers have yet to decide whether they are subjects in their own right, or whether they are part of some wider entity called 'computer law'. Nor is anyone very sure how they relate to 'information technology law' or 'the law of telecommunications', each of which has its own identity crisis. The different intellectual commitments of text writers are apparent: some are at pains to emphasise the newness of the area, others are keen to point out that much of it is simply old law in a new context. Jurisdiction is also a flashpoint, with some writers following the traditional approach of describing the law wherever they happen to live, others insisting that the net has made such parochialism obsolete. And no one can say whether new technologies, and the new social phenomena that will accompany them, will simply be more of the same, or will require lawyers to think in even stranger ways.

In this confused state of affairs, in which a huge amount is being written but a sense of the subject's identity has yet to be attained, the most compelling need seems to be to provide a map around the literature. In this book I have been detailed where the law seems to merit it, and opinionated as the spirit took me; and I have, of course, included (in Chapter 1) the standard omphaloscopic investigation of 'whether Internet law is a subject'. Nonetheless, the main aim is to sketch out the issues that have arisen in the voluminous writings in the area, and to point readers in the direction of at least some of the more noteworthy pieces. This has entailed the use of a web-based approach. Some of the references will be found in the traditional library, but the bulk of them are on the web. Rather than tediously reproducing the addresses in the text, these links are available (with footnote text) at stevehedley.com/internet. All sources marked in the notes with '(Web)' are there, and in time more will be.

This book is written from a particular jurisdictional perspective - namely, that of the three main UK jurisdictions (England and Wales, Scotland and Northern Ireland) and the Irish jurisdiction – though, of course, there will be various detours along the way. Such a multi-disciplinary exercise would in most contexts be quixotic, but the harmonising influence of EU has kept it within sensible bounds. A very basic understanding of private law, including the general law of contract and tort, is assumed.

Chapter 1 is a short general introduction to law on the Internet, focusing on sources of law and means of control, and trying to identify the role of national legal systems. It is written to be comprehensible when read first, though conceivably some readers will prefer to delay it; the issues may seem more concrete when some of the law's detail has been glimpsed.

The next four chapters contain foundational material. Chapter 2 describes the general protection of computing systems from wrongful intrusions. Chapter 3 introduces basic concepts in intellectual property law. Chapter 4 introduces privacy law and the law of data protection. And Chapter 5 considers the special role of the state in relation to data, both in its privileged access to data, and its special duties to reveal it ('freedom of information'). Those chapters lay a foundation for understanding the impact of the Internet in legal contexts. It would have been possible to treat the conflict of laws as a foundational topic also; however, it has proved more convenient to deal with it as it arises, in relation to separate topics, throughout the book.

The remaining four chapters aim to complete a rounded picture of rights and duties in the online world, drawing heavily on the principles in the earlier chapters. Chapter 6 considers the main liabilities to which the Internet user is exposed. Chapter 7 considers ownership of domain names, and related aspects of Internet administration. Chapter 8 discusses interactivity between Internet users. And Chapter 9 considers contracts that may be made over the Internet: their formation, their terms and their enforcement.

I took a deliberate decision to keep technical accounts of Internet operations to a minimum. It is assumed that readers have themselves surfed the web. It is not assumed that they understood quite what they were doing, or had any technical understanding for how the data reached their screen and their speakers. Where some sort of technical explanation is necessary to understand the legal issues, it is given in the text. There is also (at the back) a glossary of the more frequently encountered computing technicalities. It is assumed that those who want more than the bare minimum explanation will be able to find it for themselves; as the cliché has it, the best source of information about the net is the net itself. In consequence, reference to the actual technology of the Internet is extremely uneven. Readers will find little mention of it in Chapter 3 (basic intellectual property), where the main lines of the law pre-date the Internet or even electronic computing; they will find a great deal of it in Chapter 7 (domain names and network administration). If I have the balance wrong, or you have any other comments on this book, then e-mail me to say so (s.hedley@ucc.ie).

Thanks are due to many for help in writing this book. My colleagues at UCC have been most helpful throughout; particular thanks are due to Mary Donnelly, Caroline Fennell, Maeve McDonagh, William Murphy, Catherine O'Sullivan, Darius Whelan and Fidelma White. I would also like to thank some in other institutions as well, including Eoin O'Dell and Jonathan Morgan. The good people at Cavendish have been very helpful: particular thanks to Jon Lloyd, Jo Jacomb and Zoë Botterill.

This book states the law as at 1 May 2005, though a little later material is included. It is hoped that the book's web site (at stevehedley.com/internet) will include updating material as it becomes available.

Steve Hedley
January 2006

CHAPTER 1

THE INTERNET AND THE LAW

The Internet is a world-wide public access network of computers. It has no owner, though of course each of the individual pieces of hardware on which it runs has an owner. It relies for its operation on mutual comprehensibility between those various pieces of hardware. This is achieved by voluntary adherence to a single protocol – to use a human metaphor, the various machines all speak the same language.

The communications this allows for, and the laws applicable to them, are the subject of this book. 'Law and communication' would of course be an impossibly broad topic; but the peculiarities attaching to communication via the Internet seem to require distinct consideration. The use of the Internet for buying and selling – e-commerce – is a particular concern throughout.

IS 'INTERNET LAW' A SUBJECT?

There is no single code of laws applying to the Internet alone. Those who seek out the laws which apply to it meet a bewildering mix of the specific, the general and the metaphorical. There are a few (*very* few) specific references to the Internet in legislation and in international treaty. There are other laws which apply to general types of communication – trade communications, or defamatory communications, or pornographic communications – and so have some application to communication over the Internet. And the tendency to think of the Internet as a *place*, as somewhere where people do things with or to other people, invites the question of what other laws apply to this conduct.[1]

While most would now concede that there are many laws applicable to the Internet, not all conclude that 'Internet law' (sometimes called 'cyberlaw') is properly regarded as a legal topic in its own right. On one view it merely applies settled principles from different legal disciplines to certain practical, Internet-related problems; the separate legal areas remain distinct. This argument, which will be met with repeatedly in the literature, comes in two forms, which can be called the 'micro' and 'macro' forms of the argument.

The micro argument

The 'micro' denial that Internet law is a subject considers individual legal issues affecting users of the Internet, and seeks to show that they can be resolved without invoking any special legal principles. So (some argue) questions of whether a contract has been formed over the Internet simply call for the application of the principles of offer and acceptance; questions of who, if anyone, owns files transmitted across the Internet are simply questions of copyright; and so on. So

---

1   Compare Lemley, M, 'Place and cyberspace', (2003) 91 Calif LR 521.

'Internet law' is not a new subject. It is merely old wine in new bottles, and the older bottles had less confusing labels.[2]

How strong these arguments are on individual points of law must depend on more detailed consideration of each point. Much Internet law is indeed straightforward application of copyright, but copyright law has already been substantially modified to provide for the Internet; penn how satisfactory the principles of offer and acceptance are, in Internet contexts or others, is a matter of considerable debate.[3] And even if (which is not beyond question[4]) the basic structure of the criminal law can be applied unchanged to the Internet, issues of enforcement bring in unique considerations.[5] It is also worth pointing out that some of the relevant laws are, if not Internet-specific, at least computer-specific: for example, the laws on interference with computing systems.[6] If the question is whether Internet law is 'new' law or 'old' law, the answer can only be that it is a mixture of old and new.

The real answer to the 'micro' argument has to lie in the scale of the project. Suppose (contrary to the facts) that *every* legal principle which applies to the Internet were 'properly' part of some other legal discipline, a mere application of legal principles which were settled without any consideration of how they applied in this special context. *Even if that were so*, the full range of laws applicable to the Internet can only be understood by someone who treats it as a specialism in its own right. No one can be expert in contract law *and* intellectual property *and* data protection *and* freedom of expression *and* all of the other laws applicable online. There is simply too much law for the problem to be tackled that way. The 'micro' argument ultimately suggests that Internet law is incomprehensible and must remain so; an unnecessarily gloomy conclusion.

The macro argument

The 'macro' objection to 'Internet law' is less concerned with individual issues, though it draws on them to reach a grand conclusion: that there is something profoundly unlegal in using a real-world category like 'the Internet' to categorise and order legal thought. Lawyers do not concern themselves with 'the law of the horse' or 'the law of television' or 'the law of the photocopier'; rather, they apply distinctly legal categories to the real world while retaining law's unique sense of intellectual ordering. Law should not be based around particular technologies, which are essentially mutable, but around more stable legal ideas.[7]

Argument over this second issue tends to rely on deep-seated prejudices about what a 'real' legal discipline looks like, and on where lawyers should look for

---

2 Eg, McKendrick, E, 'Computers and the law – New principles or the same principles in a different context?', SCL lecture 22 September 2004 (Web); Kohl, U, 'Legal reasoning and legal change in the age of the Internet – Why the ground rules are still valid', (1999) 7 IJLIT 123.

3 Compare Savirimuthu, J, 'Code, hybrid models of consent and the Electronic Commerce (EC Directive) Regulations 2002', [2004] 2 JILT (Web).

4 Katyal, N, 'Criminal law in cyberspace', (2001) 149 U Penn LR 1003.

5 Eg, Brenner, S, 'Distributed security: Moving away from reactive law enforcement', (2005) 9 IJCLP 11.

6 Below, Chapter 2.

7 Eg, Easterbrook, F, 'Cyberspace and the law of the horse', [1996] U Chi LF 207; Sommer, J, 'Against cyberlaw', (2000) 15 BTLJ (Web). Compare Lessig, L, 'The law of the horse: What cyberlaw might teach', (1999) 113 Harv LR 501 (Web).

intellectual order in their chaotic territory. But on questions like this, lawyers are divided amongst themselves. So, for example, when we consider contract law, some see a stable and successful theory which has consistently seen off a succession of challenges, whereas others see stagnation resulting from a long refusal to engage with the economy as it actually is. And someone who is already committed to the conceptual integrity of intellectual property law or the law of defamation will resist recognition of new subjects which carve off part of their territory.

It may be wisest simply to note that intellectual growth in legal academic thought may be best served by differences of approach, and leave it at that. Nonetheless, there are important features of the current Internet legal scene that will be missed if the topic is approached largely from the perspective of other, established legal disciplines.

First, some basic understanding of the technology is necessary both for applying the law and for assessing its value. It is certainly unusual for a legal topic to be so heavily reliant on a particular technology, but then the Internet is an unusual technology. The most obvious danger from lawyers' references to technology is that they will be either incomplete or outdated. But this is a danger of which all are well aware – hence the already established tendency of legislation to be cast in 'technologically neutral' terms even when it was inspired by a particular technological development. Certainly it seems less dangerous than trying to state the law with no technological awareness at all.

Secondly, studies of distinct legal topics have a tendency towards nationalism. A student of (say) trade mark law will usually concentrate on a single jurisdiction; references to other jurisdictions and to international materials might be thought to enhance understanding of the local jurisdiction, but only by way of casting light on the main subject. Internet law is necessarily different. While it may be described from the standpoint of a particular jurisdiction, nonetheless we must look wider. So (for example) the law on ownership of .com domain names *is* part of US Federal law, or at least is so thoroughly enmeshed in it as to make no difference.[8] Internet law simply cannot be treated in the same jurisdictional spirit as other areas of law.[9]

DRAMATIS PERSONAE

What sort of people appear in problems related to Internet law? All legal liabilities are between individuals, whether these are actual individuals or pretend individuals representing collectivities or official roles of some sort ('Microsoft Corporation' or 'The Queen'). Various types of individuals will be met with again and again in this context. Ordinary users of the Internet may incur liabilities as a result of their actions. Those who make access available for others may also incur liability, whether access is provided for payment (by an Internet service provider (ISP)), or as an incidental part of a contractual arrangement (employers providing access for employees, or universities for their students) or for nothing (one family member providing for the others). Liabilities may also be incurred by those with permanent presences on the web, such as web sites of various sorts. Last but not least, liabilities may be incurred by those involved in administering computers connected to the

---

8   Below, pp 191 ff.
9   Compare McIntyre-O'Brien, R, 'Is there such a thing as cyberlaw?', (2003) 11 ISLR 118.

Internet, or involved in their management. The complex interactions between these various individuals contribute much of the complexity of the subject.

Missing from this list is any obvious role for the organs of government. While the Internet has its origins in a government-sponsored project, and significant elements of its administration are still inextricably connected to the US Department of Commerce[10], nonetheless there is no very obvious means by which any government can control it. Some aspects of Internet administration are sometimes referred to as 'Internet Governance', but while these are not unimportant, nonetheless they fall very far short of controlling what activities people are allowed to pursue over the Internet, let alone applying the law of any particular nation to those activities. To what extent is the Internet 'governed' or 'policed'? This question has no easy answer, and will be re-posed at various points throughout this book.

THE ANARCHIC INTERNET?

Given the apparent absence of government on the Internet, and equally of many of the problems that governments are supposed to solve, it is natural that the Internet would at first seem as a place without laws and without the need of laws – a sort of anarchist utopia. It seemed an entirely safe place: it was hard to conceive that your health, wealth or liberty would be threatened by anything there. And to those with even a little imagination, it seemed like another country, indeed another *sort* of country – existing in a non-physical realm, and not subject to laws considered necessary in more concrete surroundings. Certainly, earthly nations seemed to have been left far behind; national borders were not apparent on the Internet.

And so the idea grew up that the Internet gave access to a different type of space, 'cyberspace', which the law could not reach and where it was not necessary – and which could safely declare its independence from the rest of the world.[11] To the extent that any regulation was needed, it could be supplied by the community sense of Internet users.[12] 'Netiquette' was the order of the day.[13] The indifference of most law enforcement officials to the Internet was seen as beneficial; the anxiety of a few officials to extend the law's reach to cyberspace was thought politically misguided and technologically ignorant. The failure of early attempts to impose law on the net was taken to indicate that legal control was futile, rather than that states would attempt control until they succeeded.

In retrospect, the idea that the Internet was safe and devoid of anti-social behaviour was always as much a matter of perception as of fact. Hacking of various sorts, perhaps causing significant losses to the systems attacked, has always been a feature of the net. The distribution of pornography and of illegally copied materials became common as soon as the Internet was capable of it. And freedom of expression on the Internet has always gone far beyond the limits of any nation's laws. As the net has become more pervasive, the harm that can be done through it has become much worse: the damage that can be inflicted on remote computer

---

10 See below, p 169.
11 See especially Barlow, J, 'A declaration of the independence of cyberspace', 8 February 1996 (Web); for one reply to it, see Bomse, A, 'The dependence of cyberspace', (2001) 50 Duke LJ 1717.
12 For discussion, see Rowland, R, 'Cyberspace – A contemporary Utopia?', [1998] 3 JILT (Web).
13 'Netiquette guidelines', RFC 1855, October 1995 (Web).

systems has increased. The net can be used as a tool of surveillance and harassment, and it presents ever more opportunities to steal the property or even the identity of others. As these problems are increasingly raised, more governmental attention to the Internet has become apparent, and law enforcement actions become more frequent. The idea that the net does not 'need' ordinary law was always a confused one, but how that confusion is to be resolved is the stuff of early 21st century politics. Many of the controversies considered in this book are, at root, arguments about whether and how the law is to be applied to the Internet.

The apparent anarchy of the Internet has therefore yielded to a much more confused picture.[14] Some laws have indeed been imposed, publicly and harshly, on net users. Yet in other respects it remains hard to control. In some areas the problem of control seems intractable (such as the control of spam and of pornography); in others, the anxiety seems to be that it is all too easy to control (such as through governmental data retention and control of freedom of expression). Pockets where complete freedom from governments survives, such as the homes of more prolific spammers or the 'Principality of Sealand',[15] have a dubious glamour all of their own; and the problem of anonymous usage of the Internet is beginning to achieve prominence.[16] Debate as to the appropriate role for self-regulation continues.[17]

As a matter of history, the creation of the Internet happened to occur in a period where governments world-wide are exercising an increasing level of detailed control over all social activities. It is therefore not surprising that the growth of control over a potentially anarchic technology has been extremely rapid. The Internet's lawless technology has been a red rag to a family of rather large bulls. Whether the bulls' inevitable charge tramples over-much on the liberties of Internet users will be a recurrent theme in this book.

METHODS OF CONTROL

The idea that the Internet *cannot* be controlled is therefore simply wrong. But that does not mean that control is an easy or straightforward matter, still less that there is a single lawgiver who is in a position to tell net users what to do. Methods of control are a matter of intense debate, both as to what is possible and as to what is desirable. What we are witnessing now is doubtless only the start of a lengthy debate. At this stage, two insights appear to be fundamental.

Code is law

The first insight, first elaborated in detail by Lessig, is that the design of computing systems is itself a major source of control. By creating computers or programs which

---

14 Geist, M, 'Cyberlaw 2.0', (2003) 44 BCLR 323 (Web).

15 Principality of Sealand home page (Web); see also HavenCo home page (Web). For discussion, see Geltzer, J, 'The new pirates of the Caribbean: How data havens can provide safe harbors on the Internet beyond governmental reach', (2004) 10 SJLTA 433.

16 Mostyn, M, 'The need for regulating anonymous remailers', (2000) 14 IRLCT 79; du Pont, G, 'The criminalization of true anonymity in cyberspace', (2001) 7 MTTLR 191 (Web).

17 Eg, Johnson, D, Crawford, S, and Palfrey, J, 'The accountable net: Peer production of Internet governance', SSRN, May 2004 (Web); Cannataci, J and Bonnici, J, 'Can self-regulation satisfy the transnational requisite of successful Internet regulation?', (2003) 17 IRLCT 51.

make it relatively easy to do *A* and relatively hard to do *B*, users will be encouraged to do *A* rather than *B*. So the way in which programs are designed can have as much, if not more, influence over people's behaviour than legal rules – or as Lessig famously put it, 'Code is Law'.[18]

The clarity of the insight is not in doubt; its significance is however much debated. Some of the interest of the thesis is that it points to the risk of law creation by private bodies: governments do not usually create computing systems, and would be unlikely to jeopardise the profitability of computer manufacturers by telling them how to do their jobs. But, in fact, the most clear examples of this thesis in action has been the use of ICT in support of well-established laws, such as the use of digital rights management (DRM) to restrict the use of copyright material, or the deliberate recording of data so that it will be available to law enforcement authorities.[19]

While the *potential* to control the Internet through technology is undoubted, the guiding principle of the evolving technology has been almost exactly the contrary. The digital computer is probably the most general tool ever devised: a machine for processing whatever data its owner desires. And the Internet has been designed to allow rapid communication of that data on an almost entirely unrestricted basis. No doubt, there will be many pressures to redesign the Internet to make it harder to break the law, but technological conservatism is a powerful force. Lessig's principle operates mostly not as a description of the reality of Internet use, but as a warning of what governments will turn it into if their citizens let them.

Layers of control

The second insight is that the Internet can be thought of as several discrete processes or layers. At the lowest layer, 'the Internet' consists of electrical impulses passing (for the most part) along wires. At a slightly more abstract level, these impulses can be seen as packets of data, each packet with an address to which it should be delivered. It is only as significantly higher layers of abstraction are reached that it will appear what these packets are actually for, and whether they represent part of a picture, or of a document, or as instructions for the recipient computer, or whatever. So these different aspects of the technology can be considered in isolation from one another.

At root, the idea of layers relates to the mechanics of the Internet. Each layer has its own technology and management system, which operates without regard to the other layers.[20] The routers which forward packets of data to their destination need not know or care what the data represents; conversely, someone sending an image to a friend's e-mail account need not concern themselves with routers, or even know what a router is. And – significantly enough for a rapidly developing area – manufacturers can make better routers, and designers can make better images, without the need to consult one another at any point. It follows that control of the Internet is similarly layered: control of each layer is vested in very different people.

---

18 Lessig, L, *Code and Other Laws of Cyberspace*, 1999, New York: Basic Books. For reaction and criticism, see Chenwei, Z, 'In code, we trust? Regulation and emancipation in cyberspace', (2004) 1 SCRIPT-ed 617 (Web); Kesan, J and Shah, R, 'Deconstructing code', (2003) 6 YJLT 297; Wu, T, 'When code isn't law', (2003) 89 Va LR 670; Katyal, N, 'Digital architecture as crime control', (2003) 112 Yale LJ 2261.
19 Katyal, S, 'The new surveillance', (2003) 54 CWRULR 297. On DRM, see below, p 60.
20 See 'Protocols according to layers' (Web).

The only people who can make sure there is a wire for data to go down are the people physically present at the place where the wire should be. But control over other layers may be in those who manufactured the relevant equipment, or subsequently configured it. Control over the Internet is in many hands.

When we combine this notion of layers with Lessig's insight, that control over the technology is itself a source of law, it becomes apparent that control over the way the Internet is used is in fact distributed over a wide variety of people, each of whom may have a very different agenda and who may exercise control of very different sorts. So someone who owns a significant part of the cabling has control of a sort: they can disconnect that cabling, and so perhaps cut off many from the Internet. But it would be futile for that person to use that control to fight pornography: the string of 1s and 0s which represent a pornographic image are, at that level, indistinguishable from any other string.[21] Control of each level is of a very peculiar sort.

It follows that the various levels at which the Internet can be controlled are diverse, as are the people in a position to exercise control, the legal jurisdictions to which they are amenable, and the type and effectiveness of control.[22] Some of the more important levels that need to be distinguished are as follows.

Physical connection

Data cannot travel between two points unless there is a connection to carry it. So the ability to interfere with the connection can be used to control the Internet. However, this is not, in general, a very useful method of control. One basic technical feature of the Internet is that it reacts to breaks in the connection, by searching for ways to route around the break and deliver the message regardless. And even where control can be established, it is not very discriminating; someone who wishes to control exactly what is sent will have to process it all to re-assemble the data into a useful form. Indeed, the difficulty of doing this was always one reason why censorship of the Internet was considered impracticable.

However, this technical limitation can be overcome by sufficient effort, at least where the amount of data is relatively small. Some regimes, such as China and Saudi Arabia, now routinely censor Internet traffic by this means.[23] This is not done in the nations of Europe and the Americas, but this is a reflection of political freedom, not technical computing considerations.

Internet architecture and administrative institutions

If there were ever to be an international government for the Internet, it would presumably be built into the net's basic protocols, and the basic administrative institutions such as those which allocate addresses and names to machines attached to the net. There is no technical reason why control of this sort should not be

---

21 Solum, L and Chung, M, 'The layers principle: Internet architecture and the law', (2004) 79 NDLR 815.

22 Post, D, 'Anarchy, State, and the Internet: An essay on law-making in cyberspace', [1995] 3 JOL (Web).

23 See, eg, Endeshaw, A, 'Internet regulation in China: The never-ending cat and mouse game', (2004) 13 ICTL 41; 'Chinese whispers', [2004] NS (27 Nov) 40.

exercised, though it would undoubtedly be difficult. But again there is no political basis for it. Dispute over appropriate development of technical standards is vigorous enough, and shows little sympathy towards changes proposed other than for technical reasons. The central administrative bodies, principally the Internet Corporation for Assigned Names and Numbers (ICANN) and the Internet Assigned Numbers Authority (IANA), are viewed with deep suspicion whenever they step outside a purely technical role. While in a sense the entire Internet is based on a consensus – a mutual agreement by relevant technical staff to use the TCP/IP protocol – it seems inconceivable that this consensus could mutate sufficiently to permit the imposition of law throughout the net.[24]

An interesting exception to this, which is considered in more detail below, is the modification of the system of domain names to prevent breach of trade mark rights. This came about because of the curious mixture of strengths and weaknesses that ICANN has – the strength consisting of its almost unfettered power over the allocation of names, the weakness consisting of its vulnerability to legal action if it were considered complicit in a breach of trade mark. The result is a unique system of arbitration, resting heavily on concepts derived from US trade mark law, which allows the owner of a trade mark to object to the grant of a domain name which conflicts with it.[25] Whether this is or should be a model for law enforcement on the net more generally is controversial, to put it mildly.

Computer and operating system manufacture

In principle, those who design a computer and its operating system can set the limits as to what it can do and so are in an excellent position to control the activities of the ultimate users. But while there is ample opportunity for abuse here – hence the long-running battles between Microsoft and various competition authorities – there is little market incentive to place limits on what users can do. This method of control remains theoretical only.

There have been various proposals for building limitations of one sort or another into new computers. The more drastic proposals have proved too controversial: such as designing cryptographic hardware which would allow law enforcement officials to decrypt all transmissions,[26] or assigning each new processor a unique identity by which it could be identified over the net.[27] And generally all moves towards 'trusted computers' – which might, for example, be *incapable* of running copyrighted software without a proper authorisation – are regarded with great hostility.[28] However, considerable strides have been made towards preventing the use of materials in breach of copyright, and these DRM systems have been granted a limited amount of protection in law. The status of those who deliberately circumvent such controls is a matter of ongoing legal controversy.[29]

---

24 See generally below, p 165.
25 See below, p 175.
26 See *Clipper chip* (Wikipedia) (Web).
27 'So farewell then, Intel PSN', Register, 4 March 2000 (Web); Dery, G and Fox, J, 'Chipping away at the boundaries of privacy', (2000) 17 GSULR 331.
28 'MS trusted computing back to drawing board', Register, 6 May 2004 (Web); Anderson, R, 'Trusted computing – Frequently asked questions', August 2003 (Web).
29 On DRM, see below, p 60.

Internet service provision

The major weight of control and regulation has fallen on those who provide Internet access for others. ISPs exercise a considerable degree of supervision over their customers, for fear that they will be blamed for any wrongdoing by those customers. They have often found themselves the target of legal action by those aggrieved by their customers' behaviour, perhaps by distributing illegal software or data, or by defamation. An ISP who receives a complaint about a customer's behaviour has a choice – it can leave the material where it is (risking being held complicit in its customer's wrongdoing), or it can remove the material (risking legal action from the customer). Usually, the balance of inconvenience favours the party complaining. This position is rapidly becoming formalised in legislation, which specifies how quickly the ISP must act to avoid a charge of complicity with the customer.[30] Some have argued that this burden of regulation on ISPs will get more extensive with time, as the emphasis within government moves towards prevention of cybercrime, rather than mere reaction to it after the fact.[31]

ISPs have also found themselves with little alternative but to spy on their customers, as directed by national police and intelligence services. All records held by ISPs are liable to seizure to assist in official investigations, and co-operation is expected when specific customers are to be surveilled. An ongoing dispute is raging over retention of communications data covering periods of years, so that law enforcement officials can see the communications records of suspects covering a considerable period of time, before they became objects of interest.[32]

Intermediate service provision

Many who purchase Internet access from ISPs do so in order to provide it for others: most employers fall into that category. Again, fear of being held liable for the acts of those actually accessing the net provides a spur to exercise control. Mechanisms of control rely heavily on using the computers themselves to spy on their users. Provision of Internet access within the family is a related issue: as witness the anxieties of parents to keep their children from undesirable material on the Internet, which must be done either through physical supervision or by supervisory software of the 'net nanny' variety.[33]

NATIONAL OR INTERNATIONAL?

So the powers and even the relevance of nation states in this area have been seriously questioned – while it is perhaps inevitable that there will be law on the net,

---

30 Below, p 140. See Mann, R and Belzley, S, 'The promise of Internet intermediary liability', SSRN, April 2005 (Web).

31 See Brenner, S, 'Toward a criminal law for cyberspace: A new model of law enforcement?', (2004) 30 RCTLJ 1; contrast Kerr, O, 'Virtual crime, virtual deterrence: A skeptical view of self-help, architecture, and civil liability', SSRN, October 2004 (Web).

32 Below, Chapter 5.

33 For discussion of intra-family conflict, see 'Families fight over PCs shock', Register, 26 November 2004 (Web).

it is not obvious that it will be *national* law. The issues just discussed call into question whether individual states can do much to control the activities of those using the Internet, even if they can establish that the activity is occurring on their territory at all. Another challenge to the powers of states comes from the opposite direction: where control can be established, it is often not at the national level but at the international level.

So this challenge is not that control is an illusion – evidently *some* control can be brought to bear – but that *national* control is an illusion. The nations of the world can only control the Internet if they do so in concert with one another. If true, this has serious implications for the type of conduct that can be controlled. There is no universal agreement on what laws should be applied to the Internet. If international consensus is necessary for enforcing rules, then only those rules which can command such a consensus will be enforced; Internet law will then inevitably become the lowest common denominator of legal systems, consisting only of those rules that all can agree on.

The pressures towards global uniformity are clear enough.[34] Without collaboration between nations, the differences and gaps between jurisdictions become places to hide from all applicable laws.[35] Some of the problems to be tackled are intrinsically international ones – particularly combating terrorism and other transnational crimes.[36] Nations trying to attract Internet-related work from other nations may therefore find it necessary to introduce legal protections corresponding to those in those other nations. And copying the laws of other nations is often simply the path of least resistance: in many commercial areas, the needs of business are not so different across nations, and all concerned are happy to copy from prominent national or international models.[37] 'Globalisation' is often, of course, merely a code word for doing whatever the US is doing;[38] but it is clear that the US too is subject to pressures to conform.[39]

It is undeniable that Internet law has rapidly become a very international subject. A significant segment of the rules governing it are established by ICANN (which is a Californian corporation, but could not fulfil its function without taking an internationalist perspective).[40] Truly international bodies such as WIPO, the WTO and UNCITRAL have been highly influential sources of law here, and the Internet is a major factor in international negotiations at The Hague over civil jurisdiction. An international Convention on Cybercrime, agreed in November 2001, is in force from

---

34 See, eg, Cox, N, 'The regulation of cyberspace and the loss of national sovereignty', (2002) 11 ICTL 241; Hedley, S, 'Nations, markets and other imaginary places: Who makes the law in cyberspace?', (2003) 12 ICTL 215.

35 See, eg, Cox, N, 'The extraterritorial enforcement of consumer legislation and the challenge of the Internet', (2004) 8 Edin LR 60.

36 See, eg, Trachtman, J, 'Global cyberterrorism, jurisdiction, and international organization', SSRN, July 2004 (Web).

37 Diedrich, F, 'A law of the Internet? Attempts to regulate electronic commerce', [2000] 3 JILT (Web).

38 Thompson, B, 'Damn the Constitution: Europe must take back the web', Register, 9 August 2002 (Web). See also 'Bill Thompson answers critics', Register, 15 August 2002 (Web); Mueller, M, 'Who owns the Internet? Ownership as a legal basis for American control of the Internet', SSRN, March 2004 (Web).

39 Rubin, H, Fraser, L and Smith, M, 'US and international law aspects of the Internet: Fitting square pegs into round holes', (1995) 3 IJLIT 117.

40 See below, p 167.

July 2004: a Council of Europe venture, it has nonetheless solicited signatures from other leading economies; it has been ratified by 10 European nations, and has been signed (though not ratified) by 32 European governments and the governments of Canada, Japan, South Africa and the US.[41] And any significant growth in DRM seems to be at the expense of states' ability to control what happens within their borders.[42]

At the next level down, just as in the US, the more important legislation has been federal rather than state law,[43] so in Europe the major lawgiver has been the EU rather than individual nations.[44] In both instances, there is an ongoing dialogue on this issue: some individual US states have introduced their own innovative legislation, and EU debates over whether web site owners should be able to rely on the law of their country of origin have yet to reach any definitive result.[45]

However, all of this is very far from tolling the death knell for the nation state, even in matters relating to the Internet. The net facilitates international communication and trade, but much of its use is geographically local. And much of the law applicable to the Internet is national law; at ground level, it may be relatively unimportant that that national law was crafted to conform to international standards. Does this matter very much? Academic debate over the relevance of nations here has been furious if rather abstract, some insisting that a decline in the importance of the nation can lead only to a sort of anarchy,[46] others retorting that a failure to co-ordinate the activities of different nations will lead to a 'race to the bottom' as bad laws drive out good.[47]

Clearly, therefore, there are still significant national differences in relation to the laws governing the Internet, though their longer-term significance may be doubted. Various clear differences are starting to emerge:

(a) *Different degrees of toleration of freedom of expression.* A wide range of national approaches can be seen, from the intolerance of China or Saudi Arabia to the great but not unlimited liberality of the US. The differences between Europe and the US, while relatively slight in many ways, have nonetheless led to some hard fought jurisdictional battles;[48] and the difficulty of mounting a defamation action in the US has tempted several prominent plaintiffs to foreign courts.[49]

(b) *Different legislative styles.* Less dramatic, but probably more significant for trade, have been different national approaches to regulation. Comparing the US to the

---

41 See Convention on Cybercrime (signed at Budapest, November 2001) (Web). For discussion, see Goodman, M and Brenner, S, 'The emerging consensus on criminal conduct in cyberspace', (2002) 10 IJLIT 139; Hopkins, S, 'Cybercrime Convention: A positive beginning to a long road ahead', (2003) 2 JHTL 101 (Web).
42 Garlick, M, 'Locking up the bridge on the digital divide', (2004) 20 SCCHTLJ 941.
43 For discussion, see Stumphauzer, R, 'Electronic impulses, digital signals, and federal jurisdiction', (2003) 56 Vand LR 277.
44 See especially Gonçalves, M, 'Technological change, globalization, and the Europeanization of rights', (2002) 16 IRLCT 301.
45 For discussion, see Hörnle, J, 'The UK perspective on the country of origin rule in the E-Commerce Directive', (2004) 12 IJLIT 333.
46 Goldsmith, J, 'Against cyberanarchy', (1998) 65 Chi LR 1199; Ribstein, L and Kobayashi, B, 'State regulation of electronic commerce', (2002) 51 Emory LJ 1.
47 Post, D, 'Against "Against Cyberanarchy" ', (2002) 17 BTLJ 1365; Zekos, G, 'Internet or electronic technology: A threat to state sovereignty', [1999] 3 JILT (Web).
48 See below, eg, p 155.
49 Below, p 163.

nations of the EU, the economy of the EU is much more tightly regulated, with express regulation by governmental bodies being the norm; while the attitude of European national courts ultimately decides the tone of any legislation, there is no question of their having the initiative in lawmaking in the way that US federal courts do. The different legislative styles also affect the speed with which the different legal systems can react to new developments: while the process for new federal legislation is by no means speedy, it is undoubtedly faster than the tortuous debates and negotiations necessary for new EU directives.[50]

(c) *Level of enforcement.* While enforcement is nowhere at a very high level, again important differences emerge across nations. Indeed, the low level of enforcement by some nations is rapidly giving them pariah status: the amount of fraud to emerge from Nigeria, and the amount of spam to emerge from South Korea, far exceeds their fair share on most measures – a notorious fact which gives those nations undue prominence in debates on enforcement.[51]

Clearly, therefore, there is a considerable role for national legal initiatives, though also considerable uncertainty as to their importance in the long run.

NATIONAL INITIATIVES

The scramble by individual nations to enact laws providing for the Internet is very marked. There is much talk of facilitating e-trade, of not allowing the new economic opportunities created by the Internet to wither for lack of a suitable legal framework. However, some scepticism is in order, given the lack of evidence that trade over the net has been stimulated by appropriate laws or harmed by their absence. The economies of the developed nations are heavily regulated by any standard; the main impetus for legislation has been to subject electronic trading to similar or analogous controls. The wish to stimulate new forms of trading, or at least not to stand in their way, is certainly a factor, though not a very influential one. It is principally evident only in drafting style, legislatures being keen to specify their rules in technologically neutral terms, so that they do not lock those subject to them into technologies which may soon become obsolete.

So much of the legislative effort has been simply to extend existing rules and regulations to the Internet; no very novel governmental purpose has emerged, though the new environment has led to some differences of emphasis. As already remarked, the international dimension comes into play as well; regulating the Internet as if it respected national boundaries is not an option. Tax law has been surprisingly slow to change.[52] Major areas of legislative interest have been:

(a) *Fighting crime.* The novel possibilities for theft and deception in an online environment have stimulated reform of the law, as the Internet opens new possibilities both for illegal operations and for laundering the proceeds. The

---

50 May, B, Chen, J and Wen, K, 'The differences of regulatory models and Internet regulation in the EU and the US', (2004) 13 ICTL 259.

51 See, eg, 'US reveals intellectual property blacklist', Register, 4 May 2005 (Web).

52 For discussion, see Cockfield, A, 'Transforming the Internet into a taxable forum', (2001) 85 Minn LR 1171; Basu, S, 'To tax or not to tax? That is the question? Overview of options in consumption taxation of e-commerce', [2004] 1 JILT (Web).

possibilities of surveillance of online activities with a view to prosecution have also been explored extensively.

(b) *Protecting basic trading rights.* Extension of the legal protection given to intellectual property rights online has been very noticeable, not to mention highly controversial. The more general problems in enforcing contracts, both jurisdictional and substantive, have taken longer to mature, but are increasingly receiving attention.

(c) *Protecting consumers.* This has included not simply the extension of ordinary consumer rights to digital markets, but also attempts to regulate the use of personal data.

NEW TECHNOLOGIES

A dilemma for writers on Internet law is how far to speculate about improved or novel devices and programs that might be developed in the near future. The development of new technologies is always a complicated social process; the legal systems of the world may influence any part of that process. There are seven main areas where the technology can be expected to develop rapidly in the next few years, but while some reference is made to them in later chapters, overall the social and legal implications seem to this author too shady to generate much discussion in the remainder of the book. These areas are:

(a) *Improved mobile computing.* Quite powerful computers are now small enough to be carried around on a routine basis. The iPod (a music playback device) can hold up to 60GB of data. Communications are also improving: significant improvements can be expected from wi-fi; and 3G mobile telephones are themselves powerful computing machines. Obviously, these machines were all developed with a view to the improved services they can deliver to their users; but growth here seems slow and unpredictable, and the legal implications obscure.

(b) *Convergence.* For all their superficial similarities, the computer monitor and the TV screen are somewhat different from a technical point of view, and extremely different in what appears on them. This divergence can, however, be expected to diminish quite rapidly. Again, the telephone is very unlike the computer, but the gap is rapidly being closed by the development of voice over IP (VoIP) technologies. It is already becoming necessary to ask whether a computer which acts like a telephone should be subjected to the same laws as a telephone; but an answer has yet to emerge.[53]

(c) *Improved DRM.* Much ingenuity is employed in the manufacture of products which *cannot* be used in breach of intellectual property rights: say, by producing music in a form which cannot be copied, and which indeed may destroy itself when the purchased licence expires. How far this technology will be developed, and how far the legal systems of the world will permit it to be developed, are open questions.

(d) *Improved biometrics.* Most ways of identifying individuals rely on one of two techniques: testing something they know (password of some sort, etc), or measuring something about them (colour of eyes, pattern of fingerprints, etc). Of

---

53 See, eg, 'Net regulation "still possible"', BBC News, 27 January 2005 (Web).

the two, it is the latter set of techniques – the 'biometric' techniques – that seem intrinsically harder to fake and more secure. Yet developing new biometric systems, whether based on iris or face recognition or otherwise, has not proved easy. If simple, reliable and cheap biometric identification becomes available, there will doubtless be many social and legal ramifications.

(e) *Improved surveillance of people and of things.* Various emerging technologies are making it easier to track both things and people: face and number-plate recognition from CCTV data; location of mobile phones by the company which runs the network; satellite imaging; more use of GPS data; and the use of RFID chips. The latter technology is primarily used today for stock control, but there is no technological reason why it cannot be used to manage people just as well; that social choice has yet to be made. Chipping of individuals, either because they want it or because their carers want it, has already begun on a small scale.[54]

(f) *Improved cryptology systems.* Technical improvements to cryptology systems, which allow for secret electronic communications, are constantly being made. Some may even be on the verge of making practical systems of quantum encryption, which cannot be intercepted successfully, even in theory. Governments are already taking an interest in who should be allowed to use these technologies, and in the extent to which people should be allowed to keep secrets from their governments.[55] No doubt, concern over these issues will intensify.

(g) *Use of computing in legal processes.* Least predictable of all is the increasing use of computing in legal processes. Much legal work is routine, and largely concerned with sorting data into clear pre-determined categories or schemes. As such, it seems highly likely to be computerised. But actual progress in this direction is quirky at best, even in relation to legal procedure and conveyancing, where much work has been done on this problem.[56]

More generally, we have suddenly emerged into a world in which use of the Internet is the norm, not the anorak-wearing exception. Many of the implications of this are, no doubt, waiting to emerge.

FURTHER READING

Birnhack, M and Elkin-Koren, N, 'The invisible handshake: The re-emergence of the state in the digital environment', (2003) 8 VJOLT 6 (Web).

Brenner, S, 'Toward a criminal law for cyberspace: A new model of law enforcement?', (2004) 30 RCTLJ 1.

Engel, C, 'The role of law in the governance of the Internet', SSRN, August 2002 (Web).

---

54 Eg, 'First people injected with ID chips, sales drive kicks off', Register, 10 June 2002 (Web).
55 Below, p 113.
56 See e-conveyancing home page (Land Registry)(Web). For discussion, see Perry, R, 'E-conveyancing: Problems ahead?', [2003] Conv (NS) 215; Christensen, S, 'Electronic land dealings in Canada, New Zealand and the United Kingdom: Lessons for Australia', (2004) 11 E-Law 4 (Web).

Giacomello, G, 'Who is Big Brother? National governments and the regulation of the Internet', (2000) 5 IJCLP (Web).

Hughes, J, 'The Internet and the persistence of law', (2003) 44 BCLR 359.

Hunter, D, 'Cyberspace as place and the tragedy of the digital anticommons', (2003) 91 Calif LR 439.

Kesan, J, and Gallo, A, 'Optimizing regulation of electronic commerce', (2004) 72 U Cinn LR 1497.

Mariotti, R, 'Cyberspace in three dimensions', (2005) 55 Syr LR 251.

Mayer-Schönberger, V, 'The shape of governance: Analyzing the world of Internet regulation', (2003) 43 Va JIL 605.

Murray, A, 'Regulation and rights in networked space', (2003) 30 JLS 187.

Reidenberg, J, 'Technology and Internet jurisdiction', SSRN, March 2005 (Web).

Wagner, R, 'On software regulation' (2005) 78 So Calif LR 457.

CHAPTER 2

PROTECTION OF COMPUTING SYSTEMS

This chapter concerns the law's most basic protection for computing systems: criminalisation of attacks on their functioning and integrity, and of the use of computing technology to attack firms or steal their money. The chapter first considers wrongful access to computers; then damage to or impairment of computers; then computer theft and fraud; and, finally, spam. Most of this concerns the criminal law, though protection in the civil law is also briefly considered.

As will quickly become apparent, no very sharp distinction can be drawn between protecting the computer itself and protecting the data stored in it. From that perspective, this chapter can be seen as an introduction to the computer-specific ways in which data is protected, complementing the following chapter which considers its protection through more traditional and general doctrines, such as copyright law and the law of confidence.

WRONGFUL ACCESS TO DATA OR PROGRAMS

One of the most basic legal protections afforded to the owner of a computer is to protect the data on it by penalising those who access it without proper authority. Any computer owner is likely to control who has access to it, using security methods of various sorts. Even those who are prepared to grant access to the public in general (such as those running web sites) are likely to place severe restrictions on what users are allowed to do. Motives for seeking wrongful access vary: at one extreme are serious criminals, attempting to steal financial details or trade secrets, or to perpetrate some fraud; at the other would be relatively unsophisticated hackers or 'script kiddies', breaking into computers simply to prove that they can do it, and perhaps to brag about it later. Methods range from the sophisticated (such as exploiting defects in the target system's protection) to the straightforward (such as guessing the passwords of legitimate users) to the banal (such as noticing that another user has abandoned his or her computer without logging off).

Both UK and Irish law have criminal offences of wrongfully accessing computer systems. While not expressed in identical terms, these offences cover very similar ground. The offences are preparatory – that is, they are complete on proof that the defendant did an act which was meant to secure access to data, whether or not it was successful.

The UK offence is defined as follows:

A person is guilty of an offence if –

(a) he causes a computer to perform any function with intent to secure access to any program or data held in any computer;

(b) the access he intends to secure is unauthorised; and

(c) he knows at the time when he causes the computer to perform the function that that is the case.[1]

---

1   Computer Misuse Act 1990 (UK), s 1(1).

The Irish offence uses different terminology, but is quite similar in effect:

> A person who without lawful excuse operates a computer –
>
> (a) within the State with intent to access any data kept either within or outside the State, or
>
> (b) outside the State with intent to access any data kept within the State,
>
> shall, whether or not he accesses any data, be guilty of an offence ...[2]

Actus reus

The *actus reus* is in each case simply using a computer – it is committed by anyone who 'operates a computer' (Ireland) or 'causes a computer to perform any function' (UK). The slightly clumsy UK wording might seem to suggest that two computers must be involved, one to 'perform [a] function' and the other to 'access ... any program or data'; but the Court of Appeal has held that the same machine might serve for both.[3] So the offences include not only using one computer to access data held on another (such as using it to browse the Internet) but also using it to access data it already holds. No doubt, the legislatures primarily envisaged a defendant who personally queries a computer and tries to open files it holds, but the wording seems apt to cover other means of achieving the same end. So the offences probably cover use of spyware, which records data and then e-mails the result back to another machine.

Neither statute defines 'computer' – a deliberate omission in the face of a rapidly developing technology. A possible view is that a 'computer' includes any device capable of storing data in electronic form. If that view is not taken, difficult questions of degree are likely to arise – is a mobile phone a 'computer'? is a programmable VCR? a telephone-answering machine? a pocket calculator?

Mens rea

The *mens rea* of both offences is an intent to gain access to data. It does not matter that the defendant's plans were slightly hazy or mistaken: an intent to access some data or other is enough, even if the prosecution cannot identify a particular data item as one which the defendant intended to access.[4] So the offence is not confined to those who intend to look at a specific file, but also covers those on a fishing expedition to seek out anything of interest. Both offences extend not merely to data but also to programs – the UK legislation specifically refers to programs as well as data,[5] and the Irish legislation provides that 'data' includes a program.[6] The Irish legislation does not define 'access' to data; the UK legislation gives it an elaborate definition, under which data is accessed if it is used, copied, moved, displayed, outputted or (surprisingly) altered or deleted;[7] and a program is also accessed if it is run.[8]

---

2   Criminal Damage Act 1991 (IE), s 5(1).
3   *A-G's Reference (No 1 of 1991)* [1993] QB 94.
4   Computer Misuse Act 1990 (UK), s 1(2); Criminal Damage Act 1991 (IE), s 5(2).
5   Computer Misuse Act 1990 (UK), s 1(1).
6   Criminal Damage Act 1991 (IE), s 1(1) (definition of 'data').
7   Computer Misuse Act 1990 (UK), s 17(2).
8   *Ibid*, s 17(3).

It is therefore clear that the access which the legislation seeks to prevent is access *to data*, rather than access *to the computer* as such. Arguably, both offences would be improved if they were defined as offences of unauthorised use of computers, rather than unauthorised access to data. Certainly, in the current state of knowledge this would be simpler, and it is not clear what purpose the complications of the current legislation serve. As it is, the offences have a subtly different focus from that suggested by 'wrongful computer access'.

(a) On a superficial reading, the offences do not catch a defendant who merely 'steals' time on another's computer without accessing data, such as by uploading a program of his or her own and then executing it. However, this is a fine line, easily crossed. Suppose an authorised user finishes a computer session, but then neither logs off nor terminates the web browser that the user has been running. An unauthorised user then uses it to browse the web. This has been held to be an offence; presumably the data 'accessed' was the program running the web browser, namely Internet Explorer.[9] In principle, even someone executing their own program is making use of the computer's operating system; if that can be regarded as a 'program' in itself, then the legislation in effect covers mere use of another's computer. Similar questions arise where a defendant hacks into another's system purely to use it as a conduit for access to the Internet. (This has been a particular problem in recent years, as roving hackers with wireless-enabled computers have taken advantage of poorly defended wireless-access points.[10]) The intent then is not to 'access data' on the target system, but the intrusion may nonetheless do so incidentally, which may be enough to justify a prosecution.

(b) Conversely, a case could be made that even using *your own* computer to access data unlawfully is within the offences, such as by reading a disk stolen from elsewhere, or making an illegal copy of software licensed for more limited use. If the access actually effected is unlawful (for example, because it is a breach of copyright), it seems to be irrelevant that you did not misuse anyone's property, or that there were other, lawful uses for the data. This takes us very far indeed from the cases the legislation was aimed at, but it is not obvious how such an interpretation could be resisted without departing seriously from the literal meaning. It might even catch the (not uncommon) case where a defendant buys a computer second-hand and then discovers confidential files belonging to the previous owner – though on those facts there is certainly room for argument over whether access is 'unauthorised'.

Aggravated offences

Under the UK legislation, where the basic offence of unauthorised access is proved, the defendant is liable to additional penalties if the object of the unauthorised access was the commission of some further serious offence, or to facilitate the commission of such an offence by the defendant or another. The further offence must be one for which the penalty is fixed by law (murder, treason) or for which an adult can be sentenced to five years or more in prison.[11] This is therefore another preparatory

---

9   *Ellis v DPP* [2001] EWHC 362 Admin; see also *Ellis v DPP* [2002] EWHC 135 Admin.
10   'Warchalking: London wi-fi guerrillas take tips from hobos', ZDNet UK, 26 June 2002 (Web). Cf Ryan, P, 'War, peace, or stalemate: Wargames, wardialing, wardriving, and the emerging market for hacker ethics', (2004) 9 VJOLT 7 (Web).
11   Computer Misuse Act 1990 (UK), s 2.

offence – unauthorised access is subject to these higher penalties only if was a step on the way to the commission of another serious offence (albeit one that was frustrated, or may even have turned out to be impossible).

There is no equivalent provision in the Irish legislation, but many cases are caught by the higher penalties available for the distinct offence of dishonestly operating a computer, or causing it to be operated, with the intention of making a gain for himself or herself or another. 'Dishonestly' is defined as 'without a claim of right made in good faith'.[12]

Defences

General defences allowed by the criminal law can be relied on. Some of the more common cases are expressly provided for by the legislation.

The principal defence is that the defendant was authorised to access the data, or at least believed that he or she was so authorised. More precisely, the Irish legislation provides a defence where the defendant believed that those who could authorise access had done so, or would have done so if they had known the circumstances.[13] The UK legislation requires that the prosecution prove that access is *in fact* unauthorised and that 'he knows at the time when he causes the computer to perform the function that that is the case'.[14] To that extent, the offences are both parasitic on property law: the ultimate question is who has the legal right to control the computer system and so can authorise others to use it.

While it will usually be clear whether there was authorisation, difficulties can arise, especially where the defendant has been granted a password to use a particular system, but then acts in a way that the system's owner did not anticipate. One common case is that of employees who misuse the facilities to which their work password gives them access. The basic principle appears to be that while the issuing of a password to the defendant might be an important indication that the defendant's use of the system was authorised, it is only one factor. A defendant who knows that he or she is forbidden to act in the way they are now doing commits the offence, and cannot rely on a password or a generalised invitation to use the system as 'authorising' that behaviour. Equally, if the defendant knows of an unequivocal prohibition on access, the fact that there is no technological barrier ought not to be a defence. If I know I am forbidden to use a particular machine, the fact that it does not ask me for a password would not excuse me.

In the *Allison* case,[15] a credit analyst employed by American Express in Florida accessed her employer's files to steal credit card numbers and other financial details, which she passed to a confederate in Europe, enabling him to make counterfeit credit cards. He used them to defraud American Express of roughly US$1 m. As part of the extradition proceedings against the confederate, it was necessary to determine whether the credit analyst's conduct would have been criminal in the UK. As her password gave her access to all customer files, it was argued that what she had done

---

12 Criminal Justice (Theft and Fraud Offences) Act 2001 (IE), ss 2(1) and 9.
13 Criminal Damage Act 1991 (IE), s 6(2).
14 Computer Misuse Act 1990 (UK), s 1; 'unauthorised' is defined, in very general terms, in s 17(5).
15 *R v Bow Street Magistrates' Court and Allison ex p USA* [2000] 2 AC 216.

was 'authorised', and so she had committed no offence. The House of Lords rejected this argument. She had been given clear instructions to access only files relevant to her duties; this did not include the files in question. She could not be said to have been 'authorised' to look at them merely because she was in fact able to do so. But would the case have been different if she had, in fact, been instructed to work on those very files? She might argue that in such a case she was expressly 'authorised'; but the prosecution could still argue that she was only authorised to access them for the purposes of her work, and not for other, illegal purposes.

Allison calls in question the earlier decision in *DPP v Bignell* (1998).[16] Two police officers (who by the time of the appeal were married to one another) instructed a technician to access the Police National Computer, to identify the owner of a particular car. The officers were entitled to access these records for purposes connected with their work, but were in fact motivated by private concerns: one of them was recently separated from his wife, and was trying to identify her new boyfriend. The Divisional Court was not prepared to regard this use as 'unauthorised', and therefore ordered an acquittal. The officers were authorised to access information of that general type, and the fact that they did so for an improper purpose did not bring them within the legislation. The court argued that this left no gap in the law, as proceedings could be taken against the officers under the data protection legislation.[17] Yet is the wrongful access offence limited in this way? *Bignell* was criticised in *Allison* – the earlier court was said to have misled itself by asking whether the defendants could look at information of a certain type, when the real question was whether they were authorised to access the particular data in the circumstances in which they did.[18] And it seems very odd to say that the access was 'authorised' when, as the defendants well knew, it was specifically forbidden. But *Bignell* has not been directly overruled, and while the defendants' conduct is hard to defend, nonetheless in general we can expect the courts to be slow to criminalise those who merely use their work computers for their own private purposes – even purposes which they know would not have the approval of the management. This is an important issue, and it is hard to believe that these issues will remain unresolved for long.[19]

(In passing, the Lords in *Allison* suggested a different way of defending the result in *Bignell*. The data in the case had in fact been accessed by a technician, whose good faith was not in question. It is therefore arguable that there was no 'unauthorised access': the technician had full authorisation, and it is irrelevant than he was acting on orders which were, unknown to him, issued by the defendants in bad faith.[20] This is a possible reading of the UK statute, but an unnecessarily narrow one; it seems rather arbitrary to make the criminality of the defendants' conduct turn on whether they themselves pushed the keys and clicked the mouse.)

'Authorisation' may sometimes take a more technical form. When making purchases over the Internet, buyers are regularly invited to agree to terms and

---

16 [1998] 1 Cr App Rep 1.
17 Below, Chapter 4. For such a prosecution, see 'Data protection charges for sale of police data', Register, 26 April 2005 (Web).
18 *R v Bow Street Magistrates' Court and Allison ex p USA* [2000] 2 AC 216, 225 *per* Lord Hobhouse.
19 For discussion, see Hamin, Z, 'Inside cyber-threats: Problem and perspectives', (2000) 14 IRLCT 105.
20 *R v Bow Street Magistrates' Court and Allison ex parte USA* [2000] 2 AC 216, 225 *per* Lord Hobhouse.

conditions of sale; indeed, very often the sale will not proceed until the buyer has clicked an 'I agree' button. Notoriously, however, these terms are rarely read even in outline. Suppose that sellers includes a term allowing them to install software monitoring the buyer's subsequent behaviour, which it duly does, e-mailing a report back to the sellers. Clearly, the sellers have accessed the buyer's data, but they will plead authorisation or a belief in authorisation. In the current state of the law, it seems unlikely that a conviction could be secured, unless perhaps the sellers' conduct was so obviously objectionable and contrary to the buyer's interests that it would be absurd to say that it was authorised.

In his survey of how the various US jurisdictions have interpreted 'authorisation', Kerr argues strongly that authorisation to use a particular computer should be determined entirely by the way its owner has configured it. Crudely, if I protect certain data with a password, then those to whom I give the password are 'authorised' to use the data as they see fit, and all others are not. The law's function is simply to respect this technological protection, and to prevent its circumvention. Kerr is opposed to a broader look at what the owner may have agreed with others, or restrictions they may have agreed to abide by – the password should be conclusive. Kerr's slogan is therefore that 'authorisation' is code-based not contract-based.[21] There is much to be said for this view. It avoids many of the more awkward problems with 'authorisation', and keeps the concept within respectable bounds. While Kerr is probably alarmist in saying that the contrary view would 'broadly criminalize the law of contract involving the use of computers', it certainly extends it greatly and apparently unwisely. Whether Kerr's view is ultimately acceptable must depend on what other offences the law recognises to cover undesirable conduct which would be 'authorised' on this view. Conduct such as that in *Allison* must surely be illegal in any rational legal system, but perhaps a charge of assisting in a fraud is more appropriate than a charge of computer misuse.

The law is unclear on the status of 'white hat hackers', who attempt access to computer systems with a view to testing their defences, and whose intent on discovering a vulnerability is to warn the system's owner about it. Clearly, such people have no malicious intent, but the legislation does not require malicious intent before a prosecution is brought. While some of these hackers would be able to plead real or presumed authorisation, in most cases the practice seems legally dubious.

Jurisdiction and sentence

Both Acts allow prosecutions to be brought in their respective jurisdictions if either the defendant's actions were within the jurisdiction, or the data intended to be accessed was there.[22] So a hacker physically present in the jurisdiction is open to prosecution, wherever in the world the data is located; and data within the jurisdiction attracts the protection of the legislation wherever the defendant may have been when trying to access it – and whether or not the attempt succeeded. Also, UK legislation provides generally that a charge of conspiracy will lie if the act planned was criminal both in the UK and in the jurisdiction where it was to be carried out, and

---

21   Kerr, O, 'Cybercrime's scope: Interpreting "access" and "authorization" in computer misuse statutes', (2003) 78 NYULR 1596.

22   Computer Misuse Act 1990 (UK), ss 4 and 5; Criminal Damage Act 1991 (IE), s 5(1).

the conspiracy was substantially linked to a UK jurisdiction (as where the conspiracy was made there, or one party did anything relating to it there).[23]

The Irish offence is punishable by up to 3 months' imprisonment and/or a fine not exceeding €635; the aggravated offence of 'dishonest operation' carries a penalty of up to 10 years' imprisonment and/or an unlimited fine. The UK basic offence is punishable by up to six months' imprisonment, and/or a fine not exceeding £5,000. The aggravated version of the offence (access with intent to commit a further serious offence) carries up to 5 years' imprisonment and/or an unlimited fine. In one case, a bank employee was pressured by friends to access certain customer account details. They used this data to impersonate one of the account holders in an attempt to obtain money by deception. The bank employee pleaded guilty on two counts, and was sentenced at trial to 8 months in a young offender institution. The Court of Appeal agreed that detention was appropriate, even though the others had received only community punishment orders; breach of trust by a bank employee was a serious matter. However, in view of his age (19) and his previous good character, and the fact that no money had actually been lost, the term was reduced to 4 months.[24]

Subsidiary and related offences

The courts have not shown much willingness to stretch traditional offences to cover unauthorised access to computers or data. The idea that data is 'property' which can be 'stolen' has been specifically rejected.[25] Again, the courts have refused to accept that a password can be a 'false instrument' which would bring hackers within the forgery legislation;[26] when asked to do this, the House of Lords protested against '[t]he Procrustean attempt to force these facts into the language of an Act not designed to fit them', adding that it was for the legislature rather than the courts to invent new crimes to cover such conduct.[27] Indeed, it was this celebrated case, involving two journalists who hacked into the Duke of Edinburgh's mail box, that forced the UK Parliament to enact the current legislation, to target computer misuse specifically.

Nonetheless, securing unauthorised access can sometimes fall within the scope of other offences, without the need for any unnatural reading of the legislation. Accessing personal data can be a breach of the data protection legislation.[28] Copying another's data may involve breach of copyright.[29] Some types of hacking may involve unlawful interference with telecommunications.[30] And in appropriate cases (though there are probably not many of them) a computer owner who finds that their computer has been made to work full-time for a hacker might consider a charge of unlawfully using electricity.[31]

---

23 Criminal Justice (Terrorism and Conspiracy) Act 1998 (UK), ss 5–7.
24 *R v Delamare* [2003] EWCA Crim 424, (2003) 2 Cr App Rep (S) 474.
25 *Oxford v Moss* (1978) 68 Cr App Rep 183; similarly *Grant v Procurator Fiscal* [1988] RPC 41.
26 Forgery and Counterfeiting Act 1981 (E&W, NI), ss 1 and 8; cf Criminal Justice (Theft and Fraud Offences) Act 2001 (IE), ss 24 and 25.
27 *R v Gold* [1988] AC 1063, 1071 *per* Lord Brandon.
28 See Chapter 4 below.
29 See Chapter 3 below.
30 See p 83 below.
31 Eg, Theft Act 1968 (E&W), s 13; Energy (Miscellaneous Provisions) Act 1995 (IE), s 15.

Civil remedies

It seems most unlikely that the courts will treat mere access to another's computer or data, without quantifiable damage, as giving rise to a civil action. The matter is considered in more detail below.[32] Cases where actual damage is caused are considered later in the chapter.[33]

Assessment and reform

The case against the existing legislation is easy to make. It is showing its age: it was enacted before use of the Internet had spread outside communities of computer specialists, and before the web even existed. Many of the expressions used are vague and capable of improvement; as has been pointed out above, much apparently unnecessary complication has resulted from requiring an intent to access another's data, rather than an intent to use another's computer. Prosecutions are difficult, expensive and usually require the deployment of considerable computer expertise; only a handful are brought each year.[34]

Having said all that, however, it is not obvious that there is anything fundamentally wrong with this part of the legislation. There are legal technical difficulties in defining the offences, but this is inevitable when the technology is developing so rapidly: a statute precisely crafted to describe existing abuses would rapidly become obsolete. The best tactic for legislators is probably to use broad definitions that are not obviously tied to any particular technology, even though this will inevitably lead to a certain number of awkward cases a few years down the line. Much of the expense and difficulty of criminal prosecution is inherent and unavoidable. Establishing exactly what happened in any case of alleged improper access is always likely to involve difficult technical issues. Specialist bodies, such as the UK's National Hi-Tech Crime Unit[35] (formed in 2001), have a huge amount of ground to make up.[36] Yet while greater police expertise and resources would be welcome, it might only improve matters slightly. Proving the intent with which the defendant acted is also inherently difficult, yet the need cannot be avoided except by introducing offences of strict liability – probably unacceptable if the penalties are substantial. It is not obvious that this particular area of law needs desperate attention.

A criminal prosecution for wrongful computer access is a heavy tool, expensive for the prosecuting authority and usually with serious consequences on conviction. A case can therefore be made that prosecution rates for this particular offence *should* be low, and indeed that accessing another's computing system should not usually be a criminal matter.[37] Some hackers are dangerous criminals, but many others are not; arguably they should not be treated in the same way, and if (as is often the case) a hacker shows no other anti-social tendencies, it is not clear that giving them

---

32 See p 209 below.
33 Below, p 26.
34 'Computer Misuse Act: Prosecutions', *Hansard* (Lords), 7 January 2003 (Web).
35 National Hi-Tech Crime Unit home page (Web).
36 Hyde, S, 'A few coppers change', [1999] 2 JILT (Web).
37 Eg, Carr, I and Williams, K, 'Securing the e-commerce environment', (2000) 16 CLSR 295.

a criminal record serves any useful purpose. An analogy may be drawn with trespass to land: all such trespass is tortious, but it is only criminal if special circumstances are shown, such as an intention to commit a serious crime while trespassing.

A possible way forward would therefore be to reduce the scope of the offence, by requiring proof of criminal purpose before unlawful access becomes a criminal offence. This is, up to a point, the approach of the US (Federal) Computer Fraud and Abuse Act 1991, which criminalises unauthorised access to privately owned computers only where there is intent to damage national security, to further a fraud or to steal financial data.[38] This would, of course, not secure unanimous agreement. There would be irreconcilable differences of opinion over hackers who go to elaborate lengths to break into computer systems merely 'because they're there'. Many would argue seriously that this activity promotes excellence in computing skills in general and security engineering in particular. But the administrators of high-profile sites, who spend much of their time fending off hacks of that sort, would be unlikely to agree.

We should expect most cases of hacking to be dealt with in domestic forums of one sort or another and, unless serious criminality is alleged, this seems entirely appropriate. Employers can discipline employees, universities can control students, and ISPs can terminate the accounts of errant customers. In these and other cases, we would expect an organisation which provides computer access to spell out its expectations of those who use it and to take appropriate action if those expectations are frustrated. In the more serious cases, the legal system may be invoked to determine the appropriate response. Employment tribunals in both the UK[39] and Ireland[40] usually seem to treat unlawful access to important commercial data as akin to serious dishonesty, justifying dismissal after a proper enquiry.

The first line of defence against unlawful access, and very often the only effective one, is effective computer security. Maintaining effective security – patching and updating security software, monitoring usage to detect possible intrusions, attempting to educate users in safe information practices – is a significant part of any system administrator's job. New devices always lead to new problems: for example, it is currently proving much easier to make wireless access to computers available than it is to secure it against intruders. And there are always lively debates over how security can be improved. From a legal point of view, the most obvious feature of current arrangements is the assumption that security is almost entirely the responsibility of the individual company or individual whose computers are intruded upon. Indeed, a major reason why there is so little police involvement in wrongful computer access cases is the embarrassment factor, companies fearing that a successful intrusion into their systems reflects badly on their security arrangements – a matter which trusted commercial organisations may wish to hush up.

Yet – to draw an analogy with an older technology – it was no doubt obvious from the day the very first car was built that it was a dangerous tool, and that most

---

38   US Code Title 18 s 1030 (Web).
39   Eg, *Denco Ltd v Joinson* [1992] 1 All ER 463.
40   Eg, *Mullins v Digital Equipment International BV* UD 329/1989.

of the dangers could only be countered by skilful usage and regular maintenance. But it was not for several decades that legislatures insisted that users meet a certain level of skill, and that they report accidents to the proper authorities; and it was even longer before regular mechanical checks were made mandatory. How long will it take for computing technology? One US state has already introduced a mandatory reporting requirement for computer intrusions which compromise personal data;[41] and while one of the great virtues of the Internet is the ease with which new operators may connect to it, there would be obvious advantages in insisting on a basic level of security before they do so.

'Amateurs hack systems, professionals hack people'.[42] Perhaps the biggest problem in modern security arrangements is the mismatch between what security arrangements require of computer users and how those users actually behave. System administrators will always advise users to change their passwords as soon as they receive them, and regularly thereafter; not to choose a password which others may easily guess; never to write passwords down; and never to reveal them to others. Yet their grasp on reality must be weak indeed if they imagine that this advice is followed to the letter, or even in spirit, in very many cases.[43] (Though it does not appear to be true, as is commonly asserted, that passwords which are easy to remember are also easy for hackers to break.[44]) Even the ultimate security sin of leaving the password on a yellow sticky note on the computer itself (loosely equivalent to leaving your front door key on the mat outside it) is not uncommon. Not too much is to be hoped by way of educating computer users here. Inevitably, there will be a move away from passwords and towards biometric forms of identification, such as iris prints or voice identification – though, at present, this technology is of dubious utility.

DAMAGE AND IMPAIRMENT

Where a hacker goes beyond mere wrongful access and actually causes damage, it is obvious that the criminal law might be invoked by the victim. The more serious cases might involve deliberate destruction of data – perhaps out of revenge, to conceal evidence of criminality, or as part of a scheme to blackmail the data owner. The damage caused by the deliberate circulation of viruses will probably be less for each individual victim, but the total world-wide harm done by any one virus may be huge. Lesser damage, such as defacing another's web site (to harm a competitor or to make a protest), may still be expensive to remedy. Yet it is hard to define 'damage' or 'impairment', and any broad definition threatens activities which do little or no harm. The principal laws here were drafted before the web came into existence, and are widely regarded as unsatisfactory.

---

41 2002 Cal SB 1386, amending the California Civil Code (§1798.92), in force on 1 July 2003 (Web). For discussion, see Chang, J, 'Computer hacking: Making the case for a national reporting requirement', April 2004 (Web).

42 Usually attributed to the security consultant Bruce Schneier – see his home page (Web).

43 Eg, 'Brits are crap at password security', Register, 20 April 2004 (Web).

44 Yan, J, Blackwell, A, Anderson, R and Grant, A, 'The memorability and security of passwords – Some empirical results', September 2000 (Web).

Actus reus

The UK offence is committed if the defendant:

> does any act which causes an unauthorised modification of the contents of any computer ...[45]

and a 'modification' (which may be permanent or temporary) occurs if:

> by the operation of any function of the computer concerned or any other computer –
>
> (a) any program or data held in the computer concerned is altered or erased; or
>
> (b) any program or data is added to its contents; ...[46]

This includes any act which contributes towards causing such a modification.

The Irish offence is defined, not as a modification to the contents of a computer, but as damage to the data held. This is achieved by major surgery to the general offence of criminal damage to property. 'Property' is defined as including data,[47] so that 'damaging' data belonging to another is within the offence of criminal damage. Property 'belongs to another' when that other (a) has lawful custody or control of it, (b) has in it any proprietary right or interest, or (c) has a charge over it.[48] To 'damage' data includes:

> (i) to add to, alter, corrupt, erase or move to another storage medium or to a different location in the storage medium in which they are kept (whether or not property other than data is damaged thereby), or
>
> (ii) to do any act that contributes towards causing such addition, alteration, corruption, erasure or movement ...[49]

These Irish definitions are clearly broad ones, going significantly beyond what is ordinarily suggested by the word 'damage'; anything which effects a change to the data or to its location is caught. This covers a great deal that cannot be regarded as 'damaging' in any ordinary sense of the word.

It is clear therefore that the two offences have subtly different focuses. The Irish offence protects 'data', which means 'information in a form in which it can be accessed by means of a computer and includes a program';[50] whereas the UK offence protects 'the contents of any computer'.[51] This results in many small differences. Harming another's floppy disk to make it unreadable is straightforwardly within the Irish offence, but would only be within the UK offence if the disk is currently in the disk drive and so is regarded as part of the computer.[52] Under the Irish offence, it is enough if data is 'moved', whereas the UK legislation makes no mention of this. (However, in the current state of the technology this is probably of no significance: data is 'moved' from one location to another by copying it to the new location and then erasing it from the old.) The UK offence expressly catches adding new programs or data to another's system, even if they leave existing data untouched;[53]

---

45 Computer Misuse Act 1990 (UK), s 3(1)(a).

46 *Ibid*, s 17(7).

47 Criminal Damage Act 1991 (IE), s 1(1) (definition of 'property').

48 *Ibid*, s 1(2).

49 *Ibid*, s 1(1) (definition of 'to damage').

50 *Ibid*, s 1(1) (definition of 'data').

51 Computer Misuse Act 1990 (UK), s 3(1).

52 *Ibid*, s 17(6).

53 See, eg, *Re Yarimaka and Zezev* [2002] EWHC 589 Admin, [2002] Crim LR 648.

whereas the Irish offence only catches additions to existing files, or additions which wipe out existing files. The Irish definition is open-ended (it merely gives *examples* of damage, not a full definition) and so may well turn out to be broader than the UK definition.

Neither offence is straightforwardly concerned with impairing the operation of the target computer, at least not so far as the *actus reus* is concerned. There may be many such impairments which avoid criminal liability. An important current concern is with the 'denial of service' (DoS) attack, whereby a computer acting as a web server receives large numbers of bogus requests for pages, ultimately overwhelming it and putting it out of action. It is hard to see that this is within either offence; no doubt the bogus attacks are recorded in the target server's logs, and so to that extent data is 'added' to files on the target system, but this seems a rather technical way of catching behaviour that should be more clearly criminal. In October 2003, Aaron Caffrey was prosecuted in London for a DoS attack on the web server of the Port of Houston in Texas. His defence was not, however, on the scope of the offence, but rather that his machine had been taken over by a malicious hacker and had executed the attack without his knowledge. Even though Caffrey admitted some limited involvement in hacking activities, the jury acquitted, presumably because it believed his defence.[54] While the case creates no precedent, clearly it does little to encourage similar prosecutions; reform is currently being urged in some quarters.[55]

Mens rea

The UK offence requires intent to cause a modification of the contents of any computer, and further that the modification would have the effect of temporarily or permanently (a) impairing the operation of any computer; (b) preventing or hindering access to any program or data held in any computer; or (c) impairing the operation of any such program or the reliability of any such data. The intent may be quite vague in some respects: it does not matter which computer the defendant had in mind, or whether he or she had any particular data or type of data in mind, or even a particular type of modification in mind. So if an intent to do harm is established beyond reasonable doubt, it is irrelevant that the defendant had no clear idea of precisely what harm he was doing or what he was doing it to. The usual case will, no doubt, be interference with the smooth running of the target computer, but the wording is wider: so where the defendants introduced false data into a business database, this was regarded as 'impairing ... the reliability of ... data' so that the offence applied.[56] It is also irrelevant that the computer modified was not the real target; the offence plainly catches 'zombification', under which a hacker temporarily takes over a computer, which can then be used to attack others over the Internet.[57]

The Irish offence simply requires intent to damage, or recklessness as to whether damage will occur. This is significantly broader than the UK definition. First, it catches not simply those who set out to cause damage, but also risk takers who are

---

54 'Questions cloud cyber crime cases', BBC News, 17 October 2003 (Web); Mann, P, 'Mine's a Caffrey', [2003] EBL (Dec) 6.

55 Below, p 34.

56 *Re Yarimaka and Zezev* [2002] EWHC 589 Admin, [2002] Crim LR 648.

57 Computer Misuse Act 1990 (UK), s 3(2) and (3).

'reckless' as to the possibility of damage. ('For the purposes of this section a person is reckless if he has foreseen that the particular kind of damage that in fact was done might be done and yet has gone on to take the risk of it.'[58]) Secondly, given the wide Irish definition of 'damage', the offence covers many interferences with computer systems which cannot be said to impair the operation of the target computer, but nonetheless 'damage' it.

This difference of approach stands out particularly where a defendant has sneaked a program of his or her own onto a target system, perhaps by surreptitiously embedding it in a web page which the target visits, or by tricking the target into downloading it.

(a) Under the UK rules, the mere act of copying the program to the target system is 'add[ing]' the program to its contents, which is enough to establish the *actus reus*. Actually running the rogue program would almost certainly involve further additions. As to *mens rea*, an intent to impair or hinder must be established, which would involve an enquiry into the intent behind the rogue program. Obviously, malicious viruses, such as those that delete files or attempt to re-format the hard drive, are caught. But other types of program, while undoubtedly unwelcome, are not. Spyware, which monitors the owner's behaviour and reports on it elsewhere, is not obviously within the definition; nor is adware, which displays advertising material on the owner's screen. Running these programs uses computing resources, which are then not available for the owner's purposes, and to that extent they can be said to 'impair the operation' of the computer. But in most cases the impairment will be too trivial to notice, and so this seems an uncertain basis for a prosecution.

(b) Under Irish rules, the mere act of copying the program to the target system is not enough; the *actus reus* is complete only if existing data is interfered with, either because the new program overwrites it, or because the rogue program deliberately attaches itself to existing files (as viruses characteristically do). Actually running the program may or may not further interfere with existing data. Spyware or adware would not be caught, so long as it avoids interference with other files and processes. As to *mens rea*, it would be enough that the insertion of the rogue program was deliberate or reckless and, if it was, the offence is complete; the intent behind the program would go only to the severity of the crime, and hence the gravity of the penalty imposed.

While it is clear that programs which deliberately do damage are caught by both offences, matters become a little vague in other cases. It is clear, however, that if spyware and adware are to be criminalised, it is better done by the legislature than by the creative interpretation of existing laws.[59]

Defences

The main defence is that the defendant's conduct was authorised. Under the UK offence, lack of authorisation is part of the *actus reus*, and 'knowledge that any modification he intends to cause is unauthorised' is part of the *mens rea*. Under the Irish offence, the relevant data must 'belong to another' (and so there can be no

---

58 Criminal Damage Act 1991 (IE), s 2(6).
59 Below, p 35.

offence if others have no claim on it), and there is a lawful excuse if the defendant believed that those entitled to authorise it had done so, or would have done so if they knew the circumstances. This has all been considered above, in relation to the access offences; note particularly the ongoing controversy (of particular relevance where an employee harms the employer's system) over whether someone generally authorised to modify a system is still 'authorised' when that person's real purpose is improper or is forbidden.[60]

Much malevolent software spreads by means involving voluntary behaviour by the victim. The victim may be persuaded to download a program, which in fact contains a malevolent 'Trojan horse'; or the victim may open a word-processed document containing a virus. In cases of that sort, the victim had no intention of running the malicious program and so the courts would presumably be slow to say that its operation is 'authorised' – even though the victim may well have appreciated that he or she was running a program of some sort. A more difficult case is that of the 'hoax virus', where computer users are tricked into deleting essential files on their own systems, in the belief that they are removing a virus. There is no difficulty in proving 'damage' here, but as it is deliberately committed by the system's owner there would be difficulties in proving that it was 'unauthorised'.

It is sometimes suggested in the computing literature (though the matter is one of high controversy) that an attack on another's system might be justified if it was a response to an attack from that very system. The argument is that, in situations where it is hopeless to expect the police to react appropriately, it is legitimate for victims of such an attack to respond for themselves.[61] While the courts cannot be expected to be very sympathetic to vigilantism, nonetheless it is possible that there would be a defence in that situation, at least if the purpose was to prevent further attacks. Reasonable action to prevent crime or to protect property is justifiable. However, mere revenge would not be within this defence, no matter what the provocation. Again, there is a point of view that a software developer who has not been paid for their work, and has exhausted other avenues of action, would be entitled to execute a 'logic bomb' against the client, which would perhaps simply remove the unpaid software from the system, or perhaps do much more. While this is not completely unarguable as a matter of law, it is hard to believe that a defence would be found unless there was a prior warning that this might happen, and the damage was in fact extremely modest.[62]

A defence of 'computer addiction' was raised in the prosecution of three hackers in 1993. The three, who had planned their exploits via a bulletin board and who never physically met one another before the trial, allegedly caused damage costing over £30,000. Two pleaded guilty to various charges, receiving sentences of six months; but the third, Paul Bedworth (19), was said to be so hopelessly addicted to computer hacking that he was incapable of forming the necessary intent to infringe the legislation. He was acquitted.[63] While at the time the case caused extreme reactions both for and against the jury's verdict, today it seems unexceptionable. It made no new law, and recognised no new defence. Any evidence bearing the

60   Above, p 20.
61   Eg, Mullen, T, 'The right to defend', (July 2002) (Web); Moran, B, 'Vigilantes on the net', [2004] NS (12 June) 26.
62   Sewart, T, 'Software contracts – Time to drop the bomb?', (2003) 14 C&L (4) 23.
63   'Hacking "addict" acquitted', Times, 18 March 1993.

defendant's intent is obviously relevant, and this must include any psychiatric evidence of compulsive behaviour. The most that can be said is that not everyone would take such a generous view of his mental state as did that particular jury.

Jurisdiction and sentencing

Both the Irish and the UK legislation give their courts jurisdiction if either the defendant did the relevant act within the jurisdiction, or the damage occurred within the jurisdiction.[64] The generous jurisdiction on conspiracies with a link to one of the UK jurisdictions (noted above[65]) applies also. Presumably the defendant's knowledge or awareness of jurisdiction is irrelevant; it is entirely possible that someone who hacks a computer over the Internet is a little hazy as to which country it is in, but this is not and should not be a defence.

The Irish offence is punishable by imprisonment for 10 years and/or a fine of up to €12,697; the UK offence is punishable by imprisonment of up to 5 years and/or an unlimited fine. The few cases that have been brought have typically resulted in quite harsh sentences, the main factor being the amount of damage done. So in *R v Lindesay*[66] the defendant, a freelance computer developer, was sacked by the firm for which he worked. In revenge, he used his work passwords to access the sites of various clients, deleting some web pages and defacing others; he also sent e-mails to customers of one client (a supermarket) saying that it was about to raise its prices. The total cost of putting right the damage was about £9,000. The Court of Appeal was not prepared to reduce a sentence of nine months' imprisonment, despite substantial mitigation – the defendant had acted on impulse, had co-operated entirely with the police, and had pleaded guilty. Again, in *R v Vallor*,[67] the defendant had created and distributed a virus with the potential to wipe clean the hard drives of target machines; it was estimated to have infected at least 29,000 machines in 42 countries, though many more copies were intercepted by anti-virus software. Two years' imprisonment was imposed in January 2003, the court being influenced particularly by the need to deter offences of this type. Somewhat lower penalties have been imposed where the actual harm done is less, as for example in *R v Maxwell-King*,[68] which involved a largely unsuccessful attempt to circulate hardware to access cable programmes without payment.

Harsh sentences for virus writers are not unknown internationally, but a uniform approach has yet to emerge. David Smith, who wrote and circulated the 'Melissa' worm which was said to have caused about US$80 m of damage world-wide, was sentenced to 20 months' imprisonment by a US court in 2002. This was mitigated by his help in implicating not only Simon Vallor (mentioned above), but also Jan de Wit, who wrote the highly destructive 'Anna Kournikova' virus.[69] De Wit was prosecuted in the Netherlands, receiving 150 hours of community service in 2002.[70]

---

64 Computer Misuse Act 1990 (UK), ss 4 and 5, Criminal Damage Act 1991 (IE), s 1(1), (definition of 'to damage').
65 Above, p 22.
66 [2001] EWCA Crim 1720.
67 Southwark Crown Court, 21 January 2003, (2003) 3 ECLR (1) 8.
68 [2001] 2 Cr App R(S) 136.
69 'Melissa author helped Feds track other virus writers', Register, 18 September 2003 (Web).
70 'Kournikova virus author loses appeal', Register, 23 October 2002 (Web).

Subsidiary and related offences

The Irish offence is defined as a species of criminal damage, and accordingly the whole array of offences related to criminal damage apply also to 'data damage'. Damage which endangers human life (such as by interfering with hospital patient records) attracts imprisonment for life and/or an unlimited fine.[71] Unlawful threats of damage are an offence (10 years/€12,697),[72] and may in some cases amount to blackmail (14 years/€ unlimited fine).[73] Possession of anything with intent to use it to commit damage, or to allow others to do so, is also an offence (10 years/€12,697).[74] So mere possession of the code for a virus is enough for a conviction, as long as the necessary intent can be proved; presumably the same could be said of possession of passwords to which the possessor was not entitled.

The UK offence is not linked to criminal damage in this way. The offence of criminal damage does not obviously apply to 'data damage', as it requires damage to tangible property.[75] Nonetheless, the courts were initially prepared to develop the offence in that direction. In one famous case, the self-styled 'Mad Hacker' took control of JANET, the network linking UK universities with each other and with the wider Internet. He deleted or changed a number of files, including audit files recording his activities, files defining passwords and system privileges, and a worm designed specifically to trap him. He was convicted of criminal damage. The Court of Appeal noted that while the legislation requires damage to *tangible* property, it does not also require that the damage itself be tangible; accordingly, the defendant could be said to have 'damaged' the disks storing the changed or deleted files.[76] This (slightly strained) reasoning was, however, reversed by statute, which provided that 'modification of the contents of a computer shall not be regarded as damaging any computer or computer storage medium unless its effect on that computer or computer storage medium impairs its physical condition'.[77] So, while it is certainly still possible to 'damage' a computer or a disk, few hacks will do so, and the damage offence and related offences are therefore irrelevant in this context. Presumably, a threat to damage data can constitute the offence of blackmail, if the appropriate criminal intent is shown.[78]

The use of information and communications technology (ICT) to attack national infrastructure would presumably be within the scope of the anti-terrorism legislation.[79] A staple of science fiction for many years, particularly since John Badham's *Wargames* (1983) and William Gibson's *Neuromancer* (1984), it is far more talked about than actually encountered. Nonetheless, the threat has to be taken seriously. Power suppliers, air traffic controllers, and communications utilities of all sorts are necessarily reliant on computer technology.[80] Public opinion on the matter

---

71   Criminal Damage Act 1991 (IE), s 2.
72   *Ibid*, s 3.
73   Criminal Justice (Public Order) Act 1994 (IE), s 17.
74   Criminal Damage Act 1991 (IE), s 4.
75   Criminal Damage Act 1971 (E&W), ss 1 and 12(1).
76   *R v Whiteley* (1991) 93 Cr App Rep 25.
77   Computer Misuse Act 1990 (UK), s 3(6).
78   Theft Act 1968 (E&W), s 21.
79   See especially Terrorism Act 2000 (UK), s 1(2)(e).
80   See generally, National Infrastructure Security Co-ordination Centre home page (Web).

is, unsurprisingly, split, with some emphasising the massive harm that could be done by a sufficiently motivated and skilled terrorist,[81] while others emphasise the unlikeliness of most of the feared attacks, and express cynicism at panic-mongering that serves mainly to boost the profits of security consultants.[82] In the current state of the technology, the part of the national infrastructure most vulnerable to attack via the Internet is the Internet itself; particularly susceptible are the root name servers, without which machines connected to the Internet cannot know the location of other machines they wish to communicate with.[83] Many attacks on the name servers have been recorded, a handful of which have caused serious disruption; at the time of writing, none has been followed by convictions. The possible use of Internet-based attacks as a weapon of war is a matter of some interest to governments and to international lawyers.[84]

Compensation and civil remedies

Can the owner of the damaged system sue the hacker, to claim compensation for harm caused? In many cases, it will turn out that there was a contract between the two which the hacker has broken, as where an employee hacks into the employer's system, or a student into that of the university. In cases of that kind, there is a clear right to recover any provable financial loss flowing from the intrusion. Where there is no contract, the matter seems more doubtful. A conviction for any of the offences considered in this chapter may lead to a compensation order against the convicted defendant. This may not, however, be a satisfactory remedy from the victim's point of view: the court must have regard to the defendant's means, may feel it appropriate to order payment in instalments, and may be subject to jurisdictional limits. As to an ordinary civil action, it hardly seems conceivable that a court would refuse to find liability where a defendant has deliberately harmed a claimant's system, but authority is scarce. Conceivably the criminal legislation could be used as the basis of a civil action, by way of the tort of breach of statutory duty, but this is a so-far untried tactic in a rather arcane area of law.

In limited circumstances, the owner of the injured system might claim elsewhere. Many insurers are prepared to cover damage caused by hackers, though premiums have of late been very substantial. Such damage may also be within the terms of ordinary all-risk policies, unless specifically excluded.[85] If the intrusion was facilitated by a breach of security, traceable to a particular outside contractor or employee, in principle an action for breach of contract could lie.[86] If some external person or organisation made it easier for the hacker to attack, as by interfering with

---

81 Eg, Graham-Rowe, D, 'Power play', [2004] NS (15 May) 24.
82 Eg, Quinn, T, 'Electro-paranoia', [2002] Prospect (Sept) 12.
83 Eg, 'Feds investigating "largest ever" Internet attack', Register, 23 October 2002 (Web). The operation of the Domain Name System is explained in slightly more detail below, Chapter 7.
84 Delibasis, D, 'The right of states to use force in cyberspace', (2002) 11 ICTL 255; Abeyratne, R, 'Cyber-terrorism and activities in outer space', (2000) 5 Comms L 20.
85 Duboff, L and Garvey, S, 'From the Love Bug to the Stages virus: The threat of computer virus damage', [2001] Ent LR 39. For litigation, see *Tektrol Ltd v International Insurance Co of Hanover Ltd* [2005] EWCA Civ 845 (Web).
86 See 'Security contractors urged to take out personal indemnity insurance', ZDNet UK 2 June 2004 (Web).

security measures, then an action in negligence is possible.[87] However, it would take unusually strong facts before such an action was plausible: the courts are usually reluctant to allow action against those who merely failed to prevent harm actually done by others, and in most cases the loss would be regarded as purely economic.[88] Claimants would also have to be wary of the argument that they bore some responsibility for the loss themselves; a failure to take ordinary precautions against loss, such as by maintaining regular backups of important data, would be likely to reduce damages quite considerably.[89]

Assessment and reform

Many of the comments made above on the dishonest access offences apply equally to the more serious damage offences. Harmful intrusions are a common event; much of the harm is serious and deliberate, and those who do it are rightly treated as dangerous criminals; new viruses are encountered every day; computer security is a large and increasingly public concern. Against that background, the fact that prosecution rates are extremely low suggests to many that there must be something fundamentally wrong with the way the offence is defined, or the penalties for it. But this may be a hasty judgment. Most of the more serious incidents of damage are well within existing laws, whether under the computer misuse offences or the more general criminal law. The law enforcement difficulties are considerable, but extending the offences to those who do no real harm and have no real criminal intent is no solution.

As the use of ICT in general and the Internet in particular become more common and more sophisticated, it becomes harder to sum up all types of social undesirable conduct in a single neat formula. Already noted above is the ambiguity of the current law, which sometimes seeks to protect individual computers, and sometimes data *per se*. Quite possibly the time has come for a more nuanced approach, perhaps by distinguishing (as does the Cybercrime Convention) between illegal access to computer systems, data interference, system interference, and misuse of devices.[90] This might give some stability to the area. However, the politics are such as to favour a more problem-driven approach, under which particular abuses provide the motor for reform, and hence are likely to shape it even after they have been brought under control. Three examples are particularly prominent at the moment.

First, denial of service (DoS) attacks. The owner of a web site finds that it has been flooded with bogus requests for data; the web server has been unable to respond to them all, and has ultimately been overwhelmed, or has shut itself down. Very probably, an attacker with the skills to mount such an attack is also adept enough to conceal their location; a common tactic is to take over a number of 'zombie' machines, the owners of which are not complicit in the plan, and to co-ordinate a joint attack.

---

87 Faulkner, S, 'Invasion of the information snatchers: Creating liability for corporations with vulnerable computer networks', (2000) 18 JCIL 1019.

88 For general discussion, see de Villiers, M, '*Virus ex machina: Res ipsa loquitur*', [2003] STLR 1 (Web); Weston, C, 'Suing in tort for loss of computer data', (1999) 58 CLJ 67.

89 Eg, *Logical Computer Supplies Ltd v Euro Car Parks Ltd* QBD 19 June 2001.

90 Convention on Cybercrime, Arts 2 and 4–6 (Web). For yet another approach, see Nemerofsky, J, 'The crime of "interruption of computer services to authorized users": Have you ever heard of it?', (2000) 6 RJOLT 23 (Web).

(The attack is then said to be a 'distributed' denial of service, or DDoS, attack.) Such attacks may be mounted for any number of reasons; the nastier ones are part of plans to blackmail the owner of the target web site with a threat of losing their presence on the web. As noted above, it is far from clear that such attacks infringe the computer misuse legislation as it stands. A Private Members' Bill to outlaw them was introduced into the House of Lords in April 2005; this would have criminalised

> any act ... which causes ... directly or indirectly, an impairment of access to any program or data held [on a] computer ...[91]

The Bill provides for unlimited fines and for imprisonment of up to two years; this increases to five years if the intent was to facilitate further crimes. (The Bill failed, its first reading falling on the very day that a general election was announced.) This is surely much too broad. 'Impairment of access' is vague, and can cover much that is trivial. It might also criminalise possibly legitimate protests, as where many people send e-mails to the object of their protest, causing it to crash. And 'computers' are so common today that the implications are hard to foresee. Clumsily misprogramming another's microwave oven or VCR does not really seem worthy of the magistrates' attention; yet both could be said to involve 'computers'. There is no doubt that legislation is needed here, but it should be much more narrowly drafted. Article 5 of the Cybercrime Convention requires its signatories to criminalise serious and intentional hindering of functioning of a computer system, and so the matter will no doubt be revisited. The introduction of such an offence has recently been urged by the All Party Parliamentary Internet Group, in a report making a number of detailed proposals for reform of the area;[92] the government has claimed, surprisingly, that denial of service attacks are within existing legislation.[93] Whether a different attitude will be forced by the new EU framework decision on attacks against information systems remains to be seen.[94]

Secondly, there has recently been a spate of rogue diallers. Inserted onto victims' systems by spam or other clandestine means, these programs dial up premium-rate Internet services, for which the victim is subsequently billed. It is far from obvious that this is caught by existing legislation, as it may do no harm at all to the target computer, only to its owner's bank balance. Some relief from this in the UK is provided by ICSTIS, an industry body that to a certain extent regulates the premium-rate industry and can impose fines.[95] While ICSTIS is prepared to use its powers vigorously, it is currently somewhat overworked and so may not always provide an effective remedy.[96] In any event, such blatant fraud on consumers surely calls for a criminal penalty as well as financial penalties.

Thirdly, spyware and adware are becoming an increasing concern. Most of this could in principle be controlled under the data protection legislation,[97] but even if

91   Computer Misuse Act 1990 (Amendment) Bill 2005 (Web).
92   'Revision of the Computer Misuse Act', APIG, June 2004 (Web). See also 'Hacker law change gets "elevator pitch" in parliament', Register, 6 April 2005 (Web).
93   'Electronic civil disobedience', *Hansard* (Lords), 3 March 2005 (Web).
94   Council Framework Decision 2005/222/JHA on attacks against information systems, especially Art 3 (Web).
95   ICSTIS home page (Web); 'New powers granted to slam rogue diallers', ZDNet UK, 16 July 2004 (Web). For an attempt at a technological solution see 'BT cracks down on rogue diallers', Register, 27 May 2005 (Web).
96   'ICSTIS in meltdown – MPs', Register, 1 July 2004 (Web).
97   Below, Chapter 4.

this sometimes gives a satisfactory remedy, it still seems to miss the point. Running a program on someone else's machine without their permission seems objectionable whether or not that program steals personal data. Utah has already passed a law specifically criminalising those who circulate these programs[98] (though predictably enough it is being challenged as an unconstitutional interference with advertisers' freedom of speech[99]). US federal law may follow soon. As it is, these programs are proving hard to deal with; software to detect them is buggy, and there have been allegations of fraud against some of their writers. It may be prudent to extend the criminal law to catch these cases, though jurisdictional and evidential problems seem likely. The UK Government's position seems to be that spyware is caught by existing legislation.[100]

COMPUTER THEFT, FORGERY AND FRAUD

Computer-related financial crime is now at startling levels. The reason is obvious enough. As ICT is used more and more as a basic tool for managing businesses and money, any financial crime more sophisticated than a mugging is likely to involve misuse of computers at some stage. Indeed, even the mugger may very probably secure such items as credit cards, mobile phones and ID of various sorts from the victim, raising legal issues that can properly be regarded as issues of e-commerce.

Estimates for the amount of computer crime or the sums involved are abundant, but notoriously unreliable. There is no agreed definition of key terms. Bodies seeking extensions to the law, or additional powers for law enforcement agencies, have an obvious incentive to exaggerate the scale of the problem; conversely, institutions worried about customer confidence have every reason to conceal both known breaches of their security and the detail of their security measures. For many reasons, the 'dark figure' of the amount of crime committed is in practice unknowable, and talk of large rises (or indeed large falls) in criminal activity are hard to take seriously. But that it is a serious problem, no one is in any doubt.

This section does not attempt to describe all financial crimes in which ICT may play a significant role. In many areas, traditional offences have proved quite adequate for the task: theft, deception, forgery and falsification of accounts do not always assume a very different character merely because they are practised online. Crimes such as soliciting orders for goods which will not arrive, or 'pump and dump' schemes to inflate share prices, are made a great deal more easy by the Internet, but need no new legislation. However, some technical difficulties have been experienced, and the purpose of this section is to mention some of the more important issues and difficulties that have been encountered in reformulating financial criminal law in the light of the new technologies.

Irish theft and fraud law was recently reformed in detail, and the legislation contains various computer-specific provisions.[101] At the time of writing, the UK law is under review.[102] The main thrust of the new proposals is that current definitions of

---

98   Spyware Control Act 2004 (Utah Code Title 13 Chapter 40) (Web).
99   'Utah judge freezes anti-spyware law', News.Com, 22 June 2004 (Web).
100 'Spyware', *Hansard* (Lords), 10 January 2005 (Web).
101 Criminal Justice (Theft and Fraud Offences) Act 2001 (IE). See especially ss 9, 48 and 52.
102 'Fraud law reform: Consultation on proposals for legislation', Home Office, May 2004 (Web).

fraud are too specific, allowing novel types of fraud to fall between the cracks of the law. Scots law has a broad general common law offence of fraud, but England, Wales and Northern Ireland do not, and it is proposed that this gap should be filled. The Government proposes a new general statutory offence of fraud, which may be committed by false representations, by wrongful failure to disclose information, or by abuse of an official position. Also proposed are offences of obtaining services dishonestly, possessing equipment to commit frauds, and fraudulent trading by individuals (fraudulent trading by companies is already illegal). The proposals also suggest that, taken together, these new offences might be broad enough to allow abolition of the ancient catch-all common law offence of conspiracy to defraud. The proposals seem sensible enough, though if the *actus reus* of the new general fraud offence is to be so broadly drawn (particularly 'failure to disclose information'), the *mens rea* will need to be narrow to avoid criminalising unobjectionable or trivial behaviour.

Identity theft

The ability to deceive others as to his or her identity has always been an essential prerequisite for a successful con artist. 'Identity theft' and 'identity manufacture' are therefore not new ideas. However, the Internet is a relatively anonymous medium – it can be very hard to know who you are dealing with – and the increasing reliance on computer-mediated ID in commercial transactions brings problems of its own. The technology is developing all the time, and each new development has its own limitations and possibilities for avoidance. The pace of change also increases the problem of the lack of sophistication, or simple ignorance, on the part of potential victims.

Examples abound. Unlawful acquisition of others' credit card numbers or bank account details is common: methods include stealing computers or files from commercial organisations, and surveillance using spyware or packet sniffers. Deception may be used to persuade people to type in their numbers, such as by offering to sell non-existent goods on mail order or at auction, or by 'phishing' (that is, persuading the target to disclose details directly, perhaps under the pretext of a security check by a bank). The stolen numbers may be used to buy goods or services. Other personal details taken and misused may include national insurance numbers and credit profiles, which are then used to make fraudulent applications for credit cards. General details of another's life may be used to flesh out a false identity, which is then used to mislead the police and other criminal investigators.[103]

In all of these cases, the ultimate goal for which the identity was stolen is well within the criminal law. It can therefore be argued that there is no need for the creation of a new offence, the real problems rather being those of public awareness, detection and proof. This certainly seems to be the attitude of the UK and Irish Governments; there have been discussions of introducing an offence of identity theft along US lines[104] (for which the penalties have recently been

---

103 See 'New study revealing behind the scenes of phishing attacks', CircleID, 22 May 2005 (Web).
104 Identity Theft and Assumption Deterrence Act 1998, amending US Code Title s 1028 (Web). See Saunders, K and Zucker, B, 'Counteracting identity fraud in the information age: The Identity Theft and Assumption Deterrence Act', (1999) 13 IRLCT 183.

increased[105]), but there seem to be no imminent plans to do so. However, the UK's introduction of identity cards will no doubt lead to some rethinking of this area.

Defining theft and deception

Offences of theft and deception are a basic part of the protection of financial assets and there is no suggestion that they do not apply merely because a computer is involved in the case. Two major difficulties have been encountered by prosecutors, though they have largely been solved by the time of writing.

First, much trade that was previously carried out by the transfer of physical objects is now done online. So money payments or share transfers which would earlier have involved pieces of paper are now effected by the mere movement of electrons. This is problematical if the offences supposedly guaranteeing the integrity of the system are defined by reference to tangible property. So when a conman persuaded a building society to grant him a mortgage, the funds being transferred electronically, the House of Lords refused to say that he had 'obtained property by deception', as no 'property' was obtained.[106] This gap in the English law was speedily remedied by the creation of a new offence of dishonestly obtaining a money transfer.[107] The new Irish legislation sidesteps the problem by adopting an exceedingly general formulation: 'A person who dishonestly, with the intention of making a gain for himself or herself or another, or of causing loss to another, by any deception induces another to do or refrain from doing an act is guilty of an offence'.[108] This may turn out to be a continuing area of concern.[109]

Secondly, many offences against financial computing systems seem very similar to offences of deception; for example, inputting false details to secure some payment or other is remarkably like obtaining money by deception. Nonetheless, the courts have so far usually resisted the temptation to say that a computer has a mind which can be deceived.[110] Offences of deception are therefore inapplicable unless a human is involved somewhere down the line. This does not in practice seem to have reduced the scope of the criminal law to any noticeable degree; in practice, nearly all such cases fall within the general offences of theft or false accounting.

Conclusion

Fraud is always a moving target. It was not to be expected that the introduction of ICT to financial systems would reduce the problems in the short term; greater sophistication is now needed to engage in financial fraud, but it was surely never

---

105 Identity Theft Penalty Enhancement Act 2004, on which see White House press release, 15 July 2004 (Web).

106 *R v Preddy* [1996] AC 815, interpreting Theft Act 1968 (E&W), ss 4 and 15.

107 Theft (Amendment) Act 1996 (E&W), s 1, inserting new s 15A and 15B into the 1968 Act; see also Theft (Amendment) (Northern Ireland) Order 1997 (NI), SI 1997/277. For discussion, see Clements, L, 'Theft, mortgage fraud and the age of technology', [1997] 2 WJCLI (Web).

108 Criminal Justice (Theft and Fraud Offences) Act 2001 (IE), s 6.

109 Lipton, J, 'Property offences into the 21st century', [1999] 1 JILT (Web).

110 Chapman, M, 'Can a computer be deceived? Dishonesty offences and electronic transfer of funds', (2000) 64 J Cr L 89.

doubted that many would make it their business to acquire the necessary sophistication. And the Internet's international character will also lead to many difficulties of jurisdiction.[111] Yet computing technology is being adopted by the commercial world, at least in part, precisely because it makes financial auditing quicker and more efficient, and most fraud easier to detect. There is so far no reason to doubt that judgment. However, the current shift towards technology-based forms of ID is no sure-fire strategy for improving security. It is in essence a gamble that newer forms of ID will ultimately prove harder to fake than the old. Which way that gamble will turn out may not be known for many years.

SPAM

Spam is simply unrequested e-mail, sent in bulk. Jokily named by reference to a 1970s TV comedy show (and much resented by the Hormel Foods Corporation, makers of SPAM luncheon meat[112]), it is at first hard to see it as a serious threat to e-commerce. If the unauthorised access offences are quasi-trespass, and the impairment offences are quasi-damage, then sending spam can only be quasi-littering, or something equally trivial. Few spam e-mails are even read, and any spam message can be deleted by its recipient, the entire transaction involving only minimal time and cost.

Yet spam is, in fact, a matter of serious concern to legislators, police, regulators and system administrators of all sorts. This is for two reasons, both connected with the vast number of spam messages which can be sent. First, while the cost of any one message is trivial, taken in bulk spam consumes large amounts of resources. It has been reliably estimated that well over half of network traffic today consists of spam. The cost of bearing this load is ultimately reflected in the price of Internet services; it may be invisible but it is not costless. Similarly, the time necessary to deal with it is largely invisible but nonetheless substantial, whether we are talking of the efforts of ICT workers to intercept it, or the time necessary to dispose of it if it is not intercepted. Secondly, the number of potential victims from maliciously intended spam turns what would otherwise be a mere nuisance into a consumer protection problem of major proportions. Even if only one person in a thousand is stupid enough to fall for any particular deceptive spam, that is still rather a lot of people. Again, sending a single offensive e-mail may merely raise an eyebrow, whereas sending it one million times may constitute a public order crisis. Yet, despite the concentrated efforts of many, so far there is no simple solution to the problem of spam short of shutting down the Internet entirely.

Who spams, how and why?

It is usually asserted that the motivation for spamming is purely economic, and while in fact it is so cheap to do that an economic motivation does not have to be assumed, this is probably right. Much of it advertises goods and services, often

111 Gilbert, G, 'Who has jurisdiction for cross-frontier financial crimes?', [1995] 2 WJCLI (Web).
112 Hormel Foods' trademarks include SPAM, SPAMBURGER, SPAMTASTIC and any other SPAM-derived terms. See Spam home page (Web).

medical, financial or computer-related. There is a heavy concentration of sex-related offering, such as for Viagra, pornography, dubious dating services, or organ enhancement opportunities. No doubt, some of this advertising means what it says. It is hard to obtain reliable estimates for how much of this is a genuine attempt to make a sale, how much is simply meant to elicit a response (so that the spammer can be sure that the address to which the spam was sent denotes a live e-mail account), and how much is a prelude to a devious and costly fraud. Much spam is obvious as fraud to anyone with even minimal financial sophistication, such as offers to participate in pyramid schemes, or 'phishing' enquiries; particularly common is the so-called 'Nigerian fraud', which seeks help in moving funds from some remote part of the world, the object being to inveigle the helper in financial skulduggery somewhere down the line. Equally obviously malicious are spams containing viruses and other malware. Some spam carries an ideological, political or spiritual message, and so may presumably be taken at face value – unless it is really meant to denigrate those who hold that particular view.

Sending spam is relatively inexpensive, though both the cost and the computing expertise necessary to do it without being arrested are rising. E-mail addresses can be purchased by the hundreds of millions for very little; more can be obtained by harvesting likely sources on the Internet, or by using corruption or fraud to take them from major ISPs. Techniques for concealing the origin of e-mail must necessarily become second nature to any successful spammer. Some sophistication is needed in finding a location from which the spam can be sent without being stopped by a system administrator; and as administrators world-wide note the origin of major spam and then block e-mail from it, it is necessary to move on rather often. Some spammers circulate viruses which then send spam from the target machine, perhaps after raiding anything that looks like an address book. Other viruses even take over ('zombify') target machines; these machines can then later, unbeknown to their owners, be used to send out spam on their own, with no obvious link to the spammer.[113]

It is often asserted that the number of effective spammers today is low, perhaps no more than 200 across the entire globe. While it has to be pointed out that few people are in a position to know the precise number, it is certainly true that increasingly forceful tactics to root out spammers exert a Darwinian pressure: we should expect that there are only a few left, but if so, those few are evidently very good at what they do. The names of some of the more important spammers are public knowledge, at least to those who read the computing press; the anti-spam pressure group Spamhaus maintains an online public register of spammers.[114] Indeed, one prominent spammer, Scott Richter, promoted his own 'Spam King' clothing line – though he quickly found himself the subject of trademark proceedings by the Hormel Foods Corporation.[115]

Individual remedies

This section considers legal remedies that can be brought to bear on spammers. It should be said at the outset that these remedies are of limited use in tackling the

---

113 'Spammers get fussy as zombie army grows', ZDNet UK, 21 May 2004 (Web); 'The illicit trade in compromised PCs', Register, 30 April 2004 (Web).
114 Spamhaus home page (Web).
115 '"Spam King" Richter gets legal roasting', Register, 17 June 2004 (Web).

sheer bulk of spam, for which no legal remedy is currently conceivable. The remedies here are limited territorially, whereas a spammer may be based anywhere in the world. They all rely on being able to prove the guilt of a particular individual or company, often no trivial task. And the civil remedies all rely on showing that a particular person's rights have been infringed by the defendant's behaviour – usually a hopeless endeavour. That does not mean, however, that these remedies are entirely useless. First, they set limits for advertisers who wish to be considered legitimate: spam has not developed into a respectable advertising medium, and the law is one pressure to keep it that way. Secondly, they can be useful where a particular individual has been targeted and victimised by spam.[116]

The principal provision is in the Directive on Personal Data and the Protection of Privacy, which prohibits direct marketing by e-mail.[117] E-mail is defined as including text messages, and other provisions cover certain other electronic media. Marketing e-mails may not be sent to individuals without their prior consent. There is an exception for existing customers: if the customer's e-mail address is obtained in the course of a sale and in compliance with the data protection laws, then it may be used to market similar products unless or until the customer objects (each e-mail must remind them of their right to object, 'free of charge and in an easy manner'). No marketing e-mail to anyone may disguise or conceal on whose behalf it was sent, and a valid address for objections must be included. The Directive has no application unless the e-mail is an exercise in direct marketing.

There is, however, some doubt as to precisely who is protected by the Directive. While the bar on anonymous e-mail applies generally, the main prohibition protects only 'subscribers [to a public electronic communications service] who are natural persons', though it also requires EU Member States to 'ensure … that the legitimate interests of subscribers other than natural persons with regard to unsolicited communications are sufficiently protected'.[118] Plainly this covers ordinary consumers who 'subscribe' by buying net access to their home from an ISP, but where does it leave (i) members of their family, (ii) companies, (iii) individuals working within a company?

(a) The Irish regulations protect 'a subscriber […] who is a natural person'. They define a 'subscriber' as a party to a contract for the supply of electronic communications services.[119] It would appear that members of the subscriber's family are not protected, except possibly if the contract was 'expressed to be for the benefit of' the family (not impossible, given the way such services are marketed), in which case statute deems them to be parties.[120] Companies are not protected, though they, along with all non-individual subscribers, can validly object to marketing e-mail, and may not be sent it by a person to whom they have made an objection.[121] The

---

116 See below, p 152.

117 Directive 2002/58/EC, on processing of personal data and the protection of privacy in the electronic communications sector, Art 13. The Directive is implemented by the Privacy and Electronic Communications (EC Directive) Regulations 2003 (UK), SI 2003/2426 and the European Communities (Electronic Communications Networks and Services) (Data Protection and Privacy) Regulations 2003 (IE), SI 2003/535.

118 Directive 2002/58/EC, Art 13.5.

119 SI 2003/535 (IE), regs 2(1) (definition of 'subscriber') and 13(1).

120 Married Women's Status Act 1957 (IE), s 8. The legislation assumes a conventional nuclear family, the parents being married.

121 SI 2003/535 (IE), reg 13(3).

individual worker is not a subscriber but is not a non-individual either, and so has no protection, though no doubt the employer could validly object under the regulations. Unaccountably, the Irish regulations do not apply to spam from political parties.[122]

(b) The UK regulations protect 'individual subscribers'; 'individual' means a living person, and 'subscriber' again implies being a party to a contract.[123] Again, it is possible that family members may sometimes be brought within this by statutory exceptions to privity of contract.[124] There is no protection for anyone other than 'individual subscribers'; business is not protected unless conducted by a sole trader, or where for some other reason the e-mail account belongs to an individual. Even if it is, there is a suggestion that 'individual' implies a home or at least non-work address, so that the regulations would not apply.[125]

The victim of a breach of the regulations may sue for loss caused. The right of action extends to anyone who suffers damage as a result of a breach; so it would include not merely the individuals spammed but also their ISPs, if the expense resulting from the spam is quantifiable. However, any such action could be met by showing that reasonable care was taken to comply with the regulations.[126] As it is usually hard to tell whether a particular e-mail address is a business or a work e-mail, this defence may be hard to rebut. Criminal proceedings may also be taken by communications regulators (the Information Commissioner in the UK, the Data Protection Commissioner in Ireland); the maximum penalty for any one offence in Ireland is a fine of €3,000, in the UK it is £5,000 before magistrates or an unlimited amount after jury trial. While, so far, enforcement seems cumbersome and weak,[127] it is specifically the nature of the penalty that attracts the greatest criticism of the current law – Italy has made jail terms available for offences against the Directive, and it is often said that the weakness of the UK law is an incentive to spammers to relocate there.[128] Some stiff fines have been imposed for text message spam by the UK regulator ICSTIS, for spam fraudulently enticing its victims to call premium rate numbers.[129]

Other legal avenues against spam are possible, but largely untried. If the spammer turns out to be in contractual relations with one of the victims, then an action for breach of contract can be mounted; this seems to have worked on at least one occasion.[130] Spamming may involve the use of personal data,[131] and when it does so there is arguably an infringement of the data protection legislation, though whether this is true of the generality of spam seems doubtful.[132] Suggestions are occasionally made that spamming is tortious, the tort being variously said to be

---

122 See SI 2003/535 (IE), reg 1(2)–(5), and Data Protection (Amendment) Act 2003 (IE), s 2 (definition of 'direct marketing').
123 SI 2003/2426 (UK), regs 2(1) and 22(1).
124 Contracts (Rights of Third Parties) Act 1999 (E&W and NI), s 1.
125 Marchini, R, 'The new privacy and e-commerce regulations', (2003) 14 C&L (4) 26, 27.
126 SI 2003/2426 (UK), reg 30; SI 2003/535 (IE), reg 16.
127 'UK spammers set to avoid prosecution until 2005', ZDNet UK, 16 April 2004 (Web).
128 'Britain is flooding the world with spam', Times, 24 January 2004; 'Spammers consider UK a soft touch', VNUNet, 11 June 2004 (Web).
129 Eg, 'Text scammers fined £450,000', Register, 24 May 2004 (Web).
130 'Virgin spammer settles out of court', Register, 26 May 1999 (Web).
131 'Spammers use your cat's name to sell you Viagra', ZDNet UK, 22 June 2004 (Web).
132 See below, p 84.

trespass, conversion, negligence or interference with business; but there is no UK or Irish support for this yet. It is also suggested that the 'illegal impairment' offence might be invoked, but unless a deluge of spam was deliberately sent to do harm to a particular machine, this seems unlikely. Trade bodies such as the Advertising Standards Authority may sometimes be able to obtain a satisfactory outcome for victims.[133]

The content of some individual spams may be particularly objectionable. Spam aimed at a particular individual may be enough to constitute defamation or harassment, though these cases are very different from the general run of spam.[134] More generally, offensive spam may invite prosecution as pornography or racist utterances. If the spam wrongly suggests that it is connected with some legitimate firm, that firm may want to sue for defamation or breach of trade mark. More specific legislation penalises the use of e-mail to generate messages which are 'grossly offensive or of an indecent, obscene or menacing character', or sends false messages 'for the purpose of causing annoyance, inconvenience or needless anxiety'.[135]

Foreign approaches

Spam first emerged as a problem in 1994, and it impacted on all countries of the developed world at roughly the same time. A variety of responses emerged.

Much attention world-wide has been paid to the US experience. The only significant legal tool at first was the civil action, by an ISP or other body that could claim to have lost significant amounts through the activity of one particular spammer. Some sizeable awards of damages have been made,[136] though there have also been some spectacular instances of mistaken identity.[137] Then individual states began to supplement this by anti-spam statutes of various sorts: Nevada was the first, in 1997.[138]

This state legislation has, however, largely been superseded by the Federal CAN-SPAM Act 2003.[139] This created a variety of new offences of concealing the origin of e-mail or the misleading of recipients as to its content. Spam containing 'sexually oriented material' must say so in the subject line (though spam merely telling recipients how to access such material need not). Despite its title, however,

---

133 'UK advertising authority introduces anti-spam rules', ZDNet UK, 5 March 2003 (Web).
134 Ellison, L and Akdeniz, Y, 'Cyberstalking: The regulation of harassment on the Internet', [1998] Crim LR (special edition) 29.
135 Communications Act 2003 (UK), s 127 (at the time of writing this provision is not fully in force); Post Office (Amendment) Act 1951 (IE), s 13, as substituted by Postal and Telecommunications Services Act 1983 (IE), Sched 3, Pt 2, and amended by Postal and Telecommunications Services (Amendment) Act 1999 (IE), s 7.
136 Notably in *Earthlink, Inc v Carmack* 2003 US Dist LEXIS 9963 (D N Ga, 7 May 2003) ($16.4 m in damages and a permanent injunction against further spam). Theories of liability here are considered below, p 210.
137 Eg, 'Microsoft says sorry to "spammer"', BBC News, 8 August 2003 (Web).
138 For general surveys of the US position, see Kosiba, J, 'Legal relief from spam-induced Internet indigestion', (1999) 25 Dayt LR 187; Kelin, S, 'State regulation of unsolicited commercial e-mail', (2001) 16 BTLJ 435; Sorkin, D, 'Technical and legal approaches to unsolicited electronic mail', (2001) 35 USFLR 325 (Web).
139 Controlling the Assault of Non-Solicited Pornography and Marketing Act 2003 (Web), on which see Alongi, E, 'Has the US canned spam?', (2004) 46 Ariz LR 263.

the Act does not prohibit spam, but merely requires that it include a meaningful way of registering an objection so as to avoid receiving future spam.

The CAN-SPAM Act has had no noticeable impact on the problem so far; there has been one notable conviction (under a state law analogous to CAN-SPAM).[140] This comes as no surprise to anti-spam lobby groups such as Spamhaus[141] and the Coalition Against Unsolicited Commercial Email (CAUCE),[142] which opposed it as a retrograde step. Spam *per se* is not rendered illegal unless it is sent over a recipient's expressed objection; yet recipients are rightly reluctant to object, fearing that the objection will be futile, or even harmful, in that it confirms to the spammer that the e-mail address denotes a live account. Proposals for a national registry in which objections could be noted have been rejected as too likely to prove counter-productive. Proceedings under the Act have been started by the Federal Trade Commission (FTC) and several ISPs.[143] It is perhaps too early to pronounce these actions a complete failure, but the FTC is already protesting that the difficulty of identifying individual spammers ensures that prosecution cannot be a cost-effective tool.[144] Even an optimist would have to concede that the CAN-SPAM Act has proved to be an exceedingly cumbersome tool, which has yet to secure any tangible results. And if a significant number of convictions is achieved, it seems inevitable that the Act will be challenged as an illegitimate restriction on the spammers' freedom of speech.[145]

An equally gloomy picture emerges from other nations, though the details differ. The European Directive considered above is widely considered to be superior to CAN-SPAM in that it prohibits spam without prior consent (and so its regime is 'opt-in' rather than an 'opt-out'). However, it too is so manifestly ineffective that many EU nations have been reluctant to implement it, considering it worse than useless.[146] While it is fair to say that spammers have no friends in any legislature, nonetheless there are usually significant business lobbies which maintain that there is a legitimate role for properly regulated direct marketing, and which accordingly insist on exceptions to allow this.

Assessment and reform

Spam has become a problem which can only be solved at the international level. Increasing hostility by Western legislatures has ensured that most spam distribution has moved abroad, particularly to China and South Korea; this work is financed by corporations in the US and elsewhere. The more important spammers, responsible for the overwhelming bulk of the spam, are currently beyond the reach of the law, in the sense that their responsibility cannot be established (in more than a handful of cases) with the resources available to law enforcement bodies. That being so, changes to the legal system will not, for now, contribute significantly to the problem;

---

140 See 'Nine years in slammer for US spammer', Register, 8 April 2005 (Web).
141 Spamhaus home page (Web).
142 CAUCE home page (Web).
143 Eg, 'Big US ISPs set legal attack dogs on big, bad spammers', Register, 10 March 2004 (Web); 'MS sues 200 for spamming', Register, 11 June 2004 (Web).
144 'Spammer prosecutions waste time and money', Register, 16 June 2004 (Web).
145 Geissler, R, 'Whether "anti-spam" laws violate the first amendment', (2001) 8 JOL (Web).
146 'EU members ignore spam directive', ZDNet UK, 27 April 2004 (Web).

increasing the penalties or broadening the scope of the law is useless if the malefactor cannot be caught in the first place.

A pre-condition for any effective reform is therefore to establish some means by which either responsibility for spam can be effectively attributed, or by which spam can be sufficiently clearly identified and eliminated before it enters the in-box to which it is addressed. Various means for detecting forgery and for establishing the identity of an e-mail's sender are under consideration; e-mail filters are under constant development. No very obvious solution is in sight; until it is, detailed reform of the law should, properly speaking, be off the agenda.

Once effective control has been established, then the real legal battle will begin: to regulate who will be entitled to spam. Should prohibitions on spam be 'opt-in' or 'opt-out'? Should the law distinguish between different types of spam? Is the real problem one of avoiding public offence (which suggests a test based on the decorousness of the language used in the spam) or simply one of resources (which suggests that spammers should pay a small amount for each message, but otherwise be unregulated)? None of these questions really arise in the current chaos, but they may soon need to be asked.[147]

FURTHER READING

Carr, I and Williams, K, 'Securing the e-commerce environment', (2000) 16 CLSR 295.

Colombell, M, 'The legislative response to the evolution of computer viruses', (2002) 8 RJOLT 18 (Web).

Esen, R, 'Cyber crime: A growing problem', (2002) 66 J Cr L 269.

Goodman, M, 'Why the police don't care about computer crime', (1997) 10 HJOLT 465 (Web).

Kerr, O, 'Cybercrime's scope: Interpreting "access" and "authorization" in computer misuse statutes', (2003) 78 NYULR 1596.

Klang, K, 'A critical look at the regulation of computer viruses', (2003) 11 IJLIT 162.

Lee, M, Pak, S, Kim, T, Lee, D, Schapiro, A and Francis, T, 'Electronic commerce, hackers and the search for legitimacy: A regulatory proposal', (1999) 14 BTLJ 839 (Web).

Macodrum, D, Nasheri, H and O'Hearn, T, 'Spies in suits: New crimes of the information age from the United States and Canadian perspectives', (2001) 10 ICTL 139.

McIntyre-O'Brien, R, 'The current status of computer hacking offences in Ireland and their application to the Internet', [2004] COLR 7 (Web).

---

147 For discussion, see Cobos, S, 'A two-tiered registry system to regulate spam', [2003] UCLA JLT 5 (Web); Khong, W, 'Spam law for the Internet', [2001] 3 JILT (Web); Sullivan, J and de Leeuw, M, 'Spam after CAN-SPAM: How inconsistent thinking has made a hash out of unsolicited commercial e-mail policy', (2004) 20 SCCHTLJ 887.

McMahon, R, 'After billions spent to comply with HIPAA and GLBA privacy provisions, why is identity theft the most prevalent crime in America?', (2004) 49 Vill LR 625.

Philippsohn, S, 'Combating financial fraud on the Internet – An overview of current financial crimes on the internet', (May 2000) (Web).

Towle, H, 'Identity theft: myths, methods, and new law', (2004) 30 RCTLJ 237.

CHAPTER 3

OWNERSHIP OF DATA

The law in the previous chapter often protects data: by protecting the computer on which data is stored from unauthorised access or harm, the data too is safeguarded. This chapter considers more general legal institutions which protect data without much regard to the storage medium. Indeed, most of the doctrines to be considered pre-date the invention of computers by a considerable period, and their core concepts have been modified little to reflect the vastly increased ease with which both legitimate and illegitimate copies may be disseminated. How much further they should be modified in the light of new technologies is a matter of continuing debate.

Should we speak and write of 'ownership' of data? This is itself a controversial question. Legal protection of data and ideas is routinely referred to as the 'law of intellectual property', and use of that label is not seen as tying its user to any particular ideological conception of the area. And the fact (or supposed fact) that the area is becoming more property-like is often noted, whether with approbation or disapprobation. Much of this is simply a way of noting that the doctrines are increasing in scope and in severity of enforcement. But it also refers to disagreements over the rationale of the various doctrines, and whether that rationale is the same as the rationale for recognising private property. Some of the issues are introduced in the concluding section of this chapter. At this stage, it is enough to note that 'property' itself has uncertain boundaries, attracts controversies by the score, and is justified by a variety of vague theories, not all of which are compatible with one another. Therefore, argument over whether 'intellectual property' is properly so called is not very important unless (as is often the case) it is a code for discussing other, more fundamental issues as the nature of the rights at issue. From a classificatory point of view, the law of intellectual property is not very orderly, and its boundaries are unclear. Traditional doctrines such as 'copyright' and 'patent', which have in their time served a variety of purposes, have been patched up or added to as circumstances seem to require. And new doctrines have been introduced, some of great specificity (such as the legal protection of computer chip designs). The result is something of a jumble.

This chapter and the next briefly review the various ways in which the law will act to protect data. While the line is not always clear, this chapter focuses on the rights with the more straightforward economic justification, which reward those who invest resources to produce or discover useful aggregations of information, and can reasonably expect the law to protect that investment and its value in the market place. The following chapter considers rights which cut across this, demanding that data which may have been gathered at some cost is nonetheless *not* employed purely for the collector's own purposes, but is used to serve other interests.

COPYRIGHT

Copyright is probably still the most important of intellectual property doctrines. Despite its age, it is purely a creature of statute. As the name suggests, its original concern was with the making of copies of published books: the owner of the copyright had the exclusive right to produce copies, a right which could be exercised either in person, or by giving or selling permission ('licence') to others to do so. However, the right is considerably more extensive in its modern form: it is by no means confined to books, and it covers many uses for the copyrighted materials beyond simply copying them.

Much of this law is uniform world-wide – up to a point. The Berne Convention, the first version of which was adopted in 1886, standardised the law over much of the world, including nearly all of Europe. The US initially proved irreconcilable with some of its key provisions, but was party to the Universal Copyright Convention of 1952, which went much of the way towards global uniformity. The agreement on Trade-Related aspects of Intellectual Property Rights (TRIPs) of 1994 imposed Berne-like requirements on all members of the World Trade Organisation (WTO). These requirements, while demanding, are merely minimum requirements, leaving signatories free to add more: the EU has done much by way of harmonising the law across Europe, including extension of the duration of certain rights, and making considerable (and controversial) increases in enforcement powers.

Which works are protected, and for how long?

Copyright protects completed works, but not the thoughts or concepts underlying them – even where it is those thoughts and concepts that have value, rather than the work itself. So the guiding maxim is that it is not ideas that have legal protection, but rather the expression of ideas. This maxim cannot be pushed too far, though, and for some media 'ideas' and 'expression' are hard to separate. There is no legal requirement to publicly claim copyright in the work itself, whether with the © symbol or otherwise – though if the author seriously means to assert copyright later, it is a good idea to use the symbol.

Various different categories of work are protected by copyright; the period of protection differs according to the category. UK and Irish law differ in the precise definitions of the categories, though the overall effect is very similar. The categories are as follows:

(a) *Artistic works.* This includes paintings, photographs and a wide swathe of other media for artistic expression; a work of architecture, being a building (or part of a building, or any fixed structure) or a model of same; or a work of artistic craftsmanship. The Irish legislation is explicit that the court is not to make a judgment of artistic quality, whereas the UK legislation may require such a judgment if the work is claimed as an example of artistic craftsmanship. The author is taken to be the person who created the work, and the copyright subsists for 70 years from the end of the calendar year in which the author dies.[1]

(b) *Broadcasts.* Public broadcasts by wireless telegraphy, whether TV or radio, attract copyright if they were intended to be presented publicly and can lawfully be received by the public at large. Presumably this includes transmission over the Internet. Encrypted transmission can fall within this category, so long as devices for decryption are made available to the public by or with the authority of those

---

1   Copyright, Design and Patents Act 1988 (UK), ss 1(1), 4, 9(1) and 12, as modified by SI 1995/3297 and SI 2003/2498; Copyright and Related Rights Act 2000 (IE), ss 2(1) (definition of 'artistic work'), 17(2), 21 and 24.

making the transmission or providing its content. The authors are taken to be the content providers and those providing for transmission, and the copyright subsists for 50 years from the end of the calendar year in which the broadcast was made. The period of copyright cannot be extended by making a repeat broadcast.[2]

(c) *Cable programmes*. These have now, in the UK legislation, been assimilated into 'public broadcasts' and receive the same protection.[3] Ireland has not done this, but its provision is similar in effect.[4]

(d) *Film*. Despite the name, 'film' is not confined to any particular technology, but denotes any means for producing a moving image, and so includes DVD, video tape, MPEG files and much more, including many computer games. A sound track is protected as part of the film. While there is no express requirement of 'originality', nonetheless much turns on how original the film is: a mere copy of another film is not protected, whereas a truly innovative film may be protected not simply as a film but also under other heads, say as an 'original dramatic work' (below). The authors of the film are taken to be the producer and the principal director, and the copyright subsists for 70 years from the end of the calendar year of the death of the last to die of certain specified persons involved in the production.[5]

(e) *Original dramatic works*. The core idea is of something that can be, and has in fact been, performed. Dance and mime are expressly included. Considerable specificity as to performance is needed: mere dialogue is not sufficiently 'dramatic', neither is a game show format, however precise. 'Original' does not imply novelty as such – as ever, copyright subsists in the expression not in the ideas themselves – but rather it implies that the author must have used skill and effort. The author is taken to be the person who created the work, and the copyright subsists for 70 years from the end of the calendar year in which the author dies.[6]

(f) *Original literary works*. This is far broader than 'literary' writing as ordinarily understood, and may include just about any substantial piece of joined-up writing – this is discussed further below. The work must actually exist (on paper, in a data file or elsewhere) before the law's protection starts. Again, 'original' does not imply novelty, but merely skill and effort on the part of the author. The author is taken to be the person who created the work, and the copyright subsists for 70 years from the end of the calendar year in which the author dies.[7]

(g) *Original musical works*. 'Music' is taken to be self-explanatory. The work must physically exist, as musical notation or otherwise. Again, 'original' does not imply

---

2   Copyright, Design and Patents Act 1988 (UK), ss 1(1), 6 and 14, as modified by SI 1995/3297, SI 1996/2967 and SI 2003/2498; Copyright and Related Rights Act 2000 (IE), ss 2(1) (definition of 'broadcast'), 5, 6, 17(2) and 27.

3   Copyright and Related Rights Regulations 2003 (UK), SI 2003/2498, regs 4–5.

4   Copyright and Related Rights Act 2000 (IE), ss 2(1) (definitions of 'cable programme' and 'cable programme service'), 17(2) and 28.

5   Copyright, Design and Patents Act 1988 (UK), ss 1(1), 5B, 9(2) and 13B, as amended by SI 1995/3297, SI 1996/2967 and SI 2003/2498; Copyright and Related Rights Act 2000 (IE), ss 2(1) (definition of 'film'), 17(2), 21 and 25.

6   Copyright, Design and Patents Act 1988 (UK), ss 1(1), 3, 9(1) and 12, as amended by SI 1995/3297 and SI 2003/2498; Copyright and Related Rights Act 2000 (IE), ss 2(1) (definition of 'dramatic work'), 17(2), 18, 21 and 24.

7   Copyright, Design and Patents Act 1988 (UK), ss 1(1), 3(1), 9(1) and 12, as amended by SI 1995/3297, SI 1992/3233, SI 1997/3032 and SI 2003/2498; Copyright and Related Rights Act 2000 (IE), ss 2(1) (definition of 'literary work'), 17(2), 18, 21 and 24.

novelty, but merely skill and effort on the part of the author. This category does not cover words or gestures to accompany the music (though either will readily fit into other categories). The author is taken to be the person who created the work, and the copyright subsists for 70 years from the end of the calendar year in which the author dies.[8]

(h) *Published editions of literary, dramatic or musical works.* Here the copyright is not in the contents of the edition (which have their own copyright) but in the way it looks: the 'typographical arrangement' of the edition, so long as it is not simply a copy of an earlier arrangement. The author is taken to be the publisher of the edition, and the copyright subsists for 25 years (UK) or 50 years (Ireland) from the end of the calendar year in which the edition was first published.[9]

(i) *Sound recordings.* This covers any means by which sound may be reproduced (tape, CD, MP3 file, whatever), other than a mere copy of another recording. It includes (but is not limited to) sounds which reproduce literary, dramatic or musical works. The author is taken to be the producer of the recording, and copyright subsists for 50 years from the end of the calendar year in which the recording was made or (if it was made available to the public) the date on which it was first so made available.[10]

These categories can roughly be divided into 'primary' works, which are the work of creative authors and which attract the full 70–year period, and 'derivative' works, which are simply primary works copied to a new medium and which attract a lesser period of protection. It is evident that the same feat of intellectual creativity may easily result in more than one work protected by copyright. So a new song will be an 'original musical work' as soon as its notes and words are written down, and a 'sound recording' when a performance is first recorded. No copyright subsists in a derivative work if its creation involved breach of the primary copyright.

Most of the categories are self-explanatory, even though new technologies occasionally throw up difficult questions of definition. The oldest category, however, is not: 'original literary works' is one of the more opaque parts of copyright law, because of its age and the accretion of case law. As noted above, the terminology is by now hopelessly inappropriate. The most unoriginal writing imaginable is 'original' for this purpose, so long as its author did more than simply copy out the words or pictures of another.[11] Anything which provides information, instruction or pleasure, and which is written spoken or sung, is sufficiently 'literary', and there is certainly no requirement of literary merit. 'Works' is a more solid word. It emphasises that articulation is needed: no mere idea, no matter how worthy of protection, can be the subject of copyright until it has left the mind of its author, and has resulted in some material expression of a sort mentioned in the legislation. 'Work' also implies the need for something substantial: a single word, no matter how original, cannot be copyrighted.

---

8   Copyright, Design and Patents Act 1988 (UK), ss 1(1), 3(1), 9(1) and 12, as amended by SI 1995/3297 and SI 2003/2498; Copyright and Related Rights Act 2000 (IE), ss 2(1) (definition of 'musical work'), 17(2), 18, 21 and 24.

9   Copyright, Design and Patents Act 1988 (UK), ss 1(1), 8, 9 and 15; Copyright and Related Rights Act 2000 (IE), ss 2(1) (definition of 'published edition'), 17(2), 21 and 29.

10   Copyright, Design and Patents Act 1988 (UK), ss 1(1), 5A, 9 and 13A, as amended by SI 1995/3297, SI 1996/2967 and SI 2003/2498; Copyright and Related Rights Act 2000 (IE), ss 2(1) (definition of 'sound recording'), 17(2), 19, 21 and 26.

11   For an Internet case pretty close to the borderline, see *Antiquesportfolio.com plc v Rodney Fitch & Co* [2001] FSR 23.

The category of 'original literary works' is today simply a general one for the expression of concepts which seem to deserve protection and, as such, legislators have felt free to augment the definition as they see fit. Computer programs and preliminary design materials for same (such as flowcharts) are now explicitly stated to be 'original literary works', though the Irish legislation, reflecting the EU Directive it implements, demands that the program be 'the author's own intellectual creation'.[12] (Computer languages themselves are not copyright, any more than human languages are.) Dramatic and musical works are stated to be non-literary; while no doubt this requirement was inserted simply to make the legislation more orderly, it has the important (and probably unintended) effect of excluding most multi-media works from the scope of copyright – though, of course, each individual element of a multi-media presentation may be protected.

To what extent are web sites protected by copyright? The site itself is not copyright (as web sites are not mentioned as protected forms of expression in the existing legislation), but many of its elements may be. From the web master's point of view, a web site is a collection of interrelated files, some of which are code (instructions on how a web page should look) and some of which are mere data to be incorporated into the pages (such as graphic and sound files, or databases to which the web page gives access). Some individual files will attract copyright in themselves, as literary or musical works, or as sound recordings, though if they required little labour or thought to produce they might be considered insufficiently 'original'. Very probably (though the point is not settled) the code for producing the web page, whether HTML or some other code, will count as a 'computer program' and therefore qualify as a literary work. And any substantial block of text may qualify as an original literary work in itself. Some care may be needed in defining precisely what is being claimed as copyright, and in defining the first point at which it can be said to have achieved concrete expression (when it was written? when it was made available on a web server? when it was first read by a browser?). The courts have not so far proved receptive to arguments based on copying the 'look and feel' produced by another's software, at least where no actual code was copied.[13]

Various cases in UK jurisdictions have argued that web pages are within the definition of 'cable programmes', and so are copyright for that reason.[14] (The argument sounds surprising today, but was plausible given the way 'cable programme' was then defined.) The UK definition of 'cable programme' was subsequently narrowed to avoid this result,[15] though it remains an arguable point in Ireland.[16] However, in most situations it makes no difference whether the pages are protected as a 'cable programme' or as a collection of 'original literary works'. The major difference is that the copyright for cable programmes is only 50 years, whereas copyright in literary works lasts for 70 years. But if it mattered, a plaintiff could still claim the status of 'original literary work' for individual files comprising the web pages, regardless of whether they constituted part of a 'cable programme'; so it

---

12   Copyright and Related Rights Act 2000 (IE), s 2(1) (definition of 'computer program').
13   See especially *Navitaire Inc v Easyjet Airline Co* [2004] EWHC 1725 Ch (Web).
14   *Shetland Times v Wills* [1997] FSR 604; *Sony Music Entertainment (UK) Ltd v Easyinternetcafe Ltd* [2003] EWHC 62 Ch.
15   Copyright, Design and Patents Act 1988 (UK), s 6, as amended by SI 2003/2498. There are a few minor exceptions, such as simulcasts of live TV programmes over the web.
16   Copyright and Related Rights Act 2000 (IE), s 2(1) (definition of 'cable programme service').

appears that even in theory the point makes no difference. Similar considerations apply if a web page received by wireless or wi-fi connection is said to be a 'broadcast'.

What constitutes infringement of copyright?

As the word suggests, 'copyright' is infringed by the making of unauthorised copies, or (going a little wider) where anyone uses the copyright work as the model for their own work. It is usual to talk of the owner having the 'exclusive right' to exploit the work, but this is slightly misleading. To be strictly accurate, the right is *to prohibit others* from exploiting it, or to insist on the payment of a fee for permitting this.

The legislation avoids a broad conception of 'exploiting' another's work, preferring more specific language. 'Primary infringement' is said to occur if the infringer copies the work, makes it available or issues copies to the public, rents it or lends it, performs it, broadcasts it by wireless means or on cable, or makes an adaptation of it.[17] Making copies available over the Internet is specifically included by the Irish legislation,[18] and is presumably within the UK legislation too. Use of a copy made in breach of copyright attracts an additional liability for 'secondary infringement', which is committed by someone who possesses, sells, exhibits, distributes or imports an infringing copy. The copyright work must in some sense be the source of the new work. It is not enough that the new work is very similar to, or even identical with, the original work, if no process of copying was involved. It is entirely possible that two photographers or two programmers might independently produce very similar pieces of work; but unless it can be shown that the later work was copied from the earlier (perhaps even subconsciously), then the copyright in the earlier work is not infringed.

The element of copying must be substantial before infringement will be found. This is not so much a test of the amount taken, as of its importance. It is a narrower criterion than it first sounds, at least in cases where the author of the newer work has not slavishly copied the copyright work but has merely taken some elements from it. For while it is entirely accurate to say that the whole of a book or a picture is protected by copyright, nonetheless the copyright is not infringed unless something deserving of protection is taken. If the precise element taken was not original, or was not an important aspect of the copyright work, then copyright is not infringed; and, while the line is hard to draw, the courts will not act against the taking of a mere idea, as opposed to the copying of some element of its expression. Yet unoriginal elements may be used in original ways, and a new use for old elements can be protected by copyright. There are many borderline cases here, but the important point is that it is for the original copyright holder to state exactly what was copied, which can be very difficult even where the influence of their work as a model is obvious. The legislation expressly excludes certain forms of trivial copying from the scope of the law: this includes merely 'incidental' copying,[19] copying of broadcasts

---

17 Copyright, Design and Patents Act 1988 (UK), s 16, as amended by SI 1996/2967 and SI 2003/2498; Copyright and Related Rights Act 2000 (IE), ss 37 and 40–43.
18 Copyright and Related Rights Act 2000 (IE), s 40(1)(a).
19 Copyright, Design and Patents Act 1988 (UK), s 31; Copyright and Related Rights Act 2000 (IE), s 52.

merely so that they can be viewed at a time more convenient to the viewer ('time-shifting'),[20] and mere transient copying necessary for viewing a copyright work.[21]

Infringement of copyright in computer programs is a much litigated area. Simple unauthorised copying of another's computer code is clearly an infringement, as is translating it from one computer language to another,[22] or adapting, re-arranging or altering it.[23] 'Decompilation' – that is, converting a program from the 'object code' comprehensible to computers into the 'source code' comprehensible to programmers – is thus clearly an infringement. However, if the program is being used lawfully, it is not breach of copyright to try to puzzle out how it works.[24] There are also some technology-specific exemptions: some acts which would otherwise infringe copyright are permitted if the sole purpose is to make the program work on its own[25] or with other programs,[26] and there is an express right to make backup copies.[27] The difficult cases are those where only part of the code has been copied, or indeed where no code at all has been copied, but elements of the overall design have been used to write a fresh program. Here we have another example of the difficult process of identifying exactly what was taken, and whether it is a substantial and protectable part of the copyright material. The courts have toyed with a seemingly more precise test, the so-called 'abstraction and filtration' approach. The court identifies the various abstract notions that can be said to be expressed in the code; it then filters out those which are not protectable, because they are dictated by external factors or the need for efficiency, or are simply not original. The remaining 'core of protectable material', if any, is protected by copyright. While this test had some support,[28] it has more recently been ruled out as over-complicated.[29] As ever, it is the copyright owner's task to specify precisely what was taken; in some cases it will be code, and sometimes more abstract elements such as the general structure or 'architecture' of a program.

Is copyright infringed merely by viewing copyrighted aspects of another's web site? To view another's site necessarily involves copying files from that site to your own machine. However, various types of copy are in issue. There is the temporary copy held in RAM, which will disappear as soon as the user leaves that page and turns to others; there is the cached copy, held by the computer for a while in case the

---

20　Copyright, Design and Patents Act 1988 (UK), s 70, as amended by SI 2003/2498; Copyright and Related Rights Act 2000 (IE), s 101.

21　Copyright, Design and Patents Act 1988 (UK), s 28A, added by SI 2003/2498, reg 8 (but certain categories of copyright are exempt from this); Copyright and Related Rights Act 2000 (IE), s 87, as substituted by SI 2004/16, reg 3.

22　Copyright, Design and Patents Act 1988 (UK), s 21(4), as amended by SI 1992/3233, reg 5(3); Copyright and Related Rights Act 2000 (IE), s 43(3).

23　Copyright, Design and Patents Act 1988 (UK), s 21(3)(ab), added by SI 1992/3233, reg 5(2); Copyright and Related Rights Act 2000 (IE), s 43(2)(d).

24　Copyright, Design and Patents Act 1988 (UK), s 50BA, inserted by SI 2003/2498; Copyright and Related Rights Act 2000 (IE), s 82(2).

25　Copyright, Design and Patents Act 1988 (UK), s 50C, added by SI 1992/3233 and modified by SI 2003/2498; Copyright and Related Rights Act 2000 (IE), s 82(1).

26　Copyright, Design and Patents Act 1988 (UK), s 50B, added by SI 1992/3233; Copyright and Related Rights Act 2000 (IE), s 81.

27　Copyright, Design and Patents Act 1988 (UK), s 50A, added by SI 1992/3233 and modified by SI 2003/2498; Copyright and Related Rights Act 2000 (IE), s 80.

28　Eg, *John Richardson (Computers) Ltd v Flanders* [1993] FSR 497.

29　*Ibcos Computers Ltd v Barclays Mercantile Highland Finance Ltd* [1994] FSR 275; *Cantor Fitzgerald International v Tradition (UK) Ltd* [2000] RPC 95.

user wishes to see that page again; and (if the user deliberately creates it) there is a long-term copy, which can be edited or sent elsewhere. All of these are 'copies' for the purposes of copyright law.[30] If the site viewed is protected by copyright, are any or all of these copies infringing copies? The long-term copy is plainly caught, but the position of the others is less clear.

(a) In UK law, the temporary copy is not infringing so long as the sole purpose of accessing it was 'a lawful use', and the reproduction had 'no independent economic significance'. This protection applies to any 'temporary copy which is transient or incidental [and] which is an integral and essential part of a technological process', which presumably includes browsing the web. It seems doubtful that this can extend as far as cached copies (arguably not transient, pretty certainly not essential), and it cannot protect long-term copies at all. But if in fact the user did nothing with those copies, he or she could argue that no copies were deliberately made. The UK defence does not apply to the copying of programs or cable programmes, even incidentally or transiently.[31]

(b) In Irish law, again there is a general defence for 'lawful use' where the reproduction had 'no independent economic significance', though infringement occurs where the copy is subsequently 'sold, rented or lent, or offered or exposed for sale, rental or loan, or otherwise made available to the public'; the copy then becomes an infringing copy for all purposes. By implication (presumably) cached copies are in the same position.[32]

Certain categories of use are considered deserving enough to gain exemption from much of copyright law. Some of these are within the 'fair dealing' defences, which can be defeated if the particular use made is considered unfair by a court. The defences are defined in fairly narrow terms;[33] the courts have so far been unsympathetic to the argument that there are additional defences deriving from the European Convention on Human Rights.[34]

(a) *Criticism or review of other works, and reporting current events*. This exception is only for fair dealing, and the title of the work and the name of the author must be given by way of acknowledgment. The 'current events' exception does not extend to photographs;[35] events can still be 'current' if the public still displays interest in them.[36]

(b) *Education, instruction or examination*. There are a number of detailed provisions here to facilitate the use of copyright material as part of organised educational programmes.[37]

---

30 On copies in RAM, see *Kabushiki Kaisha Sony Computer Entertainment Inc v Ball* [2004] EWHC 1738 Ch (Web).

31 Copyright, Design and Patents Act 1988 (UK), s 28A, added by SI 2003/2498, reg 8.

32 Copyright and Related Rights Act 2000 (IE), s 87, as substituted by SI 2004/16, reg 3.

33 Cf Okediji, R, 'Givers, takers, and other kinds of users: A fair use doctrine for cyberspace', (2001) 53 Fla LR 107 (Web).

34 *Ashdown v Telegraph Group Ltd* [2001] EWCA Civ 1142, [2002] Ch 149 (Web).

35 Copyright, Design and Patents Act 1988 (UK), s 30, as amended by SI 2003/2498; Copyright and Related Rights Act 2000 (IE), s 51.

36 *Hyde Park Residence Ltd v Yelland* [2000] EWCA Civ 37 (Web). See generally Rowland, D, 'Whose news? Copyright and the dissemination of news on the Internet', (2003) 17 IRLCT 163.

37 Copyright, Design and Patents Act 1988 (UK), ss 32–36A; Copyright and Related Rights Act 2000 (IE), ss 53–58.

(c) *Libraries and archives.* These too have their own detailed provisions.[38]

(d) *Non-commercial research and private study.* The exception is only for fair dealing, and the title of the work and the name of the author must be given by way of acknowledgment. This defence is very limited in its application to computer programs.[39] Also useful for research is the treatment of article abstracts, which may be copied or reproduced without infringement.[40]

(e) *Parliament, judges and other official bodies.* Certain specified government officials and bodies are exempt from copyright law, so that nothing done in an official capacity can infringe it.[41]

In the UK legislation, there is also a general public interest defence, though it is rarely invoked.[42]

Ownership and licensing

Copyright *prima facie* vests in the author of the copyright work; the author is identified by slightly different rules for the different forms of copyright expression, as described above. There is detailed statutory provision for joint copyright, where more than one person had creative input and the various contributions cannot be distinguished in the work itself; also for cases where the author is unknown or cannot be identified. Where the work was produced with the aid of a computer, in such a way that no particular person or group of persons is the 'author' on ordinary principles, then copyright vests in the person who arranged for the computer to act.[43]

Where copyright work is produced under a contract, does the copyright belong to the person who actually produced it, or to their employer? This matter can be and (for those who wish to avoid subsequent litigation) should be settled in the contract itself. If it is not, then the presumption is that copyright work produced by an employee acting in the course of employment vests in the employer, whereas work produced under any other sort of contract belongs to the person who produced it. So work by freelances *prima facie* remains theirs. However, the presumption can be a weak one, and will almost certainly be displaced if the freelance's employer needs the copyright in order to reap economic advantage from the work. Work covered by government copyright vests in the government, and not in the person who wrote it.[44]

A copyright is personal property, and can be transferred to someone else by an assignment (which must be in writing and signed by the assignor), or (on death) by will or otherwise. Before the work is complete, the prospective owner may agree in

---

38 Copyright, Design and Patents Act 1988 (UK), ss 37–44A; Copyright and Related Rights Act 2000 (IE), ss 59–70.

39 Copyright, Design and Patents Act 1988 (UK), s 29, as amended by SI 1992/3233, SI 1997/3032 and SI 2003/2498; Copyright and Related Rights Act 2000 (IE), s 50.

40 Copyright, Design and Patents Act 1988 (UK), s 60; Copyright and Related Rights Act 2000 (IE), s 91.

41 Copyright, Design and Patents Act 1988 (UK), ss 45–50; Copyright and Related Rights Act 2000 (IE), ss 71–76.

42 Copyright, Design and Patents Act 1988 (UK), s 171(3).

43 Copyright, Design and Patents Act 1988 (UK), ss 9–15; Copyright and Related Rights Act 2000 (IE), ss 21–36.

44 Copyright, Design and Patents Act 1988 (UK), ss 11 and 163–167; Copyright and Related Rights Act 2000 (IE), ss 23 and 191–196.

writing to assign the copyright, and if they do so then the copyright vests in the assignee as soon as it comes into existence. The owner of a copyright may transfer part only of it, as by assigning copyright in part of a work, or assigning it only for a limited period, or assigning one of their rights (such as the right to reproduce the work) but not others. Rather than assigning the copyright, the owner may license another to do some or all of the acts restricted by copyright. The licence may be 'exclusive' – in other words, a right not merely to do the licensed act but also to prohibit others, including the owner/licensor, from doing it. An exclusive licensee is in a powerful position, having many of the remedies of an owner to protect their position. Non-exclusive licences take effect according to their terms; unlike exclusive licences, they are not required to be in writing, and can indeed be implicit. They can have rights of action against infringers if these are expressly granted to them in writing. Licensees do not lose whatever rights they have merely because the copyright passes to an assignee, unless that assignee is a *bona fide* purchaser for value without notice of the licence.[45]

Licensing and enforcement of copyright is often in the hands of trade associations, collecting societies and other private bodies. There is elaborate statutory provision for the regulation of these bodies. In some limited cases, this legislation gives a right to demand a licence on payment of the fee for it. More generally, a refusal to license or the imposition of harsh terms may be considered contrary to the principles of free trade or otherwise anti-competitive. Copyright cannot be used to segment the EU into distinct markets: if copies are lawfully made under licence, then they can be imported into any EU country, even if they were made under a licence which forbade this. (This is the so-called 'principle of exhaustion', based on respect for free trade within the EU, and it applies to property in any form.) Concerted practices leading to the prevention, restriction or distortion of competition are prohibited by Art 81 of the Treaty of Rome. Abuse of a dominant market position is prohibited by Art 82, and it is clear law that refusal to license even a direct competitor may sometimes constitute such an abuse. The detail of the law here is spelled out in the various block exemptions, which declare certain practices not to infringe the legislation; in cases falling outside them, leave must be sought from the competition authorities. Breach of the law can result in fines or an award of damages to injured parties; anti-competitive contracts are unenforceable.[46]

Not all copyright owners wish to assert their rights, or to control use of their work in every way that statute allows. There is a considerable body of opinion that computer software is best developed by allowing users to modify it as they wish. On this view, software should usually be distributed as 'open source' (that is, in the 'source code' in which it was written, rather than in 'object code' comprehensible only to computers) and without significant legal restrictions.[47] One common way of

---

45 Copyright, Design and Patents Act 1988 (UK), ss 90–93, 101 and 102; Copyright and Related Rights Act 2000 (IE), ss 120–126, 135 and 136. On contracts involving copyrights, see below, p 136.

46 Copyright, Design and Patents Act 1988 (UK), ss 116–152; Copyright and Related Rights Act 2000 (IE), ss 149–181. Fry, R, 'Copyright infringement and collective enforcement', [2002] EIPR 516; Vollebregt, E, 'EC competition law aspects of peer-to-peer networking', [2002] CTLR 63; Turner, M and Callaghan, D, 'Software licensing under the competition law spotlight', (2004) 20 CLSR 273.

47 See Copyleft (Wikipedia) (Web); see also Open Source Initiative home page (Web). For argument for and against open source, see Nikulainen, K, 'Open source software: Why is it here and will it stick around?', (2004) 1 SCRIPT-ed (Web); Strasser, M, 'A new paradigm in intellectual property law? The case against open sources', [2001] 4 STLR (Web).

doing this is the so-called 'copyleft' licence, by which the owner of the copyright licenses all users for all uses of their code, on the sole condition that any code developed from it will also be 'copyleft'. Various versions of the licence are in circulation, including the General Public Licence (GPL).[48]

Remedies

Breach of copyright in any way which prejudices the copyright owner's commercial interests is a criminal offence; various distinct offences are involved, the most serious carrying maximum penalties of 10 years/£ unlimited (UK) and 5 years/€126,973 (Ireland). Alternatively, the victim may claim an injunction against repetition, or to pre-empt a threatened breach; in sufficiently clear cases an injunction may issue even against a perpetrator whose name is unknown.[49] The victim may simply seize infringing items which are being publicly displayed for sale, though there are a number of procedural safeguards – ordinary business premises are exempt, and the local police must be told in advance of the raid. In either civil or criminal proceedings, an order can be made for forfeiture of infringing copies and of any article designed or adapted for copying the work in question. Damages are available if a civil court thinks it just to award them, and the court has great freedom in settling on an appropriate sum – it is certainly not limited to mere compensation as lawyers ordinarily understand it. The usual measure is the reasonable licence fee that should have been paid in respect of the infringement of the copyright owner's rights. In principle, damages could reflect the copyright owner's actual loss, but this is usually impossible to calculate. An action for an account of profits made through infringement is possible, though the courts tend to reserve this for the most flagrant cases.[50] In major cases, police forces and trade associations in several nations may join forces to raid infringers.[51]

A notable feature of the current landscape is the considerable number of actions against individual infringers of music copyright (mostly in the US and Europe); the plaintiffs say that they are targeting only those who are each responsible for hundreds of thousands of infringements, usually using P2P network software such as KaZaA, Gnutella or BitTorrent.[52] Considerable extensions to enforcement powers are contained in the new Directive on enforcement of intellectual property rights, including increased powers of seizure and evidence-gathering, and a power to require disclosure of the details of distribution networks.[53] To its supporters, it standardises enforcement across the EU and strikes a sensible balance between the needs of enforcers and the needs of those they investigate; to opponents, it is a major infringement of consumer privacy and other civil liberties.

---

48 See Wacha, J, 'Taking the case: Is the GPL enforceable?', (2005) 21 SCCHTLJ 451; Höppner, J, 'The GPL prevails: An analysis of the first-ever court decision on the validity and effectivity of the GPL', (2004) 1 SCRIPT-ed (Web).

49 *Bloomsbury Publishing Group Ltd v News Group Newspapers Ltd* [2003] EWHC 1205 Ch (Web).

50 Copyright, Design and Patents Act 1988 (UK), ss 96–102 and 107–115, as amended by Copyright, etc and Trade Marks (Offences and Enforcement) Act 2002 (UK), ss 1–3; Copyright and Related Rights Act 2000 (IE), ss 127–136, 140–148.

51 Eg, 'US leads Internet piracy raids', BBC News, 23 April 2004 (Web).

52 Eg, 'RIAA takes hundreds more "John Does" to court', ZDNet, 22 June 2004 (Web); 'Triple setback for music giants' global jihad', Register, 1 April 2004 (Web). On BitTorrent, see 'The BitTorrent P2P file-sharing system', Register, 18 December 2004 (Web).

53 Directive 2004/48/EC on the enforcement of intellectual property rights.

Lack of knowledge has only very limited impact as a defence. As ever, ignorance of the law is no excuse, and so a plea of ignorance of copyright law is of no utility even if true. Criminal penalties are not available if the prosecution cannot prove that the defendant knew or had reason to believe that they were infringing copyright. No damages for a primary infringement can be awarded if the defendant did not know, and had no reason to believe, that there was a relevant copyright; but such beliefs can rarely be reasonable (the defence says nothing about belief in consent). The law is more generous as to secondary infringement, that is, dealing in copies of copyrighted works: the copies are still liable to seizure, but if the infringer is prosecuted the prosecutor must prove that the accused knew the copies infringed, or had reason to think them to be infringing.[54]

It is irrelevant whether the infringement was for the infringer's own benefit. So an internet café which copies music files for customers is caught.[55] The remedies are available not merely against a person who breaches copyright, but also against someone who 'authorises' a breach.[56] But what constitutes 'authorising' another to breach copyright? The main case seems to be where one person instructs another to make one article in the style of another, copyright article; the instruction presupposes a right to make copies and so can be said to 'authorise' any breach of copyright which takes place. No doubt, someone who holds an illegal copy on their web site can equally be said to authorise any copying from there, at least if that person knew that such copying would probably occur. Very probably, this also catches someone who provides a link from their web page to an illegal copy held elsewhere, knowing that this will encourage others to follow the link and make copies for themselves; though there are substantial issues over what constitutes 'encouraging' others to breach copyright.[57]

More difficult is the case where the defendant has no access to illegal copies, but circulates software that enables those holding infringing copies to communicate and swap files with one another. In the *Napster* case,[58] the defendant circulated software with which holders of music files could log onto a central server, and thereby communicate and swap files with others in the same position. It was held that the defendant's running of the central server was sufficient involvement in the process to make it liable when copyright was breached, even though the server held no infringing copies. An injunction from a US District Court required the defendant to achieve 100% compliance with copyright law, which drove it into bankruptcy. But what if the software enables users to network with one another without any need for a central server? In that situation – where the network is a genuine 'peer to peer' (P2P) network – the defendant has no control over user activities once the

---

54 Copyright, Design and Patents Act 1988 (UK), ss 22–27, 97(1) and 107; Copyright and Related Rights Act 2000 (IE), ss 45 and 128(2). See Saxby, S, 'EU gets tough on intellectual property piracy', (2004) 20 CLSR 163; O'Brien, D, 'EU copyright law backs corporations', Irish Times, 12 March 2004; 'Anti-piracy law "stifles innovation" ', BBC News, 18 March 2004 (Web).

55 *Sony Music Entertainment (UK) Ltd v Easyinternetcafe Ltd* [2003] EWHC 62 Ch. A defence based on the 'time-shifting' rule (above, p 53) was rejected.

56 Copyright, Design and Patents Act 1988 (UK), s 16(2); Copyright and Related Rights Act 2000 (IE), s 37(2).

57 Dogan, S, 'Infringement once removed: The perils of hyperlinking to infringing content', (2002) 87 Iowa LR 829.

58 *A&M Records, Inc v Napster, Inc* 239 F 3d 1004 (9th Ct, 12 February 2001); on the case see Rayburn, C, 'After Napster', (2001) 6 VJOLT 16 (Web) and Cheval, D, 'Copyright protection in the digital age: The case against Napster', (2001) 6 WVJOLT 1 (Web). Similar issues were raised in *Re Aimster Copyright Litigation* 334 F 3d 643 (7th Ct, 30 June 2003).

software has been released. Established precedent of both the US Supreme Court[59] and the House of Lords[60] holds that merely circulating technology which enables breach of copyright does not attract liability if there are substantial lawful uses for the technology. This argument has been accepted by the courts in Holland as legitimising P2P technologies.[61] However, it has been rejected by the US Supreme Court in the recent *Grokster* case, at least where some sort of encouragement to breach copyright can be inferred; this decision rapidly led to Grokster's termination.[62] The Austrialian courts nowlook set to follow suit.[63] The matter is one of contuing controversy.[64] As noted above, the current tendency in the music industry has been to sue individual users of P2P networks rather than others involved in the process.

Internet service providers (ISPs) have always seen themselves as vulnerable here, as their customers may transmit or receive copyright material, or store it, or even make it available to others on web sites managed by the service provider. The dangers of this are so well known that it would be impossible for the ISP to claim ignorance in general terms; but identifying particular instances of infringing material is often commercially unacceptable even where it is technically possible. A common criticism of the current position is that ISPs will in practice remove material whenever a complaint is made, regardless of that complaint's merits. As the law stands, ISPs are only responsible for unlawful activities if they have 'authorised' them, or if they know or believe that particular items of data going over their network will be made into an infringing copy on receipt.[65] In addition, there is a general defence available to them: ISPs are not liable for breach of copyright where they have been the 'mere conduit' for the transmission of data between others. The definition is carefully hedged about: the ISP must not have initiated the transmission and must not be the ultimate sender or recipient, nor can the recipient have been selected by the ISP; the ISP must not select or modify the data *en route*; any data storage involved must be 'automatic, intermediate and transient' and be for the sole purpose of effecting the transmission, and must not be kept longer than is reasonably necessary for that purpose. Where a customer hires space for a web site and then uses the site to hold illegal copyright materials, the ISP has a defence if it does not know this and does not know of any facts and circumstances from which 'unlawful activity...would have been apparent', so long as it acts 'expeditiously' on acquiring this knowledge.[66] The European position is therefore similar to that in

---

59 *Sony Corporation of America v Universal City Studios, Inc* 464 US 417 (17 January 1984).

60 *CBS Songs Ltd v Amstrad Consumer Electronics plc* [1988] AC 1013.

61 'Dutch Supreme Court rules Kazaa legal', Register, 19 December 2003 (Web).

62 *Metro-Goldwyn-Mayer Studios, Inc v Grokster*, Inc 125 S Ct 2764 (Supreme Court, 27 June 2005); 'Grokster shuts downloading site', BBC News, 8 November 2005 (Web).

63 'Kazaa owners, users infringe copyright judge, Register, 5 September 2005 (Web).

64 For general reviews, see Lemley, M and Reese, R, 'Reducing digital copyright infringement without restricting innovation', (2004) 56 Stan LR 1345; Douglas, G, 'Copyright and peer-to-peer music file sharing: The *Napster* case and the argument against legislative reform', (2004) 11 E-Law (Web).

65 Copyright, Design and Patents Act 1988 (UK), ss 16(2) and 24(2); Copyright and Related Rights Act 2000 (IE), ss 37(2) and 46(2).

66 Electronic Commerce (EC Directive) Regulations 2002 (UK), SI 2002/2013, regs 17 and 19; European Communities (Directive 2000/31/EC) Regulations 2003 (IE), SI 2003/68, regs 15, 16 and 18.

Canada[67] and the US,[68] in that ISPs generally may ignore the risk that their clients are breaking the law unless a specific complaint is made; though in the US there are increasing demands for ISPs to disclose records to identify copyright infringers.[69]

ISPs are also legally exposed by practices such as caching. Where many users request the same file to be collected from some remote server, it makes technical sense for the ISP to keep a copy in a temporary store (a cache) rather than fetching it from a remote site each time it is asked for. Yet if the file contains copyright material, this is plainly a primary infringement. There is a defence for ISPs here, again narrowly drafted and subject to several conditions, including non-modification of the cached data and non-interference with the original owner's attempts to keep track of usage. If it comes to the attention of the ISP that the original data has been removed or access to it has been disabled, or that a competent court has directed such removal or disabling, then the ISP must 'expeditiously' delete, or deny access to, the cached copy.[70]

The emphasis in some areas has moved towards technological protection of copyright, the law's role being only to penalise those who try to subvert the technology. Early uses of this technology have included regional coding (so that US copies do not work in Europe and vice versa) and prohibitions on copying. This technological protection ('digital rights management' or DRM) is buttressed by specific legal provisions. Attempts to defeat such control give those with intellectual property rights in the control technology much the same remedies as are open to copyright owners whose copyright is broken. Any device used to defeat such control can be forfeited; manufacturing or marketing such devices, or possession for business purposes, is a distinct offence. A few exceptions are allowed: there is a carefully worded defence for those who subvert the control technology merely to do something they have a legal right to do; the UK version has a similarly precise defence for those engaged in research into cryptography.[71] The current position is Europe is therefore similar to that under the US Digital Millennium Copyright Act, which in general forbids circulation of software subverting rights control technology.[72]

---

67   *Society of Composers, Authors and Music Publishers of Canada v Canadian Association of Internet Providers* [2004] SCC 45 (Web).

68   See generally, Wernick, A, 'ISP: You've got mail', (2001) 17 CLSR 247; Hayes, D, 'Advanced copyright issues on the Internet – Part VI', (2001) 17 CLSR 291; Hamdani, A, 'Who's liable for cyberwrongs?', (2002) 87 Corn LR 901.

69   Ciske, M, 'For now, ISPs must stand and deliver: An analysis of *In re Recording Industry Association of America v Verizon Internet Services*', (2003) 8 VJOLT 9 (Web). For general reviews of the current position, see Unni, V, 'Internet service provider's liability for copyright infringement – How to clear the misty Indian perspective', (2001) 8 RJOLT (Web); Evans, E, 'From the Cluetrain to the Panopticon: ISP activity characterization and control of internet communications', (2004) 10 MTTLR 445 (Web).

70   Electronic Commerce (EC Directive) Regulations 2002 (UK), SI 2002/2013, reg 18, and see also Copyright, Designs and Patents Act 1988 (UK), s 97A as inserted by SI 2003/2498 (injunctions against service providers); European Communities (Directive 2000/31/EC) Regulations 2003 (IE), SI 2003/68, reg 17.

71   Copyright, Design and Patents Act 1988 (UK), s 296 and 296ZG, as inserted by SI 2003/2498; Copyright and Related Rights Act 2000 (IE), ss 370–376, as amended by SI 2004/16; Shah, A, 'UK's implementation of the anti-circumvention provisions of the EU copyright directive: An analysis', [2004] DLTR 3 (Web); *Kabushiki Kaisha Sony Computer Entertainment Inc v Ball* [2004] EWHC 1738 Ch (Web).

72   Hayes, D, 'Advanced copyright issues on the Internet – Part III', (2001) 17 CLSR 75; Foged, T, 'US v EU anti-circumvention legislation: Preserving the public's privileges in the digital age?', [2002] EIPR 525.

Jurisdictional issues

For cases governed by the Brussels Regulation[73] – roughly, cases within the EU and the EEA – any defendant can be sued in the jurisdiction where they are domiciled. Breach of copyright can be regarded as a 'tort, delict or quasi-delict' within the meaning of the Regulation, which means that action can be brought in whichever jurisdiction the wrong took place. It is usually considered that where a wrongful act occurs in one jurisdiction and its effects are suffered in another, then for this purpose the wrong takes place in both. Therefore, where electronic copies are disseminated across the EU, in principle those responsible can be sued in any of the jurisdictions where copies end up; and it should be borne in mind that if the copies were disseminated via the Internet, then both the client and the host machines will hold copies. However, where a national court has jurisdiction on the ground that the wrong occurred there, the action must be confined to that wrong alone: if the totality of a defendant's behaviour is to be looked at even though it affected more than one nation, the defendant's own domicile is the appropriate forum. Where multiple defendants are involved, the whole matter can be resolved in the courts of the domicile of any one of them.[74] Judgments made within a proper jurisdiction can then be enforced in any other Brussels Regulation jurisdiction, once registered there. Discussion of reform of the Brussels Regulation, and its possible replacement by a 'Rome II' Regulation, are ongoing.

Jurisdiction in a non-Brussels Regulation case can only be claimed as of right if the defendant is present in the jurisdiction, or accepts jurisdiction voluntarily. The court has a discretion to allow proceedings if the wrong occurred within the jurisdiction, though this discretion will not be used where the jurisdiction is not an appropriate forum for the dispute. What if the defendant's activities consisted of running a web server based outside the jurisdiction? There seems to be no case law yet on whether or when a defendant can be treated as having committed a wrong within the jurisdiction merely because they ran a web site which was contacted from within the jurisdiction.[75] This matter has been much discussed in the US. Federal jurisdiction may be established where the defendant has links with the US which are substantial, or 'continuous and systematic'. If the defendant's links are more minimal, nonetheless if it is reasonable for the plaintiff to invoke the US jurisdiction then this can be done as against a defendant who 'purposely availed himself of the benefits of the forum', as by deliberately targeting US customers. Whether such purposeful availment will be found can be a complex matter. One approach to this (the so-called *Zippo* test[76]) involves classifying web sites as 'active' (where the defendant's site clearly does business with US customers), 'passive' (where the site merely advertises) or 'interactive' (where US customers may exchange information with the defendant's site, but it falls short of an 'active' site). 'Active' sites clearly attract jurisdiction; 'passive' sites do not; 'interactive' sites may, according to the degree of interactivity. The usefulness of this test is a matter of considerable dispute; at the very least, the terminology is confusing, as *all* web

---

73 Regulation 44/2001/EC on jurisdiction and the recognition and enforcement of judgments.
74 *Pearce v Ove Arup Partnership Ltd* [1997] Ch 293.
75 Though for strongly analogous cases on trade marks, see below, p 74.
76 Named for *Zippo Manufacturing Co v Zippo Dot Com, Inc* 952 F Supp 1119 (W D Pa, 16 January 1997), a trade mark case.

sites are interactive to some degree (they never send web pages unless requested to do so).[77] International negotiations for a Hague Convention on jurisdiction in e-commerce are ongoing.[78]

Choice of law is a less important issue, given the great international convergence of national laws which culminated in the TRIPs treaty of 1994. Copyright will be protected so long as the work or its author can be said to 'qualify' by coming from a jurisdiction which has ratified one of the relevant treaties, as most have.[79] Copyright then arises in all those jurisdictions. It appears that, if it matters, it is the law of the jurisdiction where the work originated which governs, at least until the work is assigned to someone within another jurisdiction.[80]

DATABASE RIGHT

Collections of data have a slightly curious status within copyright law. In some cases, each item of data is 'original' and will be copyright. But what if this is not so, or the collection's owner seeks protection of the collection itself rather than of individual items within it? This was a difficult problem well before ICT had come to prominence. Early 20th century copyright law recognised the idea of a 'compilation', a distinct form of expression which attracted copyright. But the use of this to provide comprehensive protection for collections of data stumbled badly over the requirement of 'originality'; most notably when a telephone directory fell foul of this requirement in the US Supreme Court.[81] It is obvious that the individual data items in these cases will often be entirely banal, yet nonetheless the database as a whole will be worthy of protection because of the effort it took to compile, or its practical utility. Such collections can be objects of great commercial value. Yet substantial changes were needed to the existing law to generate appropriate protection.

Current Irish and UK laws, based on an EU directive,[82] recognise a distinct notion of a 'database', as a collection of independent works, data or other materials, arranged in a systematic or methodical way and individually accessible by any means.[83] This is not confined to electronic databases, though they are the main target of the legislation. This law also goes a long way towards protecting web sites, not merely because some web sites contain databases, but also because all but the simplest sites fall within the legal definition of a database.

'Databases' are protected in two ways. First, anything that is original in the design or arrangement of a database is protected by copyright. Secondly, the

---

77 For commentary on the modern US position, see Gray, T, 'Minimum contacts in cyberspace: The classic jurisdiction analysis in a new setting', (2002) 1 JHTL 93 (Web); Nguyen, T, 'A survey of personal jurisdiction based on Internet activity: A return to tradition', (2004) 19 BTLJ 519.

78 Gillies, L, 'The impact of the Hague Conference's proposed judgments convention for electronic commerce and intellectual property disputes', (2002) 16 IRLCT 233; Petkova, S, 'The potential impact of the draft Hague Convention on International Jurisdiction' [2004] IPQ 173.

79 Copyright Designs and Patents Act 1988 (UK), ss 153–162; Copyright and Related Rights Act 2000 (IE), ss 182–190 and Sched 3.

80 Antonelli, A, 'Applicable law aspects of copyright infringement on the Internet: What principles should apply?', [2003] SJLS 147.

81 *Feist Publications Inc v Rural Telephone Service Co Inc* 499 US 340 (27 March 1991).

82 Directive 1996/9/EC on the legal protection of databases.

83 Copyright, Design and Patents Act 1988 (UK), s 3A(1), as inserted by SI 1997/3032; Copyright and Related Rights Act 2000 (IE), s 2(1), definition of 'database'.

contents of the database, no matter how commonplace, are protected by 'database right', a distinct type of right strongly analogous to copyright. The basic principles are considered here; some of the detailed case law on the protection of web sites as databases is considered in a later chapter.[84]

Copyright in databases

Databases are recognised in the legislation as a form of expression attracting protection as copyright: the right subsists for 70 years from the death of the author. A database is only sufficiently original if, by reason of the selection or arrangement of its contents, it constitutes the author's own intellectual creation. As the Directive and the Irish Act make clear (the UK Act is silent on the point), a program to make or operate a database is not within the definition, though of course it may be protected as a 'literary work' in its own right. The drafting of the two Acts is subtly different (with various effects): in the Irish Act, an 'original database' is a distinct species of copyright work, whereas in the UK Act, a database which is original is regarded as a sub-species of 'literary work'.[85]

Ordinary definitions of copyright and its protection apply to the database, with very minor modifications. No doubt, difficult questions will arise over when copying of one idea or design principle underlying a database will be regarded as the copying of a protected expression. One form of infringement, 'adaptation', is given a special definition for databases, as meaning making an arrangement, altered version or translation of a database. Licensing is covered by the same detailed provisions for administration, discussed above.[86] There are minor differences between the Irish and the UK Acts particularly relevant to the question of whether someone who browses a database via the Internet breaches copyright:

(a) Ireland does not allow a defence of fair dealing for research and private study in respect of electronic databases; the UK allows it so long as there was no commercial purpose involved.[87]

(b) The 'mere transient copy' defence extends to databases in the Irish Act, but not the UK Act.[88]

Database right

More extensive is the 'database right', sometimes called the 'sui generis database right' to emphasise that it is a distinct entity, though highly analogous to copyright and governed by many of the same legal provisions. It is a right to prevent others

---

84 Below, pp 219 – 21.

85 Copyright, Design and Patents Act 1988 (UK), ss 3 and 3A, as inserted by SI 1997/3032; Copyright and Related Rights Act 2000 (IE), ss 17(2) and 24. For litigation see, eg, *Navitaire Inc v Easyjet Airline Co* [2004] EWHC 1725 Ch (Web).

86 Above, p 55.

87 Copyright, Design and Patents Act 1988 (UK), s 29, as amended by SI 1992/3233, SI 1997/3032 and SI 2003/2498; Copyright and Related Rights Act 2000 (IE), s 50.

88 Copyright, Design and Patents Act 1988 (UK), s 28A, added by SI 2003/2498, reg 8; Copyright and Related Rights Act 2000 (IE), s 87, as amended by SI 2004/16. On the detail of this defence, see above, p 54.

from extracting or using the data in the database, either absolutely or until a licence fee is paid. It is irrelevant whether copyright can be asserted in the database as a whole, or in any of its contents.

The leading authority on the right is the *William Hill* case and the associated cases heard at the same time before the European Court of Justice.[89] These concerned data related to sport: *William Hill* itself concerning data on horses, jockeys and races, and the associated cases concerning football fixtures. The economic rationale of the right was emphasised in the case: where a substantial investment has been made to produce commercially valuable data, then the law should protect that value. There is no pretence of requiring that the data be in any sense 'original' or protectable by law were it not drawn together into a database; it is the investment involved in drawing it all together that is protected. However, departing sharply from the opinion of the Advocate-General in the case, the Court insisted that it was only *the investment in creating the database* that was relevant – the cost of obtaining, verifying and presenting the data for that purpose. A claimant who has personally created the data cannot expect that investment to be protected by the database right; it is not what it is for. This gives a very narrow cast to the right indeed; it means (as much European case law had already suggested) that it has no application at all in a case where the data is a cheap 'spin off' from activities not aimed at producing a database at all.[90]

What is protected, and for how long?

The right applies to any database where there has been a substantial investment in obtaining, verifying or presenting its contents.[91] It makes no difference whether the data existed beforehand, or were created for the first time when they were entered in the database. The 'substantial investment' required could consist of financial, human or technical resources, and can be substantial in quality or in quantity. The investment can made at any stage in the process, and the reference to 'presenting' the data includes both the data's internal structure and the format in which it is presented to users of the database. There seems to be no reason why a web site could not be within this protection, so long as a substantial investment in making it could be shown.[92]

The maker of the database holds the right for 15 years from the end of the calendar year in which the making of the database was completed; and if, before the end of that period, the database is made available to the public, then the right is extended to 15 years from the end of the calendar year in which it was so made available. If there is a substantial change made to an existing database, which can

---

89   *British Horseracing Board Ltd v William Hill Organisation Ltd* [2001] EWCA Civ 1268 (CA) (Web); Case C-203/02 (ECJ) (Web). For commentary see Kemp, R, Meredith, D and Gibbons, C, 'Database right and the ECJ judgment in *BHB v William Hill*', (2005) 21 CLSR 108. For case law throughout the EU, see Database Right File (Web); Hugenholtz, P, 'The new database right: Early case law from Europe', (April 2001) (Web).

90   Derclaye, E, 'Databases "*sui generis*" right: Should we adopt the spin-off theory?', [2004] EIPR 402.

91   Copyright and Rights in Databases Regulations 1997 (UK), SI 1997/3032, regs 12, 13 and 15; Copyright and Related Rights Act 2000 (IE), ss 320, 321 and 323.

92   Brazell, L, 'Protection of web sites by database law', [2002] CW (Nov) 15. The case law on web sites is considered below, p 216.

itself be regarded as a substantial investment, then the database which results from the change has its own 15 year protection. Such a change need not be all at once, but could consist of the accumulation of successive additions, deletions or alterations.[93] It is not entirely clear how this applies to a database which is continually modified to keep it up with new developments – when, precisely, is the 'change' considered to happen?

What constitutes infringement of database right?

Infringement is defined as the extraction or making available to the public of the entire database or a substantial part of it; 'extraction' is defined as the permanent or temporary transfer of the database's contents to another medium. A 'substantial part' can be substantial in quality or in quantity. This implies that the extraction or making available to the public of insubstantial parts is no infringement; but nonetheless if this is done repeatedly and systematically, then the database right is infringed if this activity conflicts with the normal exploitation of the database or prejudices the interests of its maker. What are the limits of this? The court's view in *William Hill* was a narrow one. While 'extraction' by a defendant can be direct or indirect, nonetheless it must be shown to be 'substantial' by reference to the claimant's investment: so the part extracted must represent a substantial investment. It is possible for systematic extraction of insubstantial parts to add up, over time, to a substantial extraction, but only if it reconstitutes or makes available to the public a substantial part of the database. As with copyright, remedies may be available not simply against the infringer but against anyone who 'authorises' others to infringe.[94]

Those who maintain an online database may have definite ideas on how they wish the public to use it. In particular, while they may be eager for other sites to link to their site, they may resent 'deep links' which lead directly to particular data items, without the need to visit the home page. There have been several attempts in the courts of continental Europe to outlaw this, one ground being that it infringes database right. This seems doubtful, however. It is hard to say that deep linking makes the data available to the public, if it was already available before the link was created. The practice can (just possibly) be seen as an extraction of data, but this would not be enough unless the court thought the extraction was substantial and/or prejudiced the interests of the database's maker, both of which might be hard to establish even if the deep linker was in competition with the database owner. Arguments for liability attained some initial success before the German courts, but cases now have focused more clearly on what precisely has been taken by the defendant – usually to the detriment of the claim made.[95]

Various categories of use are exempt from database right, so long as the user's access to the database was lawful. There is an express right to extract insubstantial parts of a database, unless this is 'repeated and systematic' and over time amounts to a substantial extraction: this right applies even in the face of a contract term providing otherwise. There are detailed provisions for educational use,

93 Copyright and Rights in Databases Regulations 1997 (UK), SI 1997/3032, reg 17; Copyright and Related Rights Act 2000 (IE), s 325.
94 Copyright and Rights in Databases Regulations 1997 (UK), SI 1997/3032, regs 12 and 16; Copyright and Related Rights Act 2000 (IE), ss 320 and 324.
95 For European case law generally, see below, pp 219-21.

parliamentary or judicial proceedings, and some other official uses. In the Irish version, there is no 'fair dealing' defence for research or private study in respect of electronic databases. The UK version allows 'fair dealing' for research as well as teaching, so long as there is no commercial purpose.[96] There is no 'transient use' defence; presumably most of those consulting the database over the Internet will extract only an insubstantial part of the database, and so will not infringe the right.

Ownership and licensing

While the person who first owns the database is described as its 'maker', the actual definition is more obscure. The 'maker' is taken to be 'the person who takes the initiative in obtaining, verifying or presenting the contents of a database and assumes the risk of investing in that obtaining, verification or presentation'; 'investment' may consist of financial, human or technical resources. This is a complex and in many ways obscure definition, though no doubt where any substantial financial investment is involved the parties will take care to state precisely in whom the database right vests. Some special cases are spelled out in the legislation: databases made by employees in the course of their employment vest in their employer, databases made by government officials vest in the government.[97] The database can be assigned or licensed to others; the rules are the same as for assignment and licensing of copyright. Licensing of database use is subject to elaborate regulation, just as is licensing of copyright;[98] unfair licensing practice can be challenged both under this regulation and under unfair competition law.[99] The right goes a great deal of the way towards making a database a substantial asset which can readily be sold or used as collateral for a loan, though there are still technical problems here.[100]

Remedies and jurisdictional issues

Remedies are described simply by borrowing the provisions on copyright and applying them to database right. So remedies are available against anyone who infringes database right or authorises another to infringe it; criminal penalties and damages are available; seizure and forfeiture of infringing articles is allowed; and the remedies follow secondary infringement, allowing the database maker to pursue extracts from the database in a copied form.[101] The same issues emerge as to the position of ISPs caught up in infringements by their customers, and again they can only escape so long as they can plead ignorance, or that they acted expeditiously when the facts came to their attention.[102]

96 Copyright and Rights in Databases Regulations 1997 (UK), SI 1997/3032, regs 19 and 20 and Sched 1; Copyright and Related Rights Act 2000 (IE), ss 327 and 329–336.
97 Copyright and Rights in Databases Regulations 1997 (UK), SI 1997/3032, regs 12, 14 and 15; Copyright and Related Rights Act 2000 (IE), ss 320, 322 and 323.
98 Copyright and Rights in Databases Regulations 1997 (UK), SI 1997/3032, regs 23–25 and Sched 2; Copyright and Related Rights Act 2000 (IE), ss 338 and 340–361.
99 Eg, *IMS Health GmbH and Co OHG v NDC Health GmbH and Co KG* Case C-418/01, ECJ, 29 April 2004 (Web).
100 Lipton, J, 'Security interests in electronic databases', (2001) 9 IJLIT 65.
101 For injunction as a remedy see, eg, *Jobserve Ltd v Relational Designers Ltd* [2002] EWHC 176 Ch.
102 See above, p 59; the rules are the same as for copyright: see Copyright and Rights in Databases Regulations 1997 (UK), SI 1997/3032, reg 23; Copyright and Related Rights Act 2000 (IE), s 338.

The database right is a creation of EU law, with no very obvious counterpart in non-European systems of law; most conflict-of-laws issues will therefore be within the EU and governed by the Brussels Regulation.[103] Database right can be asserted only by those qualified to do so, which means (roughly) that they are citizens of, or residents of, or are based in, the EU or the EEA.[104] There are considerable difficulties in the way of non-Europeans wishing to claim the protection of database right.[105] Europeans wishing to protect databases in other jurisdictions will probably have to re-cast their claim as one in copyright, confidence or trade secret law. Whether the EU law should itself be revised,[106] or whether other jurisdictions should copy it,[107] are matters of considerable controversy.

OTHER INTELLECTUAL PROPERTY RIGHTS

Some other intellectual property rights will now be discussed briefly; they are all of lesser important to e-commerce, though their existence must be noted to give a rounded picture of the area.

Performer's right

This protects the right of performers to exploit the transmission or recording of their performance. Many varieties of performance are covered, including acting, singing, readings and recitations, musical performance, mime and variety acts. This 50 year right is infringed by authorised live broadcast, recording, or recording from a live broadcast. Much of the detailed legal provision will be familiar to those who know their copyright law; performer's right is strongly analogous to copyright.[108]

Moral right

This right is parasitic on copyright, but is nonetheless a distinct right serving rather different values. The author of a copyright work has three 'moral' rights: the right to be identified as author whenever the work is published (the so-called 'paternity' right); the right to object to derogatory treatment of the work (by distortion or mutilation of the work, or calling into question the honour or reputation of the author); and a right against false attribution of authorship. There is also a fourth moral right (applicable only to photographs and films commissioned for private or

---

103 On which see above, p 61.
104 Copyright and Rights in Databases Regulations 1997 (UK), SI 1997/3032, reg 18, as amended by SI 2003/2501; Copyright and Related Rights Act 2000 (IE), s 326.
105 Nettleton, E and Obhi, H, 'Can US companies protect their databases in Europe with database right?', [2002] CW (August) 15.
106 Lipton, J, 'Databases as intellectual property: New legal approaches', [2003] EIPR 139; Colston, C, 'Sui generis database right: Ripe for review?', [2001] 3 JILT (Web); Thönebe, C, 'The legal protection of databases in Europe – An economic analysis', Master's thesis, August 2000 (Web).
107 Conley, J, Brown, M, and Bryan, R, 'Database protection in a digital world: Why the US should decline to follow the European model', (1999) 6 RJOLT (Web); Maurer, S, Hugenholtz, P and Onsrud, H, 'Europe's database experiment', (2001) 294 Science 789 (Web).
108 Copyright, Design and Patents Act 1988 (UK), ss 180–212; Copyright and Related Rights Act 2000 (IE), ss 202–308.

domestic purposes), to privacy. The right has the same duration as copyright, except that the right against false attribution lasts until 20 years from the death of the author.[109] Unlike copyright and performer's right, moral rights cannot leave the author except by transmission on death, though they can be waived. Remedies can include an action for damages and (in the case of derogatory treatment) an injunction forcing infringers to disassociate the author from the infringing work.[110]

It is a truth, universally acknowledged, that 'moral right' is an abysmal translation of the French 'droit moral' – but the phrase is well established, and there is none obviously superior. The right is a long-standing feature of civil law systems, which was forced on semi-reluctant common law countries by international convention; indeed, it was the principal reason why the US declined to sign the Berne Convention until 102 years after its first agreed version. The UK version is noticeably narrow when compared to the Berne Convention, which it supposedly implements; the Irish version is slightly broader in several respects: for example, in that the right extends also to performers, and that the identification right need not be 'asserted' by formal declaration coming to the attention of those it is supposed to bind.[111]

Industrial designs

Protection of industrial designs generally has yet to be harmonised across the EU, and there are significant differences across nations in the protection afforded, and the relation between design rights and copyrights. There is general protection throughout the EU (and much of the world) for semi-conductor designs.[112] This regime was insisted on by the US for any nation which wanted its semi-conductor designs protected in the US; it was somewhat resented in Europe. It has been said, only half jokingly, that the creation of the database right was Europe's revenge on the US for this slight. A general Community Design Right has existed since March 2002, whereby registration of the design results in a term of up to 25 years; unregistered designs also receive Community protection, but only for 3 years.[113]

In the UK, an industrial design is very likely to attract copyright protection, but copyright is not infringed simply by making an article from a copyright design, so long as the maker resists the temptation to make a copy of the document bearing the design. Protection against the maker is given by 'design right', which is in many ways similar to copyright but has a much shorter duration: 15 years from the first recording of the design, or (if marketed within 5 years) 10 years from the first

---

109 See more generally Rajan, M, 'Moral rights and copyright harmonisation: Prospects for an "international moral right"?', SSRN, April 2002 (Web).

110 Copyright, Design and Patents Act 1988 (UK), ss 77–89, 94, 95 and 103; Copyright and Related Rights Act 2000 (IE), ss 107–119, 137, 138 and 309–319. The UK and Irish positions are contrasted in O'Hare, P, 'Protection of moral rights under the Copyright Act 2000', [2003] Comm LP 126.

111 See generally Eagles, I and Longdin, L, 'Technological creativity and moral rights: A comparative perspective', (2004) 12 IJLIT 209.

112 Directive 1987/54/EC; Design Right (Semiconductor Topographies) Regulations 1989 (UK), SI 1989/1100; European Communities (Protection of Topographies of Semiconductor Products) Regulations 1988 (IE), SI 1988/101.

113 Regulation 6/2002/EC on community designs; see also Registered Designs Regulations 2003 (UK), SI 2003/550 and European Communities (Community Designs) Regulations 2003 (IE), SI 2003/27.

marketing. During the last 5 years of protection, remedies are very limited, and in effect the right holder is forced to license its use for a fee. A different regime applies if the design is officially registered at the Design Registry. Conditions for registration are strict: the design must be novel and must have 'eye appeal'. The right is an exclusive right to make, use, import, sell or hire items based on the design; it can last up to 25 years if renewed.[114]

In Ireland, again copyright in a design is not infringed merely by making an article from the design. Provision for registration of design right is similar to that in the UK and is again strict, with requirements of novelty and 'individual character'; it can last up to 25 years if renewed. There is no provision for protection of unregistered designs.[115]

Patents

Patent rights protect new inventions; the right is a monopoly right to the use of the invention for 20 years. A patentable invention must be new, must involve an inventive step, and must be capable of industrial application. Ideas and intellectual discoveries as such are not patentable, only their industrial application. Infringement consists of employing the invention, supplying important details to others, or selling, hiring or importing its products.

In many ways, particularly in the detail of the remedies, patent is similar to copyright; but in some crucial respects it is weaker, in that an application for an official grant is required (an expensive and lengthy process), and when granted it can last for no more than 20 years. As part of the application process, the invention will have been described, and so will be publicly available at the end of the period. Nonetheless, patent rights can be much more valuable than copyright, because a patent gives a monopoly right even against someone who developed the invention quite independently; it is irrelevant whether that person copied from the patent holder. Since few patents involve really startling innovations, most being straightforward (though non-obvious) developments of the existing technology, the protection given by patent law can give a sizable industrial advantage.

Patent law was substantially harmonised across the EU by the European Patent Convention of 1973;[116] negotiations over further uniformity through a common patent code have currently stalled.[117] A patent application can be made for national protection, or at the European Patent Office (in Munich) for EU-wide protection, or under the Patent Co-operation Treaty for protection in some or all of the signatory nations.

There are substantial differences between European patent law and the patent protection in other nations. Most notably, unlike the US, the EU legislation refuses patent protection for software as such.[118] Originally, this was an attempt to ensure

---

114 Copyright, Designs and Patents Act 1988 (UK), ss 51, 52 and 213–273, and Sched 4; Registered Designs Rules 1995 (UK), SI 1995/2912; Registered Designs Regulations 2001 (UK), SI 2001/3949; Registered Designs (Amendment) Rules 2001 (UK), SI 2001/3950.

115 Copyright and Related Rights Act 2000 (IE), s 79; Industrial Designs Act 2001 (IE); Industrial Designs Regulations 2002 (IE), SI 2002/280.

116 Implemented by Patents Act 1977 (UK) and Patents Act 1992 (IE); see also Patents Rules 1995 (UK), SI 1995/2093 and Patents Rules 1992 (IE), SI 1992/179.

117 'EU patent law dies, software law lives', Register, 19 May 2004 (Web).

118 Patents Act 1977 (UK), s 1(2)(c); Patents Act 1992 (IE), s 9(2)(c).

that software would be protected, if at all, by the copyright regime rather than the patent regime. However, many applications to protect software by patent have been made, and the legislation does not say that a patent will be refused merely because it involves the use of new software. The stumbling block is rather that mere ideas or intellectual discoveries are not patentable, but only inventions capable of industrial application – in other words, inventions which produce a real-world 'technical effect' which can be specified. So software can, in effect, be patented, so long as the 'technical effect' it produces is new and can be specified; and it seems that this 'technical effect' can be purely internal to the workings of a computer.[119] Whether this restriction serves any useful purpose, and indeed whether it is compatible with the TRIPS treaty, is a matter of some debate;[120] an EU software patents directive is under active discussion.[121]

Another notable exclusion from European patent law is any protection for business methods.[122] Again, there is some wiggle-room where the method has a 'technical effect', but by and large the line has been held.[123] The US repudiated this restriction in 1998,[124] and in fact several methods for doing business over the Internet have been litigated under this head, including Amazon's 'One-Click' purchasing system.[125]

The patent regime is in many respects cumbersome, and many small enterprises could not possibly contemplate the expense and delay in making an application.[126] Most European nations recognise a lesser 'utility model' right appropriate in those circumstances: Ireland recognises a 'short-term patent' with a simplified application procedure and a 10 year duration.[127] The UK recognises no such right. There is currently an EU proposal for a community utility-model patent, which would cover computer programs as well as other inventions.[128] The UK Patent Office is considering helping small enterprises in another way, by establishing a mutual insurance association to help them enforce patent rights.[129]

Patent claims are strongly territorial, which can be a problem where the alleged infringement is over the Internet. In the *Menashe* case, an inventor acquired an EU patent in respect of a system for playing casino games: clients would install special software on their computers, which would then communicate over the Internet to a casino server, and could then play interactive games. The defendant circulated a very similar system in the UK. Could it be said that the defendant had put the inventor's process into effect within the UK, even though its server was in Curaçao?

---

119 Pila, J, 'Dispute over the meaning of "invention" in Article 52(2) EPC', (2005) 36 IRIPCL (Web).
120 Widdison, R, 'Software patents pending?', [2000] 3 JILT (Web).
121 'EC OKs software patents', Register, 7 March 2005 (Web).
122 Patents Act 1977 (UK), s 1(2)(c); Patents Act 1992 (IE), s 9(2)(c).
123 Smith, G, *Internet Law and Regulation*, 3rd edn, 2002, London: Sweet and Maxwell, pp 66–68.
124 *State Street Bank and Trust Co v Signature Financial Group, Inc* 149 F 3d 1368 (Fed Ct, 23 July 1998). See, more generally, Henderson, K and Kane, H, 'Internet patents: Will they hinder the development of e-commerce?', [2001] 1 JILT (Web); Price, D, 'Assessing the patentability of financial services and products', (2004) 3 JHTL 141 (Web).
125 *Amazon.com, Inc v Barnesandnoble.com, Inc* 239 F 3d 1343 (Fed Ct, 14 February 2001), on which see Mota, S, 'Internet business method patents', (2001) 19 JMJCIL 523.
126 Macdonald, S, 'Bearing the burden: Small firms and the patent system', [2003] 1 JILT (Web).
127 Patents Act 1992 (IE), ss 63–67.
128 See 'Utility model' (Web); Leith, P, 'Software utility models and SMEs', [2000] 2 JILT (Web).
129 *Report of the Patent Enforcement Project Working Group*, 16 June 2004 (Web).

The Court of Appeal thought so – what customers would have thought important was the input and output in the UK, even though the system was controlled and administered from abroad.[130] *Menashe* should be treated with some caution – the patent there included the communication protocols between host and client computers, whereas a more common case would be for a program to be entirely on the (foreign-based) host machine, communication being via web protocols. Nonetheless, it may be a sign that inventions which are targeted at UK audiences will be held capable of infringing UK patents.[131]

Confidence and trade secrets

The law of confidence is a rather flexible entity, a creature of case law not statute. It makes a significant contribution towards defending not only commercial confidences but also personal secrets, and there is no limit on the type of information protected by the doctrine so long as it is not illegal, immoral, hopelessly vague or manifestly trivial. The right arises wherever information has 'the necessary quality of confidentiality', which seems to mean little more than that it is known only to a few people and that those people treat it as a secret. If there is an explicit agreement to keep the secret, this will establish confidence, and such an agreement is taken to be implicit in many contracts, especially employer–employee; there is an elaborate jurisprudence on precisely where an employee's acquisition of knowledge, experience and know-how becomes participation in an enforceable confidence. However, this is simply one example of confidence, and there is certainly no requirement of a contract, though any rights deriving from confidence may be modified by contract. It is not entirely clear to what extent one person can force confidence on another, as by sending a letter or e-mail with a notice to the effect that the contents are confidential.

Confidence lasts unless or until it is destroyed by revealing the information to the wider public; if such a revelation is wrongful then it is also actionable, even though the confidence is then gone for the future. There is also a well-established 'springboard' doctrine, under which someone who steals another's valuable confidence is not allowed to profit from it even if, by the time they do so, it has become public knowledge. Whether information has become public knowledge can be a difficult question, especially in 'reverse engineering' cases where a product is widely advertised but its manufacturers claim that its inner workings are still confidential: it seems that confidence may still be retained so long as the effort required to discover the information is considerable. Merely hiding data by encryption will not usually suffice to keep it confidential for this purpose.[132] On the other hand, it has (surprisingly) been held legitimate for doctors to sell confidential medical data on their patients, so long as the identity of each patient is effectively undiscoverable.[133]

---

130 *Menashe Business Mercantile Ltd v William Hill Organisation Ltd* [2002] EWCA Civ 1702 (Web).
131 On jurisdiction generally, see Bender, G, 'Clash of the titans: The territoriality of patent law vs. The EU', (2000) 40 IDEA 49 (Web).
132 *Mars UK Ltd v Teknowledge Ltd* [2000] RPC 138.
133 *R v Department of Health ex p Source Informatics Ltd* [2001] QB 424, on which see Beyleveld, D and Histed, E, 'Betrayal of confidence in the Court of Appeal', (2000) 4 MLI 277.

Breach of confidence can be committed by anyone who knows, or ought reasonably to know, that the information is confidential. Any substantial use or disclosure of the information will be actionable; there is (probably) no requirement that the person claiming a remedy has suffered any detriment from the breach, though some breaches can be excused on public interest grounds. In many cases, it is quite unclear precisely who the confidence 'belongs to', and publication by any one of those in the know could lead to action by any of the others. The remedy may consist of an injunction to prevent further breaches and/or damages. Damages can be measured in any one of three ways, as the claimant wishes and can establish relevant figures: as the amount the claimant lost through the breach, as a reasonable licence fee for taking the secret, or as the profit gained through its misuse. It seems that for jurisdictional purposes, a breach of confidence occurs in the jurisdiction where the confidence was broken: so where an English claimant's confidence was broken by a German firm, which exploited it purely in German markets, the English courts had no jurisdiction under the Brussels Convention.[134] There is no associated criminal liability unless it is through crimes of unlawful surveillance[135] or computer misuse,[136] nor is there a jurisdiction to forfeit items made in breach of confidence. The Law Commission for England and Wales currently proposes to create a general offence of deliberate misuse of another's trade secrets;[137] the Irish Law Commission had earlier made a similar proposal, though aimed more at domestic confidences than at trade secrets as such.[138]

Several jurisdictions afford statutory protection to 'trade secrets', which are broadly equivalent to what UK and Irish lawyers call commercial confidence.[139] International standardisation here seems very distant indeed.

Trade marks

Trade marks differ from the other species of intellectual property so far considered in that, while they are indeed pieces of valuable intellectual property in themselves, their value is that they name or identify other products or services. A trade mark is a label for other items the trade mark owner wishes to sell. Traditionally, they were spoken of as a 'badge of origin', that is, an indication of who made them. Yet while trade marks can occasionally serve this function still, their primary use today is to identify brands, distinguishing particular products from other similar products. 'Origin' is not particularly relevant, especially since trade marks can readily be bought and sold; outright fraud aside, there is no reason why trade marks should have anything to do with the product's source or maker. Rather, a trade mark usually

---

134 *Kitetechnology BV v Unicor GmbH Plastmaschinen* [1995] FSR 765.

135 Below, p 83.

136 Above, p 17.

137 *Misuse of Trade Secrets*, Law Commission Consultation Paper No 150, 1997, London: HMSO (Web). For general discussion, see Freedman, C, 'The extension of the criminal law to protecting confidential commercial information: Comments on the issues and the cyber-context', (1999) 13 IRLCT 147; Lang, J, 'The protection of commercial trade secrets', [2003] EIPR 462.

138 *Privacy: Surveillance and the Interception of Communications*, LRC 57, 1998 (Web).

139 For the US position, see Babirak, M, 'The Virginia Uniform Trade Secrets Act: A critical summary of the Act and case law', (2000) 5 VJOLT 15 (Web); Johnson, A, 'Injunctive relief in the Internet age: The battle between free speech and trade secrets', (2002) 54 FCLJ 517 (Web).

denotes a brand, and so must be distinguished from a merely generic label that simply indicates a particular type of product.

Trade marks were well established by the start of the 20ᵗʰ century, but the law within the EU was recast by a Directive of 1989, now reflected in modern legislation.[140] This is probably the most uniform of the intellectual property regimes within the EU. There are also analogous, but much less used, national jurisdictions protecting business names.[141]

A trade mark must be officially registered as such. It will not be accepted for registration unless it is a sign which can be represented graphically (a term which includes words, names, and designs), and is capable of distinguishing the goods or services of one undertaking from those of others. The shape of products or their packaging can constitute a trade mark, so long as it is not dictated by the nature of the goods or the results they are to achieve. The application will state the goods or services with which the proprietor intends to use the mark; to assist, there is a classification of types of goods and services, kept and updated by the World Intellectual Property Organisation (WIPO). Registration may be refused on a number of grounds: infringement of another mark, deception, bad faith, public policy or morality. Registration is for 10 years; it may be renewed for an indefinite number of times thereafter, though in view of the fees payable there may be limits to how many times this will be worth it.

The mark must be sufficiently distinctive. Some marks are insufficiently distinctive when first created, but may become sufficiently clear in the public eye to be recognised later. This is likely to be so if the mark is purely geographical, or employs a very common name (such as 'Jones'), or is purely generic or descriptive of the product ('Froot Loops' for fruit-flavoured cereal, 'Baby-Dry' for nappies, www.primebroker.com for a broker's services). All these would be refused registration when first marketed, but may become registrable if the public begins to associate them with particular products, as their makers intend. Other marks undergo the reverse process, initially being distinctive but then coming to denote a generic type of product (Hoover, Walkman). When registered trade marks have over time become generic or descriptive, or have fallen into disuse, their registration can be revoked.[142]

Infringement is defined broadly. The principal ground of infringement is use, in the course of trade, of a sign which is identical with the trade mark, in relation to goods or services which are identical with those for which it is registered. The main target is presumably those who try to generate confusion between their own products and those the mark is intended to protect. However, this first ground requires no evidence of confusion, and on its literal wording it catches anyone acting in the course of trade who uses the mark at all, whatever their purpose – simply mentioning the product by its trade mark name brings the case within the definition. This hopelessly wide definition, if left to itself, would enable trade mark owners to censor all press references to their product. Much of the sting is drawn by the defences, though they are in narrow terms. It is legitimate to use the mark to refer to the very product it protects, so long as the usage accords with honest business

---

140 Directive 1989/104/EC; Trade Marks Act 1994 (UK); Trade Marks Act 1996 (IE).
141 Business Names Act 1985 (UK), as amended; Registration of Business Names Act 1963 (IE).
142 Trade Marks Act 1994 (UK), ss 1–8, Trade Marks Act 1996 (IE), ss 6–12.

practice and does not take unfair advantage of the mark or act detrimentally to it. Again, it is legitimate to use the trade mark to indicate the purpose of another product or service: a garage that specialises in repairing and servicing Volvos can say so without infringing the Volvo trade mark. Here too, however, the usage must accord with honest business practice, which would mean at minimum that the user of the trade mark should be careful not to suggest a commercial affiliation with the trade mark owner where there is none.[143]

Infringement can also be established even where the mark is not identical, or the products referred to are not identical. If the sign used is similar to or identical with the trade mark, and the products referred to are similar or identical to those it protects, then infringement is established if there exists a likelihood of confusion on the part of the public, which includes the likelihood of association of the sign with the trade mark. Further, use of an identical or similar sign in relation to *dissimilar* products constitutes infringement where the trade mark has a reputation in the jurisdiction and the use of the sign takes unfair advantage of, or is detrimental to, the distinctive character or the repute of the trade mark.[144]

Various defences are available. Purely descriptive use of trade-marked words is permitted: a sweet manufacturer is entitled to describe its product as a 'treat' or even to include that word in its name, even though a competitor has already registered a relevant trade mark including the word 'treat'. Use of your own trade mark in relation to the products it protects is always legitimate, even if it invites confusion with another trade mark – unless, of course, that competitor can have the registration declared improper. Use of your own name is also legitimate, provided that (in the case of a company) the whole name is given and (in all cases) the use is in accordance with honest business practices.[145]

Trade marks can be assigned in writing, or particular uses of them can be licensed. In the modern law, there is no objection to free assignment or franchising of trade marks and, so long as there is no deception of the public, there is no reason why the trade mark should belong to the same company as lawfully places the mark on its products.[146]

Remedies can include civil actions for injunctions or damages. Infringing items can be forfeited. Criminal sanctions are narrowly defined, only protecting trade marks on goods not services, and even there not extending to all instances of infringement; their main use is against the production of counterfeit goods. The making of groundless threats of infringement proceedings is a criminal offence.[147]

National trade marks protect use of the trade mark only within that nation. (Note that registration under the UK system is good for all the UK jurisdictions.) If an alleged infringer is based abroad, do the home courts have jurisdiction based on the fact that the infringer's web site can be seen by those surfing in the home jurisdiction? The courts have consistently rejected the argument that a defendant can be said to 'use' the mark in a particular jurisdiction merely because it can be viewed from there. Rather, there must be evidence of commercial activity by the defendant

---

143 Trade Marks Act 1994 (UK), s 10, Trade Marks Act 1996 (IE), s 14.
144 Trade Marks Act 1994 (UK), s 10, Trade Marks Act 1996 (IE), s 14.
145 Trade Marks Act 1994 (UK), ss 10 and 11, Trade Marks Act 1996 (IE), ss 14 and 15.
146 Trade Marks Act 1994 (UK), s 24, Trade Marks Act 1996 (IE), s 28.
147 Trade Marks Act 1994 (UK), s 14, Trade Marks Act 1996 (IE), s 18.

in, or aimed at, the jurisdiction. So where it was clear that the main commercial impact of the defendant's activities would be in Scotland, the Scottish courts had jurisdiction.[148] However, where a Dublin shop's web site did nothing in particular to attract UK customers, the shop itself having no significant trade outside Ireland, an English court found it had no jurisdiction.[149] The precise point at which the line will be drawn is not altogether clear, but it seems to be enough that the defendant's web site is designed to attract trade from the home jurisdiction amongst others.[150] It seems clear that the general approach is comparable to that of the US courts, under the *Zippo* test.[151]

Protection across a wider range of jurisdictions may be obtained by application under the Madrid Protocol (to which both the UK and Ireland are parties) for international registration, which will cover all countries which are parties to the Protocol – 77 at the time of writing, including (from November 2003) the US. Registration may be opposed by the owner of a conflicting mark, but this will only prevent registration in the countries to which that mark applies. Alternatively, a trade mark user may apply for a Community Trade Mark, covering all jurisdictions within the EU. However, if such an application is successfully opposed by a prior mark holder in an EU state, the application fails completely. There is community-wide provision for protection of well-known marks in jurisdictions where they are not registered, where the use is likely to cause confusion.

Passing off

Passing off is a common law tort. The central idea is that the defendant gave the impression that the goods they were selling were those of the claimant: the defendant 'passed off' their goods as the claimant's. As such, the tort is in essence a law of unregistered trade marks. But in several respects the tort goes wider, and it has been suggested that it is, or might grow into, a general tort of unfair competition.

The tort protects the reputation and market position of the claimant's goods and business generally – the claimant's 'goodwill' as it is usually called. No tort is committed if there is no injury to goodwill. If the claimant's products are not sold in the UK, then nothing the defendant can do will injure the claimant's goodwill there, because they have none. However, it makes no difference whether the public knows whose the goodwill is: the tort protects product branding whether or not the public appreciates who owns the brand. There is also no requirement that claimant and defendant be competitors, though in most cases they are.

---

148 *Bonnier Media Ltd v Smith* 2002 SCLR 977, on which see Edwards, L, 'The Scotsman, the Greek, the Mauritian company and the Internet: Where on earth do things happen in cyberspace?', (2004) 8 Edin LR 99.

149 *Euromarket Designs Inc v Peters and Crate & Barrel* [2001] FSR 288; similarly *1–800 Flowers, Inc v Phonenames Ltd* [2001] EWCA Civ 721 (Web).

150 *V&S Vin and Sprit Aktiebolag AB v Absolut Beach Pty Ltd* (England and Wales, Chancery Division, 15 May 2001). For general discussion, see Bainbridge, D, 'Trademark infringement, the Internet and jurisdiction', [2003] 1 JILT (Web).

151 Discussed above, p 61; see Simonyuk, Y, 'The extraterritorial reach of trademarks on the Internet', [2002] DLTR 9 (Web). For discussion and criticism of the US position generally, see: Bakken, E, 'Unauthorized use of another's trademark on the Internet', [2003] 3 UCLA JLT (Web); Kaiser, B, 'Contributory trademark infringement by Internet service providers: An argument for limitation', (2002) 7 JTLP (Web); Dogan, S and Lemley, M, 'Trademarks and consumer search costs on the Internet', SSRN, June 2004 (Web).

Infringement consists of a false statement to the public about the defendant's goods. The statement may be implicit, as where the defendant wrongly suggests a connection with the claimant by imitating their packaging or advertising. The law is usually stated to require a false statement that goods of the defendant are goods of the claimant, but the courts have not confined themselves to that: the tort is also committed if the defendant passes off inferior examples of the claimant's goods as being superior, or wrongly suggests that there is some connection between their goods and the claimant, as by falsely suggesting that the claimant is endorsing the defendant's products. The tort has also been extended to cover 'reverse passing off', where the defendant passes off the claimant's products as being their own. And (most controversially) the tort has been applied where no particular trader is targeted; wrongly describing your drink as 'champagne' is actionable by any or all of the producers and importers who really do deal in champagne. At its outer edges, the tort fades into the tort of malicious falsehood or trade libel, which catches any harmful statement about the claimant's products. A mere reference to the claimant's brand is not enough if there is no real danger that members of the public will assume that the product is the claimant's, though the courts are reluctant to overestimate the degree of perspicacity that members of the public will show. Defences to the tort are few and narrow: there is no absolute rule that a defendant may use their own name if it leads to confusion with the claimant.

An injunction will be available to prohibit infringement. Damages are awarded if a substantial number of people are misled and sufficient fault by the defendant is shown: intent to deceive the public is not required, so long as it was a probable consequence of what the defendant did. Damages can be awarded for lost business, or more generally for injury to trading reputation, as where the claimant's goods have been associated with goods of inferior quality. In one Irish case, where the defendant seems to have created general public confusion between its business and that of the plaintiff, damages included the cost of an advertising campaign to establish the difference in the public mind.[152]

'Goodwill' is territorial: an action within the jurisdiction must be based on injury to goodwill within the jurisdiction. So where a German company's web site allegedly damages the goodwill of an English company, then an action for injury to English goodwill can be brought in England, because that is where the damage occurs.[153]

ASSESSMENT

For a legal area of its considerable age, the law of intellectual property shows remarkable uniformity across the world. The reasons for this have much to do with the mobility of the written word. In the mid-19th century, when much legal energy was going into the creation and consolidation of *national* legal codes, continental European publishers were already concerned at the ease with which their products could be copied and their income stolen abroad. The incentive this gave to private firms to lobby for international legislation was considerable; and this remains the case today. It is very hard for opponents to fight new claims to extend the rights yet

---

152 *Falcon Travel v Falcon Leisure Group* [1991] 1 IR 175.
153 *Mecklermedia Corporation v DC Congress GmbH* [1998] Ch 40.

further.[154] The international intellectual property regime is gaining sharper and sharper teeth, and indeed there is every sign that enforcement powers will get nastier again before too long.

Yet what is the nature of these rights? Clearly, they have gone a long way from their rather humble origins.[155] Have the legal systems of the world in effect recognised a new species of property: ownership of ideas? This is a question with many facets. One is simply terminological: can we or should we use the same legal language for breach of intellectual rights that we do for property generally? Overwhelmingly, the answer given to this today is 'yes', though it would be a mistake to read too much into this, let alone to regard it as determining any substantive legal question.[156] Another facet is the legal–philosophical one: given that 'property' is a label for a pretty substantial legal subject, is it proper to apply that label to 'intellectual property' as well? In many cases, the legislation itself is clear that it is, but any argument on that question rapidly turns into one on the more general questions of what 'property' is, why it is treated as valuable by the law, and whether the protection now afforded to it is set at the appropriate level.[157] It would be a mistake to assume that those who particularly wish to apply the 'property' label are also particularly keen on wide enforcement; on the contrary, many do so in order to stress the difficulties and ambiguities of property law, the multiple claims there may be to any one piece of property, and the precautions against unfair competition and market failure that must accompany any powerful property regime.[158]

The main complaint about these rights (one which is often obscured by calling them 'property') is simply that they are now too extensive: that it is too easy to gain protection for a relatively trivial innovation, the advantage given is too great, the term too long, and the tools of enforcement too heavy-handed. Intellectual property law is in practice only rarely concerned with protecting great leaps of the imagination; the lesser intellectual creations with which it usually deals arguably do not need the law's protection, or at least not to the degree they have received. Whether there is too much protection or too little is in principle unknowable, as we cannot say what the economy would have been like if a different intellectual property regime had been in place 50 or 20 years ago. Each side of the argument can invent scenarios of horror. Those who support the rights can paint a picture of a world where technical and intellectual innovation grinds to a halt because of the lack of a law protecting new ideas; their opponents, such as Lawrence Lessig, can posit a world where no parent dares to tell bedtime stories to their children for fear that the Disney Company will assert copyright in 'their' story. And debate still rages over whether software development is superior under an 'open source' regime or a proprietary regime.

---

154 See particularly *Eldred v Ashcroft* 537 US 186 (15 January 2003) (refusal of the US Supreme Court to declare further copyright extension unconstitutional). On the case, see Murphy, S, 'Unlimited congressional power under the copyright clause in Article I of the Constitution', (2004) 38 USFLR 525; Kretschmer, M, 'Digital copyright: The end of an era', [2003] EIPR 333.

155 Liu, J, 'Regulatory copyright', (2004) 83 NCLR 87.

156 See, eg, Kelleher, D, 'Stealing information', (2001) 2 TELJ 8.

157 Lipton, J, 'Information wants to be property: Legal commodification of e-commerce assets', (2002) 16 IRLCT 53; Druey, J, 'Information cannot be owned: There is more of a difference than many think', SSRN, April 2004 (Web); Lemley, M, '*Ex ante* versus *ex post* justifications for intellectual property', (2004) 71 Chi LR 129.

158 Carrier, M, 'Cabining intellectual property through a property paradigm', (2004) 54 Duke LJ 1; Lipton, J, 'Information property: Rights and responsibilities', (2004) 56 Fla LR 135.

Particularly in the spotlight is the increasing reliance on technology to enforce intellectual property rights. There is nothing really new in this – many 20th century innovators protected their innovative technology by deliberately obstructing those who would copy it. But the greater ease with which this is now done raises fundamental questions. The use of software to control what your users do is effectively the assumption of legal authority over them; or (as Lessig more pithily puts it) 'Code is Law'.[159] This is particularly obvious where the creators of that software manage to have it declared a criminal offence to circumvent it. It would be naïve to regard this encryption software as merely protecting its owner's rights, for the effectiveness of the protection effectively turns those rights into something very different, and much more threatening, than they were before.[160] A great deal of money and effort is being expended to create effective digital rights management (DRM), though what percentage of users will prove able to break through the new constraints remains to be seen; the debate on when or whether copyright owners should be allowed to use such constraints has hardly begun.[161]

FURTHER READING

Awoyemi, B, 'Zippo is dying, should it be dead?', (2005) 9 MIPLP 37.

Bollinger, L, 'Protect this work of expression', (2004) 44 SCLR 1287.

Dinwoodie, G, 'TRIPs and the dynamics of intellectual property lawmaking', (2004) 36 CWRJIL 95.

Douglas, D, 'Copyright and peer-to-peer music file sharing: The Napster case and the argument against legislative reform', (2004) 11 E-Law (Web).

Katyal, S, 'The new surveillance', (2004) 54 CWRULR 297.

Kowalski, H, 'Peer-to-peer file sharing and technological sabotage tactics: No legislation required', (2004) 8 MIPLP 297.

Ku, R, 'Copyright, the Constitution and progress', SSRN, June 2004 (Web).

Lemley, M and Reese, R, 'Reducing digital copyright infringement without restricting innovation', (2004) 56 Stan LR 1345.

Lessig, L, Free Culture, 2004, New York: Penguin (Web).

Radin, M, 'Regulation by contract, regulation by machine', SSRN, April 2004 (Web).

Wagner, R, 'On software regulation', (2005) 78 So Calif LR 457.

Yu, P, 'The escalating copyright wars', (2004) 32 Hof LR 907.

---

159 Above, p 5.
160 Picker, R, 'From Edison to the Broadcast Flag: Mechanisms of consent and refusal and the propertization of copyright', SSRN, September 2002 (Web).
161 Roemer, R, 'Trusted computing, digital rights management, and the fight for copyright control on your computer', [2003] UCLA JLT 8 (Web); Loren, L, 'Technological protections in copyright law: Is more legal protection needed?', (2002) 16 IRLCT 133; McCullagh, D and Homsi, M, 'Leave DRM alone: A survey of legislative proposals relating to digital rights management technology and their problems', [2005] MSLR 317.

CHAPTER 4

RIGHTS OVER DATA: PRIVATE RIGHTS

The previous chapter covered ownership of data: the right to produce or to accumulate data, often with a view to restricting access to others, or permitting it only on payment. This chapter and the next concern rights which cut across ownership rights, or even run completely counter to them: rights to access or control data accumulated by others. Starting with the right to see your opponent's data in hostile litigation, this chapter then proceeds to personal privacy law generally, and then (the main topic of the chapter) to the specific safeguards for personal data in the data protection legislation. This treatment of private rights to data is complemented by the next chapter, which covers the extensive rights of the state to demand data from those within its territory.

In a sense, the line between this chapter and the previous one is arbitrary. Both concern rights to control data, and indeed some legal institutions (especially the law of confidence) feature in both. Nonetheless, there is a very real difference in philosophy between them. The motivation for data ownership law is at root economic. By protecting accumulations of data and the investment they represent, the law encourages further investment in data, and thus promotes economic activity. But the controls in this chapter and the next quite deliberately undermine those incentives, either to fine-tune the precise types of data which may be accumulated, or to serve some other purpose which has higher priority. A society where everyone lived in a virtual goldfish bowl might well turn out to be financially richer, but many would prefer to be poorer if privacy could be safeguarded. And we do not always value the accumulation of data so highly that we wish its owners to be able to conceal evidence of wrongdoing. The balance that is struck here, and whether it is the right one, is the problem addressed by this and the following chapter.

DISCOVERY IN PRIVATE LITIGATION

As business records are increasingly kept in electronic form, inevitably there is more of an electronic aspect to the pre-trial process of discovery under which relevant documents held by each side are listed and, if necessary, copied to the other litigant. This has all happened within a traditional framework, however. While there has been the occasional 'smoking gun', where a case turns on an electronic record of a type that could never have existed in pre-computer days,[1] overall there has been relatively little fuss. Eventual explicit recognition of problems with electronic data in the rules of court is of course inevitable, and proposals are being drafted.[2]

Standard discovery (or disclosure, as it is now known in England and Wales) requires each party to search for documents relevant to the case, to list them and to supply that list to the other party, to produce the documents when requested, and to permit copies to be made unless privilege is claimed.[3] There

---

1   Eg, ' "Busty blonde" email lawyers face lawsuit', Register, 6 September 2001 (Web).
2   Eastham, L, 'Documents, disclosure and direction', (2004) 14 C&L (6) 4; Withers, K, 'Computer-based disclosure and discovery in civil litigation', [2001] 1 JILT (Web); Sautter, E, 'The new rules on e-disclosure', (2005) 155 NLJ 1618.
3   See, eg, Superior Court Rules, Order 31 (IE); Civil Procedure Rules, Pt 31 (E&W) (Web).

appears to be no serious doubt that data files constitute 'documents' for this purpose.[4] Problems may arise because of the sheer bulk of data retained by modern computing systems, bearing in mind back-up copies, e-mail archives and automatically generated logs. This may include much that was wrongly assumed by its authors to be long gone. A sensible attitude needs to be taken to the degree of diligence used during the search for relevant data.[5]

The admissibility of electronic documents, if disputed, depends on rules which are rather different in each jurisdiction. Speaking very generally, any electronic file or document would have to be classified for the purpose of the dispute as real evidence, as hearsay, or as a copy of another document. If the document is real evidence – a physical thing which supposedly 'speaks for itself' – then in a case of doubt there would have to be an account of the process by which it was produced. If it is hearsay – such as a record of what someone said, in a case where the issue is whether that statement was true – then the admissibility or weight of the document may clearly be in doubt. (In civil proceedings in the UK jurisdictions, the hearsay rule is almost dead as regards admissibility, though of course it is still important as to the weight of the evidence; the rule survives as to admissibility in Ireland, though with numerous exceptions.) And if the data constitutes a copy of a relevant document, then questions may be asked about the accuracy of the copying and the location of the original. The detail of the law in each jurisdiction is complex, and beyond the scope of this book. Suffice it to say that if there is no particular reason to suspect tampering, then ICT-based evidence is as good as any other – though an explanation of the process involved in producing it may be needed to clarify what it means, and how reliable it is as evidence on the point actually in issue.[6]

Most electronic documents can be taken at face value, and there is usually no need to lead technical computing evidence to verify them. Doubts may arise, however, in particular cases, as where there is a suspicion that a file may have been clandestinely altered; or if there is some issue as to the file's metadata which may indicate its source and other details about its making; or if the file has been concealed or encrypted; or if crucial data has been deleted. (Most deletion involves, at most, marking the relevant memory sector as available for re-use; a 'deleted' file may therefore be recovered unless that sector has actually been re-used for other data.) Such cases will probably involve seizure of relevant hardware under search orders (still called *Anton Piller* orders in some jurisdictions). This is a rapidly evolving area.[7]

Various other avenues are sometimes available for obtaining data held by others. Rights under the data protection legislation and the freedom of information legislation may sometimes be useful in that regard.[8] Circumstances which do not warrant a search order may nonetheless warrant an order for the preservation of

4   See, eg, *Derby and Co Ltd v Weldon (No 9)* [1991] 1 WLR 652.
5   On all these issues, see Harrison, R, 'The e-mail of the species', (2002) 12 C&L (6) 25; Taylor, R and Richardson, M, 'E-mails: Service by e-mail and disclosure of e-mails', (2001) 151 NLJ 1364.
6   See generally Nicoll, C, 'Should computers be trusted? Hearsay and authentication with special reference to electronic commerce', [1999] JBL 332; Leroux, O, 'Legal admissibility of electronic evidence', (2004) 18 IRLCT 193.
7   See, eg, Turner, M, 'Beware: Computer evidence quicksand', (2001) 11 C&L (6) 36; 'Forensic computing uncloaks industrial espionage', Register, 15 July 2004 (Web).
8   Eg, *McK v Information Commissioner* (Irish High Court, 14 January 2004).

data.[9] And where particular data very probably identifies a wrongdoer, the victim of that wrong may be able to demand access to the data, whether or not the person holding it was partly responsible for the wrong. So where a contributor to a bulletin board commits defamation, the defamed individual may be able to demand data from the board's owners to help them identify the defamer.[10] (Indeed, this may be necessary even where the board owner is in principle willing to help without an order, but fears that without one it might be in breach of the law of data protection or confidence.) Finally, the aid of foreign courts may sometimes be obtained to acquire relevant evidence held within their jurisdiction.[11]

PERSONAL PRIVACY LAW GENERALLY

Control of privacy is increasingly a matter of controlling electronic data acquired by others. This is partly because of the rise of electronic forms of communication: laws to preserve privacy are of little use if they cannot reach the swiftest and most pervasive channels, such as e-mail and the web. But it is also a matter of technological convergence. Computers are no longer mere calculating engines, but the vectors of a polymorphous 'information technology', enveloping ever more methods of recording and communicating ideas. The first camera was made over a century before the first computer, yet today digital cameras are increasingly replacing the older technology. Telephone, radio and TV are similarly becoming digital technologies. And even newspapers (surely the most low-tech form of mass communication) are increasingly becoming creatures of ICT, both at the production stage, and through online dissemination and archiving.

It can accordingly be argued that data protection law (which is considered in the following section) is already the main avenue for protecting privacy; it may in time become the only one. But we are certainly not at that point yet. Legal protection of privacy has much older roots. And there are dangers in focusing too closely on particular technologies. While data protection law is not confined to electronic data, nonetheless that is its main focus, and there is a worry that wider ideas of protection may accordingly be lost. More pragmatically, there is a considerable body of privacy protection law which either does not mention ICT at all, or is not yet fully integrated into the data protection regime. These rules and liabilities are the subject of this section.

Protection of privacy *per se* often has a prominent place in declarations of rights. The European Convention on Human Rights (ECHR) declares that '[e]veryone has the right to respect for his private and family life, his home and his correspondence',[12] and it is an important (if unenumerated) right in the Irish constitution. Yet translating this into actual remedies when privacy is violated has proved to be a different matter. There is no recognised common law tort of invasion

---

9   Susman, P, 'Court orders for the preservation of computer data', (2001) 12 C&L (2) 20.
10   *Takenaka (UK) Ltd v Frankl* [2001] EWCA Civ 348 (Web); *Totalise plc v The Motley Fool Ltd* [2001] EWCA Civ 1897, [2002] 1 WLR 1233 (Web), on which see Brimstead, K, (2002) 9 ITLT (10) 3. For intellectual property cases, see Suzor, N, 'Privacy v intellectual property litigation: Preliminary third party discovery on the Internet', (2004) 25 ABR 228 (Web).
11   Eg, Wessel, J, 'Stars, stripes and section 1782', (2001) 145 Sol Jo 56; Carey, G and Leonowicz, S, 'Letters rogatory and the new European regime', [2003] Comm LP 287.
12   Art 8.1.

of privacy, and attempts to create one by reference to the European Convention have so far not met with success.[13] A recent judgment of the ECHR criticising UK privacy law (by no means the first) has not resulted in reform.[14] In their failure to recognise either explicit privacy rights or rights to the protection of personality, the UK and Irish jurisdictions are noticeably more reluctant to protect their citizens' rights than are either the rest of Europe[15] or the US.[16] It is too early to give up on either system, but the signs are not good.[17] The issue is particularly controversial in connection with cross-border disputes, where much may turn on which nation's laws are applied.

Rather more success has been achieved through the equitable concept of confidence. This was discussed in the previous chapter as one means by which business parties can protect and capitalise on data in their possession.[18] But the concept is flexible, and can be used for precisely the opposite purpose, of *forbidding* data collection or exploitation, on the ground that it represents something the claimant is entitled to keep confidential. Recent English cases have emphasised this, especially the *Naomi Campbell* case, where the supermodel was allowed to sue for publication of pictures and details of her therapy for drug addiction.[19] Confidence cases may therefore involve details of the claimant's private life as well as valuable commercial secrets. Indeed, some cases involve both, as the private lives of the rich and famous may be marketable assets of considerable value to the press. In one recent case concerning photographic rights over a celebrity wedding, the happy couple received a mere £14,600 for a wrongful press intrusion. The trial judge also awarded the newspaper to whom they had sold the rights over £1 m; however, this did not survive appeal, the Court of Appeal holding that no wrong had been committed against the newspaper which had bought the rights.[20] If there is to be a tort of breach of privacy, it looks very much as if it will be a variant of the law of confidence.[21]

Confidence has also been invoked in some high-profile criminal cases, where criminals who have served their sentences have sought to prevent revelation of their new whereabouts, or current appearance, or details of new identities they have assumed. The courts have been largely sympathetic to this, and injunctions have issued to prevent publication by anyone of prohibited details. Where such an order was issued in respect of James Bulger's killers, however, Butler-Sloss P was prepared to modify the effect of the order so that ISPs would not be put in breach of the injunction if one of their clients posted such details on their web site. Nonetheless, the injunction insisted that ISPs who became aware that such material was on the web should take 'all reasonable steps' to suppress it – if necessary by

---

13   See especially *Wainwright v Home Office* [2003] UKHL 53, [2004] 2 AC 406 (Web).

14   *Peck v United Kingdom* [2003] ECHR 44 (Web).

15   Weber, O, 'Human dignity and the commercial appropriation of personality: Towards a cosmopolitan consensus in publicity rights?', (2004) 1 SCRIPT-ed (Web).

16   Bohlman, E, 'Privacy in the Age of Information', [2002] 2 JILT (Web).

17   See especially Bhogal, M, 'United Kingdom privacy update 2003', (2004) 1 SCRIPT-ed (Web).

18   Above, p 71.

19   *Campbell v Mirror Group Newspapers Ltd* [2004] UKHL 22, [2004] 2 AC 457 (Web), on which see Wacks, R, ' "Private facts": Is Naomi Campbell a good model?', (2004) 1 SCRIPT-ed 460 (Web).

20   *Douglas and Zeta-Jones v Hello!* [2005] EWCA Civ 595 (Web).

21   See Forde, G, 'A right to privacy and intellectual property law', (2001) 2 TELJ (4) 9.

blocking customer access to that particular URL.[22] Similar orders might also issue on the basis of an inherent jurisdiction to protect the young, or in the interests of a fair trial.[23]

Wrongful interception of telecommunications on a public system is a criminal offence: the penalty is 5 years' imprisonment/€63,487 in Ireland, 2 years' imprisonment/£ unlimited in the UK. The Irish legislation covers only public systems. The UK legislation covers all public and private systems. However, it provides that the controller of a private system commits no offence by intercepting communications on its own system. If those listened to have not consented to this, then they have an action in tort for this interference with their privacy; detailed regulations provide the controller with a defence so long as the surveillance is for certain specified purposes, and all reasonable steps have been taken to inform users of the risk of monitoring.[24]

Extensive duties are imposed on all those who run electronic communications networks, to safeguard security and confidentiality, to inform users of the risk of security breaches, to prevent misuse, and to provide for the timely erasure of traffic data, location data and billing data. Breach of these duties gives a civil action to the victim, though proof that all reasonable care was taken to comply is a defence. Breach can also be treated as an offence, punishable within the same procedural framework as offences against the data protection legislation.[25]

DATA PROTECTION: THE STATUTORY FRAMEWORK

Data protection law, inspired by the growth of computing power available to government and business in the 1970s, can be traced to a Council of Europe Convention of 1981, which led the UK to enact legislation in 1984 and Ireland to do the same in 1988.[26] The law was broadened and refined by an EU Directive of 1995, leading to UK legislation in 1998 and Irish legislation in 2003.[27] The modern legislation avoids technology-specific provisions, and indeed extends the regime to data held on paper-based filing systems. Those provisions, which are not covered in

---

22 'Internet firm wins Bulger protection', Guardian, 11 July 2001 (Web).
23 See especially *In re S (FC) (a child)* [2004] UKHL 47 (Web).
24 Regulation of Investigatory Powers Act 2000 (UK), ss 1–3 and Telecommunications (Lawful Business Practice) (Interception of Communications) Regulations 2000 (UK), SI 2000/2699, as amended by SI 2003/2426; Postal and Telecommunications Services Act 1983 (IE), s 98. Despite the specific reference to 'Telecom Éireann' (Eircom) in the Irish legislation, the provisions also catch other licensed operators: Postal and Telecommunications Services (Amendment) Act 1999 (IE), s 7.
25 Directive 2002/58/EC, on processing of personal data and the protection of privacy in the electronic communications sector. The Directive is implemented by the Privacy and Electronic Communications (EC Directive) Regulations 2003 (UK), SI 2003/2426, and the European Communities (Electronic Communications Networks and Services) (Data Protection and Privacy) Regulations 2003 (IE), SI 2003/535.
26 Data Protection Act 1984 (UK); Data Protection Act 1988 (IE).
27 Directive on the protection of individuals with regard to the processing of personal data and on the free movement of such data, 1995/46/EC; enacted as Data Protection Act 1998 (UK) and Data Protection (Amendment) Act 2003 (IE). The Irish Act merely amends the previous 1988 Act; for the principal changes, see Boyle, D, 'Data Protection (Amendment) Act 2003 – An overview', [2003] ILT 234. A few minor provisions of the 2003 Act are not in force at the time of writing: see SI 2003/207 (IE).

this book, are not fully in force until 2007; the UK courts are taking a very narrow line as to when the legislation applies to non-electronic data.[28]

Overview of the legislation

The data protection legislation is complicated – especially in its UK implementation – and hard to sum up briefly. While there is a deeply based fear as to how data processing will develop, which cannot be dismissed as merely a fear of the unknown, nonetheless it is not very clear exactly what we are afraid of, or which data practices we wish to ban. And (obviously enough) the legislation does no one any favours if it blindly bans beneficial technologies merely out of a fear that harmful uses may be made of them.

In all the detail of the legislation, two recurrent themes are apparent. First, it seeks to identify a few core rights of data subjects, such as the right to know what data is held on them. Secondly, it restricts data controllers by making them specify the purpose for which the data is collected, and then insisting that their subsequent use of it is reasonable in the light of the purpose. (Note the unusual regulatory technique: the data controller has a wide range of choice as to purpose but, having made the choice, must stick with it or be in breach of the law.) These two themes are returned to again and again in the bulk of detailed regulation.

This legislation will no doubt be amended constantly for the foreseeable future, as new uses for personal data emerge and as enforcement strategies change; the data protection legislation should therefore be regarded as a work in progress.

Personal data

The legislation protects 'personal data', which means information relating to a person who can be identified.[29] The 'person' must be a human being (a 'natural person'); dead people and artificial people (such as companies and governments) are not protected, though of course their employees are protected in their own right.

Data is plainly caught where it is enough *in itself* to identify a particular individual, such as his or her name, or a good picture of the person. It is not entirely clear whether postal addresses, telephone numbers or e-mail addresses fall into that category: does it matter whether the name can be guessed from the address alone (as would be the case with steve.hedley@xyz.com but not user3498@xyz.com); and does it matter whether the particular address is used by more than one person?[30] Most data does not clearly identify its subject, but nonetheless is within the legislation if its subject can be identified from that data and from other information which is, or is

---

28   See especially *Durant v Financial Services Authority* [2003] EWCA Civ 1746 (Web); *Johnson v Medical Defence Union Ltd* [2004] EWHC 347 (Ch) (Web), though note that the claimant was later able to obtain the data by discovery: [2004] EWHC 2509 (Ch) (Web).

29   Data Protection Act 1998 (UK), s 1(1) (definition of 'personal data'); Data Protection Act 1988 (IE), s 1(1) (definition of 'personal data') as amended by Data Protection (Amendment) Act 2003 (IE), s 2.

30   Carey, P, 'E-mail addresses: Are they personal data?', [2000] Ent LR 11; Harrington, J, 'Data protection and e-mail addresses revisited: Is the DPA workable?', [2000] Ent LR 141.

likely to come into, the possession of the data controller. This can potentially include a wide variety of data, including genetic data, images produced by CCTV or otherwise, and location data produced by mobile telephones, RFID chips implanted or carried, or otherwise.[31] In principle, the legislation does not apply to data that has been anonymised to make identification of the subject impossible, though there are considerable doubts as to what is required.[32]

The precise scope of 'personal data' is controversial. Taken literally, the expression seems to suggest a broad meaning: any reference to the data subject is caught so long as he or she is identifiable. And such a literal reading seems compatible with the broad purposes of the legislation. But in the *Durant* case, the Court of Appeal suggested that the data must be 'personal' in a stricter sense: it must have the data subject as its focus, as opposed to simply mentioning him or her incidentally to some other topic; and, further, it must be biographical, in the sense of describing the data subject personally, rather than merely describing events with no personal connotations. Accordingly, when Michael Durant made a complaint about his bank to the Financial Services Authority, the Authority's file on his case was not within the legislation: it related to Durant's complaint, not to Durant personally, except insofar as personal views on him were expressed.[33] If correct, this suggests a very narrow ambit for the legislation indeed. It seems impossible to square with the Directive's definition ('any information relating to an identified or identifiable natural person').[34] After a complaint by Durant to the European Commission, the Commission is now enquiring whether the UK Act complies with EU law.[35]

Particularly strong controls apply to one subset of 'personal data', namely 'sensitive personal data'. This phrase denotes the data subject's racial or ethnic origin, membership of a trade union, physical or mental health or condition, sex life, or political or religious opinions (the Irish legislation adds 'philosophical' opinions, the UK legislation 'other beliefs of a similar nature'). It also includes data on the subject's commission or alleged commission of any offence, and details of any criminal proceedings. The list is a curious one, and includes much that is in practice not private. (Ask yourself how long you could successfully conceal your racial origins, or whether your freedom of belief is adequately protected *merely* by recognising that your beliefs are private.) The aim of the legislation is not 'privacy' as such, but the prevention of misuse of personal data – an overlapping but nonetheless distinct objective.[36] The definition is likely to need clarification if biometric forms of identification become more common – for example, does 'physical ... condition' cover copies of fingerprints or retina images?

---

31   Brown, A, 'RFID tags: An unlawful, or just unwanted, invasion of privacy?', (2004) 14 C&L (5) 27.

32   Walden, I, 'Anonymising personal data', (2002) 10 IJLIT 224; Beyleveld, D and Townend, D, 'When is personal data rendered anonymous?', (2004) 6 MLI 73.

33   *Durant v Financial Services Authority* [2003] EWCA Civ 1746 (Web). For commentary, see Chalton, S, 'The Court of Appeal's interpretation of 'personal data' in *Durant v FSA*', (2004) 20 CLSR 175; Coppel, J, 'Data access requests: What was all the fuss about?', (2003) 153 NLJ 1908.

34   Directive 1995/46/EC, Art 2(a).

35   'European Commission suggests UK's Data Protection Act is deficient', OUT-LAW, 15 July 2004 (Web).

36   Data Protection Act 1998 (UK), s 2; Data Protection Act 1988 (IE), s 1(1) (definition of 'sensitive personal data') as inserted by Data Protection (Amendment) Act 2003 (IE), s 2.

Processing

The broad topic of the legislation is the 'processing' of personal data; but this is construed very widely, to include just about any activity involving the data. 'Processing' includes obtaining, keeping, organising, storing, altering, adapting, retrieving, using, or destroying data; in short, data is 'processed' continually and without a break from the time it is acquired to the time it is erased.[37] (Even if the relevant PC or server has been turned off, the data is still stored, and so is being 'processed' for this purpose.) A full description of the duties imposed during 'processing' is beyond the scope of this book, though more detail is given below of the main provisions applicable to e-commerce. The Directive sums itself up in five 'principles relating to data quality'; UK law covers the same ground in eight 'data protection principles'; the Irish law has no such neat summary.[38] Shortly, the structure is as follows:

(a) No processing should occur at all unless one of the general conditions for processing is satisfied. The principal condition is the consent of the data subject (the Irish legislation provides for family members to give consent where the subject cannot). Other conditions that can justify processing are that the processing is necessary for entering into or performing a contract with the subject, for complying with a legal obligation, or to protect the data subject's vital interests. Various public interest purposes are also allowed, as is pursuit of legitimate interests without prejudice to the data subject's rights.[39]

(b) The conditions for processing are even more strict in relation to sensitive personal data: *explicit* consent of the data subject, or other very specific conditions, including prevention of injury or damage to property, or that 'the information contained in the data has been made public as a result of steps deliberately taken by the data subject'.[40]

(c) Personal data must be obtained fairly, and the purpose of acquiring it must be notified to the data subject along with the identity of the data controller and other data required by fairness, unless this is considered impractical. The type and quantity of data is governed by the purpose: it must be relevant, adequate and not excessive, subsequent processing must not be incompatible with the purpose. Data cannot be kept for longer than is required for the purpose for which it is held, but must be deleted when the purpose is satisfied.[41]

(d) Simply holding personal data attracts duties: the data must be accurate, and updated where necessary; measures must be taken to guard the data against loss or

37   Data Protection Act 1998 (UK), s 1(1) (definition of 'processing'); Data Protection Act 1988 (IE), s 1(1) (definition of 'processing') as inserted by Data Protection (Amendment) Act 2003 (IE), s 2.

38   Directive 1995/46/EC, Art 6; Data Protection Act 1998 (UK), Sched 1. For the Irish legislation, see O'Dowd, M, 'Data protection – An overview', [2004] COLR 14 (Web).

39   Data Protection Act 1998 (UK), Sched 1 Pt I (first data principle), Pt II para 1, and Sched 2; Data Protection Act 1988 (IE), s 2A, as inserted by Data Protection (Amendment) Act 2003 (IE), s 4.

40   Data Protection Act 1998 (UK), Sched 1 Pt I (first data principle), Pt II para 1, Sched 3 and SI 2000/417; Data Protection Act 1988 (IE), s 2B, as inserted by Data Protection (Amendment) Act 2003 (IE), s 4.

41   Data Protection Act 1998 (UK), Sched 1 Pt I (second, third and fifth data principles), Pt II paras 2, 3 and 5, and SI 2000/185; Data Protection Act 1988 (IE), ss 2(1) and 2D, as amended by Data Protection (Amendment) Act 2003 (IE), ss 3 and 4.

damage. Data subjects have a right to know if data is held on them; they may have the right to see it and insist on corrections where it is inaccurate.[42]

(e) Certain uses of personal data are considered particularly objectionable. This includes direct marketing and automated decision-taking. More generally, data subjects have the right to object to processing which causes them distress.[43]

(f) Transfer of the data to others must be justified in the light of the purpose for which it was acquired. Control is particularly strict where the transfer is outside the EU, to jurisdictions without similarly broad legal controls.[44]

Exempted activities

Certain activities are exempt from the legislation, or are regulated to a lesser extent. The detail of this is beyond the scope of this book, but in outline the exceptions in respect of electronic data are as follows:

(a) Domestic use, such as recreation and household family administration, is not caught by the legislation. This exception does not, however, apply to personal web pages if open to the entire world.[45]

(b) Journalists, artists and writers of literary works benefit from a broad exemption for freedom of expression. The exemption applies if the data processing is solely for a journalistic, literary or artistic purpose, compliance with the legislation is incompatible with the purpose, and the data controller reasonably believes that publication would be in the public interest. In the UK legislation, this exemption carries a sting in its tail: if the exemption is relied on but a court rejects it, the data subject can claim aggravated damages for the infringement of his or her rights. There is little case law on the exemption so far, and fundamental questions about it are unanswered. Does it apply to all personal data, or only to data other than sensitive personal data? And does it provide a defence in all cases, or merely for activities leading up to publication but not the publication itself? (Morland J held the latter in *Campbell*, the Court of Appeal the former.) The importance of freedom of expression, and its protection in the Human Rights Convention (Art 10), may be significant here.[46]

---

42 Data Protection Act 1998 (UK), Sched 1 Pt I (fourth, sixth and seventh data principles), and Pt II paras 7–12; Data Protection Act 1988 (IE), ss 2(1), 2C, 3 and 4, as amended by Data Protection (Amendment) Act 2003 (IE), ss 3–5.

43 Data Protection Act 1998 (UK), ss 10–12; Data Protection Act 1988 (IE), ss 2, 6A and 6B, as amended by Data Protection (Amendment) Act 2003 (IE), ss 3 and 7.

44 Data Protection Act 1998 (UK), Sched 1 Pt I (eighth data principle) and Sched 4; Data Protection Act 1988 (IE), s 11, as amended by Data Protection (Amendment) Act 2003 (IE), s 12.

45 Data Protection Act 1998 (UK), s 36; Data Protection Act 1988 (IE), s 1(4)(c); *Lindqvist* (2003, ECJ, Case C-101/01) (Web).

46 Data Protection Act 1998 (UK), s 32; Data Protection Act 1988 (IE), s 22A, as inserted by Data Protection (Amendment) Act 2003 (IE), s 21; *Campbell v Mirror Group Newspapers Ltd* [2002] EWHC 499 QB, Morland J (Web); [2002] EWCA Civ 1373, [2003] QB 633, Court of Appeal (Web) (the House of Lords opinions do not consider data protection issues). For commentary, see Simon, I, '*Campbell* condensed', [2003] EIPR 146; Turle, M, 'Altered images', (2003) 19 CLSR 54.

(c) Health[47] and social work[48] each has its own special rules, modifying the rights under the legislation and providing some exemptions.

(d) Research of various sorts is exempt.[49]

(e) National security and police work is exempt, though the precise limits are unclear.[50] It has been held in the UK that refusals to allow individuals to see files on them held by the security services must be justified on a case by case basis, rather than by a blanket ban.[51] An official certificate that national security exempts particular data from the requirements of the legislation is conclusive.[52] Voluntary transfer of data relevant for national security or the detection or prevention of crime is encouraged by providing that disclosing such data to appropriate authorities is no breach of the data protection legislation.[53] The administration of justice generally is exempt; data caught by legal professional privilege is also exempt,[54] and the Irish Department of Justice is considering exempting lawyers from the need to register client records at all.[55]

(f) There are numerous exemptions for particular governmental functions.

Enforcement

The enforcement regime is centred on the requirement that data controllers must register as such, identifying themselves, briefly describing the personal datasets they hold as well as (in general terms) those to whom they disclose the data. In the UK, the duty to register applies to all data controllers who process personal data; in Ireland, the duty is being implemented more slowly, at present covering only certain types of controller and certain types of data.[56] Processing data before registration is an offence.[57] The registers are available online.[58] The legislation already has a (well-deserved) reputation for complexity; indeed, promotion of the need for

---

47 See especially Data Protection (Subject Access Modification) (Health) Order 2000 (UK), SI 2000/413, and Health Service (Control of Patient Information) Regulations 2002 (UK), SI 2002/1438; Data Protection (Access Modification) (Health) Regulations 1989 (IE), SI 1989/82, and Data Protection Act 1988 (IE), s 4(8), as amended by Data Protection (Amendment) Act 2003 (IE), s 5; Case, P, 'Confidence matters: The rise and fall of informational autonomy in medical law', (2003) 11 Med LR 208.

48 Data Protection (Subject Access Modification) (Social Work) Order 2000 (UK), SI 2000/415, as amended by SI 2005/467; Data Protection (Access Modification) (Social Work) Regulations 1989 (IE), SI 1989/83, and Data Protection Act 1988 (IE), s 4(8), as amended by Data Protection (Amendment) Act 2003 (IE), s 5.

49 See especially Data Protection Act 1998 (UK), s 33; Data Protection Act 1988 (IE), ss 1(3C), 2(5) and 5(1)(h), as amended by Data Protection (Amendment) Act 2003 (IE), ss 2, 3 and 6.

50 Data Protection Act 1998 (UK), ss 28 and 29; Data Protection Act 1988 (IE), ss 1(4)(a) and 5(1)(a).

51 *Baker v Home Secretary* (Information Tribunal, 1 October 2001) (Web).

52 Data Protection Act 1998 (UK), s 28; Data Protection Act 1988 (IE), s 27.

53 Data Protection Act 1998 (UK), ss 28 and 29; Data Protection Act 1988 (IE), s 8.

54 Data Protection Act 1998 (UK), Sched 7 para 10; Data Protection Act 1988 (IE), s 5(1)(g).

55 'Special data exemption for legal clients', Sunday Business Post, 11 April 2004.

56 See Data Protection Act 1988 (IE), s 16(1); and note especially the addition of ISPs and telcos to the list of those who must register, in the Data Protection (Registration) Regulations 2001 (IE), SI 2001/2. The new, more general provision for registration (inserted by Data Protection (Amendment) Act 2003 (IE), s 16) is not yet in force: see SI 2003/207.

57 Data Protection Act 1998 (UK), ss 16–26; Data Protection Act 1988 (IE), ss 16–20, as amended by Data Protection (Amendment) Act 2003 (IE), ss 16–18.

58 Data Protection Public Register (UK) (Web); Registry (IE) (Web).

data controllers to register has necessarily involved attempts to suppress scammers who charge large amounts to register naïve customers.[59]

Enforcement of the rights and duties in the legislation is primarily carried out by the Information Commissioner (UK) or Data Protection Commissioner (IE), against any data controller within the jurisdiction. The Commissioners have the power to investigate complaints, if necessary by conducting searches and seizing documents.[60] There is also a power to ask relevant questions by Information Notice, non-compliance with which is an offence.[61] The Commissioners can prosecute for any of the offences in the legislation, which include processing personal data without a valid registration, or obtaining or disclosing the data without the authority of the data controller; the more extensive UK provision also criminalises selling personal data or offering to sell it.[62] Where certain conduct is an infringement of rights under the legislation, but it falls short of an offence, the Commissioner can nonetheless serve an enforcement notice on the data controller concerned, requiring compliance with the law; non-compliance with the notice is an offence.[63] If the defendant in any of these cases thinks that the Commissioner is acting beyond his or her powers, then the point can be taken to the Circuit Court (Ireland) or the specialist Information Tribunal (UK).[64] Penalties for infringement of the legislation consist of fines only; there is no provision for imprisonment. Offenders in the UK may be fined up to £5,000 on summary conviction, or an unlimited amount if convicted before a jury; in Ireland the figures are € 3,000 and € 100,000 respectively.[65]

Where a particular individual's breaches of data protection law (or other laws) are so substantial, or affect so many consumers, that the collective interests of consumers can be said to need protection, then enhanced powers are available under the Injunctions Directive.[66] An appropriate enforcement body may consult with the individual concerned with a request not to infringe consumers' interests; if dissatisfied with the outcome, then two weeks from beginning the consultation, the enforcement body may apply for an order against the individual, requiring them to desist from the conduct complained of. The court has unlimited powers to enforce the order. In the UK, the Information Commissioner is designated for the purposes of the legislation to act as such an enforcement body; in Ireland, the Data Protection Commissioner is not so designated, and the powers are vested in the Director of Consumer Affairs.[67]

---

59 Eg, 'Firms duped over data registering', BBC News, 16 February 2003 (Web); 'Injunction granted against data protection adverts', OFT Press Release, 6 February 2004 (Web).

60 Data Protection Act 1998 (UK), s 50 and Sched 9; Data Protection Act 1988 (IE), s 24, as amended by Data Protection (Amendment) Act 2003 (IE), s 22.

61 Data Protection Act 1998 (UK), ss 43, 44 and 47; Data Protection Act 1988 (IE), s 12.

62 Data Protection Act 1998 (UK), s 55; Data Protection Act 1988 (IE), ss 21 and 22.

63 Data Protection Act 1998 (UK), ss 40, 41 and 47; Data Protection Act 1988 (IE), s 10, as amended by Data Protection (Amendment) Act 2003 (IE), s 11.

64 Data Protection Act 1998 (UK), ss 48 and 49; Data Protection Act 1988 (IE), s 26.

65 Data Protection Act 1998 (UK), s 60; Data Protection Act 1988 (IE), s 31, as amended by Data Protection (Amendment) Act 2003 (IE), s 19.

66 Directive 1998/27/EC on injunctions for the protection of consumers' interests; Enterprise Act 2002 (UK), ss 210–236; European Communities (Protection of Consumers' Collective Interests) Regulations 2001 (IE), SI 2001/449.

67 For enforcement bodies, see Enterprise Act 2002 (Part 8 Designated Enforcers: Criteria for Designation, etc) Order 2003 (UK), SI 2003/1399, and Enterprise Act 2002 (Part 8 Domestic Infringements) Order 2003 (UK), SI 2003/1593; 'Commission communication concerning Article 4(3) of Directive 98/27/EC', OJ, 31 December 2003, C 321/26 (Web).

Individuals who have been refused their rights under the legislation may complain to the Commissioner, who is under a statutory duty to consider their complaint.[68] Alternatively, individuals themselves may take the relevant data controller to a civil court, where the data controller is within the jurisdiction. Remedies under the UK legislation are relatively broad: a court can instruct the data controller to grant access to the data, or restrain some types of unlawful processing, or order the erasure or correction of inaccurate data, and (where that data had already been sent out to others) that those others be notified of the error.[69] There is a right to compensation for any damage caused by an infringement of the UK legislation, subject to a defence that all reasonable care was taken to comply. Damages can include a figure for distress where there is also damage, or if the infringement related to one of the 'special purposes' (art, literature or journalism).[70] Remedies in the Irish Courts are more limited: the legislation merely provides that the data controller owes a duty of care to the data subject '[f]or the purposes of the law of torts and to the extent that that law does not so provide': this presumably gives a right to damages for actual loss and (possibly) for nervous shock (though not distress *per se*), though it would be for the plaintiff to prove that the duty of care was broken by negligence of some kind.[71]

More generally, the Commissioners have a role in promoting good practice in matters of data protection, particularly by promoting codes of practice.[72]

DATA PROTECTION, THE INTERNET AND E-COMMERCE

The provisions of the legislation are complicated, and a slightly more detailed look is needed. The legislation can be made a little more concrete by considering the life cycle of personal data, starting with its acquisition by the data controller, through the various possible forms of processing and its eventual erasure, and its afterlife as data transferred to a new data controller. The focus here is on the use of customer and other data in e-commerce, especially where the data is collected or used on a web site.[73]

Obtaining data from the data subject by asking for it

There are four requirements when asking data subjects for personal data about themselves: that the data subject be properly informed of the nature and purpose of the processing; that there be a sufficient legal condition for processing; that the data requested must be adequate and not excessive in the light of the purpose; and that the data be obtained fairly.

As will quickly become apparent, in practice these four requirements telescope into a single requirement of informed consent. Accordingly, where data is collected

---

68   Data Protection Act 1998 (UK), s 42; Data Protection Act 1988 (IE), ss 6A, 10 and 12A, as inserted by Data Protection (Amendment) Act 2003 (IE), ss 8, 11 and 13.
69   Data Protection Act 1998 (UK), ss 7, 8, 10, 12, 14 and 15.
70   *Ibid*, s 13.
71   Data Protection Act 1988 (IE), s 7.
72   See generally Data Protection Act 1998 (UK), ss 51–54; Data Protection Act 1988 (IE), ss 9 and 13–15, as amended by Data Protection (Amendment) Act 2003 (IE), ss 10, 14 and 15.
73   For a general review, see Grant, H and Brownsdon, E, 'Web sites: New guidance from the Information Commissioner – Pt 1', (2001) 1 PDP (8) 8 and 'Pt 2', (2001) 2 PDP (2) 6.

from customers or potential customers at a web site, the question is whether the customer knows what the data will be used for, or at least has easy means of knowledge. In most cases, the most practical solution is a lucid and prominently signposted privacy policy on the site.

(a) Proper information about the processing includes certain statutory details: the identity of the data controller, and the purpose or purposes for which the data is collected. If the data controller is established abroad, a local representative must also be identified. The requirement to state the purpose of the processing is not confined to the *main* purpose: if a company means to sell consumer details it collects to other firms, this will have to be mentioned, however the data is to be used first. The information must be 'provided' to the data subject or 'made readily available to' him or her; issues of how prominently or conveniently the information is displayed are bound to arise here. The legislation dispenses with this duty where it is not practicable to give the information required.[74]

(b) 'Satisfactory condition for processing' can be established by consent, and if the data is being given voluntarily by the data subject then consent may be easy to establish. But the consent must be consent *to the processing* (to everything the data controller does with the data); and so either the nature of the processing will have to be explained, or it must be obvious from the circumstances. Another relevant condition is that the data is necessary to prepare for the making of a contract, which is at the request of the data subject. If the data is requested on a form in a web page, it may be necessary for the web site owner to arrange matters so that the data subject cannot proceed further without some explicit indication of agreement, such as by checking a box stating 'I agree to the conditions'. Particular care is needed where the details constitute 'sensitive personal data', where 'explicit consent' is required. The consent of children is also problematical: the web site owner will have to consider whether children can truly be said to consent to the processing of their personal details, or whether there is some other ground on which the processing can be justified.[75]

(c) The data requested must be adequate and not excessive in the light of the data controller's purpose – not too much and not too little, given the purpose for which it is requested. Particular care is needed here when the web site owner decides whether to make revelation of certain data compulsory for particular transactions.[76]

(d) The statutory requirement of fairness cannot be satisfied until the previous two requirements are fulfilled. But even when they are, there is a requirement of fairness on top. Both UK and Irish legislation add that fairness may require that additional information be disclosed to the data subject. The requirement of fairness is evidently meant to be open-ended, to avoid sharp practices which the framers of the legislation have not anticipated. The Irish legislation is explicit that fairness may require the data controller to say whether the request for personal data is obligatory, and to inform the data subject of the possible consequences of failure to

---

74   Data Protection Act 1998 (UK), Sched 1 Pt II para 2; Data Protection Act 1988 (IE), s 2D, as inserted by Data Protection (Amendment) Act 2003 (IE), s 4.

75   Data Protection Act 1998 (UK), Sched 1 Pt I para 1, and Scheds 2 and 3; Data Protection Act 1988 (IE), s 2A and 2B, as inserted by Data Protection (Amendment) Act 2003s 4. See Ambrose, M and Jeffrey, I, 'Children and the net', [2001] EBL (Nov) 4.

76   Data Protection Act 1998 (UK), Sched 1 Pt I para 3; Data Protection Act 1988 (IE), s 2(1)(c)(iii), as amended by Data Protection (Amendment) Act 2003 (IE), s 3.

give the data as requested. The UK legislation is explicit that fairness must have regard to the method by which the data is obtained, including in particular whether any person from whom it is obtained is deceived or misled as to the purpose or purposes for which it is to be processed.[77]

In summary, the data subject must give his or her informed consent to the processing at the time the data is given to the data controller. There are only very limited exceptions, as where notification of purpose involves disproportionate effort, or where the collection of the data is required by law. It is not at all clear how much attention must be drawn to the purpose before the data subject's willingness to proceed constitutes consent, though as a rule of thumb the more important, non-obvious or potentially objectionable the purpose is, the more would have to be done to satisfy the legislator's requirements. Where the data is given at a web site, certain aspects of page design will be crucial: how prominently the privacy policy is signposted, how clear it is, and how the data subject's consent to it is signified. Proper records may have to be taken if it will be necessary to establish consent at some later time.

There is an awkward gap in the legislation, on the relation between its requirements as to data privacy, and any contract the parties may have made on that matter. In principle, the parties can contract out of the Acts. A written contract could constitute adequate notice of the statutory particulars, and processing data in order to satisfy a contract between the data subject and the data controller satisfies the conditions for processing. But, in practice, a contract which made major inroads into data rights will be of doubtful validity under consumer protection legislation. If contracts have a role here, it is to trim or channel the rights, not to make major modifications to them.[78]

Obtaining data from the data subject without asking for it

A certain amount of data is necessarily transferred during communication using ICT, and much of it may be recorded. Mobile telephony necessarily includes transfer of traffic data, including data from which the location of the phone (and therefore its user) may be ascertained. Communication over the Internet will similarly involve some information about the sender of any message. And all of these records will include the time at which the message was sent. Traffic data has its own special legal regime, which prohibits many abuses.[79] The data protection regime applies also: to the extent that the data is personal data (that is, where the person to whom it relates is identifiable), the Data Protection Acts must be respected.[80] Little commercial use has so far been made of mobile phone data beyond the obvious uses of billing the owner; current legislation prohibits its use, except with the consent of the data subject as part of a value-added service.[81] In principle it could be used for proximity advertising (such as texting a special offer to those passing the shop where the offer

---

77   Data Protection Act 1998 (UK), Sched 1 Pt II paras 1 and 2; Data Protection Act 1988 (IE), ss 2(1)(a) and 2D(2)(d), as inserted by Data Protection (Amendment) Act 2003 (IE), ss 3 and 4.
78   Sanders, J, 'Personal data as currency', (2002) 2 PDP (4) 7.
79   Above, p 83.
80   Rowe, H and McGilligan, R, 'Location technology and data protection', (2001) 17 CLSR 333.
81   Privacy and Electronic Communications (EC Directive) Regulations 2003 (UK), SI 2003/2426, reg 14 and the European Communities (Electronic Communications Networks and Services) (Data Protection and Privacy) Regulations 2003 (IE), SI 2003/535, reg 9; above, p 83.

is being conducted), and for tracking the location of a mobile phone; questions of consent should be raised with clients.[82]

How do owners of web sites keep track of those who visit the site? In principle, the log file produced by any web server could be used to identify those who have visited and to analyse what they were interested in, but in practice particular individuals are hard to identify from such data; keeping track of visitors is done by means of cookies, which are small files sent from the web server to the web browser. To consider the extent to which cookies fall within the legislation, we must distinguish between 'session cookies', which are meant to persist for only a short while, and 'persistent cookies'. The former are simply meant to identify the visitor during a single visit to a site: having looked at one page of a site and perhaps given personal details, the session cookie ensures that the visitor is still recognised as he or she moves to other pages. Persistent cookies are used to recognise the visitor when they return at a later date. Cookies are sometimes used for authentication purposes, and sometimes to gather data about shopping habits. Is all of this compatible with the legislation? The identity of the data controller, the fact that cookies are being used, and the purpose of so doing, would have to be displayed on the web site; if the condition for processing is 'consent', the display would have to be quite prominent. The purpose matters a good deal (the more non-obvious or potentially objectionable the purpose, the more would be needed to bring the data subject's attention to it).

Some sites make their use of persistent cookies more obvious than do others. Regular users of amazon.com cannot fail to notice that the site greets them by name, recommends books based on previous purchases, or even offers to buy back old purchases second-hand. Consent through repeated use in those circumstances would be hard to deny, though this would not justify the use of the personal data for non-obvious purposes. It is sometimes argued that consent to cookies can be presumed, inasmuch as web browsers can be configured to refuse cookies; but the argument is a weak one, as it presupposes an unrealistic degree of computing sophistication in most visitors. The UK legislation disapplies the duty to inform the data subject where this would involve 'disproportionate effort', though the data controller's reasons for believing that disproportionate effort is involved must be recorded.[83]

The use of spyware, or other clandestine gathering of personal data is plainly a breach of the legislation: by definition, there is no information as to the identity of the data controller or the purpose of the data collection.

If cookies or spyware are used by foreign data controllers, there is obviously a jurisdictional problem. It has been argued, plausibly enough, that these mechanisms cause data to be processed on the target's own machine, and therefore there is processing on a computer within the jurisdiction, and the legislation applies with full force.[84] If that is so, in principle the foreign data controller would have to nominate a representative within the jurisdiction, and to give its name as part of the notification to data subjects. This seems in practice unenforceable, however.

---

82   For vendors of relevant products see, eg, FleetOnline (Web); 'Microsoft to open up mobile phone location data', ZDNet UK, 29 June 2004 (Web).

83   Data Protection (Conditions under paragraph 3 of part II of schedule 1) Order 2000 (UK), SI 2000/185, reg 5.

84   *Working document on determining the international application of EU data protection law to personal data processing on the Internet by non-EU based web sites*, Article 29 Data Protection Working Party, 30 May 2002 (Web), on which see Scherzer, D, 'EU regulation of processing of personal data by wholly non-Europe-based web sites', [2003] EIPR 292.

Obtaining data from elsewhere

Personal data may arrive from a number of sources other than from data subjects themselves. One firm may sell customer data to another, or perhaps swap customer lists. Many e-commerce sites encourage consumers to recommend friends who might appreciate their services, and no doubt a few do. A difficult case, for which there is currently no satisfactory provision, is the purchase of a gift: on the letter of the law, when flowers or other goods are purchased for delivery to a named recipient, the supplier ought to contact the recipient to say 'A gift is on the way, please try to look surprised when it arrives'. Given the low level of enforcement of data protection law, however, this problem remains theoretical rather than actual.

The legal duty is to notify the person whose data is transferred at the time of transfer or as soon as is practical thereafter. The notification must include the identity of the data controller, and the purpose or purposes for which the data is collected; also any other information necessary to make the new data controller's possession of the data fair. Again, the UK legislation disapplies the duty to inform the data subject where this would involve 'disproportionate effort', though the data controller's reasons for believing that this is so must be recorded.[85] Assuming that the transferor of the data complied with the legislation, very little more may be needed from the transferee: the data subjects will already have had the purpose of the data collection made known to them, and all that is needed is that they be provided with a means of identifying the new data controller.

Duties while holding data

The data controller must take reasonable steps to keep the data secure: to guard against unauthorised taking, alteration or other processing, and against accidental loss or destruction of the data. The degree of care depends on the nature of the data and the harm done if security is violated. The content of this duty will change with time: different measures will become appropriate as the technology develops, as old threats diminish or can be routinely dealt with and as new threats emerge. Reasonable steps must be taken to ensure that all employees and others involved are aware of the law and comply with it. The legislation demands particular care when the processing is sub-contracted to another: the work must be done under a written contract under which the sub-contractor takes orders from no one but the primary data controller; and there must be satisfactory organisational and technical guarantees of security in place.[86]

The legislation states that the data shall be accurate; but this is then considerably qualified. The duty is only to make an accurate record of the data as it is received, and to include an indication of its source. As to its correspondence to

---

85   Data Protection (Conditions under paragraph 3 of part II of schedule 1) Order 2000 (UK), SI 2000/185, reg 5.

86   Data Protection Act 1998 (UK), Sched 1 Pt I para 7 and Pt II paras 7–12; Data Protection Act 1988 (IE), ss 2(1)(d), 2C and 21, as amended by Data Protection (Amendment) Act 2003 (IE), ss 2 and 3.

objective reality, no remedy will be available for the inaccuracy if the data controller has taken reasonable care, in the light of the purposes of the processing, to ensure accuracy. If the data subject complains that the data is inaccurate, the data controller must make sure that the data indicates that fact.[87]

The duty is not static. The duty of accuracy may require checking and updating of data. Data must be no more and no less than is required by the purpose; so any change affecting the data controller's purpose may affect the amount of data that may be retained. Fulfilment of the purpose, or its abandonment, may mean that there is no longer a justification for retaining the data, and so it must be erased. A complete data protection strategy for the controller must take into account all the ways in which personal data is recorded, including its presence on old machines which are to be thrown away; it will not usually be considered enough merely to delete the data, if it is then still recoverable.[88]

Anyone who suspects that another holds personal data relating to them may demand confirmation whether that is so; the demand must be answered within 21 days (Ireland) or 40 days (UK), stating whether such data is held and, if so, describing it and the purpose for which it is held.[89] Any data subject may demand a copy of the actual data held on them, in intelligible form; the data controller must comply within 40 days, and must include a detailed description of the data, as well as any information held on the source of the data. The data controller may, however, charge a fee for this, within statutory limits.[90] There are certain cases where the data controller need not hand over the data demanded: where the data controller is not reasonably satisfied that the person demanding the data is in fact the data subject, or where revealing the data would compromise the rights of others, such as those who handed over data in confidence.[91] Any data subject is entitled to complain if the data is held in breach of the legislation, and to demand correction, erasure or 'blocking' (that is, marking it so as to prevent it from being processed). The data controller has 40 days in which to comply but, as noted above, a complaint that the data is inaccurate can be met simply by marking the data to that effect.[92] Failure to comply with a legitimate demand can be brought to the attention of the Commissioner, who may then issue an enforcement notice, or may prosecute, unless a defence of due diligence can be raised. Civil remedies may also be available to the data subject, as described above.[93]

---

87 Data Protection Act 1998 (UK), Sched 1 Pt I para 4 and Pt II para 7; Data Protection Act 1988 (IE), ss 2(1)(b) and 7, as amended by Data Protection (Amendment) Act 2003 (IE), s 3.

88 Data Protection Act 1998 (UK), Sched 1 Pt I paras 3–5; Data Protection Act 1988 (IE), s 2(1)(c)(iii)–(iv), as amended by Data Protection (Amendment) Act 2003 (IE), s 3. See Warner, J, 'Data culling', [2002] SLT (37) 303; Middleton, R, 'Data retention policies – Data protection considerations', (2003) 19 CLSR 216.

89 Data Protection Act 1998 (UK), s 7(1); Data Protection Act 1988 (IE), s 3, as amended by Data Protection (Amendment) Act 2003 (IE), s 2.

90 Data Protection Act 1998 (UK), ss 7 and 8, and on fees see SI 2000/191 and SI 2001/3223; Data Protection Act (IE) 1988 s 4, as amended by Data Protection (Amendment) Act 2003 (IE), s 5.

91 Data Protection Act 1998 (UK), s 7(4)–(7); Data Protection Act 1988 (IE), s 4, as amended by Data Protection (Amendment) Act 2003 (IE), s 5.

92 Data Protection Act 1998 (UK), s 14 (which gives the court power to order the correction of inaccurate data); Data Protection Act 1988 (IE), s 6, as amended by Data Protection (Amendment) Act 2003 (IE), s 7.

93 Above, p 90. For possible reforms to subject access rights, see *Response to the Consultation Paper 'Data Protection Act 1998: Subject Access'*, Department for Constitutional Affairs, July 2003 (Web).

Particularly objectionable types of processing

In three areas, data subjects are given a right to object to particularly annoying or worrying types of personal data processing.

(a) Data subjects have a right to object to the use of personal data for the purposes of direct marketing. A data subject may object to the data controller, who must cease using the data for that purpose within a reasonable period (UK) or 40 days (Ireland). The Irish provision goes further, both in explicitly requiring erasure of the data except where it is held for other purposes, and also in requiring data controllers who intend to use data for direct marketing to inform the data subjects concerned to give them a chance to object. Oddly, the Irish legislation exempts political advertising from all these controls.[94] As to marketing by e-mail, these provisions are effectively superseded by the spam regulations, replacing the data protection legislation's 'opt-out' provisions with a new 'opt-in' regime.[95]

(b) The use of personal data as the sole criterion for the purposes of automated decision-taking is prohibited, where the decision significantly affects the data subject and which is meant to evaluate certain personal matters such as, for example, his or her performance at work, creditworthiness, reliability or conduct. The Irish legislation states this as an outright ban, though there is an exception where the data subject consents (an opt-in regime); the UK legislation, by contrast, requires the data controller to give notice to the data subject, who then has a right to object to such decisions, exercisable either before they are taken or within 21 days of their being taken (an opt-out regime). Where the decision is a contractual one (a decision whether to enter into a contract with the data subject, or with a view to entering into such a contract, or in the course of performing such a contract), then effectively there must be a right of appeal to a human being: either the automated decision must be as the data subject has requested, or 'adequate steps [must be] taken to safeguard the legitimate interests of the data subject by, for example (but without prejudice to the generality of the foregoing), the making of arrangements to enable him or her to make representations to the data controller in relation to the proposal'.[96] There is also a more limited right in these cases, to be told the logic on which such an automated decision is made, unless this would reveal the data controller's trade secrets.[97]

(c) More generally, data processing which causes substantial and unwarranted damage or distress can be objected to by anyone (whether or not they are the ones suffering the damage or distress). The data subject may serve a written notice on the data controller complaining of the processing; the data controller has 21 days in which to comply or to state grounds for failing to comply; proceedings may then be

---

94   Data Protection Act 1998 (UK), s 11; Data Protection Act 1988 (IE), ss 1(1) (definition of 'direct marketing') and 2(7) and (8), as amended by Data Protection (Amendment) Act 2003 (IE), ss 2 and 3. See especially *R (Robertson) v Wakefield Metropolitan District Council* [2001] EWHC 915 Admin, [2002] QB 1052 (Web).

95   Above, p 41.

96   Data Protection Act 1998 (UK), s 12; Data Protection Act 1988 (IE), s 6B, as inserted by Data Protection (Amendment) Act 2003 (IE), s 8. See Bygrave, L, 'Minding the machine: Article 15 of the EC data protection directive and automated profiling', (2001) 17 CLSR 17.

97   Data Protection Act 1998 (UK), ss 7(1)(d) and 8(5); Data Protection Act 1988 (IE), s 4(1)(a)(iv) and (12), as inserted by Data Protection (Amendment) Act 2003 (IE), s 5.

taken by the Commissioner or (in the UK version) before a court.[98] There are various exceptions:

- where the data subject has given explicit consent;
- where the processing is necessary for the performance of a contract to which the data subject is a party, in order to take steps at the request of the data subject prior to his or her entering into a contract, for compliance with any legal obligation to which the data controller or data subject is subject (other than one imposed by contract);
- to protect the vital interests of the data subject.

Pitilessly, the Irish legislation also exempts processing in the course of political activities carried out by political parties, or holders of or candidates for elective office.

Allowing for developments in the technology, the legislation gives some flexibility here: regulations may be made to reduce the scope of the 'damage or distress' provisions by exempting stated types of processing; but there is also provision to toughen them, by allowing regulations to identify stated damaging or distressing types of processing and to deal with them at the registration stage, allowing the Commissioner to refuse registration to that would-be data processor until satisfactory safeguards are in place.[99]

Transferring data to others within the jurisdiction

The recipients of personal data must be indicated as part of the data controller's registration, and one of the conditions for processing (consent, or whatever) must be satisfied in respect of the transfer of data to another. If a customer database might be treated as a saleable business asset, then this point must be addressed when personal data is gathered to constitute it.[100]

Placing personal data on a web site is an extreme example of transferring it to others, in that the data is available to anyone who accesses the site, unless password or other arrangements are in place to narrow access. Consent to this, or some other way of establishing a condition for processing, must be present. The consequences of this can be a little startling to those unfamiliar with the legislation, especially as the exception for personal or domestic computing has been held not to apply to data disseminated this way. In *Lindqvist*, the defendant created a page on her personal web site to help those preparing to take their first communion at her local church. This included some personal details of people they could turn to for help. This was held to be an infringement of the data protection legislation on several counts of wrongly disclosing personal data, including sensitive personal data (she had incidentally revealed that one of the people had been ill). The European Court of Justice held that she was quite properly fined € 450 for this.[101] Fines would also no doubt be payable in the various cases where online retailers and banks have

---

98 Data Protection Act 1998 (UK), s 10; Data Protection Act 1988 (IE), s 6A, as inserted by Data Protection (Amendment) Act 2003 (IE), s 8.
99 Data Protection Act 1998 (UK), s 22; Data Protection Act 1988 (IE), s 12A, as inserted by Data Protection (Amendment) Act 2003 (IE), s 13.
100 Miller, N, 'Sellers beware!', (2002) 146 Sol Jo 384.
101 *Lindqvist* (2003, ECJ, Case C-101/01) (Web).

accidentally revealed customer data to the wrong person on their web sites, unless a 'due diligence' defence could be made out.[102]

Exporting data outside the EU and EEA

In general, personal data may not be transferred outside the EU or EEA; this is on the ground that jurisdictions which do not apply the Data Protection Directive cannot be relied upon to provide adequate protection for the rights of data subjects. There are two general exceptions to this. First, the European Commission may certify that particular jurisdictions meet the required standards, so that data transfers are not objectionable merely because they go to those jurisdictions. At the time of writing, the following jurisdictions have been certified as supplying adequate protection to personal data: Argentina, Canada, Guernsey, Isle of Man, Switzerland. Secondly, the Commission can provide standard contract clauses, such that a recipient in a named jurisdiction gives adequate protection to data by agreeing to those clauses.[103]

Outside those cases, it is to be taken that a transfer out of the jurisdiction usually infringes the rights of the data subject concerned. For particular jurisdictions, the European Commission can determine that transfers are safe if the transferee will sign up to certain standard terms; such a 'safe harbour' arrangement is in force in respect of the US.[104] Standard contract clauses for transferring personal data to other nations have been drafted by the EU.[105] There are also some particular situations where transfers are nonetheless regarded as justifiable, even though the jurisdiction concerned is not a safe one. These are:[106]

(a) that the transfer is required or authorised by any enactment or international convention;

(b) that the data subject has consented;

(c) that the transfer is necessary for the performance of a contract between the data subject and the data controller, or for the taking of steps at the request of the data subject with a view to entering into a contract with the data controller;

(d) that the transfer is necessary for the conclusion of a contract between the data controller and a person other than the data subject that is entered into at the request of the data subject, and is in the interests of the data subject, or for the performance of such a contract;

---

102 Eg, 'UK Web shoppers' details exposed', ZDNet UK,13 August 2002 (Web).

103 Data Protection Act 1998 (UK), Sched 1 Pt II paras 13–15; Data Protection Act 1988 (IE), s 11(1)–(3) as amended by Data Protection (Amendment) Act 2003 (IE), s 12. See Commission Decisions on the adequacy of the protection of personal data in third countries (Web).

104 Data Protection Act 1998 (UK), Sched 1 Pt II para 15, and Sched 4 paras 8 and 9; Data Protection Act 1988 (IE), s 11(4)(a)(ix) and 11(6), as amended by Data Protection (Amendment) Act 2003 (IE), s 12. See *Commission Staff Working Document*, SEC (2004) 1323 (Web); Zinser, A, 'International data transfers between the US and the EU', (2004) 20 CLSR 182; DiLascio, T, 'How safe is the safe harbor?', (2004) 22 BUILJ 399.

105 Commission Decision of 27 December 2001 on standard contractual clauses for the transfer of personal data to processors established in third countries (2002/16/EC) (Web); *Working Document Establishing a Model Checklist Application for Approval of Binding Corporate Rules*, Article 29 Working Party, WP108 (Web). See Rowe, H, 'Transfers of personal data to third countries: The role of binding corporate rules', (2003) 19 CLSR 490.

106 Data Protection Act 1998 (UK), Sched 4; Data Protection Act 1988 (IE), s 11(4), as amended by Data Protection (Amendment) Act 2003 (IE), s 12. See generally Pullan, T, 'Data protection and offshore outsourcing', (2005) 16 C&L (1) 32.

(e) that the transfer is necessary for reasons of substantial public interest;

(f) that the transfer is necessary for the purposes of obtaining legal advice or in connection with legal proceedings;

(g) that the transfer is necessary to protect the data subject's vital interests and informing the data subject of, or seeking his or her consent to, the transfer is likely to damage those vital interests.

THE DATA PROTECTION REGIME: ASSESSMENT

Any attempt to assess the law of data protection immediately runs into a problem: it is quite unclear what that law covers or should cover. It is exceedingly technical and, in crucial respects, unclear. The motivation for the legislation and its constant development is fear: fear that personal data in the wrong hands will be abused. But who will be doing the abusing, and what it will consist of, is vague at best. Attitudes to the legislation depend entirely on how seriously that threat is taken. If its target is unclear, many will respond that this only emphasises the need for very general legislation, which can quickly be deployed against new threats as they become concrete. Many others will retort that the dangers at which it is aimed may well turn out to be illusory; whereas its costs, and the brake it places on innovation, are very real. Let us wait until real dangers emerge, runs the argument; costly bureaucratic restrictions with no clear aim are precisely the sort of legislation that free societies should avoid.

To the extent that the legislation has a clear point, it seems to be aiming at a number of targets simultaneously. Some of them are in the general area of privacy: inhibiting the collection and use of personal details. This aspect is increasing in scope as ever more personal data is collected in machine-readable form. Others are more in the area of defamation: if personal details are to be collected and used in commerce then they should be accurate; if people are to be refused credit because of past lapses, then it is vital that the refusal is based on accurate information. Yet other targets of the legislation are more in the area of discrimination. There can be no real secret about your age, sex or racial origins, but it may be legitimate to insist that no account is taken of them in certain situations. These and other purposes are effected through data protection law; proposals for reform must take account of its diverse character.

It is also quite unclear to what extent people *want* their privacy protected. The norm throughout the late 20th century was for commerce and consumer transactions to be largely anonymous, through the decline of the inefficient, friendly local shop in favour of the faceless megastore. Shoppers who changed from one brand to another would not expect their supermarket to notice, or to solicit their reasons; a new parent who received, out of the blue, offers of discounts on nappies and baby food would probably experience surprise at being noticed before they felt anything else. That old privacy has gone. The great unanswered question is: when transparency of consumer transactions becomes routine, will the public like this or loathe it? When the shock of the new has passed, will the attentions of data-driven commercial firms be welcomed or shunned? It is not obvious that *all* consumers will hate receiving targeted offers carefully designed to appeal to them in particular. It is more likely that some such offers will be deemed more objectionable than others, so the law will have to distinguish between offers; it is also more likely that some consumers will object more than others, and so the law will have to distinguish between consumers. If people truly have a right to privacy, then it must include an entitlement to give it up for something they value more; and if business is prepared to offer them this, then it will rarely be the law's function to stand in the way of an exchange that both sides deem profitable.

The current legislation in its own terms

The data protection legislation provides a highly elaborate code, the scope of which has been progressively extended, even though it is (as one eminent lawyer has remarked) 'almost incomprehensible'.[107] Many rights are stated in strong terms, but they are usually then subject to broad exceptions. Indeed, it is often asserted that there are too many escape clauses for the general principles to be taken seriously.[108] Enforcement is extremely weak. Of the tens of thousands of cases referred to the UK Commissioner per year, over half receive advice on the application of the law. What use is made of this advice is not recorded; the latest annual report records the successful prosecution of seven individuals and one company. In other words, data controllers who are willing to comply with the law of their own motion receive advice on the finer points; and it appears that over 90% of data controllers contacted in this connection already show an understanding of the rights of data subjects. However, any real element of compulsion is lacking, unless the individual data subject cares enough about it to commence a civil action.[109]

There is also a significant problem in keeping the legislation up to date. The current legislation is based on a Directive of 1995, which was implemented across the EU, the UK doing so in 1998 and Ireland (one of the last) in 2003. The governing legislation is therefore, if not pre-Internet, certainly pre-web, and (as was described above) is not easy to apply to a world of interconnected computers. This is not to deny the merit of some of the EU bodies involved; for commentary on topical data protection issues, the EU's Article 29 Working Party is usually an excellent source.[110] But the amount of time it takes to amend EU legislation does not encourage its use in this area. And the lack of fit between what the law requires of web sites, and what they actually do, is obvious.

The data protection legislation is rapidly becoming a byword for unnecessary complexity; you do not have to search far for anecdotes of bizarre data protection practices supposedly based on the legislation. It is true that most of these anecdotes do not stand up to investigation. Many are urban myths, and most of the rest suggest merely that some compliance officers are not very good at advising on the detailed application of the legislation. And it is certainly true that much of the criticism of the legislation is badly informed. But with Acts this complex, it is difficult to be anything other than badly informed.[111] The message that personal data is subject to control has gone out loud and clear; but as to the nature of that control, and the 'safe harbours'

---

107 'Government FOI Act chief trails Data Act "reform" ', Register, 18 October 2004 (Web).
108 Eg, Oxman, S, 'Exemptions to the EU personal data privacy directive: Will they swallow the directive?', (2000) 24 BCICLR 191 (Web).
109 For annual reports, see *Information Commissioner Annual Report for 2004* (Web) and *Data Protection Commissioner Annual Report for 2004* (Web).
110 Article 29 Data Protection Working Party (Web).
111 'Data protection in the spotlight again', [2004] EBL (April) 16.

to achieve compliance, the message is getting lost. Current proposals for gentle relaxation of the legislation do not seem to go far enough.[112]

Other approaches

The EU model is similar to that adopted in several other jurisdictions, such as Canada. But more minimalist regimes will also be found. The Latin American 'habeas data' model is perhaps the narrowest: this consists solely of a personal right of action to force a data controller to reveal what data it holds on the data subject, and (if it is inaccurate) to correct it. This addresses two key concerns of the European model of legislation – it provides a remedy for *inaccurate* personal data, and (inasmuch as knowing what data a company holds enables you to guess what it wants to do with it) it gives publicity to the way in which data is being used. But it does nothing to address privacy concerns as such.[113]

The US legal system, suspicious as ever of grand regulatory schemes, has gone for a different sort of minimalism. The most general legislation, the Electronic Communications Privacy Act 1986, concentrates on interception and wrongful storage of data, and so misses many contemporary concerns.[114] By and large, calls for a data protection law have been neglected, but individual scandals have led to schemes aimed at particular problems or particular market sectors.[115] In particular there is:

(a) The Video Recordings Act 1988, which protects individuals from revelations about which videos they have hired.[116]

(b) The Children's On-line Privacy Protection Act 1998, which restricts the collection of personal data from children under 13.[117]

(c) The Gramm-Leach-Bliley Financial Modernization Act 1999, regulating customer privacy in interstate financial transactions.[118]

This neatly indicates the regulatory dilemma. Uncertainty as to the precise nature of the problem, and a suspicion that over-enthusiastic regulation will kill useful innovation along with the more malign sort, ensures that the US legislature intervenes only where a particular scandal forces it to do so. The result is a crazy patchwork of inconsistent controls. Whereas attempts to exercise more uniform control often means that the European system attacks non-problems (such as

---

112 See *Proposals for Amendment made by Austria, Finland, Sweden and the United Kingdom (Explanatory Note)*, September 2002 (Web).

113 Guadamuz, A, 'Habeas Data: The Latin-American response to data protection', [2000] 2 JILT (Web); Guadamuz, A, 'Habeas Data vs the European Data Protection Directive', [2001] 3 JILT (Web).

114 Cooper, H, 'The Electronic Communications Privacy Act: Does the answer to the Internet information privacy problem lie in a 15-year-old Federal statute?', (2001) 20 JMJCIL 1.

115 See Cain, R, 'Global privacy concerns and regulation – Is the US a world apart?', (2002) 16 IRLCT 23; Bohlman, E, 'Privacy in the Age of Information', [2002] 2 JILT (Web); Solove, D, 'The origins and growth of information privacy law', SSRN, October 2003 (Web).

116 US Code Title 18 s 2710.

117 US Code Title 15 s 6501. See Dixon, T, 'Children's Online Privacy Protection Act: America's privacy patchwork grows', [1999] PLPR 52 (Web); Hertzel, D, 'Don't talk to strangers: An analysis of government and industry efforts to protect a child's privacy online', (2000) 52 FCLJ 429 (Web).

118 US Code Title 15 ss 6801–6810.

restricting the use of personal data even where no harm seems likely), or the system is made to tackle problems to which it is plainly unsuited (such as control of spam). There cannot be any very tidy solution until we have a clearer understanding of the problems, and legislate for them. The main point in favour of the US system is that it places few unnecessary restrictions on innovation (but that is because it has few restrictions at all); the main point in favour of the EU system is that it forces data controllers to admit what they are doing (though at what cost to speed of innovation is unclear).

The differences between national regimes are significant not simply because they provide a basis for comparison, but also because of the economic pressure those differences bring to bear. Certainly, nations which expect to obtain significant work through outsourcing from European businesses are under immense pressure to achieve EU recognition as having adequate data protection regimes, though this is not the only pressure on them.[119] What effect the EU and the US are having on one another, and whether the effect will be a 'ratcheting up' of transnational privacy standards or a 'race to the bottom', is a matter of considerable debate.[120]

What should we be aiming for?

In this early stage of the game, the law needs to deal with obvious abuses, but otherwise needs to admit its ignorance of current practice and of future development. Where there seems to be a real possibility of abuse, the initial reaction should not be to prohibit, but to learn more. The 'habeas data' approach should therefore be fundamental: individuals should have the right to know what information is held on them and to correct it if it is wrong; it is clear that incentives on business parties to check the accuracy of data are low, and that considerable harm can be done to individuals by inaccurate data. The next priority is to clarify what is being done with personal data. It is an open question how real are the dangers posed by unrestrained processing of personal data; knowledge of what is actually being done is vital, both in individual cases and as part of a broader picture.

In time, this knowledge will allow the establishment of regulation for particular market sectors. With a clearer understanding of the problems and the appropriate incentives, no doubt regulation on a sectoral basis will be easier than it is now, and some of the weaknesses of the current regime can be avoided. Industry and consumer involvement should make it less oppositional, not being imposed on an unwilling industry by a remote Commissioner, but recognising values more broadly accepted. And where it is necessary to give consumers rights, they should be rights that can in practice be exercised, not mere theoretical entitlements to litigate.

Present trends indicate that consumer privacy is a valuable asset. It has value not simply because consumers themselves value it, but because commercial entities do so too: greater knowledge of their consumers enables them to produce more tempting products, and therefore to benefit both consumers and themselves. In

---

119 See, eg, Carey, P, 'E-commerce: Does the Data Protection Act 1998 apply to offshore e-business?', (2000) 11 C&L (3) 23.

120 Eg, Shaffer, G, 'Globalization and social protection: The impact of EU and international rules in the ratcheting up of US privacy standards', (2000) 25 YJIL 1; Clear, M, 'Falling into the gap: The EU's Data Protection Act and its impact on US law and commerce', (2000) 18 JMJCIL 981; Vitale, A, 'The EU Privacy Directive and the resulting safe harbor' (2002) 35 Vand JTL 321.

circumstances where there is no reason to do otherwise, this development should surely be encouraged. Some consumers will prefer privacy, others value more the goods and services which surrendering their privacy brings. That choice must be built into the law and given force. This choice also throws into relief the cases where free choice should not be the governing criterion. When does legitimate informed commercial decision-taking end and unlawful discrimination begin? These cases will be the truly difficult ones.

FURTHER READING

Bainbridge, D and Pearce, G, 'Tilting at windmills – Has the new data protection law failed to make a significant contribution to rights of privacy?', [2000] 2 JILT (Web).

Burk, D, 'Privacy and property in the global datasphere', MLSRP 05–17 (Web).

Hahn, R and Layne-Farrar, A, 'The benefits and costs of online privacy legislation', (2002) 54 ABA ALR 85.

Hann, I, Hui, K, Lee, S and Png, I, 'The value of online information privacy: An empirical investigation', SSRN, 2003 (Web).

Hetcher, S, 'Norm proselytizers create a privacy entitlement in cyberspace', (2001) 16 BTLJ 877 (Web).

Karas, S, 'Privacy, identity, databases', (2002) 52 AULR 393 (Web).

Lugaresi, N, 'Principles and regulations about online privacy: "Implementation Divide" and misunderstandings in the EU', SSRN, 2002 (Web).

Moshell, R, '… And then there was one: The outlook for a self-regulatory United States amidst a global trend toward comprehensive data protection', (2005) 37 TTLR 357.

Safier, S, 'Between Big Brother and the bottom line: Privacy in cyberspace', (2000) 5 VJOLT (Web).

Schwartz, P, 'Property, privacy and personal data', (2004) 117 Harv LR 2055.

Solove, D and Hoofnagle, C, 'A model regime of privacy protection', SSRN, 2005 (Web).

Walker, K, 'Where everybody knows your name: A pragmatic look at the costs of privacy and the benefits of information exchange', [2000] 2 STLR (Web).

CHAPTER 5

RIGHTS OVER DATA: SECURITY AND BIG BROTHER

The previous two chapters covered rights to own data, and the rights of individuals to demand data relevant to them or to their interests. Some contrasting themes are now examined. First, there is a brief discussion of encryption law and practice, showing how data owners may identify data as theirs but also hide it from those they do not wish to see it.

The chapter then considers the special position of governmental data and governmental rights. The general principles discussed in earlier chapters can of course apply to government. The government owns much intellectual property, and must respect the intellectual property rights of others. As a party to litigation, the government has the same rights to discovery as private litigants; government can also be the target of actions brought to protect individual rights, whether privacy rights or rights to data protection. Nonetheless, the government is not simply a private individual writ large. This chapter considers the government right to seize data to assist with law enforcement and other core governmental functions. This includes not simply such data as individuals happen to hold, but also the widening category of data which individuals are required to keep precisely so that law enforcement bodies can inspect it. It concludes with sections on the sharing of data within government, and the freedom of information legislation, which gives individuals rights to view government documents.

This is a boom time for government acquisition of data about its citizens, and for the sharing of that information between otherwise unrelated government departments. Concern about terrorism has provided a ready justification for this, even though it is a justification which is sadly lacking in many respects; it is pure speculation whether a single terrorist incident to date could have been prevented by increasing governmental surveillance on individuals, nor does it take much knowledge of ICT to be able to evade current surveillance techniques. While full considerations of these questions would take us into controversial territory, it is undeniable that combating terrorism is very far from the only goal of the new legislation.

SECURITY AND AUTHENTICATION

Most electronic commerce is not possible unless the parties to transactions have a reliable method for ascertaining one another's identity. It is also highly desirable that publicity be kept to a minimum. In practice, these two requirements are bound together, and the need for secure and authenticated communications is well recognised. This section discusses first the main technologies currently available to meet this need, and then the legal framework within which the technology is used.

It is common to refer to authentication methods for electronic documents as 'digital signatures'.[1] The point of the expression is obvious enough: just as a signature

---

1   For a review of authentication methods, see Ford, M, 'Identity authentication and E-Commerce', [1998] 3 JILT (Web).

on a written document is meant to authenticate it and designate its author, so a 'digital signature' fulfils the same functions for an electronic document. Nonetheless, it is a misleading expression. There is as yet no standard for converting a written signature into a 'digital signature'; the digital technology may perform similar functions to that of a signature, but it is a very different thing, as will become apparent. 'Digital signatures' perform additional functions, by no means analogous to ordinary signatures: in particular, they are designed as part of the process of encryption, to ensure not only that the recipient of an electronic communication can know its author, but also that no one but the intended recipient be able to access it.

In summary, 'digital signatures' rely on knowledge of or access to a key, and so are fundamentally different entities from ordinary signatures, which are really a species of biometric identification. Nonetheless, use of the phrase 'digital signature' appears to have become firmly established.

The technology

In theory, security and authenticity could be guaranteed with reasonable certainty by the use of a private key system of encryption. Two people who wish to communicate electronically could agree on a (numerical) private key, which would then be used to encrypt and decrypt messages between them. Messages intercepted by others would be unintelligible without the key. This is a very secure method, even if someone intercepting the method knows the algorithm or procedure used to encrypt the message; and security can be increased as necessary, by increasing the length of the key (and therefore increasing the computing power necessary to break the encryption). However, this 'private key' encryption is not a very practical method for e-commerce, because it can only work after the parties have already agreed on a private key – the communication of the key from one to the other must either be insecure, or must be rendered secure by some other means.

More practical, though resting on abstruse mathematical formulae, is the so-called 'public key' system. One party uses a mathematical procedure to generate two (numerical) keys. These keys are related via the encryption and decryption algorithm: a message which is encrypted using the first key can only be decrypted using the second, and vice versa. (The mathematical concepts which make this possible are beyond both the scope of this book and the comprehension of its author.) The first key is then made public by its owner, while the second is kept secret. The owner may then initiate communications by a message encrypted using the private key: this message can then be decrypted by anyone who knows the public key. But as only the possessor of the private key can produce such a message, there is a guarantee of authenticity. A reply to the message can be encrypted using the public key; as it can only be decrypted using the private key (which only its owner has) there is a guarantee of security. The reasonable needs of the parties for secure communications are thus met, even though nearly everything about the process is public knowledge; only the private key is kept confidential.[2]

Any encryption using either the 'private key' or 'public key' methods can be broken if sufficient computer power is brought to bear on the encrypted message. However, attempts to break encryption become progressively more demanding as

---

2   See, eg, 'What is public-key cryptography?', RSA Laboratories (Web).

longer keys are used. A very common system for online transactions is the Secure Sockets Layer (SSL) system, a public key system that enables secure communications over the Internet. Keys for this system can either be 40-bit or 128-bit. The shorter 40-bit keys are numbers between 0 and (roughly) 10^{12} (one million million), a significant number but by no means insoluble for a sufficiently determined attempt to break the encryption. The longer 128-bit keys are between 0 and (roughly) 3×10^{26} (three hundred million million million million), which in practice means that the encryption is unbreakable by existing computers, unless those trying to break the encryption have some clue which enables them to shorten the enquiry.[3]

Practical use of this technology in the market place involves various intermediaries. This notably includes those who make the technology available to their customers and provide administrative and support services as required. These 'cryptography service providers' are subject to a certain amount of regulation, as detailed below. Further aid for secure transactions can be provided by 'certification service providers', which can confirm the identity of their clients and their clients' public keys.[4] Regulation of these entities is so far minimal, but a legal framework is there, and legislation will probably grow.

Legislation worldwide

There has been a rush to make provision for encryption technologies in the legal systems of the world, driven by acute national anxieties about being left behind as the technology develops. Part of the anxiety is over misuse of the technology: this has been reflected in attempts to restrict the export of encryption software, and attempts to ensure that it is not used to conceal criminal activity from law enforcement authorities. Another anxiety is the wish to avoid artificial legal barriers to the use of encryption technology, particularly by ensuring that contracts effected through encrypted messages are as valid as those made by more traditional means. A third anxiety has been to provide support for emerging markets and institutions related to encryption – a difficult task, as the uncertainty in how the technology will develop makes it hard to say what market controls will help more than they hinder. Most of these issues are dealt with in this section, though issues relating to contract formation – and particularly the extent to which a 'digital signature' will be equated with a signature made with pen and paper – will be considered below.[5]

International co-operation and uniformity is particularly desirable in matters such as encryption, which affect how businesses communicate – surely one of the most basic of market fundamentals.[6] And some international standards have emerged, particularly the UNCITRAL *Model Law on Electronic Signatures* (2001).[7] But individual nations have been reluctant to wait for such standards to emerge, and indeed have regarded enactment of their own digital signature law as a totem for

---

3 Sites employing SSL have web addresses beginning 'https://'. Cf '64-bit encryption broken after four years', VNUNet, 30 September 2002 (Web).

4 For a brief introduction, see Lim, Y, 'Digital signature, certification authorities and the law', (2002) 9 E-Law (Web).

5 Below, p 253.

6 Lincoln, A, 'Electronic signature laws and the need for uniformity in the global market', (2004) 8 JSEBL 67.

7 For documents, see 'UNCITRAL – Electronic Commerce' (Web).

prowess in e-commerce.[8] Within the EU, several nations have not waited for the slow process leading to Europe-wide regulation but have pressed ahead with their own rules; the result is a plethora of national regimes that are now slowly being absorbed into a harmonised regime.

Export controls

The principal international treaty affecting cryptography is the Wassenaar Arrangement, which was agreed by 33 nations in July 1996, though not subsequently ratified. The UK and Ireland are both parties, as are most of the major industrial nations. The object of the Treaty is to control the availability of 'dual-use' goods (that is, goods with both military and civilian uses), in particular by prohibiting their export except under licence. The lengthy list of 'dual-use' technologies includes cryptographic software and equipment. Only the more powerful forms of encryption are covered. There are a number of exceptions: routine and inflexible software on sale to consumers; equipment used for pay television services or copy protection on audio or video data; certain types of cordless phones. The nations that are party to the Arrangement are required to maintain 'fully effective' export controls, and to exercise 'vigilance' in authorising export of the technologies concerned.[9]

Within the EU, uniformity and mutual recognition of Member States' export licences has been guaranteed by Regulation since June 2000.[10] The decision whether to grant a licence in any one case still rests with the nation state concerned. The aim of the Regulation is to promote uniformity of practice and exchange of information between governments; it specifies criteria and procedures for nations to decide on exports, but leaves the decision with them, though general policy is reviewed by the Council of Ministers.

The UK legislation, which on matters relevant here mirrors the Wassenaar Arrangement, is spread over a number of statutes, culminating in the Export Controls Act 2002. It has repeatedly been amended, both to keep track of new technologies and following a major scandal in the 1990s over export of munitions to Iraq, and with an eye to compliance with the EU Regulation mentioned above; it is long overdue for consolidation. It applies expressly to the transmission of software by electronic means.[11] Increasingly (and particularly in relation to cryptography) it defers to the Regulation, at least in defining dual-use technologies. Some exemptions are created by Open General Export Licence, which are executive orders authorising the export of general categories of goods.[12] All other items within the Regulations require individual licence. Any grant of a licence is subject to conditions, including guarantees as to the use of the item, and duties to keep records. Various offences are created by the Regulations, including making misleading applications for licences and failing to comply with licence conditions; penalties are a fine of up to £5,000 before magistrates, or an unlimited fine and up to two years' imprisonment before a jury.

---

8   For the US position, see Zemnick, S, 'The E-Sign Act', (2001) 76 CKLR 1965.
9   For documentation, see The Wassenaar Arrangement home page (Web).
10 Regulation 1504/2004/EC, on setting up a Community regime for the control of exports of dual-use items and technology.
11 Export of Goods, Transfer of Technology and Provision of Technical Assistance (Control) Order 2003 (UK), SI 2003/2764, reg 6.
12 DTI Export Control Organisation (Web).

Irish law is to very similar effect, though it is content to rely on the EU Regulation rather than making domestic provision.

Regulation of risks and intermediaries

The use of encryption involves a variety of risks, particularly in cases where the encryption is compromised. Theft of passwords or encryption keys, hacking and interception of messages, all have their dangers. As one of the main objects of encryption is to engender trust between commercial entities, we might expect the problems caused when that trust is shattered to be acute. However, regulation of the risks is largely being left to ordinary background legal rules; some tentative steps are being made towards quality control of cryptographic services, but fears of over-regulation are leading governments to agree to industry control rather than explicit regulation. There is as yet no internationally agreed set of rules; we might therefore expect that different jurisdictions will allocate risks differently, though there is now an element of uniformity within the EU.[13] What follows is a necessarily general and tentative sketch of the likely legal issues.

Allocation of risk between signature user and service provider

The signature user will have made a contract with their service provider, and that contract will presumably settle what is expected of both parties, and how the more obvious risks are to be allocated. In practice, the contract will be on the service provider's standard form, and is likely to restrict the service provider's liability to a considerable extent. Each case will need analysis of its individual facts, but the following general legal principles are likely to be relevant:

(a) Full information on contract terms will be required, either under consumer protection legislation or on the ground that the service provider is supplying an 'information society service'.[14] These regulations may also give a limited right to cancel the contract.

(b) The quality of the service provider's performance is almost certainly regulated by statutory implied terms, though we await clear rulings on whether the customer is to be regarded as purchasing 'goods' or 'services', which may affect the detail of the obligation.

(c) Exemption clauses are strongly controlled by statute, though the detail depends on the identity of the customer ('consumer' or no?), on whether the provider has been negligent, and on the type of loss the exemption clause covers (an exclusion for personal injury or property damage is harder to justify than an exclusion in respect of financial loss). In a consumer case, other restrictive terms may also come under the judicial spotlight.

In addition, a cryptography service provider will almost certainly hold personal data relating to its customer, and so the data protection regime applies; common law duties of confidence will also cover this ground.

---

13 See Directive 1999/93/EC on a Community framework for electronic signatures, on which see further Siems, M, 'The EU Directive on Electronic Signatures – A worldwide model or a fruitless attempt to regulate the future?', (2002) 16 IRLCT 7.

14 See below, p 133.

Allocation of risk between signature user and third party

No doubt, situations could arise where a company's signature is wrongly attached to a document, on which a third party then relies to their detriment. It is difficult to predict what form this might take. If the signature was stolen from the company and then used in a criminal manner, an action in negligence might be possible. If the signature was misused by an employee of the company, then principles of agency or vicarious liability would probably be in issue.

Allocation of risk between third party and service provider

As mentioned above, the practical operation of the public key system must in practice involve the participation of a certification service provider (CSP), who can confirm the public key of its client. Suppose then that a CSP certifies its client's public key as requested by the third party, who then suffers loss after relying on the certificate: perhaps the key given is inaccurate, or has been compromised. Is the CSP liable to the third party for loss resulting from reliance on the certificate?[15]

A preliminary question is the nature of the legal relations between CSP and relying party. As the CSP has expressly invited the third party to rely on its certificate – indeed, the certificate has no other purpose – a duty of care is likely to be established. It follows that the CSP is liable in cases where negligence by the CSP can be established, the third party's reliance on the certificate was reasonable, the third party's loss flowed from the CSP's negligence, and that loss was not too remote a consequence. Could a more extensive liability be established though the law of contract? This is a less obvious argument, though not an impossible one. It might be argued that the contract between the signature user and the CSP was a contract for the benefit of those such as the third party, thus allowing the third party to sue. Alternatively, it is arguable that the CSP's certificate is itself a contractual promise or offer of terms, which is accepted by reliance on it. Some CSPs go to great lengths in their standard terms to deny the existence of any such contract; but the invitation to rely is clear (indeed, it is inherent in the role of the CSP) and so a contract may be found despite this.

CSPs wishing to limit their liability on certificates will probably do so by explicitly limiting the scope of the certificates. In particular, they will alert those asking for certificates to sources of insecurity in electronic communications, place strict time limits on any certificate they issue, and insist that the third party should also consult certain specified stop lists and revocation lists. In accordance with general contract and tort principles, the courts are unlikely to regard such limitations as legally binding unless they were expressly brought to the attention of those contemplating reliance on the certificate, presumably by posting the limitations prominently so that they cannot fail to be noticed by reasonable users. The precise detail of this remains to be worked out by judicial decisions.

---

15 For discussion, see Hindelang, S, 'No remedy for disappointed trust – The liability regime for certification authorities towards third parties outwith the EC Directive in England and Germany compared', [2002] 1 JILT (Web); Balboni, P, 'Liability of certification service providers towards relying parties', (2004) 13 ICTL 211.

Accreditation

Legislative provision has been made for official accreditation of CSPs. However, it is the lightest of light-touch legislation. It is not even in force yet – and indeed the UK version has already expired[16] – the object is not so much to register providers as to pressure CSPs into establishing their own professional control.[17] Under this (inert) statutory regime, no provider is obliged to seek accreditation. However, a provider which does so may be certified by the state as accredited, and such a provider may then issue 'qualified' certificates, which will (presumably) be regarded as especially trustworthy. The obligations of accredited providers may be spelled out by regulation; no sanction for non-compliance is mentioned beyond the threat that accreditation will be withdrawn. Accredited providers are also subject to various liabilities in favour of third parties who rely on their certificates, unless negligence can be disproved. Legislative inaction here is a sign of official satisfaction with tScheme, which is precisely the sort of industry body which the legislation was designed to encourage.[18]

SEIZURE OF DATA

In a networked world, traditional powers of search and seizure must extend also to data in electronic form. But the matter is not simply one of traditional situations in new technological dress. The new possibilities for data accumulation and dissemination lead to unprecedented problems: hugely increased scope for tax evasion and other financial crimes, not to mention intellectual property and pornography offences. Networking by criminals requires a networked response, especially given the increasing modern focus of legislation (not entirely as a consequence of ICT) on criminal organisation and accounting, and seizure of criminal assets. This section is concerned with governmental powers to seize and collate data to further its objects.

Data can often be seized under ordinary powers of search and seizure, typically by taking control of relevant hardware or disks. PCs can readily be removed to police custody if that seems appropriate. It may sometimes be easier to act against intermediaries, such as ISPs, who hold copies of the relevant data. Such intermediaries may be reluctant to co-operate, not least because letting the police help themselves to a customer's data may put the ISP in breach of contract or breach of the data protection legislation; indeed, one English ISP found it necessary to refuse access to customer data until a court would formally rule that granting access to it was no breach of the Regulation of Investigatory Powers Act.[19] To assist the police, there are exceptions in the Data Protection Acts, to provide a safe harbour for those who help police authorities voluntarily;[20] nonetheless, some ISPs have insisted on search warrants.

16 'Sun sets on UK encryption regulation powers', Register, 26 May 2005 (Web).
17 See Electronic Communications Act 2000 (UK), ss 1–6 and Electronic Signatures Regulations 2002 (UK), SI 2002/318; Electronic Commerce Act 2000 (IE), ss 29 and 30.
18 See tScheme home page (Web); Mason, S, *Electronic Signatures in Law*, 2003, London: LexisNexis, Chapter 10; 'Digital certificate regime wins UK gov plaudits', Register, 22 April 2004 (Web).
19 *R (NTL Group Ltd) v Crown Court at Ipswich* [2002] EWHC 1585 Admin, [2003] QB 131.
20 Data Protection Act 1998 (UK), s 29(3); Data Protection Act 1988 (IE), s 8, as amended by Data Protection (Amendment) Act 2003 (IE), s 9.

If a prosecution is to be based on seized data, then some care is needed at the stage when the seizure is planned, and thereafter. Any argument that the seizure was illegal can affect its admissibility in evidence: whether it is admitted is at the discretion of the trial judge, and a seizure which was consciously in excess of powers requires strong facts to justify it. So where the Irish Gardai raided the home of Judge Curtin and removed his PC, which was said to hold child pornography, the prosecution failed because the warrant for seizure had expired slightly over two hours before the seizure took place;[21] whether that evidence can be used to remove him from his judgeship has not, at the time of writing, been determined.

Dealing with a suspect's computer is not a simple matter of turning it on and looking for evidence: computing experts are necessarily involved.[22] The more sophisticated criminals may have booby-trapped their machines; the more damning files may be hidden or encrypted; the most crucial evidence may consist of metadata or deleted files.[23] Where a prosecution is based on the defendant's possession of compromising documents or images, it will always be open to the defendant to argue that they were planted by the police or by some sort of trojan, or were an unwanted popup, and the police will have to be ready to counter this argument if made.[24]

Criminal evidence law is of some subtlety, and cannot be treated in detail here. Any data tendered in evidence must be classified as real evidence, as hearsay, or as a copy of another document, and different rules apply to each.[25] The hearsay rule is very much alive in criminal cases, though by statute the data is usually admissible if it is relevant and there is an adequate explanation for the failure to call the original maker of the statement.[26] Both Irish and English law have experimented with additional requirements as to the reliability of the computer which produced the data, though England has recently abolished its specific provision and reverted to a rebuttable presumption that the computer was working properly.[27] Technical evidence of this sort has played an important role in high-profile prosecutions, such as those of Harold Shipman and Ian Huntley, not to mention the Hutton enquiry.[28]

---

21   'Outcome of case inevitable, says judge', Irish Times, 24 April 2004; 'Exclusion of unconstitutionally obtained evidence', (2004) 14 ICLJ 25.

22   See *Lord Advocate's Reference (No 1 of 2002)* [2002] SCCR 743; Lambert, P, 'The search for elusive electrons: Getting a sense for electronic evidence', (2001) 1 JSIJ 23.

23   See Sommer, P, 'Downloads, logs and captures: Evidence from cyberspace', [2002] CTLR 33; Knight, W, 'Chasing the elusive shadows of e-crime', [2004] NS (8 May) 26; Clark, A, 'Hard drive evidence', (2004) 148 Sol Jo (Expert Witness Supp, Summer) 14.

24   See Hill, S, 'Driving a trojan horse and cart through the Computer Misuse Act', (2004) 14 C&L (5) 30; Brenner, S, Carrier, B and Henniger, J, 'The Trojan Horse defense in cybercrime cases', (2004) 21 SCCHTLJ 1.

25   *R v Governor of Brixton Prison ex p Levin* [1997] UKHL 27, [1997] AC 741 (Web), on which see Fitzpatrick, B, 'Computers, hearsay, and the status of extradition proceedings', [1998] 1 WJCLI (Web); *R (O'Shea) v Coventry Justices* [2004] EWHC 905 Admin (Web).

26   For the modern English and Welsh law of criminal hearsay, see Criminal Justice Act 2003 (UK), ss 114–133.

27   Criminal Evidence Act 1992 (IE), ss 4–11. For the position in England and Wales, see Quinn, K, 'Computer evidence in criminal proceedings: Farewell to the ill-fated s 69 of the Police and Criminal Evidence Act 1984', (2001) 5 IJEP 174; Tapper, C, 'Electronic evidence and the Criminal Justice Act 2003', [2004] CTLR 161.

28   'Footprints on the disk', Guardian, 5 February 2004 (Web).

Forced disclosure of cryptographic keys

There has been much official concern at the prospect that cryptographic techniques might be used to conceal criminal activity. However, it has proved difficult to reconcile government's need to know the content of messages with the public's need for a reasonable level of confidentiality; most proposed compromises would either allow government to see the content of all messages unaccountably, or could easily be circumvented by those determined to do so. In 1993, the US government proposed the 'Clipper Chip', which would facilitate encryption but which would also allow government to break that encryption as it chose. However, massive opposition to such a gross invasion of privacy defeated the proposal. The matter is one of continuing debate.[29]

Most legal systems around the world have made no specific provision for the problem, in the knowledge that there is no easy solution; no doubt, ordinary police powers of search and seizure are adequate in most cases where a police enquiry requires encryption to be broken. The UK is unusual in enacting express powers in that regard, though at the time of writing the powers have not been brought into force. As drafted, the powers can be exercised wherever this is necessary in the interests of national security, the prevention or detection of crime, or the economic wellbeing of the UK. A formal notice is served on anyone who is in possession of a key, or who has an immediate right of access to it; the recipient of the notice must then either surrender the key, or use it to decrypt the data in question. Failure to comply with the notice is an offence, punishable with up to two years' imprisonment and/or an unlimited fine. There is a complicated definition of 'possession' of the key, and detailed provision on the burden of proof if the recipient of the notice denies that they had possession at the time of the notice. If the notice requires it, the recipient is required to keep the authorities' attempt to decrypt the data a secret.[30]

These powers are, unsurprisingly, exceedingly controversial, and the UK government's official position is that there is so far no 'pressing operational need' to bring them into force.[31] Various groups of programmers have plans to render the powers unenforceable, using encryption with keys held outside the jurisdiction.[32] This is unfinished business: in principle, governments cannot accept that some forms of communication can be kept secret even from them, whereas some of their citizens demand precisely that. The issue is ongoing, and is likely to remain so while the technology continues to develop.[33]

---

29 Ackerman, W, 'Encryption: A 21st century national security dilemma', (1998) 12 IRLCT 371; Andrews, S, 'Who holds the key? – A comparative study of US and European encryption policies', [2000] 2 JILT (Web).

30 Regulation of Investigatory Powers Act 2000 (UK), ss 49–56; 'Government backtracks on encryption enquiry', ZDNet UK, 4 April 2001 (Web).

31 'Regulation of Investigatory Powers Act 2000', *Hansard* (Lords), 16 July 2004 (Web).

32 See, eg, m-o-o-t home page (Web).

33 For background and a selection of views, see Mostyn, M, 'The need for regulating anonymous remailers', (2000) 14 IRLCT 79; Brown, I and Laurie, B, 'Security against compelled disclosure', (Web); du Pont, G, 'The criminalization of true anonymity in cyberspace', (2001) 7 MTTLR 191 (Web).

SURVEILLANCE OF SPECIFIC INDIVIDUALS

Relatively little is publicly known about methods used to spy on those in whom the police have a particular interest; the authorities are not keen to have attention focused on how common this is, or on the precise operational details of so doing. However, where the main evidence in a case is electronic, it is impossible to avoid revealing quite a bit about the process. A well-documented case is the prosecution of the mobster Nicodemo Scarfo in New Jersey in 2001. Acting under a confidential court order, FBI employees broke into Scarfo's office and installed key-logging software. This recorded Scarfo's encryption pass phrase, enabling the FBI to decrypt documents which might otherwise have remained unintelligible.[34] The FBI has subsequently developed a superior key-logging program called *Magic Lantern*, which apparently can be installed by sending it as an e-mail message.[35]

An easier, and presumably much more common, way of spying on individuals is to require their ISP to monitor them. By this means, telephone conversations, e-mails and the content of web pages viewed can be recorded. The US appear to have been first here, monitoring specific individuals by insisting that their service provider route traffic through a machine running packet sniffing software. This software searches for data to or from specific addresses. The FBI's own *Omnivore* software, working from 1997, could capture e-mails; an improved version, called *Carnivore*, available from 1998 onwards, could also reconstruct web pages viewed, and was well integrated with the FBI's custom data mining program *CoolMiner*. Apparently, *Carnivore* could be a highly useful tool, especially if the target did not appreciate that he or she was under surveillance. But it had obvious weaknesses: it sometimes gathered too much data, both in the sense of bulk and in the sense of going beyond the precise data requested; and it was defeated by encryption, unless the cryptographic key could be determined by other means.[36] It has since been phased out in favour of other software.[37] Whether the legal limits for the use of this technology have been correctly set is a controversial question, to put it mildly.[38]

A peculiarity of the UK system (which sets it apart from the US and most of Europe, including Ireland) is that while the powers of monitoring are extensive, nonetheless the product of the monitoring is not usually admissible in court, nor indeed is anyone in court allowed to mention the possibility of such monitoring.[39] This rule, which strikes many as bizarre, is justified as part of a policy of de-emphasising

---

34   Murphy, A, 'Cracking the code to privacy: How far can the FBI go?', [2002] 2 DLTR (Web).

35   Hartzog, N, 'The "Magic Lantern" revealed: A report of the FBI's new "key logging" trojan', (2002) 20 JMJCIL 287.

36   On the technical and legal issues, see particularly Nabbali, T and Perry, M, 'Going for the throat: Carnivore in an Echelon World – part 1', (2003) 19 CLSR 456 and 'part 2', (2004) 20 CLSR 84.

37   'FBI retires Carnivore', Register, 15 January 2005 (Web).

38   Eg, Barrett, C, 'FBI Internet surveillance: The need for a natural rights application of the Fourth Amendment to insure Internet privacy', (2002) 8 RJOLT 16 (Web); Dunham, G, 'Carnivore, the FBI's e-mail surveillance system: Devouring criminals, not privacy', (2002) 54 FCLJ 543 (Web); Kerr, O, 'Internet surveillance law after the USA-PATRIOT Act: The Big Brother that isn't', (2003) 97 Nw ULR 607; Kollar, J, 'USA PATRIOT Act, the Fourth Amendment, and paranoia: Can they read this while I'm typing?', (2004) 3 JHTL 67 (Web).

39   Regulation of Investigatory Powers Act 2000 (UK), ss 17 and 18; *A-G's Reference (No 5 of 2002)* [2004] UKHL 40 (Web); *R v E* [2004] 1 WLR 3279. See generally Ormerod, D and McKay, S, 'Telephone intercepts and their admissibility', [2004] Crim LR 15.

electronic monitoring, to lull criminals into a false sense of security. It also prevents the defendant's legal team from seeing the transcript of the monitoring. Whether the policy is a sensible one is a matter on which the security services and the prosecution service are famously (and given the context, remarkably publicly) at odds.[40] Monitoring of telecommunications is ordered by warrant addressed to the telecommunications provider; the warrant must specify either a particular person or particular premises as the target of the warrant. The warrant must be considered necessary in the interests of national security or economic wellbeing, or to prevent or detect serious crime, or be authorised under an international mutual assistance agreement. Warrants can only be issued by the Home Secretary on the application of the police, the security services and the customs service.[41] Oversight of the system, such as it is, is provided by an Interception of Communications Commissioner,[42] and individual complaints are handled by an Investigatory Powers Tribunal.[43] Complaints to the tribunal are few – unsurprisingly, as it would be an offence for anyone involved in the monitoring process to reveal to its subject what was going on.[44] To date, no complaints to the tribunal have been upheld, though a certain number of errors in monitoring are admitted to in annual reports of the Commissioner.[45]

There is no detailed public statement of what UK ISPs must do to comply with the legislation on monitoring,[46] but inferences may be drawn from the capability requirements with which all telcos with more than 10,000 UK customers must comply. Amongst other things, these companies must be ready to implement interception within one working day of the warrant; to ensure complete interception of all relevant communications and simultaneous handover to the relevant contact; to enable simultaneous surveillance of up to one customer in 10,000; and to allow auditing to check that the right data is being intercepted.[47] A Technical Advisory Board, which includes representatives both from those who order monitoring and those who provide it, advises on technical detail; grants may be made to help defray the cost of monitoring.[48]

Even less is publicly known about the Irish system. Interception is governed by pre-Internet provisions covering the transmission of 'telecommunications messages', which is presumably taken to include Internet traffic of all sorts. Special cases aside, interception must be authorised by ministerial warrant, which can only issue for the

---

40 '"Phone-tapping" evidence vetoed', BBC News, 18 February 2005 (Web).
41 For the powers generally, see Regulation of Investigatory Powers Act 2000 (UK), ss 5–20; Akdeniz, Y, Taylor, N and Walker, C, 'Regulation of Investigatory Powers Act 2000 (1): BigBrother.gov.uk', [2001] Crim LR 73.
42 Regulation of Investigatory Powers Act 2000 (UK), ss 57 and 58.
43 *Ibid*, ss 65 and 69; Investigatory Powers Tribunal Rules 2000 (UK), SI 2000/2665 (both as amended).
44 Regulation of Investigatory Powers Act 2000 (UK), s 19.
45 'Intelligence and security service tribunals', *Hansard* (Commons), 18 March 2004 (Web).
46 A little more detail is given in the Covert Surveillance Code of Practice (Web).
47 Regulation of Investigatory Powers (Maintenance of Interception Capability) Order 2002 (UK), SI 2002/1931. Official figures for the number of warrants do not distinguish between warrants for letters, the Internet and data; see *Report of the Interception of Communications Commissioner for 2003*, HC 883 (July 2004) (Web).
48 Regulation of Investigatory Powers Act 2000 (UK), ss 12–14; Technical Advisory Board home page (Web). For general discussion of the legislation, see Best, K and McCusker, R, 'The scrutiny of the electronic communications of businesses: Striking the balance between the power to intercept and the right to privacy?', [2002] 1 WJCLI (Web).

purpose of investigation of serious crime or in the interests of state security. The warrant must relate to a particular 'postal address' or 'telecommunications address'; presumably this is interpreted as including a particular e-mail account, or activity from a particular customer account. Oversight is provided by a judge of the High Court, and there is a Complaints Referee.[49]

DATA RETENTION BY PRIVATE BODIES

Modern business generates and retains huge amounts of data for a variety of reasons, including management needs and a desire to keep a close eye on customers. Legal constraints also play a role: such as (for example) the duties on companies to retain tax records and accounting records – a duty which (if the UK and Ireland follow the course set by the post-Enron US) may expand considerably.[50] From the government's point of view, it is usually enough that this data is stored and can be accessed if particular cases call for investigation. Nonetheless, there is a noticeable recent trend of calling for more data to be retained, or even asking for it to be transferred in bulk. A certain amount of governmental interest has been shown in supermarket loyalty card data, which (if cross-referenced with health records) might reveal important links between eating habits and health. Requests for such data have been refused in the past,[51] but possibly attitudes are changing.[52]

Communications traffic data: access and retention

Telecommunications providers have no reason to record the content of their customers' transmissions, but they retain a certain amount of 'traffic data', not amounting to the entire datastream but typically including data on individual messages: sender, recipient, time, and duration. In the case of mobile phones, this will include data which could be used to identify where the phone actually was at particular times. The obvious reason for retaining this data is in case the eventual bill is disputed by the customer, though this varies with the channel of communication: telephone calls are charged by the nature and duration of the call, whereas ISPs typically do not charge by the number of sites visited or the amount of data transferred, and so may have no need to retain the detail of this. Length of retention after the customer has paid their bill paid varies considerably, some small telcos deleting the data immediately but other larger ones retaining it for several years. Data protection law applies to all of this data, and so, in principle, customers could complain at over-zealous retention, or if the data were revealed to others without their consent.

---

49   Postal and Telecommunications Services Act 1983 (IE), ss 98 and 110; Interception of Postal Packets and Telecommunications Messages (Regulation) Act 1993 (IE). Despite the specific reference to 'Telecom Éireann' (Eircom), the provisions also catch other licensed operators: Postal and Telecommunications Services (Amendment) Act 1999 (IE), s 7.

50   Middleton, R, 'Data retention policies after Enron', (2002) 18 CLSR 333; Chan, M, 'Paper piles to computer files: A federal approach to electronic records retention and management', (2004) 44 SCLR 805.

51   'Retailers reject gov't plea for data', Campaign, 29 January 1999.

52   'Loyalty cards may help switch to healthy eating', Scotland on Sunday, 4 January 2004.

What if law enforcement authorities seek access to this traffic data? If the authorities plead national security, then the telco can voluntarily hand it over without infringing the data protection legislation;[53] the telco sends a bill to cover its costs. If the telco refuses, a warrant could be sought under the ordinary law.

The question then arises whether telcos can be compelled to retain this data in bulk, so that when the authorities develop an interest in a particular individual they will be able to access not merely current data but past data also. Yet both the practical objections to this (cost to telcos) and the legal and political objections (confidentiality, privacy and other data rights) are obvious enough, and have been repeatedly urged by opponents of data retention. Some of the legal objections have been relieved by a controversial amendment to the Data Protection Directive, permitting data retention 'for a limited period'. But the amendment provides, as it must, that the retention must be justified as a 'necessary, appropriate and proportionate measure within a democratic society to safeguard national security (that is, state security), defence, public security, and the prevention, investigation, detection and prosecution of criminal offences or of unauthorised use of the electronic communication system'.[54] As the complaint against data retention is precisely that it is a disproportionate and unnecessary response to the problems it addresses, the amendment arguably does nothing to legalise it.[55] But the argument from illegality is merely one weapon in the dispute, which is ongoing.

The UK government has created a general duty on telcos to hand over such data as they happen to have, on demand.[56] Such data can be demanded for a wide variety of purposes, including national security, prevention or detection of crime, the economic wellbeing of the UK, public safety or public health, or the assessment or collection of tax. Other purposes can be added by Parliamentary resolution. The bodies entitled to demand access were specified in the original legislation as any police force or any of the intelligence services, as well as the tax and customs authorities. This was all controversial enough when first introduced; even more controversial were subsequent attempts to extend the list, including a notorious draft instrument of May 2002 that would have added all local authorities and a number of minor investigatory agencies such as the Office of Fair Trading and the Food Standards Agency. After an outcry, this draft was withdrawn;[57] a later draft, more carefully defining the purposes for which data was needed, but incorporating an even longer list of authorities who could demand data, was enacted in December 2003;[58] more were added in April 2005.[59] It appears that the more minor agencies can in practice obtain access to traffic data, by making a case to that effect to one of the bodies officially listed; indeed, one of the defences made to the withdrawn draft order was that it

---

53 Above, p 111.
54 Directive 2002/58/EC on the processing of personal data, Art 15.
55 See especially 'Memorandum of laws concerning the legality of data retention with regard to the rights guaranteed by the European convention on human rights', prepared by Covington and Burling for Privacy International, 10 October 2003 (Web).
56 Regulation of Investigatory Powers Act 2000 (UK), ss 21–25, in force 5 January 2004: see SI 2003/3140.
57 'Blunkett shelves access to data plans', Guardian, 19 June 2002 (Web).
58 Regulation of Investigatory Powers (Communications Data) Order 2003 (UK), SI 2003/3172. See Munir, A and Mohd, S, 'Access to communications data by public authorities', (2004) 20 CLSR 194.
59 Regulation of Investigatory Powers (Communications Data) (Amendment) Order 2005 (UK), SI 2005/1083.

simply regularised the real position.[60] The government has persistently refused to quantify the amount of data appropriated under these provisions, saying that too many agencies are involved. The pressure group, Privacy International, has conservatively estimated that data on 100 m telephone calls and subscriber data on 1 m customers is handed over each year (and that in a period before the new powers were in force!);[61] the government admits to about half a million specific requests.[62] Given the amount of data involved, the oversight of the system by the Interception of Communications Commissioner is presumably no more than nominal. There is still considerable argument over whether telcos' costs are adequately met under current arrangements; to what extent the law is compatible with privacy rights is an open question.[63]

The UK government means to insist that telcos retain all traffic data for a significant period, whether or not there is a commercial justification for so doing, so that it may be accessed under the provisions just discussed. But the legislative scheme is that these matters should be dealt with non-coercively. By legislation in force in December 2001,[64] the Home Secretary may negotiate a code of practice with telcos to regulate the retention of this data and access to it by government officials. There is elaborate provision for the negotiations and for the approval of the resulting code by Parliament. Breach of the code does not attract legal penalties, though the code is admissible as evidence in a case where the justification for retaining the data is in issue. The legislation includes a power to make compulsory directions to retain data, but this power has not yet been invoked and has only a limited lifespan if unused. The code now in force[65] discusses the relationship between retention and the data protection legislation, and the need to distinguish between retention for business reasons and retention for national security reasons. The period set for retention for security reasons varies with the type of data: subscriber details and telephony data are to be retained for 12 months, e-mail and ISP data for 6 months, web activity logs for 4 days. Payments can be made to compensate for the cost of retaining the data; negotiations over this have been stormy, not least because of disagreements about how much data would have been retained by telcos for their own purposes. It is not entirely clear from publicly available sources how much of this in place: some telcos are said to be working on providing facilities for data retention, others are opposed to it in principle, and yet others are opposed to it unless a more generous attitude is taken towards their costs.[66] The government evidently means to press ahead with this, and has (ominously) extended the lifespan of its compulsory powers over telcos,[67] though it has yet to use them.

60 'UK snoop charter: We're already getting all the data anyway', Register, 18 June 2002 (Web); 'How ISP surveillance currently works, Pt 1', (Web).

61 'UK gov seizes data on 100m calls, 1m users, a year', Register, 14 May 2003 (Web).

62 'Communications data', *Hansard* (Lords), 9 June 2003 (Web).

63 'Snooping laws may be illegal', Guardian, 31 July 2002 (Web).

64 Anti-terrorism, Crime and Security Act 2001 (UK), ss 102–107. See more generally Walden, I and McCormack, E, 'Retaining and accessing communications data', (2003) 8 Comms L 256; Walker, C and Akdeniz, Y, 'Anti-terrorism laws and data retention: War is over?', (2003) 54 NILQ 159 (Web).

65 Voluntary Code of Practice (Web). The Code is authorised by Retention of Communications Data (Code of Practice) Order 2003 (UK), SI 2003/3175.

66 'Communications data code of practice', *Hansard* (Commons), 14 May 2004 (Web); Vine, S, 'The data retention regime: The ISP's point of view', [2003] EBL (Dec) 5.

67 Retention of Communications Data (Extension of Initial Period) Order 2003 (UK), SI 2003/3173, by which the period now ends on 13 December 2005.

The compatibility of any of this with basic privacy or other human rights is doubtful; national and international criticism of the entire exercise has been loud and long.[68]

The Irish scene has been no more satisfactory. In April 2002 the cabinet issued a secret order to telcos to retain data for three years, to allow access only to Garda Síochána (police) and army officials, and not to mention the existence of the order publicly. No plausible legal basis for the order has been suggested.[69] The existence of the order only became public knowledge when the Information Commissioner revealed it in February 2003; legal proceedings were threatened, but then stalled.[70] The Minister for Justice defended the order as an interim solution while public consultation on a more permanent scheme was conducted. Then, unexpectedly, legislation authorising data retention for three years was proposed and quickly passed.[71]

Proposals for EU-wide data retention have received much discussion, not to mention denunciation by a number of bodies, including Europe's Data Protection Commissioners.[72] A public consultation is currently in progress.[73] Negotiations are secret, and details are obscure. It is clear, however, that the impetus for the proposal comes not from the European Commission but from certain Member States, particularly those that have tried to introduce data retention at home but have encountered opposition. It seems that this proposal will be pushed on only as political circumstances permit; and that any resulting directive will be fairly loose, to permit nations with little interest to achieve bare compliance easily, but to allow nations which wish to engage in fuller surveillance of their citizens to do so, claiming that they are merely complying with the requirements of EU law.[74]

DATA SHARING WITHIN GOVERNMENT

In the UK especially, there seems to be a positive mania for data sharing, following the report, *Privacy and Data Sharing*, in April 2002.[75] It is praised in government circles as promoting efficiency (though the counter-argument, that it will result in information overload and paralysis, is little mentioned). The debates over it usually receive little public coverage, and do not dig very deeply into the issues. This is

---

68 See especially 'Communications data: Report of an Inquiry by the All Party Internet Group', APIG, January 2003 (Web).

69 Some reference has been made to statutory interception powers (above, pp 115–16), but these evidently apply only to investigations of particular suspect individuals, not the entire population.

70 'State secretly retaining phone data', Irish Times, 25 February 2003; 'Move to retain phone call data deplored', Irish Times, 6 March 2003; 'Court threat for State over data privacy', Irish Times, 26 May 2003. See generally Woods, A, 'We know what you did last summer!', [2005] COLR 3 (Web).

71 Criminal Justice (Terrorist Offences) Act 2005 (IE), ss 61–67, in force 8 March 2005.

72 'EU data protection chiefs oppose data retention moves', Register, 17 September 2002 (Web).

73 *DG InfSo – DG JAI Consultation Document on Traffic Data Retention*, 30 July 2004 (Web). See also Opinion 9/2004 of the Article 29 Data Protection Working Party, 9 November 2004 (Web).

74 'EC calls for rethink of data retention proposals', Register, 10 December 2004 (Web).

75 *Privacy and Data Sharing: The Way Forward for Public Services*, Cabinet Office, 11 April 2002 (Web). See also *Privacy and Data Sharing: The Way Forward for Public Services – An Update on Progress*, Department for Constitutional Affairs, November 2003 (Web) and *Public Sector Data Sharing: Guidance on the Law*, Department for Constitutional Affairs, November 2003 (Web).

partly because those issues are so arcane, and partly because most debates are sparked by individual crises which might indeed have been prevented by more intelligent use of government data. Oversight of data sharing is with the Department for Constitutional Affairs;[76] the e-Government Interoperability Framework (e-GIF) is an ongoing project.[77] Some more specific developments are worthy of particular attention.

(a) Computerisation of NHS records is proceeding.[78] Central government has powers to appropriate patient records without the consent of the patient or the GP holding them.[79] All babies born in NHS hospitals in England on or after 29 October 2002 are allocated a lifetime number to help identify their records.[80] No one has suggested that access to the records will be restricted to health personnel; there are many complaints that access is too easy, and that such constraints as exist are too easily evaded.[81] Occasionally, evidence of systematic police access to data emerges.[82] There are repeated complaints that the restrictions in the data protection legislation impede legitimate medical research;[83] and while there is as yet no one issue in the UK or Ireland to rival the controversy over genetic privacy in Iceland,[84] this is probably only a matter of time.[85]

(b) The Police National Computer was upgraded in 2002. There is much emphasis on data sharing with various partners, including the Criminal Records Bureau (which holds the National Firearms Forensic Intelligence Database and the National DNA Database) and the Criminal Records Bureau. Collection and availability of local data came in for considerable criticism in the wake of the Soham case, where the murders could possibly have been prevented if local police data on the murderer had been matched more quickly with police data from his home town. After official criticism of the 'fundamental failures' in police intelligence practices,[86] the Home Office promises a national intelligence system.[87] An attempt by one of the chief constables involved to blame the data protection legislation for the intelligence failure has been largely rejected, though certain minor amendments seem likely.[88] As a rule, data protection law does not seem to impose significant constraints here.

---

76 See *Privacy and Data Sharing: The Way Forward* (Web).

77 See e-GIF (Web).

78 'Patient records go on database', Times, 21 July 2003.

79 Health and Social Care Act 2001 (E&W), s 60; Health Service (Control of Patient Information) Regulations 2002 (E&W), SI 2002/1438.

80 See 'NHS numbers for babies' (Web); 'NHS "numbers for babies" goes live', VNUNet, 29 October 2002 (Web).

81 'How safe is your medical record?', Register, 23 June 2004 (Web).

82 Eg, 'Data sharing calls time on Cardiff bar brawls', VNUNet, 13 July 2004 (Web).

83 Eg, 'Data protection, informed consent and research', (2004) 328 BMJ 1029 (Web).

84 Gertz, R, 'An analysis of the Icelandic Supreme Court judgement on the Health Sector Database Act', (2004) 1 SCRIPT-ed 2 (Web); Potts, J, 'At least give the natives glass beads: An examination of the bargain made between Iceland and deCODE Genetics with implications for global bioprospecting', (2002) 7 VJOLT 8 (Web).

85 Hsieh, A, 'A nation's genes for a cure to cancer: Evolving ethical, social and legal issues regarding population genetic databases', (2004) 37 Col JL & Soc Prob 359.

86 See the Bichard Inquiry Report, 22 June 2004 (Web).

87 'Home Office promises national intelligence system', ZDNet, UK 23 June 2004 (Web); 'Data federation and the police', Register, 6 July 2004 (Web).

88 Wildish, N and Nissanka, V, 'A deletion too far: Huntley, Soham and data protection', (2004) 14 C&L (6) 28; Tomlinson, H and Thomson, M, 'Policing the use of data', (2004) 154 NLJ 338; Room, S, 'Meeting the challenges of Climbié and Soham – part 3', (2004) 154 NLJ 590.

(c) A crackdown on uninsured drivers is planned, by collating the insurance industry's own motor database with the records of the DVLA. As automatic number plate recognition becomes a routine technology, this too can be brought into the scheme to identify offenders quickly.[89]

(d) The use of CCTV cameras as a tool for public surveillance grew throughout the 1990s.[90] This generates large amounts of personal data in official hands. As image-recognition technology improves, it will become easier to match images with particular individuals: areas where significant improvements may be expected are in relation to vehicle recognition (used at tolls and in road-pricing schemes such as London's congestion charge[91]) and face recognition.[92] Scanning of individuals for suspect packages seems likely to improve dramatically as it becomes possible to exploit the terahertz band of the electromagnetic spectrum; it is already becoming necessary to limit this technology so that it cannot be used to show what the scanned individual looks like naked, as it can easily do.[93] The data protection issues here are immense.

The crowning glory of governmental data sharing would be the introduction of a system of national identity cards, which would provide a focus for identifying all individuals, and hence matching all data relating to individuals.[94] Again, while this proposal has become a matter of public debate, that debate has tended to be diverted into marginal questions, such as whether there will be a physical card which citizens will be obliged to carry (not central to the project, and largely irrelevant if face-recognition technology continues to improve), or whether continental Europe's experience of identity cards suggests any difficulties (largely irrelevant, as cumbersome paper-based systems do not pose the same threats to privacy). The current debate over the scheme lacks public recognition both that it necessarily involves hugely increased surveillance of the entire population, and that the supposed public benefits have been expressed only in the vaguest and most question-begging of terms.[95]

INTERNATIONAL DATA SHARING

International co-operation and exchange of data is an increasing factor in policing, though it is rarely publicised. In one of the more noticeable products of such co-operation, the US Postal Inspection Service in 1999 seized a Texas web server that

---

89 'Linked databases to beat uninsured drivers', VNUNet, 11 August 2004 (Web).

90 Fay, S, 'Tough on crime, tough on civil liberties: Some negative aspects of Britain's wholesale adoption of CCTV surveillance during the 1990s', (1998) 12 IRLCT 315.

91 'Congestion charging – enforcement technology', (Web); 'Does London mayor's "ring of steel" breach UK Data Act?', Register, 19 February 2003 (Web); Lerouge, J, 'Road tolling and privacy', (1999) 15 CLSR 379.

92 Luk, J, 'Identifying terrorists: Privacy rights in the US and the UK', (2002) 25 HICLR 223.

93 'Anger over airport security scans that reveal all', Sunday Telegraph, 11 August 2002.

94 For current info see 'Identity cards' (Web); 'ID cards to use "key database" of personal info', Register, 26 April 2004 (Web).

95 For discussion, see Holderness, M, 'Every step you take', [2002] NS (25 May) 50; 'Policing by plastic', Guardian, 30 May 2003 (Web); 'Information Commissioner publishes concerns on identity cards', Information Commissioner, 30 July 2004 (Web); 6, Perri, 'Entitlement cards: Do the Home Secretary's proposals comply with data protection principles? Part I', (2003) 3 WDPR 18 (Web), and 'Part II', (2003) 3 WDPR 13 (Web).

had been selling child pornography to customers across the world. The data recovered, which included credit card numbers for 150,000 suspects, was passed on to relevant national police forces, including those in the UK (7,200 names) and Ireland (130 names). Prosecutions have been slow in coming, but have been substantial, and have included some prominent individuals.[96]

European and US police forces seem keen to share more data, and protection against abuses is weak in the extreme.[97] However, two factors operate against unrestrained data sharing. The first is the inability of many legislators to believe that other countries have fair legal systems; this means that there is substantial opposition whenever new proposals to share data with foreigners are proposed.[98] The second is that conflicting interests or goals between different nations may impede willingness to share data; while all nations have an interest in attempting to suppress theft, tax evasion and drug dealing, differences of approach may prevent co-operation on other matters. The result is an array of overlapping alliances, sometimes in open conflict with one another. Much co-operation takes place at the EU level, particularly through EUROPOL.[99] Sub-groups of nations within the EU are also relevant, particularly the parties to the Schengen Convention.[100] Each nation within the EU has its own network of alliances with neighbours and others.

In two areas, controversy over data sharing has spilled into the public arena.

(a) A US-led intelligence-gathering coalition called ECHELON, to which the UK is a significant contributor, has been the object of protest by several EU nations, not least because they allege that they are themselves its major targets.[101] ECHELON is believed to spy on communications traffic, especially satellite traffic, potentially catching most Internet traffic (though of course only a tiny fraction of it can be retained). Vigorous protests have been made by the EU; the US has refused even to acknowledge ECHELON's existence, though some of its partners have not; the main effect of the protests seems to have been a greater US willingness to negotiate intelligence sharing agreements with individual European nations, perhaps in the hope of preventing any significant independent European intelligence capability.[102]

(b) In November 2001, US legislation required electronic transfer of passenger data for all flights inbound to the US, to be sent within 15 minutes of the plane's departure. Compliance by EU carriers was, however, postponed pending negotiations. In February 2003, it was agreed with the EU Commission that US authorities would be allowed to access the computer systems of European airlines to secure this data; US Customs undertook to respect EU data protection laws, but no legal remedy

---

96 'Web raids help to put 3,000 on sex crimes register', Times, 29 July 2004; 'Operation Ore puts children "at risk" ', BBC News, 27 January 2003 (Web); *R (O'Shea) v Coventry Justices* [2004] EWHC 905 Admin (Web).

97 Kennedy, D, 'In search of a balance between police power and privacy in the Cybercrime Treaty', (2002) 9 RJOLT 3 (Web); 'EU–USA agreements – the drafts on the table', Statewatch, April 2003 (Web).

98 Eg, 'US cybercrime push "imperils personal security" of Americans', Register, 20 November 2003 (Web).

99 EURPOL home page (Web).

100 On which, see Karanja, S, 'The Schengen information system in Austria', [2002] 1 JILT (Web); Colvin, M, 'The Schengen information system: A human rights audit', (2001) 151 NLJ 895.

101 'E-mail users warned over spy network', BBC News, 29 May 2001 (Web).

102 For some background, see Nabbali, T and Perry, M, 'Going for the throat: Carnivore in an Echelon World – part 2', (2004) 20 CLSR 84; Sloan, L, 'ECHELON and the legal restraints on signals intelligence: A need for re-evaluation', (2001) 50 Duke LJ 1467 (Web).

was given to ensure compliance with this.[103] After a public outcry, the Commission changed its position, saying that the agreement manifestly infringed data protection law; it began to renegotiate the agreement, apparently to restrict the amount of data transferred, but also (according to some informed observers) to secure access to the data itself. An amended agreement was reached, accompanied by an official determination by the Commission that data rights were now adequately safeguarded; having secured the unanimous consent of EU governments, it entered into force in May 2004.[104] The EU Parliament is still not content, and is challenging the agreement before the European Court of Justice;[105] meanwhile, reporting of advance travel data to EU Member States themselves is gradually being put in place.[106] The US is now calling for transfer of data an hour *before* each flight leaves.[107]

FREEDOM OF INFORMATION

As was described above, the growth of government data on its citizens has been very substantial, but little publicised. Public access to government information is rather the reverse: trumpeted as an important addition to the rights of citizens, but in fact rather narrowly stated, and shot through with numerous and broad exceptions. The Irish Freedom of Information Act 1997, in force April 1998, has achieved a modest success in this area; it was not however quite modest enough for the Irish government, who in 2003 introduced legislation limiting its scope and substantially increasing the fees payable by those who invoke it.[108] The UK Freedom of Information Act 2000 was the subject of serious disputes both inside and outside the cabinet during its passage; the resulting detailed provisions are nowhere near as generous as those originally proposed, though they are somewhat broader than the terms initially proposed to Parliament. It is in force on 1 January 2005. The legislation does not, however, extend to Scottish public authorities, which have their own rules: the Freedom of Information (Scotland) Act 2002 was fully in force on 30 April 2004.[109] Freedom of information within the EU is of earlier vintage; the current Regulation dates from 2001.[110]

Only the Irish and the general UK legislation will be considered in detail here. The detail of the different legislative schemes is rather different, and each demands separate treatment.

---

103 'Flying to the US? Give US gov all your personal data', Register, 20 February 2003 (Web).
104 'Ministers thwart MEPs, OK EU–US airline data deal', Register, 18 May 2004 (Web).
105 'EU move to have US air data pact annulled', Irish Times, 26 June 2004.
106 Directive 2004/82/EC on the obligation of carriers to communicate passenger data, to be implemented by 5 September 2006. For some of the issues in the controversy, see Baker, S, Shenk, M, Kuilwijk, K, Chang, W and Mah, D, 'Flights and rights: Anonymisation, data-matching and privacy', (2004) 14 C&L (6) 35; Asinari, M and Poullet, Y, 'The airline passenger data disclosure case and the EU–US debate', (2004) 20 CLSR 98; and see the same authors' 'Airline passengers' data', (2004) 20 CLSR 370.
107 'US calls for increased and earlier passenger data transfers', OUT-LAW, 24 May 2005 (Web).
108 Freedom of Information (Amendment) Act 2003 (IE).
109 See Freedom of Information (Scotland) Act 2002 (Commencement No 3) Order 2004 (Sc), SI 2004/203.
110 Regulation 1049/2001/EC.

The Irish legislation[111]

The legislation gives a right of access to most government records created after the Freedom of Information Act 1997 came into force (21 April 1998); for some bodies the date is set a little later, and for others no date has yet been set.

Where a record is requested, a decision whether to allow access to it must be made within four weeks (extensible up to eight weeks in certain limited circumstances). A request may be refused if it is invalid, or if one of the exemptions applies. Invalidity is established if there are no sufficient particulars to identify the requested record, or if producing it would create substantial and unreasonable interference with, or disruption of, the other work of the public body concerned; however, before access can be refused on either of those grounds, there must be an offer to assist in rewriting the request to avoid the problem. Invalidity is also established where the record requested does not exist or cannot be found; or where the record is to be published; or where the request seems frivolous or vexatious; or where the fee has not been paid.[112]

There are a number of exemptions. Some government organs are not within the scope of the legislation at all, though it provides a framework for bringing them in at a later time; in this category is the Garda Síochána. Various categories of records are exempted from the right of access; some are in absolute terms, others involve a public interest test, balancing the right of access against the other interests involved.[113]

(a) Cabinet papers may be withheld for five years from the time when the relevant cabinet decision was made, where the public interest is thought to require it. Certain categories of papers can in any event only be disclosed after consultation with the political parties of the cabinet members at the relevant time. Even the existence or otherwise of the requested record need not be revealed unless the public interest is satisfied.

(b) The deliberations of public bodies generally are exempt, where the public interest is thought to require it. There are exceptions for technical or purely factual records.

(c) Access may be refused on the ground that it would interfere with investigations, audit or management procedures, or if it would disclose the detail of ongoing negotiations.

(d) Access must be refused where it would infringe legal professional privilege, or would constitute contempt of court. Certain papers of the Oireachtas are also exempt from disclosure, as are the private papers of a representative in the European Parliament or a member of a local authority or a health board.

(e) The public interest may be invoked to deny access where it would prejudice the investigation of crime, the prosecution of offenders or the fairness of criminal trials. Public safety, and the security of buildings or of communications, are also grounds for refusing access, as is protecting the identity of police informants. A certificate may be issued, making the decision to deny access effectively unchallengeable.

---

111 For general discussion, see Irish FOI Links (Web).

112 Freedom of Information Act 1997 (IE), ss 6–18, as amended by Freedom of Information (Amendment) Act 2003 (IE), ss 4–13.

113 Freedom of Information Act 1997 (IE), ss 19–32, as amended by Freedom of Information (Amendment) Act 2003 (IE), ss 14–24.

(f) Adverse interference with the security or defence of the state, international relations or matters relating to Northern Ireland are all grounds for refusal of access, and indeed for refusing to disclose whether a requested record actually exists. A certificate may be issued, making the decision to deny access effectively unchallengeable.

(g) Information given in confidence cannot be disclosed.

(h) Commercially sensitive records are exempt, unless the person to whom they relate consents or knew all along that they might be disclosed, or if the disclosure is necessary to avoid serious and imminent danger to life, health or the environment.

(i) A request which would reveal personal information (except that relating to the person making the request) must be refused. This protects both living and dead individuals. If alive, the person to whom the information relates may waive this protection; it may also be disregarded if necessary to avoid serious and imminent danger to life or health.

(j) Access may be refused where it would prejudice research or researchers, or any cultural heritage or natural resource.

(k) Unwarranted interference in financial and economic interests is another ground for refusal.

Access to the record may be given in any one or more of a variety of forms, though if the requester has specified a preferred form, this can only be departed from for stated reasons. If the requester is dissatisfied with a refusal or partial refusal of their request, the initial remedy is an internal review of the decision; if the result of the review is equally unsatisfying, then an appeal can be taken to the Information Commissioner.[114]

Where personal information is held by public bodies, the person concerned can insist that it be amended where it is incomplete, incorrect or misleading. The legislation also gives a right to those with a material interest in a decision by any public body to claim a written statement of facts and reasons in respect of the decision.[115]

In addition to access to particular records, the legislation contains more general duties to provide information. Every public body is obliged to publish a reference book setting out its structure, organisation and functions, and the detail of the services it provides. It must also describe the classes of records it holds, and procedures for exercising rights under the legislation. The so-called 'internal law' of each public body – its rules, guidelines and precedents for exercising its powers – must also be published.[116]

The changes introduced by the 2003 Act restrict access in a number of ways. In addition to the fees contained in the 1997 Act for search and retrieval of records and for reproduction, new fees are now to be demanded for most applications under the legislation, and for appeals. Several of the exempted categories have also been

---

114 Freedom of Information Act 1997 (IE), ss 7, 8 and 12, as amended by Freedom of Information Act 2003 (IE), ss 5 and 6.

115 Freedom of Information Act 1997 (IE), ss 17 and 18, as amended by Freedom of Information Act 2003 (IE), ss 12 and 13.

116 Freedom of Information Act 1997 (IE), ss 15 and 16, as amended by Freedom of Information Act 2003 (IE), ss 10 and 11.

broadened. Informal methods have also been used to discourage what have been seen as abusive applications; for example, one department took to publishing all applications under the legislation on its public web site, powerfully discouraging journalists from making applications to support a possible exclusive. Applications under the legislation have fallen dramatically since the introduction of the amendments, as seems to have been the intention.[117]

The UK legislation

The (much delayed) Freedom of Information Act 2000 is in force on 1 January 2005.[118] It covers all information held on or after that date, whenever it originated. One of the many controversies that has surrounded the implementation of the legislation has been the late introduction of penalties for destroying information before the deadline: the specific offence of alteration or concealment of records with intent to prevent disclosure has been delayed along with the bulk of the legislation.[119]

The right under the Act is stated in broad terms, as a right to be informed by public authorities whether requested information exits, and if so, to have that information communicated. Requests must be complied with within 20 working days, though regulations may provide for a longer period in specified types of cases. A request may be refused if it falls into one of the exempt categories. It may also be refused if it is not in the right form, if the fee is not paid, or if the request is vexatious. If a request is the same as, or is substantially similar to, an earlier request by the same person, then the public authority can insist on a 'reasonable interval' before it must comply with the new request. Regulations may be made to define a financial limit for complying with requests: where the cost of complying with the request would exceed the limit, then it may be refused or a higher fee may be charged for complying with the request. Public authorities are under a duty to provide advice and assistance in relation to the making of requests, and must conform to a code of practice in so doing.[120]

The public bodies subject to the legislation include all government departments, local authorities in England, Wales and Northern Ireland, publicly owned companies, and a variety of other bodies listed at length in the Act. The list can be added to by order. In a few cases, only certain categories of information held by particular authorities is subject to the Act; and the list can be amended by order, to limit the categories of information further.[121]

The exemptions are defined as either absolute exemptions, or as 'public interest' exemptions.[122] Most of the exemptions prohibit not merely disclosure of the

---

117 Woods, A, 'Adding another glass block to the barrier of transparency: The media and the Freedom of Information Acts', [2004] COLR 1 (Web).

118 Freedom of Information Act 2000 (UK), s 77, in force 1 January 2005. See 'Freedom of Information Act 2000: Section 77', *Hansard* (Lords), 24 June 2002 (Web).

119 See, eg, 'Mayor Ken boasts of pre-FOIA "juicy bit" shredfest', Register, 21 March 2005 (Web).

120 Freedom of Information Act 2000 (UK), ss 8–17; Freedom of Information and Data Protection (Appropriate Limit and Fees) Regulations 2004 (UK), SI 2004/3244.

121 Freedom of Information Act 2000 (UK), ss 1–7 and Sched 1.

122 *Ibid*, ss 21–44.

information but also disclosure of whether particular requested information even exits. Absolute exemptions cover the following topics:

(a) Information reasonably accessible by other means, even if it must be paid for.
(b) Information supplied by, or relating to, security authorities, which include the Security Service, the Secret Intelligence Services, GCHQ, the National Criminal Intelligence Service, and the various tribunals which have oversight of these bodies.
(c) Documents filed with a court, or created for the purposes of legal proceedings.
(d) Information covered by parliamentary privilege, or which is held by one of the Houses of Parliament, and disclosure of which is considered to prejudice advice or deliberation.
(e) Personal data. Where the data subject is the person now making the Freedom of Information request, the request is dealt with under the Data Protection Act. In other cases, a balancing test applies to weigh the claims of the data subject against the claims of the person making the request.
(f) Information obtained in confidence.
(g) Information disclosure of which is prohibited by statute, would breach EU law, or would constitute a contempt of court.

For the 'public interest' exemptions, a decision must be made whether the public interest in disclosure outweighs the public interest in preventing it. The categories of information affected are:

(a) Information held with a view to future publication.
(b) Information required to safeguard national security. A ministerial certificate that non-disclosure is necessary to safeguard national security is conclusive evidence to that effect; such a certificate can be expressed to cover general categories of information.
(c) Defence information, or information on the capabilities, effectiveness or security of the armed forces.
(d) Information likely to prejudice the UK's international relations or the promotion of the UK's interests abroad. Relations between the governments of the constituent parts of the UK are also covered, in similar terms.
(e) Information disclosure of which is likely to prejudice the UK's economic interests or the financial administration of the government.
(f) Criminal investigations and prosecutions have an exemption for their files. There is also a more general exemption for information disclosure of which is likely to prejudice the prevention or detection of crime, the prosecution of offenders, the administration of justice, the assessment and collection of taxes, immigration controls, and other related governmental functions.
(g) Information disclosure of which would prejudice the audit of public authority accounts.
(h) Information which relates to the formulation or development of government policy is exempt, as are ministerial communications, advice from the Law Officers, and the operation of any ministerial private office. Once a policy decision has been made, the exemption continues to apply to information other than statistical information, which becomes disclosable.
(i) There is a general exemption for information disclosure of which may prejudice effective conduct of public affairs, as by prejudicing collective responsibility, or inhibiting the free and frank provision of advice or exchange of views.

(j)   Information relating to communications with the monarch or other members of the royal family or the royal household, or relating to the conferring of any royal honour or dignity.

(k)   Information disclosure of which is likely to endanger health or safety.

(l)   Environmental information of certain sorts is exempted (to reduce the overlap with the Åarhus Convention).

(m) Information covered by legal professional privilege.

(n)   Trade secrets.

There is no exemption for the privacy of commercial dealings, and so the Act may entail a significant degree of disclosure for companies that do business with government.[123]

The form in which the information is communicated is at the discretion of the public authority, though where the requester has expressed a preference, the authority must give effect to that preference so far as is reasonably practical. A refusal to provide information must be accompanied by a statement of which exemption is invoked and why it applies, except where that reply would itself reveal information which is exempt from disclosure. Appeals against a refusal to supply information go to the Information Commissioner, who has power to require information (by information notice) and to insist on enforcement (by enforcement notice), as well as having powers of search and seizure. Where the public authority claims one of the public interest immunities but the Information Commissioner rules that the public interest requires disclosure, a complex and controversial provision applies: in essence, the public authority may insist on keeping the information secret so long as a sufficiently important official (typically a minister who is a member of the cabinet) signs a certificate ruling that the public interest requires it. In principle, this certificate could be challenged by judicial review. A further appeal lies from the Information Commissioner to the Information Tribunal. It remains to be seen how this will work out in practice, and whether any significant use is made by the Information Commissioner of the broader powers in the Act (the Commissioner need not wait for a formal application before acting, but has a general brief to ensure compliance with the Act).[124]

To facilitate the exercise of rights under the Act, each public authority must adopt, maintain and comply with a publication scheme for its information available to the public. Many of these schemes are available online.[125] The Department for Constitutional Affairs has produced various codes of practice to provide guidance on compliance with the legislation.

EVALUATION

When the histories of government in the early 21st century are written, the race to improve data surveillance capacities will be a notable feature. Also notable will be the neglect, bordering on contempt, for principles of law so recently imposed on

---

123 Turle, M, 'Free information, business threat?', (2004) 154 NLJ 1258.

124 Freedom of Information Act 2000 (UK), ss 50–54.

125 Information Asset Register (Web).

non-state bodies – for example, the principle that data gathered for one purpose shall not be used for different and incompatible purposes. Most notable of all will be the weakness of the reasons proffered for the change. 'Prevention of terrorism' is used to justify changes which have no obvious connection with terrorism, and have no demonstrable effect on it; 'efficiency of government' is put forward as an unquestionable good, without asking whether government can ever be too efficient for its citizens' good. The result is a massive assumption of power by government, with no clear statement of purpose or legal limitation, and with no effective redress should it be abused. Whether these extensive entitlements of the state against its citizens will be balanced, by similarly broad and effective entitlements of citizens to information from the state, hangs in the balance.[126]

FURTHER READING

Birkinshaw, P, *Freedom of Information – The Law, the Practice and the Ideal*, 3rd edn, 2001, London: Butterworths.

Birnhack, M and Elkin-Koren, N, 'The invisible handshake: The re-emergence of the state in the digital environment', (2003) 8 VJOLT 6 (Web).

Black, T, 'Taking account of the world as it will be: The shifting course of US encryption policy', (2001) 53 FCLJ 289 (Web).

Case, P, 'Confidence matters: The rise and fall of informational autonomy in medical law', (2003) 11 Med LR 208.

Cornford, T, 'The Freedom of Information Act 2000: Genuine or sham?', [2001] 3 WJCLI (Web).

Curtin, D, 'Citizens' fundamental right of access to EU information: An evolving digital *passepartout?*', (2000) 37 CML Rev 7.

Levi, M and Wall, D, 'Technologies, security and privacy in the post-9/11 European information society', (2004) 31 JLS 194.

Murray, J, 'Public key infrastructure, digital signatures and systematic risk', [2003] 1 JILT (Web).

Palfrey, T, 'The hidden legacy of Scott', (1999) 13 IRLCT 163.

Price, S, 'Understanding contemporary cryptography and its wider impact upon the general law', (1999) 13 IRLCT 95.

Reid, A and Ryder, N, 'For whose eyes only? A critique of the UK's Regulation of Investigatory Powers Act 2000', (2001) 10 ICTL 179.

Steele, J, 'Freedom of Information: Is privacy winning?', (2004) 13 Notts LJ 17.

---

126 Jones, N and Marchant, J, 'Here comes Big Brother', [2001] NS (22 September) 12; 'For whom the Liberty Bell tolls', [2002] Economist (31 Aug) 19 (Web).

CHAPTER 6

RIGHTS AND LIABILITIES ONLINE

This chapter discusses the law that is, or could be, encountered when acquiring a presence online, including simple access to the Internet, but concentrating on those acquiring their own web site. It also discusses the liabilities that may be encountered once that presence is established, such as if offence is given by the content of e-mail or web pages coming from that domain.

The problem is considered from the point of view of the commercial organisation acquiring a presence online. The chapter's scope is narrow: it focuses on legal aspects (even though they would by no means always be the main consideration); and within the law, the focus is on those aspects that are especially relevant to e-commerce. The division of the material is by legal criteria: acquiring hardware, software and relevant services and software, and the legal liabilities that may follow (for harassment, defamation or whatever). The case of the business is primary here; additional legislation may protect the consumer who enters into similar or analogous arrangements, and this legislation will be mentioned briefly.[1]

Much is said about the tasks to be performed and the procedures to be followed, and very little about the people who are to do them, or the management structures through which jobs are allocated. Employment law and corporate governance law are not e-commerce-specific, and are not discussed here. It should be borne in mind that some of those doing the work will be employees, whereas others will be freelances working under contracts for advice or for services; and this will be highly relevant if legal liability for their actions becomes an issue. It is particularly common in the ICT industry for individual workers to form small companies or partnerships, this status being in many ways preferable to that of employee, even if the work is substantially the same. In response, the UK tax authorities have introduced provisions deeming such workers to be 'employed' for tax and employers' contribution purposes.[2] However, for other purposes they are not so deemed, a point which will be relevant in considering employer responsibility for misbehaviour. This area is currently in flux, as negotiations continue over a proposed EU Agency Workers' Directive, which would require employers to treat independent contractors no less favourably than ordinary employees.

CONTRACTS TO ACQUIRE AN ONLINE PRESENCE

Hardware

A purchase of computer hardware is a sale of goods, for which there is a well-established legal framework as to obligations and remedies.[3] The obligations as to

---

1   For another survey of the issues here, see Burnett, R, 'The changing context of IT contracts', (2004) 154 NLJ 343.

2   Income Tax (Earnings and Pensions) Act 2003 (UK), ss 48–61; 'MPs put the boot into IR35', ZDNet UK, 30 July 2003 (Web).

3   Sale of Goods Act 1979 (UK), Sale of Goods Act 1893 (IE). Both Acts are significantly amended; amending legislation is referred to below where especially relevant.

the quality of goods supplied are stated in broad terms, which permit the courts to take into account a variety of factors: the general expectations which buyers are entitled to have of goods, specific things that may have been said (or not said) in relation to them, and any contractual document to which both parties assented. The obligations of the seller as to quality are as follows:

(a) Goods sold by description must conform to the description given. The parties should clarify precisely what is being sold, to avoid disputes later. Not every contract term describing the goods is part of the 'description' as a matter of law, though this point is usually relevant only to the precise remedy available on breach. The seller may sometimes be able to escape from liability for misdescription by arguing that the buyer did not rely on the description.[4]

(b) Goods must be fit for any particular purpose for which the seller knows the buyer means to use the goods. Again, the seller may sometimes be able to escape from liability by arguing that the buyer did not rely on the seller in this regard.[5]

(c) More generally, goods must meet a certain minimum standard of quality ('merchantable quality', in Ireland, 'satisfactory quality' in the UK). Goods do not conform with this standard if a reasonable buyer would not regard them as satisfactory; all relevant circumstances must be taken into account, including anything said about the goods. Price is also relevant: the seller may argue that low-priced goods can be of low quality.[6]

(d) Any further express obligations in the contract as to quality must also be respected.

An ordinary sale of goods is simply a contract to supply conforming goods. Any obligations as to installation, maintenance, repair or subsequent upgrading would be additional, and must be stipulated for specifically. If these obligations are substantial, then it may be possible to argue that the contract is no longer one for the sale of goods; however, the obligations in respect of the goods themselves are likely to be similar in any event.[7]

Some care needs to be taken over the formal contract between the parties, which should ideally include a statement of the obligations on both sides. The seller may wish to qualify or exclude obligations which would otherwise arise under the sale of goods legislation, or to insert an 'entire agreement' clause which will state that the contractual document is to be the sole authentic record of the parties' agreement, so that reference to other documents or to discussions between the parties cannot correct or qualify it. In general, commercial parties may agree whatever they wish, though terms which qualify obligations which would otherwise arise are interpreted narrowly, and liability for breach of the quality obligations or for misrepresentation can be excluded only where it is reasonable to do so.[8] Consumer law, if it applies, is

---

4   Sale of Goods Act 1979 (UK), s 13; Sale of Goods Act 1893 (IE), s 13, as inserted by Sale of Goods and Supply of Services Act 1980 (IE), s 10.

5   Sale of Goods Act 1979 (UK), s 14(3); Sale of Goods Act 1893 (IE), s 14(4), as inserted by Sale of Goods and Supply of Services Act 1980 (IE), s 10.

6   Sale of Goods Act 1979 (UK), s 14(2)–(2B), as inserted by Sale and Supply of Goods Act 1994 (UK), s 1; Sale of Goods Act 1893 (IE), s 14(2) and (3), as inserted by Sale of Goods and Supply of Goods Act 1980 (IE), s 10.

7   See, eg, Supply of Goods and Services Act 1982 (UK); Sale of Goods and Supply of Services Act 1980 (IE), s 39.

8   Unfair Contract Terms Act 1977 (UK), ss 6, 8, 17 and 20, as amended by Sale of Goods Act 1979 (UK), s 63 and Sched 2 para 19; Sale of Goods Act 1893 (IE), s 55, as inserted by Sale of Goods and Supply of Services Act 1980 (IE), s 46.

even more generous to buyers: all exclusions are subject to tests of reasonableness or good faith, and the basic obligations under the sale of goods legislation cannot be excluded at all.[9]

Remedies on breach by the seller can include a right for the buyer to reject and return the goods. The primary remedy is damages, which will include all loss naturally resulting from the breach, and additional losses that should reasonably have been foreseen before the event. Much of this can be anticipated at the contract stage: if the buyer has particular vulnerabilities, then the seller can be put on notice of them; or the seller may seek to limit its liability by excluding certain kinds of damage ('no liability for consequential loss' is a common stipulation), or by stating that its only liability is to replace defective equipment. Again, if consumer law applies, it prohibits most attempts to restrict consumer rights.

Access to the net and other 'information society services'

Access to the Internet is governed by a broad regulatory regime.[10] However, relatively little of this affects those purchasing this service, who simply deal on a contractual basis with those holding themselves out as internet service providers (ISPs). Suppliers of 'information society services' (or 'ISSs') are the subject of special provisions, which partly benefit them but also provide some protection for their customers. Provision of access to the Internet is the archetypical ISS, though the definition is in fact considerably wider. An ISS is a service which is provided:

(a) *at a distance*: that is, without the parties being simultaneously present; and

(b) *by electronic means*: that is, they are provided solely by electronic equipment for the processing and storage of data; and

(c) *at the individual request of the recipient*.

This includes providers of access to the net, but can also include just about any service provided over it. There is a statutory 'indicative list' of services which, for one reason or another, are considered not to fall within the definition. The list generally takes a conservative view of what is an ISS, excluding many services that fall within the literal definition (such as those provided by voice over the telephone) and many (though not all) of those which require the consumer to be in a particular place. Unfortunately, no particular logic to the exclusions is explained in the legislation.[11]

Where a particular service is considered to be an ISS, certain protections apply; some of these protect suppliers of the service (particularly the 'mere conduit' defence[12] and the general entitlement to rely on the laws of their home jurisdiction[13]), and others

---

9   In addition to the provisions referred to in the previous note, see Unfair Terms in Consumer Contracts Regulations 1999 (UK), SI 1999/2083; European Communities (Unfair Terms in Consumer Contracts) Regulations 1995 (IE), SI 1995/27.

10   For overviews, see van Duijevoorde, G and Oudejans, R, 'European competition law, the new e-communications framework, and the consumer in the information society: More than a virtual position?', (2003) 12 ICTL 179; Dodd, S, 'Competition law and the Internet', (2000) 6 BR 133; Smith, G, *Internet Law and Regulation*, 3rd edn, 2002, London: Sweet and Maxwell, Chapter 8.

11   See Directive 1998/34/EC, Art 1(2), as inserted by Directive 1998/48/EC, Art 2(a) and Annex V. For commentary, see Harrington, J, 'Information society services: What are they and how relevant is the definition?', (2001) 17 CLSR 174.

12   Below, p 140.

13   Moeral, L, 'The country-of-origin principle in the e-commerce directive', [2001] CTLR 184.

protect their customers. (The Directive also includes anti-spam provisions, but these are obsolete now that more general provision has been made for spam.[14]) The pro-customer provisions consist mainly of obligations to provide information:

(a) Advertising and other commercial communications sent to customers or potential customers need to be clearly labelled as such, with the person on whose behalf they are made clearly identifiable. Promotional offers, competitions and games must be clearly indicated as such, and their conditions clearly presented and easily accessible.[15]

(b) Suppliers of ISSs must make available 'easily, directly and permanently' the following information to recipients of their services: their name, geographic address and e-mail address, VAT identification number, and certain other details specific to particular types of service suppliers.[16]

(c) Before a contract is made with a customer, the ISS supplier must indicate the technical steps leading to the formation of the contract, whether the concluded contract will be accessible by the customer, the technical means for correcting errors before the placing of the order, and the languages in which the supplier is prepared to deal. Where there is a relevant code of conduct, the supplier must say how this may be consulted electronically. However, none of these restrictions apply where the contract is concluded exclusively by exchange of e-mail.[17]

(d) Any contract terms or general conditions provided must be made available in a way that allows the recipient to store and reproduce them.[18]

Where an order is placed by technological means (say, via a web site), then it must be acknowledged electronically (again, this does not apply to contracts concluded exclusively by exchange of e-mail).[19]

Where ISSs are supplied to a consumer, then the consumer may also have the benefit of the regulations on distance contracts, which impose different (and more extensive) informational requirements.[20] Trade bodies such as the Advertising Standards Association may also occasionally be able to provide a remedy for misrepresentation or sharp practice.[21]

As access to the Internet becomes a basic business necessity rather than an optional extra, the precise terms as to security and continuity of service may be a matter of intense negotiation. On the customers' side, some understanding of what is

---

14   Above, p 41.
15   Directive 2000/31/EC on certain legal aspects of information society services, Art 6; Electronic Commerce (EC Directive) Regulations 2002 (UK), SI 2002/2013, reg 7; European Communities (Directive 2000/31/EC) Regulations 2003 (IE), SI 2003/68, reg 8.
16   Directive 2000/31/EC, Art 5; Electronic Commerce (EC Directive) Regulations 2002 (UK), SI 2002/2013, reg 6; European Communities (Directive 2000/31/EC) Regulations 2003 (IE), SI 2003/68, reg 7.
17   Directive 2000/31/EC, Art 10; Electronic Commerce (EC Directive) Regulations 2002 (UK), SI 2002/2013, reg 9; European Communities (Directive 2000/31/EC) Regulations 2003 (IE), SI 2003/68, reg 13.
18   Directive 2000/31/EC, Art 10(3); Electronic Commerce (EC Directive) Regulations 2002 (UK), SI 2002/2013, reg 9(3); European Communities (Directive 2000/31/EC) Regulations 2003 (IE), SI 2003/68, reg 13(3).
19   Directive 2000/31/EC art 11; Electronic Commerce (EC Directive) Regulations 2002 (UK), SI 2002/2013, reg 11; European Communities (Directive 2000/31/EC) Regulations 2003 (IE), SI 2003/68, reg 14.
20   Below, p 262.
21   Eg, 'Ruling raps broadband definition', BBC News, 13 August 2004 (Web).

at stake if security or continuity is comprised will be necessary to determine how much they are prepared to pay. On the suppliers' side, much depends on their own position within the network, as no company will be very willing to guarantee a service over which they do not have control. An ISP which owns part of the national 'backbone' of telecommunications facilities is therefore in a stronger position to guarantee service than is an ISP who merely pays another ISP for access; if necessary, the customer may find it necessary to review the ISP's own contractual arrangements before accepting this additional risk.[22]

Similar issues apply to contracts for web services, which allow computing systems in different places to interact with one another. These services, which allow for interoperability between computers running very different software or indeed different operating systems, are increasingly necessary for integrating business activities with one another. A contract to provide web services will have to address questions such as performance standards, apportionment of certain risks, security and privacy.[23]

A contract for space on the web would have to address issues of the reliability of the service; likely amount of traffic and provision in the event that it temporarily reaches a higher level; provision of usage statistics and other data as the customer requires; back-ups and other disaster recovery provision; confidentiality and security. Few web sites worth visiting remain static; there must be adequate provision either for the ISP to refresh web site content, or to permit its customer to do so.[24]

The actual name of the web space as it appears on the Internet – the domain name – must itself be purchased from a name registrar. This is a straightforward transaction, and while there are some complex issues of law over rights to domain names,[25] there is very little difficulty in the ordinary case – though some consideration may need to be given to relevant trade mark rights.[26] Some care as to who, precisely, owns the domain name is sometimes required.[27] There seems to be a significant consumer protection problem in relation to the purchasing of domain names – there are many complaints of 'domain slamming' and other frauds, such as attempts to panic customers into buying particular domain names by claiming that others are about to do so.[28]

Provision of code: software and web design

Provision of code for applications and web pages is regulated by very little law beyond the general law of contract.[29] Given that a business may have little

---

22 McCrum, A, 'Getting started: ISPs and domain names', (2000) 11 PLC (2) 15.
23 Endeshaw, A, 'Web services and the law: A sketch of the potential issues', (2003) 11 IJLIT 251.
24 Kang, J, 'Web hosting', (2004) 12 ITLT 9. For litigation see, eg, *Youatwork Ltd v Motivano Ltd* [2003] EWHC 1047 Ch; Douglas, M, Charlton, A and Drew, J, 'Mandatory injunctions in IT disputes', (2004) 15 C&L 18.
25 Below, Chapter 7.
26 See generally Osborne, D and Palmer, S, 'Domain name registration strategy', (2002) 12 C&L (6) 18.
27 Maclachlan, A, 'Who owns your domain name?', (2000) 150 NLJ 700.
28 See, eg, 'Alert over invoices from "Domain Registry Services" ', Register, 27 July 2004 (Web); 'Domain slammer promises to turn over new leaf', Register, 5 January 2005 (Web).
29 For a general and comparative account, see Girot, C, *User Protection in IT Contracts*, 2001, The Hague: Kluwer Law International. For discussion, see Macdonald, E, 'Bugs and breaches', (2005) 13 IJLIT 118; Callaghan, D and O'Sullivan, C, 'Who should bear the cost of software bugs?', (2005) 21 CLSR 56.

knowledge of or experience with ICT, and its software provider may know equally little about its customer's business, a precise and comprehensive division of responsibility will be necessary. Code may be provided 'off the peg', or may have been written for the particular transaction. In practice, most cases will fall between these extreme cases. Even software purchased from a supplier will usually need to be configured for the needs of a particular user, and software written for a particular occasion is almost certain to contain recycled code which has its origins elsewhere.

Contracts for code generally

It is not always obvious how the law will categorise a contract for the provision of computer code. This will probably not matter in a case where the parties have taken the trouble to spell out every detail of their bargain; but where they have not, it may be necessary to decide what sort of a contract it is, and therefore what terms should be implied by law.[30] There are a number of possible contract models:

(a) The contract may constitute a contract for services, particularly if it calls for the supplier to write a good deal of code itself, or to perform other tasks beyond merely supplying pre-existing code; if so, an obligation to use reasonable care and skill may be implied by statute.[31] Where the buyer is paying for software to be written, a number of issues should be settled: the precise specification to which the software is to conform; how conformity to the specification is to be tested;[32] time limits for performance on both sides; ownership of the resulting code, both after the transaction is completed and during it (in case of disputes or insolvency); and liability for mishaps of one sort or another.[33] If necessary, provision must be made for training the customer's staff to use the new software.

(b) Some such contracts will be regarded as sale of goods; this is particularly likely to be so if the contract is one for the provision of software and hardware together, or of an entire system meant to achieve a particular result. This approach has also (controversially, and *obiter*) been taken where the contract is one for the provision of software to be delivered on a physical medium such as a CD: the CD is taken to be the goods.[34] If this is so, the sale of goods warranties of fitness for purpose and of merchantable/satisfactory quality will apply.

(c) Sale of computer code alone is almost certainly sale of an intellectual property right, but no warranty accompanies that by operation of law. The view has been expressed, *obiter*, that a fitness for purpose warranty might be implied into sales of software at common law, but there is little support for this.[35]

---

30 See generally Douglas, M and Pilling, B, 'Implied terms in computer contracts', (2001) 12 C&L (3) 28.

31 Supply of Goods and Services Act 1982 (UK), s 13; Sale of Goods and Supply of Services Act 1980 (IE), s 39.

32 Hughes, G, 'Reasonable design', [1999] 2 JILT (Web).

33 See generally Yates, J, 'Sympathy for the devil?', (2004) 15 C&L (2) 6. For litigation see, eg, *Cyprotex Discovery Ltd v University of Sheffield* [2004] EWCA Civ 380 (Web).

34 *St Albans City and District Council v International Computers Ltd* [1995] FSR 686 (Scott Baker J), [1996] 4 All ER 481 (CA). For a contrary view, see *Beta Computers (Europe) Ltd v Adobe Systems (Europe) Ltd* [1996] SLT 604. For discussion, see Hedley, S, 'Defective software in the Court of Appeal', [1997] CLJ 21.

35 For discussion, see White, A, 'Caveat vendor?', [1997] 3 JILT (Web).

(d) A common transaction is the sale of a licence to use software for a period. It is most unlikely that any kind of a warranty will be implied into such a transaction, though an express promise of suitability for a particular purpose might be enforceable.

(e) There may be a sale of a licence, but with an obligation on the seller to maintain, renew and upgrade it during the contract period. This so-called 'application service provision' (ASP) contract usually provides software for a fixed period, with an obligation to upgrade it as new versions become available, usually over the Internet with no need for intervention by the buyer.[36]

As discussed above in relation to hardware, the parties' obligations as to software will depend on the contract itself and what is said before entering into it; attention will be needed to the precise drafting and to principles of misrepresentation. The precise responsibilities of the parties, and provision for the more obvious risks, may need to be clarified. Whether the software was or was not produced specially for this transaction often turns out to be a crucial issue. In all cases, it is well recognised that the reliability of software can only really be ascertained by use; so statements that software is 'tried and tested' may well import a warranty that it is free of bugs.[37] However, if the customer pays for general purpose software or for software produced for someone else, then it is often hard to complain that it is not appropriate for their precise needs.[38]

Contracts for web site code

Web site provision or development raises similar problems. A statement of tasks to be performed and an allocation of responsibilities must be agreed.[39] In particular:

(a) The web site must be specified in some detail, so that it is clear what constitutes performance of the contract. If the completed site is meant to perform particular tasks, those tasks must be described in the contract.

(b) The same web site may look different when viewed with different browsers. If this matters, it may be better for the contract to specify which browser is being provided for.

(c) Provision of content for the site must be cleared up. Typically, a web site developer will know little of the detailed workings of its customer's business. Descriptive text will therefore have to come from the customer, as will photographs and other images unless they are entirely generic. Content provision by third parties will again need careful definition; appropriate warranties to accompany them may have to be drafted.[40]

---

36   Bickerstaff, R and Sourgnes, A, 'Application service providers – Negotiating the best deal', (2001) 12 PLC (May) 37; Morris, G, 'Digging … with ASPade, and other new tools', (2001) 11 C&L (6) 16.

37   See, eg, *SAM Business Systems Ltd v Hedley and Co* [2002] EWHC 2733 TCC (Web). On the facts, however, any warranty was excluded by an 'entire agreement' clause, which was held to be a reasonable one.

38   Eg, *Anglo Group plc v Winther Browne and Co Ltd* [2000] EWHC 127 Tech (Web).

39   See generally Holder, C, 'Outsourcing your web site – Contractual issues', [2002] EBL (July) 8. For litigation over whether the parties made a contract at all, see *Co-operative Group (CWS) Ltd v International Computers Ltd* [2003] EWHC 1 Tech (Web), noted by Atkins, R, (2004) 12 IJLIT (2) 157.

40   Brock, A, 'Web site content agreements', [2000] EBL (Dec) 6.

(d) If it is intended that consumers viewing the site should actually be able to buy goods or services online, then the full business and legal implications of this need to be worked out when the site is being planned. Any proper solution to this problem is likely to involve links to the seller's existing marketing and accounts systems, of which the web developer must acquire an adequate grasp.

(e) Any necessary permissions must be obtained, such as licences to use certain software, images, trade marks or databases, as well as registration to handle any personal data under the data protection legislation. It is unlikely that the average web development company can give detailed legal advice; any doubts on the need for permissions must be clarified somehow.[41]

(f) The contract might also require the developer to register the site with search engines.

(g) It must be clear who owns the intellectual property rights to the site's code.

(h) Provision may also be made for maintaining and enhancing the site, correcting errors, and adapting it for future developments, such as changes in the law.

Web site development contracts also typically make provision for variations, as customers develop new needs, or simply have second thoughts as work on the site proceeds.

On breach, the most likely remedy is damages for breach of contract, though ownership of any valuable intellectual property rights may also be in issue. An injunction is an unlikely remedy, at least where the object is to force the parties to work together co-operatively.[42]

A Software Transactions Act?

For what is increasingly an important area, the law has surprisingly little to say on sales of computer code and similar transactions. Many have suggested that a Software Transactions Act is now as obviously and as badly needed as the Sale of Goods Act, and that the law is seriously deficient in its provision here. While it is true that issues which are purely between commercial contracting parties should usually be left to them, it is not unreasonable to expect default provisions that should apply in the absence of contrary agreement, as well as provisions protecting third party rights and consumer interests.

However, the US experience is not encouraging. A new code on software licences was proposed by the American Law Institute in the mid-1990s (Art 2B of the Uniform Commercial Code). After furious lobbying and discussion, it was disowned by the Institute, then re-born as the Uniform Computer Information Transactions Act (UCITA), proposed by the National Conference of Commissioners on Uniform State Laws. A draft of this was eventually enacted (in slightly different ways) by Maryland and Virginia in 2000; four other states then passed legislation that was not simply incompatible with UCITA, but was expressly aimed against its supposedly pernicious effects. After the argument on its merits or demerits continued to rage,

---

41   For litigation see, eg, *Antiquesportfolio.com plc v Rodney Fitch & Co* [2001] FSR 23.

42   For litigation on assessment of damages see, eg, *Pegler Ltd v Wang (UK) Ltd* (1999) 70 Con LR 68; for litigation over the right to terminate the contract see, eg, *Peregrine Systems Ltd v Steria Ltd* [2005] EWCA Civ 239 (Web), discussed (2005) 16 C&L 18.

the National Conference of Commissioners eventually abandoned the project in July 2003.[43] This does not necessarily doom subsequent attempts, on either side of the pond, but clearly the strength of the interests involved will make agreement on a single text difficult.[44]

LIABILITY FOR SELF AND OTHERS: INTRODUCTION

Access to the Internet is a significant source of legal liability. The remainder of this chapter considers some of the more important ways in which legal liability may be incurred over the Internet (though the most important for e-business, the possibility of making contracts over the Internet, is postponed to a later chapter). The most important heads of liability are those for distributing and viewing pornography and liability for defamatory utterances; though in fact there is a wide swathe of offensive behaviours that may result in liability and which differ in their legal definition across the world's legal systems.

Liability for others

For an organisation of any size, the problems resulting from liability over the Internet are considerable, because of the significant risk that the organisation will be held legally responsible for the behaviour of those working for it or within it. Many of these risks will be remote from the core concerns of the organisation itself: often, the risk is not so much that those seeking to do their jobs will accidentally commit legal wrongs, as that employees and others will come to see Internet access as a perk, and will commit wrongs in the course of their own activities. Or again, organisations which sell access to the Internet may find that their customers use this access in ways which breach the law. All of this can be illustrated with material on intellectual property, considered above: an employer may find that it is liable for its employee's breach of the law in a case where it can be said to have 'authorised' that breach; and those who make Internet facilities available for others may be held complicit in breaches of the law if they took no steps to prevent them.[45]

Generalising about liability for others is an unsafe activity in the current state of the law. Actively assisting another in a breach of the law will incur liability, both civil and criminal, alongside the principal wrongdoer; but outside that clear case, the theories of liability are too various to permit of easy statement, and individual types of liability must be considered separately. Civil liability might flow from theories of

---

43 For drafts of the proposed legislation, see UCC Article 2b Licenses (Web) and Uniform Computer Information Transactions Act (Web). There is a considerable literature pro and con. See, eg, Tuomey, D, 'Weathering the commercial storm: Why everyone should steer clear of the UCITA', [2002] 1 JILT (Web); Clarke, L, 'Performance risk, form contracts and UCITA', (2001) 7 MTTLR 1 (Web); Neboyskey, D, 'A leap forward: Why states should ratify the UCITA', (2000) 52 FCLJ 793 (Web); Zohur, A, 'Acknowledging information technology under the civil code', (2004) 50 Loy LR 461.

44 For local commentary, see Rowland, D and Campbell, A, 'Supply of software: Copyright and contract issues', (2002) 10 IJLIT 23; Kawawa, N, 'Contract law relating to liability for injury caused by information in electronic form: Classification of contracts – a comparative study, England and the US', [2000] 1 JILT (Web).

45 Above, p 58.

agency, or authorisation, or vicarious liability; criminal liability may flow from notions of incitement, conspiracy, or abetting another's wrongdoing. Clearly, therefore, any sizable organisation will need a thorough audit of the legal risks to which it may be exposed as a result of Internet access, and this should be thoroughly integrated with its document retention policy and its codes of conduct for those who use its computing facilities.[46] The appropriateness and level of monitoring will also have to be considered. Individual web sites may require a similar audit.[47]

The closest that European law has to general provisions are those which attempt to isolate ISPs (and other providers of information society services) from liability for the wrongdoing of their customers. ISPs are not liable where they have been the 'mere conduit' of illegal material (that is, they have merely relayed, cached or hosted the material, with no knowledge of any wrongdoing); they are not responsible for the content of Internet traffic, provided that they act expeditiously if wrongdoing comes to their attention; and they have no duty to monitor that traffic. These are valuable general defences for telcos, universities and others who provide Internet facilities which can then be used without control.[48]

In the specific case of an organisation and its employees, any code of conduct for Internet use will have to be drawn up with care. If the employer expects to be able to dismiss employees for misconduct in relation to the Internet, some precision will be needed in specifying the conduct that is regarded as objectionable and the consequences that may follow. There will also have to be an adequate paper trail, so that it will be undeniable that the organisation's policy on the matter was brought to the attention of whichever employee it turns out to be relevant to. Policies on monitoring of Internet use must also be explicit and brought to the attention of those monitored, and (preferably) signed by the employees to show their consent to them. The law here is complex and so far largely untested in litigation, involving detailed issues of privacy, human rights and data protection law.[49] It has been a matter of concern across the whole of the EU.[50] A code of good practice for the UK has been produced by the Information Commissioner.[51]

When these liabilities are looked at from the point of view of the organisation – as this chapter does – there is a risk that they appear random or even absurd. From the business point of view, indeed, the liabilities have no more purpose or predictability than the weather or the movements of markets, against which the organisation must also seize what protection it can. However, this imposition of liability is very purposeful from a governmental perspective, and it is important not to lose sight of this. Liability is imposed on secondary parties because the alternative is to impose no effective liability at all. Governments do not have the will, the means or the money to keep an eye on every user of the Internet. But by imposing secondary liabilities on

---

46   Burden, K, '"E-risk" and insurance', (2000) 6 CLSR 258; Hamzah, Z, 'Strategies to manage legal risks and designing an effective risk management framework', (2002) 12 C&L (6) 37.

47   Cailloux, J and Roquilly, C, 'Legal security of web sites: Proposal for a legal audit methodology and a legal risks classification', [2001] 2 JILT (Web).

48   See especially Directive 2000/31/EC, Arts 3, 4, 12–15. For discussion, see Hörnle, J, 'Country of origin regulation in cross-border media', (2005) 54 ICLQ 89.

49   For general discussion, see Ford, M, 'Two conceptions of worker privacy', (2002) 31 ILJ 135; Oliver, H, 'E-mail and Internet monitoring in the workplace', (2002) 31 ILJ 321.

50   See particularly *Working Document on the Surveillance of Electronic Communications in the Workplace*, Article 29 Data Protection Working Party, May 2002 (Web).

51   The Employment Practices Data Protection Code: Part 3: Monitoring at Work (Web).

those who grant access to it, a certain level of control is exercised: ISPs and employers become surrogate police officers, insisting on rules which the police themselves are in no position to enforce. The discipline thereby imposed can be harsh: students can be expelled, or employees sacked, for offences that might merit only a warning or a minor penalty if brought to the attention of magistrates.[52] And the signs are that it is only too easy to frighten intermediaries into restricting Internet content to that to which someone else objects.[53] Those who provide Internet services for others are effectively forced to watch over those others as well.[54]

PORNOGRAPHY

The desire of some Internet users to circulate pornographic images has had a surprisingly large impact on its development. It has significantly increased the demand for bandwidth: high-quality images can involve considerable quantities of data. The notorious difficulties of policing the Internet have made it a natural haven for those who wish their activities to escape the attention of the authorities. At times, the needs of pornographers and the considerable profits some of them make have proved powerful spurs to technological development, particularly in the creation of online stores. And companies which have made considerable investments in new communications technologies – such as 3G mobile phones – are inevitably driven to consider the marketing of pornography as one way of exploiting the technology they have so expensively acquired.[55]

The current moral panic over Internet pornography is therefore unsurprising. Yet the almost universal public distaste does not reflect any consensus on what pornography is, on who needs to be protected from it, or why. Perceptions of what is 'pornographic' differ sharply between individuals, as well as between nations; justifications for legal intervention differ starkly, from religious injunctions, to arguments based on public taste, to arguments based on harm supposedly done in its making or consumption (arguments which tend to be solid enough when children are involved but rather nebulous otherwise). In fact, the issue over what images should be banned is really at least three issues, which should almost certainly receive very different answers: (i) what images should children be prevented from seeing, (ii) what images should adults be prevented from seeing if they have not sought out indecent images, and (iii) what images should adults not be allowed to seek out at all. It can be seen that the problem could largely be alleviated by some system of zoning, so that Internet pornography becomes something that must be deliberately sought out and cannot be merely stumbled across.[56] But recent debate has been dominated by pornography recording sexual abuse of children, and which would very probably not have been made at all but for the chance to distribute it over the net; zoning is obviously no answer to this.[57]

---

52 For discussion, see Morris, E, 'Sacked for surfing', (2005) 149 Sol Jo 16.
53 See, eg, Nas, S, 'The Multatuli Project – ISP notice and take down', October 2004 (Web).
54 See above, p 9.
55 See, eg, 'Wireless porn set to be $1bn market,' ZDNet UK, 26 October 2004 (Web).
56 See, eg, Furlow, C, 'Erogenous zoning on the cyber-frontier', (2000) 5 VJOLT 7 (Web).
57 For criminological issues, see Taylor, M and Quayle, E, *Child Pornography – An Internet Crime*, 2003, Sussex: Brunner-Routledge; Burke, A, Sowerbutts, S, Blundell, B and Sherry, M, 'Child pornography and the Internet: Policing and treatment issues', (2002) 9 PPL 79.

Methods of control

Part of the air of panic surrounding the whole question of Internet pornography distribution reflects the difficulty of control – for who, other than the person actually consuming the pornography, has any idea that an offence is being committed? Desperation at this has even led to the circulation of a virus to seek it out and send reports on those found to possess it – though this approach has proved controversial (to put it mildly) and has not had much effect.[58] It also appears that an international collaboration between police forces produced a fake child porn web site to ensnare potential paedophiles.[59] The more effective methods turn out to be rather tamer; various points or methods of control have emerged, in a somewhat irregular pattern.

Communications providers have found themselves under strong pressure to prevent their customers from accessing pornographic sites or downloading pornographic images. An early wake-up call here came in the form of the conviction of Felix Somm, President of CompuServ Germany, before a Munich criminal court in May 1998, for wilful distribution of pornographic material.[60] While that conviction was reversed on appeal, the prosecution having conceded that there was no practical means then available for an ISP to distinguish pornographic from other traffic, nonetheless the pressure on ISPs was considerable. Attention has recently focused on an attempt by BT to catalogue pornographic sites and to block their customers' access to them with its 'Cleanfeed' filter. At one point, BT claimed to be preventing some 20,000 attempts per day to access porn (the company has about 2 m customers for its Internet services);[61] however, the validity of that statistic was rapidly called into question;[62] the overall success of the scheme is currently unclear. Meanwhile, as advances in mobile phone technology make the downloading of high-grade images relatively easy, concern is increasing at the widening access to porn this represents,[63] and mobile operators have introduced a new code of practice as a first step.[64]

If effective filtering technology can be developed, it would not merely be of interest to ISPs, but also to public and private organisations of various sorts. There has been much enthusiasm for the general notion of filtering, but actual implementation is another matter, and there has been much opposition on human rights grounds.[65] The legal difficulties are considerable; the technological ones worse.[66] Classifying and cataloguing sites as pornographic is labour-intensive work, and is a huge operation if the number of sites is to be large enough to make a significant impact; and there is no defence against sites which simply change location to avoid the filter.

---

58   See 'Virus Name: VBS/Pedpoly@MM', McAfee Virus Information Library (Web); 'Computer virus tackles child porn', BBC News, 30 May 2001 (Web).
59   'Police in paedo porn sting', Register, 18 December 2003 (Web).
60   Bender, G, '*Bavaria v Felix Somm*: The pornography conviction of the former CompuServ manager', (1998) 1 IJCLP (Web).
61   'Extent of child net porn revealed', BBC News, 20 July 2004 (Web).
62   'BT on child porn stats', Register, 22 July 2004 (Web).
63   See, eg, 'Vodafone blocks access to porn', BBC News, 2 July 2004 (Web).
64   UK code of practice for the self-regulation of new forms of content on mobiles, 19 January 2004 (Web).
65   Garry, P, 'The flip side of the 1st amendment; a right to filter', [2004] MSLR 57.
66   Maravilla, C, 'The virtual Red Light District: Filtration software and the zoning of the Internet', (2001) 5 WVJOLT 2 (Web); 'A starting point: Legal implications of Internet filtering', OpenNet Initiative, September 2004 (Web).

Supervision by employers of their staff has placed something of a brake on those who would use their work computers to look for porn; this approach has netted some very high-profile offenders indeed.[67] Publicly threatening firms with prosecution for failing to curb their employees has seemed to some a useful approach.[68] To others, this is the most objectionable part of the entire anti-pornography campaign. Many organisations seem to be undiscriminating in the images they are objecting to; it is odd that an image which can lawfully be bought over the counter at a newsagent's becomes a sacking offence when looked at over the net. A sense of perspective seems to be lacking.[69]

Hotlines are available, so that pornographic sites can be reported by concerned net surfers. In the UK, the principal hotline is run by the Internet Watch Foundation.[70] This body was formed in 1996 at the initiative of ISPs, and its close links with ISPs mean that it may be able to have pages removed or even whole sites shut down. Whether it is appropriate for a private body, effectively indeed an industry body, to be acting as an unaccountable censor, is a matter of opinion.

An unexpected but nonetheless frequently effective mode of control is through credit cards and other forms of payment used online. This is increasingly being used in a preventative manner. Banks are in any event unhappy at dealing with pornographers, who often seem more prone to fraud than other types of trader;[71] many banks are anxious to avoid the use of their cards for such transactions,[72] even to the extent of cancelling cards held by known purchasers of porn.[73] Credit card numbers have also proved important after the event, providing strong evidence of criminal involvement. In 1999, the US Postal Inspection Service seized a Texas web server that had been selling child porn to customers across the world. Evidence that computers belonging to particular suspects had visited the site would probably not have carried much weight; after all, the visit could have been accidental, or someone else might have been using the computer in question. However, where it is clear from the server logs that the visitor had downloaded pornography after giving the suspect's credit card number to effect payment, the number of innocent explanations begins to decline rapidly. While the overall number of convictions resulting from the seizure of the Texas server does not appear to be impressive, nonetheless it clearly indicates one route by which distribution of pornography can be controlled.[74]

Enforcement of controls on Internet pornography imposes unique challenges. Detection is extremely difficult. Even where a clear suspect presents himself, proving the case involves difficult technical and legal issues.[75] Complaints by the police that

67   Eg, 'BoI chief resigns over access of "adult" web site', Sunday Business Post, 30 May 2004. For some less famous cases, see Pay v Lancashire Probation Service [2004] ICR 187 and Council for the Regulation of Health Care Professionals v General Dental Council [2005] EWHC 87 (Web).
68   'Work porn risk for businesses', BBC News, 17 May 2004 (Web).
69   For discussion, see 'We have become bigger hypocrites than Victorians', Irish Times, 1 June 2004; 'Internet porn: Guilty till proven innocent', ZDNet, 1 September 2004 (Web).
70   See Internet Watch Foundation home page (Web).
71   'Third-party bill payers won't cover sex items, cite fraud risk', Cincinnati Enquirer, 8 May 2003 (Web).
72   'Banks urged to ban credit card use for Internet porn', Guardian, 3 July 2004 (Web).
73   'Paedophiles face credit card blacklist', Register, 9 June 2004 (Web).
74   On this case, see also above, pp 121–22.
75   Cox, D, 'Litigating child pornography and obscenity cases in the Internet age', (1999) 4 JTLP 2 (Web); Sommer, P, 'Evidence in Internet paedophilia cases', [2002] CTLR 176.

Internet porn has given them significant additional burdens, without any significant new resources being made available, are loud and long.[76]

Detailed consideration is now given to the law in England and Wales, and in Ireland, before turning to the international scene.[77]

England and Wales

The current law is a mess, with a wide variety of separate offences (modified more or less to allow for the Internet) restrained by some very general defences, in the form of the 'mere conduit' defences for suppliers of net services,[78] and human rights guarantees of respect for privacy and freedom of expression.[79] Offences related to obscenity are various, and include publishing 'stories told in pictures' in such a way as to corrupt children;[80] or sending indecent or obscene matter over a public electronic communications network.[81] There are also offences specifically connected with the abuse of children in the making of the original images.[82]

An important offence, evidently meant to restrict pornography to zones of privacy rather than to outlaw it entirely, is the Indecent Displays (Control) Act 1981, which prohibits public displays of indecent matter: 'Any matter which is displayed in or so as to be visible from any public place shall, for the purposes of this section, be deemed to be publicly displayed'; and a public place means 'any place to which the public have or are permitted to have access (whether on payment or otherwise) while that matter is displayed'. There are defences for art galleries and museums, and for displays to adults who are paying to see the indecent display and where certain steps have been taken to exclude those under 18.[83] The Act is pre-Internet. However, if a court were to accept that web sites may be 'places' to which web surfers 'have access', then there seems to be no difficulty in applying it to indecent web sites. Even if that point were not accepted, nonetheless it would be hard to deny its application to publicly available web browsers, such as those in public libraries or cybercafés.

The principal pornography offences cover a variety of activities – distribution or possession of obscene matter, with separate offences of distribution or possession of child pornography – and to these I now turn.

---

76 'Out of control', Spectator, 19 April 2003, p 18; 'UK police tackle mounting Internet porn caseload', Register, 22 April 2005 (Web).
77 For the Scottish position, see Civic Government (Scotland) Act 1982, ss 51 and 52A; *Longmuir v HM Advocate* 2000 SCCR 447; *Arnott v McFadyen* 2002 SCCR 96; *McGaffney v HM Advocate* 2004 SCCR 384.
78 Above, p 140.
79 For unsuccessful attempts to invoke human rights principles here, see *R v Bowden* [2001] QB 88; *R v Perrin* [2002] EWCA Crim 747 (Web).
80 Children and Young Persons (Harmful Publications) Act 1955 (E&W and Sc).
81 Communications Act 2003 (UK), s 127 (this provision is not fully in force at the time of writing).
82 Sexual Offences Act 2003 (E&W), ss 47–51.
83 Indecent Displays (Control) Act 1981 (E&W, Sc); much of the detail is amended by subsequent legislation.

Obscenity

The main offence, under the Obscene Publications Act 1959, relates to 'obscene' articles. An article is obscene 'if its effect ... is, if taken as a whole, such as to tend to deprave and corrupt persons who are likely, having regard to all relevant circumstances, to read, see or hear the matter contained or embodied in it'.[84] The offence has two limbs: publication of the obscene articles, or possession with a view to publication for gain.

A defendant can be said to 'publish' an article if he or she '(a) distributes, circulates, sells, lets on hire, gives, or lends it, or ... offers it for sale or for letting on hire; or (b) in the case of an article containing or embodying matter to be looked at or a record, shows, plays or projects it, or, where the matter is data stored electronically, transmits that data'.[85] This is plainly a broad offence.

(a) Making obscene matter available for others to download, by putting it on a web site, is plainly within that definition. Making an image available for downloading is 'showing' it, whether or not it is also 'distributing' it.[86] And where a defendant based in England uploaded obscene images to a US server, from where they were downloaded by a police officer in London, there were two 'publications': namely, the uploading and the downloading.[87]

(b) Providing a hyperlink to another server, where obscene matter may be downloaded, is not so plainly caught – it is hard to say that the defendant 'distributes', 'shows' or 'transmits' data which never goes via his server. However, if it is made sufficiently clear what the link will lead to, providing the link may be said to aid and abet any use of it, and so there is secondary liability for the offence committed by the controller of the site linked to.

(c) Actual downloading is not obviously caught, unless it can be said that someone who deliberately produces an image on their own screen 'shows, plays or projects it'. As the offence is so clearly aimed at distributors, it would be odd if it were held to catch also those who merely look.

Possession, ownership or control of obscene articles is within the offence if it is with a view to publication for gain.[88] It is unclear whether someone in the jurisdiction who controls data held on a foreign machine can be said to be 'controlling' it within the jurisdiction. It is also unclear whether merely viewing an obscene image over the Internet amounts to 'possession, ownership or control' of it; certainly any such viewer is in a position to copy it if they wish, and in that sense can be said to 'possess' or 'control' it, but this does not appear to be the situation at which the section was aimed.

There is no defence that the defendant does not personally regard the image as obscene or corrupting, and it is irrelevant whether the defendant intended to corrupt anyone else. However, there is a defence if the defendant can show that he never examined the article in question and had no reasonable cause to suspect that he was

---

84 Obscene Publications Act 1959 (E&W), s 1(1).
85 *Ibid*, s 1(3), as amended by Criminal Justice and Public Order Act 1994, s 168(1) and Sched 9 para 3, and Broadcasting Act 1990, ss 162(1), 203(3), and Sched 21.
86 *R v Fellows, R v Arnold* [1997] 2 All ER 548.
87 *R v Waddon* (Court of Appeal, 6 April 2000).
88 Obscene Publications Act 1964 (E&W), s 1.

in breach of the Act.[89] This is clearly a useful defence for commercial web site hosters (who obviously 'possess' the site files for gain, but very probably have no idea of their contents). Those who supply Internet services of any sort may also benefit from the general 'mere conduit' defence.[90] However, neither defence will apply if obscene matter is brought to their attention and they do nothing.

Penalties for breach of the section can be up to £5,000 and six months' imprisonment on conviction before magistrates, or an unlimited fine and three years' imprisonment before a jury. Any profits made from the breach can also be seized, whether made in the UK or abroad, and whether or not any foreign laws were broken.[91]

Indecent images of children

A separate offence, under the Protection of Children Act 1978, relates to indecent photographs or pseudo-photographs of children. 'Indecent' is not defined. 'Child' means someone under 18, though pseudo-photographs which give the predominant impression that their subject is under 18 are caught whatever the actual age. Four activities in relation to such articles are criminalised: making them, distributing or showing them, possessing them, and advertising them. The offence can be committed by companies as well as by people.

'Photograph' is an unfortunate word here, as it suggests that a particular technology is being targeted rather than a particular type of conduct. In fact, the courts found no difficulty in extending the notion of 'photograph' to include graphic images from which photographs could be reproduced,[92] and subsequent amendments have extended the Act's scope even further. 'Photograph' now includes a film, a copy of a photograph or film, a photograph comprised in a film, a film negative, and any form of video recording; it also includes data stored on a computer disc or by other electronic means which is capable of conversion into a photograph. 'Pseudo-photograph' means an image, whether made by computer graphics or otherwise, which appears to be a photograph, and includes a copy of a pseudo-photograph, as well as data stored on a computer disc or by other electronic means which is capable of conversion into a pseudo-photograph.[93] There is a notable contrast here with the US law, which insists on harm to children in the making of the image, and so does not penalise production of images that merely *appear* to involve child abuse.[94]

The offence is committed by taking or making the photograph or pseudo-photograph, or distributing or showing it. 'Distributing' it includes parting with possession of it to another, or exposing or offering it for sale to another.[95] This is

---

89   Obscene Publications Act 1959 (E&W), s 2(5); Obscene Publications Act 1964 (E&W), s 1(3).
90   Above, p 140.
91   *R v McKinnon* [2004] EWCA Crim 395, [2004] 2 Cr App R(S) 234.
92   *R v Fellows, R v Arnold* [1997] 2 All ER 548.
93   Protection of Children Act 1978 (E&W), s 7, as amended by Criminal Justice and Public Order Act 1994 s 84(3).
94   Peysakhovich, S, 'Virtual child pornography: Why American and British laws are at odds with each other', (2004) 14 ALJST 799.
95   Protection of Children Act 1978 (E&W), s 1, as amended by Criminal Justice and Public Order Act 1994, ss 84 and 168, and Sexual Offences Act 2003, s 139 and Sched 6, para 24.

broad enough to catch anyone who distributes child pornography images over the Internet; it also seems broad enough to catch many who download it, though the limits are not absolutely clear. Where the defendant downloads an image, deliberately saving the image file on the hard drive for later retrieval, he is clearly making a copy of a pseudo-photograph, and the offence is committed.[96] Controversially, it has been held that the same result follows even when the defendant does not save a permanent copy. In a case where the defendant deliberately viewed a pornographic site, it was held that he had deliberately 'made' a pseudo-photograph, and it was irrelevant whether he had the intent or the technical skill to save that image for later use.[97] Matters would be quite otherwise, however, if the defendant merely stumbled on the images without making a deliberate search.

The offence is also committed by 'possession' of the indecent images, if this is with a view to their being distributed or shown to others. It seems to be accepted that storing a data file which is a pseudo-photograph can constitute possession; but the fact that the file exists is not enough in itself, as intent to possess must be shown. If the defendant viewed an indecent image and deliberately saved a copy, then the offence is committed. But computers often save files without a direct command from their operators, and so there can be innocent explanations for the presence of an indecent file, as where it was sent as an unrequested e-mail attachment, or merely seen transiently while browsing the web. In those circumstances, there would be no intent to possess the data file, and so no offence of possession.[98]

Possession only attracts the Act's penalties if the defendant meant to distribute or show the image to others. In passing, however, note the lesser offences of mere possession of child pornography, where no intent to distribute is required. The defences to this lesser crime are as for the more serious offence, and also that 'the photograph or pseudo-photograph was sent to [the defendant] without any prior request made by him or on his behalf and that he did not keep it for an unreasonable time'. The penalty can be an unlimited fine and/or five years' imprisonment on conviction by a jury.[99]

Defences are available for those who can prove that they had legitimate reasons for their conduct, or who had not themselves seen the images and did not know, nor had any cause to suspect, that they were indecent.[100] If the defendant knows that the image is indecent, he may nonetheless be entitled to the defence if he has no reason to think it is an image of a child.[101] In addition, ISPs charged with aiding and abetting the offence can plead that they were 'mere conduits' for the illegal images.[102] Making an indecent image can also be justified on the ground that it was necessary for the 'prevention, detection or investigation of crime, or for the purposes of criminal proceedings, in any part of the world'.[103]

---

96   *R v Bowden* [2001] QB 88; *Atkins v DPP* [2000] 1 WLR 1427.
97   *R v Smith* [2002] EWCA Crim 683, [2003] 1 Cr App Rep 212.
98   *Atkins v DPP* [2000] 1 WLR 1427.
99   Criminal Justice Act 1988 (E&W), s 160, as amended.
100 Protection of Children Act 1978 (E&W), s 1(4), as amended by Criminal Justice and Public Order Act 1994, s 84.
101 *R v Collier* [2004] EWCA Crim 1411.
102 Above, p 140.
103 Protection of Children Act 1978 (E&W), s 1B, inserted by Sexual Offences Act 2003, s 46.

Penalties are fairly severe. Magistrates can impose a fine of £5,000 or up to 6 months' imprisonment, or both; conviction before a jury brings an unlimited fine and/or up to 10 years' imprisonment. The Court of Appeal has developed a classification of images to assist in determining the severity of offences, ranging from level one (erotic posing with no sexual activity) to level five (sadism or bestiality); in cases involving large numbers of images, strict guidelines must be followed to ensure that they are classified fairly.[104] Other factors are also taken into account: such as the defendant's degree of responsibility for the original abuse, the extent of any commercial gain, and the extent of distribution. The penalty would take all these factors into account; prison would usually be justified by evidence of distribution, or possession of a large amount of level 2 material, or a small amount of level 3 material.[105] The sentence can also include a restraining order forbidding the defendant from accessing the Internet and other relevant technologies.[106]

Ireland

The Irish law on obscenity generally is somewhat antique. Most obviously applicable to the Internet is the offence of sending 'any message or other matter which is grossly offensive or of an indecent, obscene or menacing character' over any telecommunications system.[107] This provision seems, however, to be aimed at those who are engaged in harassment, and it is not entirely clear whether it applies where the message was actually requested by the recipient. The offence carries a penalty of €1,015 and/or 12 months' imprisonment on summary conviction, €63,487 and/or 5 years before a jury.[108] Pornography circulated on CD-ROM and involving moving images may possibly be caught by the Video Recordings Act 1989, which imposes a system of classification of content.[109] There are also the old and highly uncertain common law offences of obscene libel, outraging public decency, and conspiring to corrupt public morals; though we can expect that any attempt to revive those ancient offences will result in strong challenges based on constitutional freedoms and human rights.

Child pornography is, however, dealt with by specific modern legislation. 'Child pornography' is extensively defined, in terms which include any depiction of sexual activity by a child, or by someone appearing to be a child. A 'child' is someone under 17; anyone who appears to be a child or has been depicted as such, is presumed to be a child unless the contrary is shown. The core definitions are vague, but probably wide enough to cover files sent over the Internet; for example, a 'visual representation' of prohibited content includes 'any document', and 'document' includes 'any tape, computer disk or other thing on which data capable of conversion into any such document is stored'.[110] There are two offences.

---

104 *R v Thompson* [2004] EWCA Crim 669 (Web).

105 *R v Oliver* [2002] EWCA Crim 2766, [2003] 2 Cr App R (S) 64.

106 Eg, *R v Collard* [2004] EWCA Crim 1664.

107 Post Office (Amendment) Act 1951 (IE), s 13(1), as substituted by Postal and Telecommunications Services Act 1983 (IE), Sched 4 and as amended by Postal and Telecommunications Services (Amendment) Act 1999 (IE), s 7.

108 Postal and Telecommunications Services Act 1983 (IE), s 4.

109 Video Recordings Act 1989 (IE), especially s 1(1) (definition of 'video recording' and 'video work').

110 Child Trafficking and Pornography Act 1998 (IE), s 2.

(a) The *distribution* offence catches anyone who knowingly produces, distributes, prints, publishes, imports, exports, sells or shows any child pornography, or who possesses it for the purpose of distributing, publishing, exporting, selling or showing it. Advertising, encouraging or facilitating such activity by others is also within the offence. The offence is not absolute, but can only be committed knowingly. The penalty is €1,904 and/or 12 months' imprisonment on summary conviction, or an unlimited fine and/or 14 years' imprisonment on conviction before a jury.[111] Sentences have included orders forbidding access to the Internet for lengthy periods.[112]

(b) The *possession* offence is committed simply by knowing possession of child pornography. There is a defence if it can be shown that the possession was for the purpose of *bona fide* research. The penalty is €1,904 and or 12 months imprisonment on summary conviction, or €6,348/or 5 years' imprisonment on conviction before a jury.[113]

As both offences can only be committed 'knowingly', innocent third parties such as ISPs will be safe so long as they act on whatever knowledge they have, and it will be unnecessary to rely on the European 'mere conduit' defence.

United States

Pornography was already a much litigated area of US law even before the Internet. Pre-Internet authority established that 'obscene' communications were not protected by the constitutional guarantee of freedom of speech. 'Obscenity' was defined as referring to communications that were patently offensive, were aimed at prurient interests, and were without redeeming social value. It was accepted that individual communities might render different judgments in applying this test; each community was entitled to apply its own standards, even though this meant that what was 'obscene' varied across different states.[114] It follows that pornographers can be prosecuted by local standards in any state where their products are downloaded, and if necessary can be extradited from the state where they happen to be.[115] There has been some judicial disquiet at this, as it means that the entire Internet is governed by the values of the most conservative states; there has, however, been no noticeable support for the view that Internet users should be regarded as the relevant 'community', rather than the traditional approach of looking for geographical communities.[116]

Much recent legislation has attempted to go beyond this, to protect children even in cases where no 'obscenity' is involved; however, these statutes have fallen foul of important constitutional values. The Child Pornography Protection Act 1996

---

111 *Ibid*, s 5. On sentencing, see also Conroy, B, 'Sentencing under the Child Pornography and Trafficking Act 1998', (2004) 14 ICLJ (2) 8.

112 *DPP v Muldoon* (Court of Criminal Appeal, 7 July 2003).

113 Child Trafficking and Pornography Act 1998 (IE), s 6.

114 *Miller v California* 413 US 15 (21 June 1973) (Web).

115 Eg, *US v Thomas* 74 F 3d 701 (6th Ct, 29 January 1996), cert denied 117 S Ct 74 (7 October 1996).

116 Karniel, Y and Wismonsky, H, 'Pornography, community and the Internet: Freedom of speech and obscenity on the Internet', (2004) 30 RCTLJ 105; Walters, L and DeWitt, C, 'Obscenity in the digital age: The re-evaluation of community standards', (2005) 10 Nexus 59; Whitehead, R, ' "Carnal knowledge" is the key: A discussion of how non-geographic *Miller* standards apply to the Internet', (2005) 10 Nexus 49.

('CPPA') attempted to broaden the range of child pornography prohibited by law. The earlier precedents were encouraging, as it had been held that child pornography was by definition obscene.[117] But the Supreme Court, while recognising that the abuse involved in the production of child pornography justified that inroad into the right of free speech, refused to apply this to 'virtual' pornography which did not in fact portray actual children. It followed that much of CPPA was invalid.[118] Congress returned to the issue with the Prosecutorial Remedies and Other Tools to end the Exploitation of Children Today Act 2003 ('PROTECT'); it is hard to see how it can be valid if CPPA was invalid, but the matter has yet to be determined.[119] Again, an attempt was made in the Communications Decency Act 1996 ('CDA') to criminalise material which was 'indecent' when viewed by children, even though it was not 'obscene'. However, the Supreme Court held this to be unconstitutional: it went far beyond protecting children from sexual harm, and too far towards imposing on adults standards designed for children.[120] Congress responded with the Child On-line Protection Act 1998 ('COPA'), more narrowly drafted legislation towards the same end. This too was quickly challenged and, at the time of writing, proceedings under it are restrained pending a full determination of its constitutionality.[121]

International approaches

It seems hopeless to expect international co-operation to go very broadly here, given the huge differences in standards on what constitutes pornography – from the stricter Islamic nations which condemn almost any gratuitous display of bare flesh, to Nordic nations which are reluctant ever to describe adult nudity as pornographic. The suspicion that some nations are using complaints of 'pornography' to suppress political dissent does not encourage international co-operation either. Even on child pornography, where the best chance of unanimity might be expected, the drafters of the Convention on Cybercrime felt it necessary to cut individual nations plenty of slack, providing a broad definition of 'child pornography' but allowing signatory nations to modify much of it.[122]

An EU Framework Decision requires legislation on production, distribution, dissemination, transmission, supply and possession of child pornography. Member States must bring themselves into conformity with the decision by 20 January 2006. A certain amount of leeway is given for different approaches, such as how to treat images of those over 18 but appearing to be younger, or material produced entirely for personal private use, or possessed without intent to distribute.[123] A further

---

117 *New York v Ferber* 458 US 747 (2 July 1982).

118 *Ashcroft v Free Speech Coalition* 535 US 234 (16 April 2002). See Loewy, A, 'Taking free speech seriously: The United States Supreme Court and virtual child pornography', SSRN, November 2002 (Web); Kreston, S, 'Defeating the virtual defense in child pornography prosecutions', (2004) 4 JHTL 49 (Web).

119 Kosse, S, 'Virtual child pornography – A US update', (2004) 9 Comms L (2) 39.

120 *Reno v ACLU* 521 US 844 (26 June 1997).

121 Kosse, S, 'Try, try again: Will Congress ever get it right?', (2004) 38 URLR 721; Nist, T, 'Finding the right approach: A constitutional alternative for shielding kids from harmful materials online', (2004) 65 OSLJ 451; Gearan, J, 'Preliminary injunction against enforcement of Child Online Protection Act upheld', (2005) 38 Suff ULR 741.

122 Convention on Cybercrime, Art 9 (Web).

123 Council Framework Decision on combating the sexual exploitation of children and child pornography (2004/68/JHA), 22 December 2003 (Web).

decision is planned for the promotion of hotlines and other means to assist removal of harmful content from the Internet.[124]

PERSONAL SAFETY AND FREEDOM FROM HARASSMENT

Individuals may be targeted over the Internet with an eye to harassment, bullying or worse. In many cases, perpetrator and victim may come from the same area, and may indeed already know each other offline; in others, perpetrator and victim meet online.

Child victims

The Internet has proved a powerful tool for bullying and deception.[125] Virtual chat rooms especially are likely sites for abuse. Cases have often included bizarre elements, such as where one teenager invented a false personality which he used to persuade another to attempt to murder him.[126] More mundane, and much more common, are attempts at sexual entrapment of one sort or another.[127] Public anxiety at these cases is acute, but enforcement is difficult.

The substantive evils here – child abduction and sexual abuse – were, of course, criminalised long ago. The trend of legal reforms here has been to increase the scope of preparatory offences, to allow police intervention at an earlier stage. This must be seen alongside practices such as covert police presences in chat rooms; the preparatory offences justify action based on what appears on the net itself. Traditional preparatory offences such as incitement and attempt are of some value.[128] The UK has extended this, so that incitement which occurs in the UK is punishable there even if what is incited was to occur abroad.[129] The UK has also recently introduced an offence of meeting a child (under 16) after communication. This offence is aimed at 'grooming' – that is, preparing the minor to accept that sex with the defendant would be natural and appropriate – but in fact is merely defined as meeting the minor following communication on at least two occasions, with intent to commit one of certain sexual offences.[130] It remains to be seen how satisfactory this will turn to be. The offence relies entirely on proof of intent – the communications themselves will in many cases appear quite innocent – and the question of what level of proof is required will be crucial.

The secondary offences of assisting abusers require proof of intent, and so those who provide Internet facilities are safe so long as they act on any evidence of wrongdoing. The 'mere conduit' defence also applies.[131] Nonetheless, pressure on

---

124 *Establishing a Multiannual Community Programme on Promoting Safer Use of the Internet and New Online Technologies*, 12 March 2004 (Web).

125 Eg, 'Modern bullies are seeking victims through cyberspace', Times, 25 September 2004.

126 'Boy, 14, makes an Internet appointment to be murdered', Times, 29 May 2004.

127 Eg, *A-G's Reference (No 54 of 2003)* [2003] EWCA Crim 3948, [2004] 2 Cr App R(S) 196; *Robertson v HM Advocate* 2004 SCCR 180.

128 Gillespie, A, 'Children, chatrooms and the law', [2001] Crim LR 435.

129 Sexual Offences (Conspiracy and Incitement) Act 1996 (UK).

130 Sexual Offences Act 2003 (E&W, NI), s 15. See Ost, S, 'Getting to grips with sexual grooming? The new offence under the Sexual Offences Act 2003', (2004) 26 JSWFL 147.

131 Above, p 140. The defence applies to the grooming offence by virtue of the Electronic Commerce (EC Directive) (Extension) Regulations 2004 (UK), SI 2004/1178.

ISPs and chat room operators to be seen to be doing something is intense, whether by controlling access to chat rooms, providing safety warnings and virtual panic buttons, moderating chat room discussions, or random monitoring.[132] Various attempts have been made to establish child-friendly areas of the Internet, such as kids.us in the US, with mixed success.[133] It seems to be generally accepted that a large part of the answer has to consist of education, both of the potential victims and of their parents.[134]

Adult victims

Conversations over the Internet are not always noted for their politeness. Indeed, in some forums deliberate insults or 'flaming' are commonplace. However, it seems unlikely and impractical that the criminal law would intervene in these cases unless much more were proved. Where, however, an organised campaign of abuse against a specific individual appears to have been conducted, there are some offences that may be relevant.

(a) Harassment is a criminal activity, and while the legislation does not specifically mention the Internet or e-mail, there is no reason why it cannot be applied to such behaviour online.[135] Civil remedies, including injunctions, may also be available[136] – one case involved the grant of an injunction against e-mail harassment to a resident of Thailand against an English defendant.[137] Aggravating elements such as racial abuse or threats to kill may bring in other, more serious offences.[138]

(b) There is a specific offence of using a telecommunications network to send anything which is 'grossly offensive or of an indecent, obscene or menacing character', or sending false messages or persistently using the network 'for the purpose of causing annoyance, inconvenience or needless anxiety to another'.[139] England and Wales also have a related offence of 'malicious communication', which has been amended to apply to electronic communications.[140]

Secondary liability is possible, subject to the 'mere conduit' defence. In a famous case in Virginia, an unknown perpetrator targeted the plaintiff by using an AOL bulletin

---

132 See, eg, 'MSN torches chatrooms', Register, 23 September 2003 (Web).

133 Under the Dot Kids Implementation and Efficiency Act of 2002, on which see Browne, M, 'Play it again Uncle Sam: Another attempt by Congress to regulate Internet content', (2004) 12 CLC 79.

134 See think U know, Home office site (Web); 'Online child safety drive launched', BBC News, 6 January 2003 (Web); Book, C, 'Do you really know who is on the other side of your computer screen?', (2004) 14 ALJST 749.

135 Protection from Harassment Act 1997 (UK); Non-Fatal Offences against the Person Act 1997 (IE), s 10. See 'Jail for mobile stalker', VNUNet, 21 November 2002 (Web); Merschman, J, 'The dark side of the web: Cyberstalking and the need for contemporary legislation', (2001) 24 HWLJ 255.

136 Eg, *Chiron Corp Ltd v Avery* [2004] EWHC 493 QB.

137 *Potter v Price* [2004] EWHC 781 QB. See also *Inter-Tel Inc v Ocis plc* [2004] EWHC 2269 QB (Web).

138 See, eg, *R v Norman* [2003] EWCA Crim 3878 (racially aggravated harassment).

139 Communications Act 2003 (UK), s 127 (at the time of writing this provision is not fully in force); Post Office (Amendment) Act 1951 (IE), s 13, as substituted by Postal and Telecommunications Services Act 1983 (IE), Sched 3 Pt 2 and amended by Postal and Telecommunications Services (Amendment) Act 1999 (IE), s 7.

140 Malicious Communications Act 1988 (E&W), as amended by the Criminal Justice and Police Act 2001, s 43.

board to advertise T-shirts glorying the Oklahoma bombings, giving the plaintiff's home telephone number as that of the supplier. The plaintiff was accordingly deluged with outraged calls, including death threats, particularly after his number was read out on KRXO, a local rock station. After a complaint by the plaintiff, AOL removed the original posting (though precisely how quickly is disputed), but declined to issue a public retraction; KRXO did issue a retraction. In separate actions, the Federal Court of Appeals held that both AOL and KRXO had done everything the law required, and no action lay.[141] For defendants entitled to the 'mere conduit' defence, European law seems to reach the same result, provided the defendant acts expeditiously.

In the special case of harassment at work by co-employees, discrimination law may provide remedies for the harassed claimant, and employers may find themselves liable for the way in which their other employees have misused Internet facilities.[142] Typical cases often do not involve direct targeting of the claimant, but rather the creation of a hostile working environment in which the claimant is made to feel unwelcome or uneasy.[143]

OFFENSIVE SPEECH AND CONDUCT GENERALLY

The human capacity for disgust at certain utterances by others seems to be universal. However, this disgust is levelled at a bewilderingly diverse range of targets, with tolerance differing markedly both between individuals and between cultures. That the use of the Internet would generate considerable offence was obvious from the start; yet no nation with even modest technological aspirations dares keep it out entirely. A distressingly large number of nations – most prominently perhaps China, Iran, and Saudi Arabia – attempt to limit their citizens' access to the net, usually by a combination of Internet filtering technology (the rich nation's solution) and vicious threats to local ISPs (the poor nation's solution).[144] This fact, and the tendency of some nations to treat information uncongenial to their government as worse than the vilest pornography, inhibits international collaboration. And even nations which are happy to acknowledge one another's democratic credentials may nonetheless differ sharply in particular instances, as the *Yahoo!* litigation (below) illustrates. Widespread agreement on more than a handful of matters seems unattainable, almost unthinkable.

Gambling is yet another flashpoint. Both Ireland and the UK have elaborate provision for gambling, defining which sorts of games are lawful and the conditions under which they can be played; the UK legislation has recently been modified to make express provision for gambling over the Internet, as part of a general

---

141 *Zeran v America Online, Inc* 129 F 3d 327 (4th Ct, 12 November 1997) (Web); *Zeran v Diamond Broadcasting* 203 F 3d 714 (10th Ct, 28 January 2000).
142 For actual disputes, see Harrington, C, 'No surfing', (2002) 146 Sol Jo 682.
143 Volokh, E, 'Freedom of speech, cyberspace, and harassment law', [2001] STLR 3 (Web); 'Protect us from smut, whimper trembling workers', Register, 16 September 2004 (Web).
144 See, eg, 'China urges ISPs to sign "self-disciplinary" pact', Register, 21 June 2004 (Web); Bambauer, D, and others, 'Internet filtering in China in 2004–2005: A country study', SSRN, April 2005 (Web). On national Internet filtering, see the OpenNet Initiative site (Web).

liberalisation of the law.[145] For those nations which permit gambling at all, it is a valuable source of revenue; for those which do not, it is the more dangerous because of the high potential returns for those who run it.[146] Open conflict between different national approaches has occasionally surfaced in international tribunals.[147]

Free speech world-wide is too massive a topic to be considered here in full, and it is not easy to select particular topics as ones to which the Internet is particularly appropriate (or inappropriate). The general timidity of ISPs on receiving a complaint of offending is well known. Given the choice between starting a legal battle of unknown length and cost, and simply losing the customer whose site has created offence, the latter will almost invariably seem the cheaper and wiser option. The overwhelming tendency is therefore to remove offending material without a fight. It is the bizarre or the poignant cases that make it into the newspapers. A mother who advertised and agreed to sell her unborn baby over the Internet received a prison term from a Leeds court.[148] A site protesting against over-zealous traffic enforcement in Canterbury was suspended, after police complaints at harassment of particular traffic wardens.[149] And various sites, supposedly blaspheming God and the Madonna, were closed by Rome police – apparently by seizing account details from their arrested authors, and using them to remove the material from the US-based servers.[150] A rather more worrying site, providing resources and encouragement for anti-abortionists attempting to murder abortion providers, was the target of an injunction and a US$107 m damages award.[151]

More consistent international distaste has been shown for sites that promote racist views. Racism has long been recognised as a problem on the net. The German and French authorities particularly have been active in prosecuting neo-Nazi site owners; German courts have even convicted owners of foreign web sites,[152] and local ISPs have been instructed to block access to particular sites.[153] Indeed, the search engine Google has felt obliged to remove certain objectionable sites from its indexes at google.de and google.fr (though those sites remain available from google.com).[154]

While there is undoubted zeal for opposing racism across Western nations, it is unevenly spread. Draft provisions in the Convention on Cybercrime, criminalising

---

145 Gambling Act 2005 (UK); see s 4, definition of 'remote gambling'. See more generally Paton, D, Siegel, D and Williams, L, 'A policy response to the e-commerce revolution: The case of betting taxation in the UK', (2002) 112 EJ F296.

146 See, eg, Essa, A, 'The prohibition of online casinos in Australia: Is it working?', (2004) 4 QUT LJJ 1 (Web); Andrle, J, 'A winning hand: A proposal for an international regulatory schema with respect to the growing online gambling dilemma in the United States', (2004) 37 Vand JTL 1389.

147 Thayer, J, 'The trade of cross-border gambling and betting: The WTO dispute between Antigua and the United States', [2004] DLTR 13 (Web); 'WTO rules against US gambling laws', Register, 11 November 2004 (Web).

148 'Internet baby sale mother jailed', BBC News, 21 May 2004 (Web).

149 'Web site censored over pictures of traffic wardens', Register, 9 July 2002 (Web).

150 'Italian police shut down blasphemous web sites', OUT-LAW, 12 July 2002 (Web).

151 *Planned Parenthood of the Columbia/Willamette, Inc v American Coalition of Life Activists* 41 F Supp 2d 1130 (D Or, 14 March 1999), affirmed 290 F 3d 1058 (9th Ct, 16 May 2002); cert denied 539 US 958 (27 June 2003); McSpadden, N, 'Slow and steady does not always win the race: The Nuremberg files web site and what it should teach us about incitement and the Internet', (2001) 76 Ind LJ 485.

152 'German court bans foreign Nazi web sites', InfoWorld, 13 December 2000 (Web).

153 'Frankfurt: *Nein* to Neo-Nazi sites', Wired, 20 December 2002 (Web).

154 'Google excludes controversial sites', ZDNet UK, 24 October 2002 (Web).

racism and xenophobia online, were ultimately withdrawn, the US making it clear that it could not sign up to provisions so clearly in conflict with its constitutional guarantee of free speech. (Incitement to racist violence is prohibited in US law, but speech short of that is not; 'hate speech' is still speech, and so is protected by the 1st amendment to the constitution.[155]) An optional protocol to the Convention was proposed, and adopted by 11 European nations in January 2003.[156] It seems unlikely that either the UK or Ireland will accede to it: while much of it is compatible with existing laws on inciting racial hatred, the specific provisions on Holocaust denial are thought unpalatable. (Signatories must prohibit 'material which denies, grossly minimises, approves or justifies acts constituting genocide or crimes against humanity', though derogation is possible.[157])

These subtle but important differences in reconciling freedom of speech with opposition to racism inhibit international co-operation, as is well illustrated by the Yahoo! Nazi Memorabilia controversy, which is now recounted.

L'affaire 'Yahoo!'

This arose out of the auctioning on Yahoo!'s sites of various items of Nazi memorabilia, including coins, emblems and flags; the pages advertising the material also included extracts from famous Nazi and racist texts, including *Mein Kampf*. Anti-racist groups in France objected to this, relying particularly on local statutes criminalising displays of Nazi propaganda and sales of Nazi artefacts. Yahoo! France rapidly removed the items from yahoo.fr, but the parent company (Yahoo! Inc, the headquarters of which are in California) declined to alter its main site, yahoo.com.

The subsequent legal proceedings were of some complexity.

(a) On 5 April 2000, La Ligue Contre le Racism et l'Antisemitisme (LICRA) commenced civil proceedings in France for a fine against Yahoo! Inc. Process was served on Yahoo! Inc in California.

(b) On 22 May 2000, the Tribunal de Grande Instance de Paris ordered Yahoo! Inc to 'dissuade and render impossible' access by people in France to the Nazi auction on yahoo.com.[158]

(c) On 22 November 2000, after further argument, the Tribunal re-affirmed its earlier order. As to Yahoo! Inc's protest that it was not technically possible to bar French access to the site, Judge Gomez accepted evidence that French access could be reduced by 90% through a combination of barring access from sources known to be French and, in certain instances, requesting those wanting access to state their nationality. (Justifiable scepticism has been expressed about the 90% figure, though there is no doubt that such filtering reduces access markedly.) Yahoo! Inc was given three months in which to comply; non-compliance was to result in a fine of 10,000

---

155 For discussion, see Tsesis, A, 'Prohibiting incitement on the Internet', (2002) 7 VJOLT 5 (Web); Nyberg, A, 'Is all speech local? Balancing conflicting free speech principles on the Internet', (2004) 92 GLJ 663.

156 Additional Protocol to the Convention on cybercrime, concerning the criminalisation of acts of a racist and xenophobic nature committed through computer systems (28 January 2003) (Web).

157 *Ibid*, Art 6.

158 'France – Liability – Auction of Nazi objects', [2000] EBL (July) 15.

francs (roughly £1,000/€1,500) per day. However, Judge Gomez stipulated that this fine was not recoverable from Yahoo! France.[159]

(d) On 21 December 2000, Yahoo! Inc started proceedings against LICRA in a Federal court in California, seeking a declaration that any attempt to enforce a penalty imposed by the French court would violate their 1st amendment (free speech) rights. LICRA moved to dismiss the action for lack of jurisdiction against them, but Judge Fogel held on 7 June 2001 that LICRA had deliberately targeted Yahoo! Inc in its home jurisdiction, by serving process on it there in the French action, and so were amenable to the Federal jurisdiction.[160]

(e) On 7 November 2001, Judge Fogel granted the declaration sought by Yahoo! Inc. Free speech in the US by a US resident was protected by the 1st amendment; the fact that the 'speech' could be 'heard' in France made no difference.[161]

(f) On 26 February 2002, another anti-racist group, L'Amicale des Deportes d'Auschwitz, persuaded the Tribunal Correctionnel de Paris to conduct criminal proceedings for 'justifying war crimes' against Tim Koogle, Yahoo! Inc's chief executive, at the time the controversy blew up. Defences based on limitation and lack of jurisdiction were rejected.[162]

(g) On 11 February 2003, the Tribunal Correctionnel acquitted Koogle, noting that neither he nor Yahoo! Inc had done anything to portray war crimes in a favourable light.[163]

(h) On 23 August 2004, the Federal 9th Circuit Court of Appeals, by a majority, reversed Judge Fogel's ruling and refused the declaration sought by Yahoo! Inc. The French court had not yet imposed a fine for breach of its order, and further French proceedings would be necessary before it did so; LICRA had no plans to put this process in motion, and gave as their opinion that Yahoo! Inc was not in breach of the French court's order. Accordingly, there was no issue to be tried, and the Federal court had no jurisdiction over LICRA. If the French court imposed a fine and LICRA attempted to enforce it in a US court, then and only then would it be necessary to determine whether doing so would violate Yahoo!'s 1st amendment rights.[164]

(i) On 10 February 2005, the 9th Circuit Court of Appeals ordered a re-hearing of the case, directing that its earlier ruling should no longer be regarded as a legal precedent.[165]

(j) On 6 April 2005, Koogle's acquittal was confirmed on appeal in Paris.[166]

While the saga may not be completely over, it is clear that it has been much less momentous for the international development of the Internet than had earlier

---

159 'France – Jurisdiction – Auction', [2001] EBL (February) 13; Hugot, J and Dalton, N, 'The universal jurisdiction of the French courts in civil and criminal cases: The road to digital purgatory?', [2002] Ent LR (3) 49; Bodard, K, 'Free access to information challenged by filtering techniques', (2003) 12 ICTL 263.

160 *Yahoo!, Inc v LICRA* 145 F Supp 2d 1168 (ND Ca, 7 June 2001).

161 *Yahoo!, Inc v LICRA* 169 F Supp 2d 1181 (ND Ca, 7 November 2001).

162 'Yahoo! faces criminal charges over Nazi auction sites', [2002] WILR (4) 19; 'France – Jurisdiction', [2002] EBL (July) 14.

163 'Court clears Yahoo in Nazi case', Wired, 11 February 2003.

164 *Yahoo!, Inc v LICRA* 379 F 3d 1120 (9th Ct, 23 August 2004).

165 *Yahoo!, Inc v LICRA* 399 F 3d 1010 (9th Ct, 10 February 2005).

166 'Ex-Yahoo! CEO's Nazi auction acquittal upheld in France', OUT-LAW, 7 April 2005 (Web).

been feared. It is also clear that the intention behind most of the litigation was largely symbolic, rather than to obtain the remedies asked for. This is particularly so in relation to the prosecution of Tim Koogle – which was surely of calculated futility, as it would be impossible to extradite him from the US for acts which are not criminal there.

The case has resulted in a considerable literature.[167] Many have argued that it shows the need for an international treaty, to resolve otherwise hopeless differences between national courts. However, the case could be used to argue precisely the contrary: that certain types of difference cannot possibly be smoothed away by international treaty (can a nation occupied by the Nazis possibly have the same attitude to them as a nation an ocean away?), and yet national courts can still manage to avoid head-on collisions with one another.

DEFAMATION

As the web increasingly becomes a standard source of information about the contemporary world, it is not too surprising that some individuals become concerned that it might be a source of misinformation about them. If anything, it is surprising how few cases of Internet defamation there have been, though no doubt the considerable expense of such actions goes a long way towards explaining this. Certainly, some corners of the net seem designed to attract hostile attention from those alleging that they have been defamed. Many discussion forums allow for fast and furious discussion, especially if they are 'unmoderated' (that is, contributions to the discussion are not vetted by a human editor). Some sites – such as www.is-a-cheat.com – give a platform to those highly likely to make defamatory comments. And some bloggers are given to making pungent remarks about identifiable individuals. No doubt, the limitations of search engines make it harder for those with common names to notice defamation – a Joseph Gutnick might realise that defamatory things are being said about him well before a John Smith might – but most net-literate people are curious enough to search for their own name sooner or later, and they may not always like what they find.

As might be expected, attacking individual defamers is usually a far more difficult and costly task than attacking the organisation that provided them with access to the Internet. So employers, universities and ISPs have lost far more sleep (and far more in legal fees) than the employees, students and customers who have done the defaming; and the issue of intermediary liability has dominated the discussion of the issue. Very often, the victim of defamation can obtain a quite satisfactory remedy by attacking the intermediary alone.[168] Some have been determined to push it further: one of the first plaintiffs to issue defamation proceedings for statements on the Internet insisted on knowing the identity of the

---

167 See especially Reidenberg, J, 'The *Yahoo!* case and the international democratization of the Internet', SSRN, April 2001, (Web); Okoniewski, E, '*Yahoo!, Inc v LICRA*: The French challenge to free expression on the Internet', (2002) 18 AUILR 295; Manolopoulos, A, 'Raising "cyber-borders": The interaction between law and technology', (2003) 11 IJLIT 40; Dawson, C, 'Creating borders on the Internet: Free speech, the United States, and international jurisdiction', (2004) 44 Va JIL 637.

168 See, eg, 'How Posh and Becks silenced the rumour mill of the Internet', Independent, 30 November 2002 (Web).

actual defamer.[169] In general, however, control of net access providers gives as much control as most plaintiffs need.

In some respects, as use of the net becomes more routine, Internet defamation issues are coming closer to mainstream, pre-Internet defamation law. The celebrated *Gutnick* case is in this mould: it involved newspaper allegations against a prominent businessman, which he wished to dispute.[170] Perhaps litigation would have been less likely had the newspaper not been available on the Internet; but such an internationally read publication as the *Wall Street Journal* might well have been the subject of litigation by an Australian even in pre-Internet days. The Internet may be adding a new dimension to forum shopping for libel, but not so far a very significant one. In the event, the Australian courts asserted jurisdiction over the claim, which was then settled without any ruling on liability.[171] It has not been followed by a significant number of other such claims, though (as will be mentioned below) there are already suggestions that the courts in London may be beginning to assert a similarly wide jurisdiction.

United Kingdom

The law of defamation is similar in all of the UK jurisdictions. Internationally speaking, the focus is on London, long dubbed the 'libel capital of the world' for its specialist libel bar, its willingness to accept jurisdiction, and its reputation for high damages awards. These pro-claimant features have attracted a good deal of business, from a number of prominent figures and celebrities who might have been expected to sue in other jurisdictions.[172]

Defamation involves the publication of a statement which tends to lower the claimant in the estimation of reasonable people. Scotland apart, a distinction is drawn between libel (written defamation) and slander (spoken defamation): the latter is treated as less serious, and is actionable only on proof of resulting harm, or if the case falls within certain especially dire categories of utterance, such as allegations of dishonesty. Almost certainly, electronic communications of all types are libel rather than slander, though the point has never been resolved by case law. Much defamation litigation turns on the precise meaning to be attributed to the statement in question. Ultimately, this is a question for a jury to resolve, though in recent years there have been concerted attempts in the English jurisdiction to divert matters away from juries, both by resolving some matters before the main trial, and by removing juries altogether from the more technical cases.

Various defences are available, though they are notoriously narrow. Truth ('justification') is a defence if the defendant can prove it; this is a highly technical

---

169 *Totalise plc v The Motley Fool Ltd* [2001] EWCA Civ 1897, [2002] 1 WLR 1233 (Web), considered above, p 81. For subsequent proceedings, see 'Anonymity no protection for online libellers', Register, 24 March 2005 (Web).

170 *Dow Jones and Co Inc v Gutnick* [2002] HCA 56 (Web). For commentary, see Garnett, R, '*Dow Jones and Company Inc v Gutnick*: An adequate response to transnational Internet defamation?', (2003) 4 MJIL 196 (Web); Kohl, U, 'Defamation on the Internet – Nice decision, shame about the reasoning', (2003) 52 ICLQ 1049; Werley, B, 'Aussie Rules: Universal jurisdiction over Internet defamation', (2004) 18 TICLJ 199.

171 'Dow Jones settles defamation lawsuit', ABC News, 15 November 2004 (Web).

172 See, eg, 'Perle's wisdom shows by suing for libel in London, not the US', Times, 15 March 2003.

defence, however, especially as what the defendant must justify is not the literal truth of the statement but rather its defamatory 'sting'. 'Fair comment' is also a defence, though again it is rigorously defined – any factual statement must be independently justified, and the comment must stay within fair bounds. There is a narrow category of 'absolute privilege', which immunises the makers of certain official pronouncements from liability for defamation; there is also a rather wider category of 'qualified privilege', where those making statements out of duty receive immunity, unless they can be shown to be motivated by spite against the claimant. Lack of intent to defame is not a defence, though an innocent defamer who is prepared to tender an immediate apology and make reasonable amends is able to limit their liability considerably. The influence of human rights principles is beginning to be felt in this area, and has already led to a significant widening of the defence of fair comment; however, there is still a long way to go before the English law will be able to shrug off its unenviable pro-claimant reputation.

Liability turns on the publication of the defamatory statement to third parties (though in Scots law, publication to the pursuer personally may sometimes suffice). A distinction is drawn between the primary publisher (who actually made the defamatory statement), and secondary publishers (who merely repeated or disseminated it). Primary publishers are fully liable for their utterances, whereas secondary publishers can defend an action in defamation by proving that they did not know, and could not reasonably have known, of the defamatory content. Anxieties about liability for statements made in electronic media led to a restatement of the law here. It now provides that:

In defamation proceedings a person has a defence if he shows that –

(a) he was not the author, editor or publisher of the statement complained of,

(b) he took reasonable care in relation to its publication, and

(c) he did not know, and had no reason to believe, that what he did caused or contributed to the publication of a defamatory statement.[173]

It might be a difficult question whether a particular defendant was or was not the 'author, editor or publisher' of a particular statement appearing in some Internet medium. If the statement appears as part of a site deliberately on show to the public as part of a commercial operation, the site's controller is likely to be regarded as publisher, defined as 'commercial publisher, that is, a person whose business is issuing material to the public, or a section of the public, who issues material containing the statement in the course of that business'.[174] This is also clearly broad enough to cover online newspapers, which therefore cannot plead secondary publisher status.

For ISPs and others who have simply made Internet access available to the defamer, the matter is less clear cut. The ISP would probably easily be able to avoid being treated as the 'author' ('the originator of the statement'[175]) but might in some circumstances be treated as an 'editor' ('a person having editorial or equivalent responsibility for the content of the statement or the decision to publish it'[176]). The legislation gives ISPs a positive incentive *not* to exercise any prior control over what

---

173 Defamation Act 1996 (UK), s 1(1).
174 *Ibid*, s 1(2) (definition of 'publisher').
175 *Ibid*, s 1(2) (definition of 'author').
176 *Ibid*, s 1(2) (definition of 'editor').

their customers say, as exercising such a control might make them 'editors' and thus primary publishers. This is undoubtedly a dilemma for those moderating controversial chat rooms or discussion groups, who risk charges of irresponsible conduct if they do not monitor every message, but may be treated as primary publishers if they do. It is clear that simply making the statement available on the net is not in itself grounds for primary liability: primary liability does not arise simply from 'operating or providing any equipment, system or service by means of which the statement is retrieved, copied, distributed or made'; nor is the 'operator of or provider of access to a communications system by means of which the statement is transmitted, or made available, by a person over whom he has no effective control' to be regarded as a primary publisher.[177]

Secondary publishers can therefore escape liability for defamatory statements by taking reasonable care in relation to the publication, so long as they did not know, and had no reason to know, that defamatory statements would be made. In applying this test, statute directs the courts to have regard to '(a) the extent of his responsibility for the content of the statement or the decision to publish it, (b) the nature or circumstances of the publication, and (c) the previous conduct or character of the author, editor or publisher'.[178] Case law on what this requires is lacking. Before the event, it plainly may require some pre-emptive procedures to be in place, perhaps including random monitoring. After the event, it clearly requires swift action when a complaint is made. At the instant the complaint is received by the ISP, it can no longer say that it 'did not know' – the defence is gone, and defamatory material is being 'published' by the ISP for as long as it remains publicly available from its server.[179] There are various uncertainties in the defence, though this may be of little consequence, as ISPs who fall just outside it will be able to plead the 'mere conduit' defence.[180]

The common criticism here is that ISPs are only too ready to act on complaints, removing apparently defamatory material as soon as legal action is threatened; the risk of legal action by the complainer if the ISP leaves it there is far more serious than the risk of action by the customer if it removes it. It is unrealistic to expect ISPs to show much knowledge of the law of defamation, or (in cases where the truth of the statement is disputed) to expend significant resources checking its veracity. The cost of securing the removal of awkward material on the net is therefore, in most cases, merely the cost of a forceful solicitor's letter to the ISP; which is cheap indeed as a way of suppressing criticism. The Law Commission of England and Wales has pointed to this highly unsatisfactory aspect of the law, though it admits that it is unclear precisely what balance should be struck between free speech and the legitimate interest of companies and celebrities in maintaining their reputations.[181]

A related problem is that of Internet archives. In one case, the London *Times* published an article accusing Grigori Loutchansky of international criminal activities, including mafia activity and money-laundering. The article was archived

---

177 *Ibid*, s 1(3).

178 *Ibid*, s 1(5).

179 *Godfrey v Demon Internet Ltd* [1999] EWHC QB 244, [2001] QB 201 (Web).

180 Above, p 140.

181 *Defamation and the Internet*, Scoping Study No 2, December 2002, Part II (Web). For comment, see Hendrie-Liaño, J, 'Playing Canute with defamation law', (2003) 14 C&L (4) 34; Hurst, A and McDermott, J, 'Defamation in cyberspace: Hope of reform for ISPs?', (2003) 8 Comms L (2) 261.

on the newspaper's web site. In the subsequent libel proceedings, the main issue was whether the original article was defamatory; ultimately the newspaper failed on this, being able to establish neither the truth of its story nor a qualified privilege to report the facts as it saw them.[182] Regardless of this, however, was the continued inclusion of the article in its archive defamatory? This was a distinct issue, and indeed it fell to be decided before the issue of privilege for the original article was settled. The Court of Appeal held that *even if* privilege could be established for the original article, nonetheless it was not available in respect of the archive version. Inclusion in the archive constituted the repetition of allegations which were disputed, and which *The Times* did not intend to defend as true; conceivably the inclusion could have been justified if some qualification had been attached to notify readers of the dispute, but without it there could be no privilege.[183] *The Times* also relied on the short limitation period in defamation cases, saying that action should have been brought within a year of the original publication; it suggested that inclusion in the archive should be viewed as a single publication on the date when it was first added, not a series of multiple publications since that time. This argument too was rejected: repeated public access to the archive was properly treated as a series of multiple publications.[184] The court rejected the argument that this broad liability was an infringement of *The Times'* right of free expression. The right did not apply so strongly to archives as it did to daily publications – 'Archive material is stale news' – and the proper course for *The Times* would have been to add a disclaimer warning readers that the article's truth was disputed.[185]

The usual remedy in defamation cases is damages. Some quite large sums have changed hands in Internet defamation cases. The days of six-figure awards merely for ruffling a celebrity's dignity seem to have gone, but significant interference with another's business may still result in a large award. In 1997, Norwich Union settled a claim brought by Western Provident, a rival firm, with a public apology and a payment of £450,000 in damages and costs; employees of Norwich Union had circulated false rumours that Western Provident was in financial difficulties and was under investigation by government inspectors.[186] And an ex-employee of British Gas successfully sued after the company circulated a defamatory e-mail to staff of one of its subsidiaries, warning them not to have dealings with the claimant's new firm; £101,000 was agreed as damages, without an apology.[187] These large awards are exceptional, however. More typical is a case in 2000, for circulation of malicious rumours: £1,000 was awarded to the company involved and £25,000 to the individual personally defamed.[188] Injunctions are sometimes available, where the allegation is either made without belief in its truth or has not been substantiated at trial. There is no right of reply.

In what circumstances will the courts of the UK accept jurisdiction when the facts of the case cross borders either within the UK or further afield? A key issue is

---

182 See *Loutchansky v Times Newspapers Ltd* [2001] EWCA Civ 1805, [2002] QB 783 (Web); 'Times to appeal after setback in libel test case', Times, 27 November 2002.

183 *Loutchansky v Times Newspapers Ltd* [2001] EWCA Civ 1805, [2002] QB 783, para 79 (Web).

184 *Ibid*, para 57.

185 *Ibid*, para 74. For discussion, see *Defamation and the Internet*, Scoping Study No 2, December 2002, Part III (Web); Edwards, L, 'Times for a change: *Loutchansky v Times Newspaper*', (Web).

186 'NU to make e-mail libel payout', Times, 18 July 1997.

187 'Email costs BG £101,000', Register, 25 June 1999 (Web).

188 *Takenaka (UK) Ltd v Frankl* (QBD, 11 October 2000).

whether the publication of a defamatory article on the Internet will be treated as a single tort, occurring wherever the server was physically located (the 'single publication rule'), or whether each separate downloading of the article should be treated as a tort, occurring wherever it was downloaded (the 'multiple publication rule'). Logically, either rule has something to be said for it. The opinion of the House of Lords in *Berezovsky v Michaels*[189] was that the multiple publication rule was to be preferred: if the claimant in the case had a reputation to protect in one of the UK jurisdictions, then he could do so by legal action, notwithstanding that both claimant and defendant were based elsewhere. So the claimant, based in Russia, was able to sue the editor of *Forbes Magazine*, based in New York, in an action in London, but solely in respect of his reputation in England. The defendant's English readership was about 2,000, as opposed to a Russian readership of 13 and a US readership of about 785,000; the article in question had been downloaded in England about 6,000 times. The *Berezovsky* ruling accords with rulings of the ECJ[190] and of the High Court of Australia in the *Gutnick* case;[191] the US 'single publication' rule was rejected as making sense in a federal context, but as inappropriate for international disputes.

In the light of the 'multiple publication' approach, therefore, a number of possible forums exist for the publication on the Internet of a single defamatory document:

(a) For disputes *within* the Brussels Convention (disputes within EU and EEA states), the plaintiff has a choice. A single action in relation to all the harm resulting from the statement within the EU may be commenced in the defendant's state of domicile. The 'double actionability' rule applies: so if the plaintiff complains of a statement on a server in country A affecting her reputation in country B, she must prove that both legal systems recognise her entitlement to a remedy. Alternatively, a plaintiff may sue in the state where her reputation was affected; if so, then the only law that is relevant is the law of that country, but the action must be confined to harm done in that country and no further.[192]

(b) For disputes *outside* the Brussels Convention, and thus falling to be resolved by traditional rules, a claimant may seek leave to commence proceedings against a foreign defendant in respect of damage to reputation within the jurisdiction.[193] The action would be limited to the damage sustained within the jurisdiction. It is not entirely clear how or whether 'double actionability' applies, though there is a loose assumption by many that it does not apply at all, as the only publication complained of is within the jurisdiction. But even if there was clearly damage within the jurisdiction, a defendant may argue that there is a more appropriate forum to resolve the dispute, and that the domestic action should be stayed accordingly. The principles are well settled.[194] The UK court will stay its proceedings only if there is another court with jurisdiction, which can more

---

189 [2000] UKHL 25, [2000] 1 WLR 1004 (Web).

190 *Shevill v Presse Alliance SA* (Case C-69/93), [1995] 2 AC 18.

191 *Dow Jones and Co Inc v Gutnick* [2002] HCA 56 (Web).

192 *Shevill v Presse Alliance SA* (Case C-69/93), [1995] 2 AC 18. It is unclear how this fits with the entitlement of an ISS to rely on its home jurisdiction's laws (above, p 133). See discussion in *Defamation and the Internet*, Scoping Study No 2, December 2002, paras 4.37–4.49 (Web).

193 See Civil Procedure Rules, r 6.20(8) (E&W).

194 See *Spiliada Maritime Corp v Cansulex Ltd, 'The Spiliada'* [1987] 1 AC 460.

suitably try the case. The burden of proof is on the party seeking a stay of proceedings. Relevant factors include the location of both parties, expense, availability of witnesses, and the question of which law will govern. A stay will also be refused if the claimant can show that justice will not be obtained in the proposed alternative jurisdiction. These are difficult criteria to satisfy, but this happened in a case where the plaintiff, a New Yorker appointed as American Ambassador to Ireland, was criticised in the *Irish Voice*, a New York publication with no circulation in Ireland; fewer than 1% of downloads to its web site went to the UK. The plaintiff sued in Belfast, the writs being served with the High Court's leave in New York. However, a stay was ordered, Higgins J ruling that the US would be the natural forum for the action.[195]

Considerable debate surrounds the area, which is in any event under review as part of the preparations for a fresh re-statement of EU rules on jurisdiction for non-contractual liability ('Rome II').[196] Meanwhile, the London courts seem very willing to allow service out of the jurisdiction in respect of US publications on the net,[197] though in one case they were prepared to stay an action where it was clear that damage to the claimant within the jurisdiction was minimal.[198]

Ireland

Most of the basic principles resemble those of the UK. The principal difference is the lack of any legislation on the position of secondary publishers. It seems likely, however, that similar conclusions would be reached at common law.[199]

Conflict between jurisdictions

Differences between jurisdictions are marked. Those between the English jurisdiction and the US federal jurisdiction are especially noteworthy, as the relative liberality of the former regularly attracts claimants who might more naturally have sued in the latter.[200] In particular, US law has more generous protection for journalists (though also ongoing disputes as to who counts as a 'journalist' in Internet contexts), and wider defences for mere secondary publishers[201] (though no noticeable reluctance to

---

195 *Tracy v O'Dowd* (NI QB, 28 January 2002).
196 See discussion in *Defamation and the Internet*, Scoping Study No 2, December 2002, Part IV (Web); Ludbrook, T, 'Defamation and the Internet: Where are we now and where are we going?', [2004] Ent LR 173 and 203. See more generally *The Rome II Regulation*, House of Lords EU Committee, 7 April 2004 (Web).
197 See especially *Lewis v King* [2004] EWCA Civ 1329 (Web); *Richardson v Schwarzenegger* [2004] EWHC 2422 QB (Web).
198 *Dow Jones and Co Inc v Jameel* [2005] EWCA Civ 75 (Web).
199 See Mullooly, P, 'Liability for defamatory statement in the Internet: A comparative overview', (2000) 1 HLJ 202, 215–218.
200 See generally Socha, M, 'Double standard: A comparison of British and American defamation law', (2004) 23 PSILR 471.
201 Patel, S, 'Immunizing Internet Service Providers from third party Internet defamation claims: How far should courts go?', (2002) 55 Vand LR 647; Deturbide, M, 'Liability of Internet Service Providers for defamation in the US and Britain: Same competing interests, different responses', [2000] 3 JILT (Web).

force those secondary publishers to identify the primary defamer[202]). Direct conflict between the jurisdictions rarely surfaces, though there is an obvious reluctance to allow claimants successful in London to enforce the judgment in the US. Some in the US urge persuading the rest of the world of the merits of free speech,[203] whereas others decry this as 'exporting the constitution'.[204] Meanwhile, international negotiations for a satisfactory jurisdictional regime continue.[205]

FURTHER READING

Dawson, D, 'Creating borders on the Internet: Free speech, the United States, and international jurisdiction', (2004) 44 Va JIL 637.

Hughes, H, 'Reasonable design', [1999] 2 JILT (Web).

Kawawa, N, 'Contract law relating to liability for injury caused by information in electronic form: Classification of contracts – a comparative study, England and the US', [2000] 1 JILT (Web).

Kohl, U, 'Who has the right to govern online activity? A criminal and civil point of view', (2004) 18 IJLCT 387.

Merschman, J, 'The Dark Side of the web: Cyberstalking and the need for contemporary legislation', (2001) 24 HWLJ 255.

Patel, S, 'Immunizing Internet Service Providers from third party Internet defamation claims: How far should courts go?', (2002) 55 Vand LR 647.

Peysakhovich, S, 'Virtual child pornography: Why American and British laws are at odds with each other', (2004) 14 ALJST 799.

Rosen, M, 'Should "un-American" foreign judgments be enforced?', (2004) 88 Minn LR 783.

Socha, M, 'Double standard: A comparison of British and American defamation law', (2004) 23 PSILR 471.

Tripp, T, 'Interception of communications', (2001) 10 ICTL 285.

Werley, B, 'Aussie Rules: Universal jurisdiction over Internet defamation', (2004) 18 TICLJ 199.

Williams, K, 'Child pornography law: Does it protect children?', (2004) 26 JSWFL 245.

---

202 Stiles, A, 'Everyone's a critic: Defamation and anonymity on the Internet', [2002] DLTR 4 (Web); Naples, G and Maher, M, 'Cybersmearing: A legal conflict between individuals and corporations', [2002] 2 JILT (Web).

203 Sutton, M, 'Legislating the Tower of Babel: International restrictions on Internet content and the marketplace of ideas', (2004) 56 FCLJ 415 (Web).

204 Rosen, M, 'Exporting the constitution', (2004) 53 Emory LJ 171.

205 Svantesson, D, 'At the crossroads – The proposed Hague Convention and the future of Internet defamation', (2002) 18 CLSR 191.

CHAPTER 7

DOMAIN NAMES

This chapter discusses the system by which the names of Internet domains are allocated and administered, and the impact upon it of legal principles.

Acquiring a domain name is usually problem-free: simply a question of registering the name online and making the first payment – a transaction that can be performed in a few moments. But the system which lies behind this is mired in controversy, and the relationship of the law relating to domain name ownership with the rest of the world's legal systems is problematical at best. Disputes over names are relatively rare, but can be of considerable complexity when they arise. Domain name ownership must be considered against the background of several legal systems, including the legal micro-systems constituted by the internal dispute resolution schemes established by the domain name administrators themselves. This chapter first describes the technical and political structures for allocating domain names and administering related aspects of the Internet. It then considers various systems of arbitration for resolving disputes over domain names. Finally, it asks how these disputes will fare if brought to the ordinary domestic courts.

While, of course, the entire Internet is a human creation with human needs in mind, the system of domain names caters peculiarly to human weakness. The routers which control Internet traffic do not use them: machines talk to machines using numbers, not words, and for each machine attached to the net there is an IP number to identify it. What is described here is a peripheral matter for the machines, but vital for the humans: the link between the IP numbers and the domain names by which the humans refer to them.

DOMAIN NAME ADMINISTRATION

The system of domain names is one of the more important ways in which the Internet is humanised and made comprehensible to non-specialists. A typical address such as www.ucc.ie is easy to understand and to remember, in a way that 143.239.1.60 cannot be; and for experienced Internet users many addresses are obvious, in the sense that the address can easily be guessed by those who know the organisation concerned, and vice versa.

There is a price to be paid, however, for a system which is both convenient and intuitive. It requires two parallel sets of names – numerical IP addresses for the convenience of the computers and domain names for the convenience of the humans – and a bureaucracy to match the two. Moreover, there is a certain lack of logic in the top-level of the structure for names, some of which are denoted by country codes (such as .uk for the UK and .ie for Ireland) and others by more generic labels (such as .com, .org and .info). The system allows for several different top-level domains which can reasonably be claimed by any one organisation; habit and fashion play a great part in deciding which will be used. For example, few US sites use .us domains, their owners preferring more generic names; .com is very much associated with US or international business, and is for that reason shunned by many non-US companies who seek local customers.[1]

The key to the system is the allocation of top-level domains, each of which is assigned to a particular registrar. The country-code top-level domains (ccTLDs), of which there are 251 at the time of writing, are each assigned to a national registrar, which may (within limits) make its own rules for sub-domains and for registering names within it.[2] So the .uk domain is administered by Nominet, a private company the members of which are drawn from various Internet and business-related industries; new domain names are granted only within sub-domains, such as .co.uk,. org.uk, .ac.uk, and .me.uk (for personal domains).[3] In the .ie domain, second-level domains are granted freely, and there is no attempt to distinguish different types of domain name owners.[4] Again, each of the 14 generic top-level domains (gTLDs) has its own administering body; for example, the .com domain is administered by VeriSign Global Registry Services, a California corporation.[5] Would-be domain name owners buy their registration from a registrar, which has the right to add names to the appropriate registry. For many of the ccTLDs, there is only one registrar. Such a monopoly is not considered satisfactory for the more popular gTLDs: a number of registrars have been appointed to handle routine applications, and for the more popular domains there is vigorous price competition between them.

While there is a certain amount of logical method in the assignment of domain names, it does not go very far. How many gTLDs are to be recognised, and which ones, is a question which can be answered many ways, and is in fact a question that has remained controversial for some time now. Different domains have their own rules, with no pretence at consistency. If University College Cork sought to own, in addition to ucc.ie, the domain ucc.com, there is no reason why it should not have it (always assuming that it evicts Upper Canada Consultants of Ontario); acquiring ucc.edu would require not only evicting Union County College of New Jersey but also satisfying the administrators of the .edu domain that it fell within its rules; ucc.uk is simply not available, whether or not some substantial connection with the UK could be demonstrated, as the UK administrators no longer grant second-level domains to individual organisations. Inconsistencies are sharpened because some codes lend themselves to uses quite different from those originally intended:

(a) Those who wish their domain name to hint that they come from Latin America, Los Angeles or Louisiana may be tempted to buy a domain within .la, even though technically this denotes the People's Democratic Republic of Laos.

(b) Scots who are miffed at the lack of a ccTLD for Scotland may settle for a domain within .sc, even though it is actually the code for the Seychelles.[6] (A proposal for a .scot.uk second-level domain was rejected by Nominet in June 2001.)

---

1   See, eg, 'UK users ignore dot com web sites', VNUNet, 17 February 2000 (Web).
2   See Root-Zone Whois Information (Web).
3   Nominet home page (Web). For a recent doubt as to the precise status of Nominet, see 'Cohen disputes UK registry's legitimacy', Register, 27 May 2005 (Web).
4   .ie domain registry home page (Web).
5   Generic Top-Level Domains (Web).
6   Wieworka, E, 'Uniting Scottish businesses with their Internet domains', (2002) 13 C&L (1) 21.

(c) Those who want to purchase an address within .co.uk can expect to have to explain their credentials as UK commercial entities. Those who purchase an address within uk.com need not, as it is owned by a private company which acquired that domain, and which makes freedom from restrictions a prime selling point. (The same company, which is based in London, also owns eu.com and us.com.)[7]

While the scheme for each TLD is different, the majority place no restriction on who may apply for domains, though (as is discussed below) someone who picks a name to which they have no possible legitimate claim is vulnerable to eviction by someone who does.

This part of the chapter first discusses the administration of domain names generally, and particularly the role of the Internet Corporation for Assigned Names and Numbers (ICANN). The chapter then progresses to the handling of disputes over domain names and, in particular, the Uniform Dispute Resolution Procedure (UDRP) through which most disputes are resolved. This sets the scene for the final part of the chapter, which considers cases where these disputes spill over into the ordinary courts.

Names and numbers

As explained above, domain names are a human convenience; actual network administration is based rather on IP numbers. Each machine connected to the Internet is (temporarily or permanently) assigned an IP number, which is used by other machines to communicate with it. Unlike telephone numbers, IP numbers are of no particular significance to those outside the technical community, and there is no question of certain numbers being particularly desirable or useful. IP numbers are assigned and administered uncontroversially by the four Regional Internet Registries, central records being kept by the Internet Assigned Numbers Authority (IANA).[8] There is the occasional scandal when numbers are used without permission but, by and large, the matter is free from controversy.[9]

The main problem with IP numbers is that there are not enough of them. Under the current system, numbers run from 0.0.0.0 to 255.255.255.255, which in theory allows for 4,294,967,296 distinct addresses on the Internet. (In practice, the number is rather less, as some addresses are reserved for technical purposes.) This seemed like an adequate number when version 4 of the Internet Protocol was introduced in January 1983, but the rapid reduction in size and cost of computers, the growth of mobile computing, and the general adoption of the Internet Protocol as the standard for communication between computers, have resulted in a huge demand for new IP numbers. Version 6 of the Protocol allows for numbers to run from 0:0:0:0:0:0:0:0 to FFFF:FFFF:FFFF:FFFF:FFFF:FFFF:FFFF:FFFF (in hexadecimal, that is, base 16). How many addresses this will in practice make available is not entirely clear, though even the most bleakly pessimistic views suggest that there will be billions of usable addresses for every person on the planet. Version 4 and version 6 are currently both in use across the world, as the migration from the old system to the new is carried

---

7   CentralNic home page (Web).
8   IANA home page (Web). On IANA's role, see especially 'Abuse issues and IP addresses' (Web).
9   'Cracking down on cyberspace land grabs', Register, 11 June 2003 (Web).

through, largely invisibly to those outside technical computing communities; the migration is not expected to be complete until well into the century.[10]

Control of the root

Proper functioning of the Internet requires there to be some sort of an index, to define which IP number corresponds to each domain name. For a number of practical reasons, however, this index cannot be held in one place: the index is divided across a variety of different machines: in the jargon, the index is 'distributed'. This distributed index system (the Domain Name System or DNS) therefore relies on communication between the various registries where the index is kept. Where a message is directed at www.ucc.ie, the first local registry to receive the message may already hold the corresponding IP number; if it does not, it may have the IP number for the registry holding IP numbers for *.ie, to which it will forward the request; if this does not work, the request will go to one of the root servers, which can say where the registries are for *.ie and other root domains. Eventually, a machine which holds the requested IP number will be located, and the message sent to its proper destination. The DNS relies on the existence of a single authoritative root server, which designates registries for the top-level domains, which can in turn authoritatively designate second-level domains, and so forth. (Actually, there are 13 authoritative root servers, 12 of which take their cue from the 'A' root server, based in Herndon, Virginia.)[11] An address on the Internet does not exist, for practical purposes, unless it is recognised within and by the authority of this system: in the same way that no one would ever phone you if there was no way of discovering your telephone number, so a machine the domain name of which is not accepted by the DNS system can expect no communication from others.

In theory, then, control of the root is control of the Internet: those who use the Internet must do as the root controller says, or be cut out of the system. Who rules the root, rules the entire Internet. In practice, however, that would be a wild overstatement of the powers of the root controller. The Internet relies on close technical co-operation and compliance with common technical standards and protocols. But there is no legal compulsion involved – there is no relevant national or international legal mechanism to compel anyone – and massive resistance would be encountered if those in control of the root were seen to be exceeding their proper bounds. In practical political terms, it is hard to see what one of the major registries could do, short of deliberate sabotage, to justify removing its domain from the root server. The most dire threat imaginable in practice is to refuse to change details in the root server file, so that current arrangements continue even where one of the registrars would prefer a different arrangement. In principle, computer operators throughout the world could decide to recognise a different root server, if current arrangements proved unpalatable. It would take extreme circumstances to make this an attractive option, as it risks the destruction of the entire Internet, but the fact that it could be done is a potent factor in debates on reform.[12]

---

10   'IPv6 domains primed for launch', ZDNet UK, 26 July 2004 (Web).
11   See 'Root Name Servers' (Web).
12   See, eg, Kitz, V, 'ICANN may be the only game in town, but Marina del Rey isn't the only town on earth', (2004) 8 CLRTJ 281 (Web).

If push ever came to shove, the root belongs to the US Department of Commerce. It was originally created by a team headed by Jon Postel (a major figure in the development of the Internet), acting under a contract for the Department; in time, this was formalised by the creation of IANA, the body which now administers it. As the increased commercial and social importance of the Internet became clearer throughout the 1990s, as did its increasingly international nature, various models of Internet governance were debated. This led to the creation in 1998 of the Internet Corporation for Assigned Names and Numbers (ICANN), which now has control of IANA and hence of the root. Its operation and legal powers are described in the next section. The fact that the root actually belongs to a branch of the US government is the starting point for the international politics of the issue. The US government places as little emphasis on this as it can, publicly distancing itself from control of the Internet while holding fast to that control; other nations regard this as a standing grievance. The current deeply unsatisfactory constitutional arrangements are the inevitable consequence of an international stand-off, with some members of the US Congress being unwilling to accept that the Internet is not American, and the politicians in the rest of the world being unwilling to accept that it is.

The Internet Corporation for Assigned Names and Numbers (ICANN)

From a strictly legal point of view, ICANN is a non-profit corporation registered in California, formed in October 1998. It is constrained, in addition to the ordinary law of California and the US, by its own internal bylaws,[13] and by the terms of contracts it has signed. These include its contract with the US government to perform certain technical functions related to the running of the Internet, its contracts with the individual registrars for each top-level domain, and a Memorandum of Understanding with the US Department of Commerce.[14] There is no ICANN-specific legislation (though it is sometimes threatened);[15] but, as a California corporation, it is undoubtedly bound by relevant US law, however unsatisfactory that might seem to non-US Internet users.

The precarious (and indeed downright weird) constitutional position of the ICANN becomes clear when we ask: Is it a private body or a public body? Its primary functions seem to involve regulating the Internet in the public interest; important aspects of the Internet are under its sole control. This strongly suggests that it is a public body. If true, however, then it is and always has been an *illegal* body, for the US federal government can only delegate its functions by open and formal grant, not by a mere nod and wink to a private corporation. On that view, therefore, administration of the Internet is in a legal vacuum that can only be filled by appropriate US federal legislation. The other view – formally accepted by most relevant parties – is that ICANN is a purely private body, that the contracts it has entered into with other free agents are simply that and are not regulatory tools, and that while ICANN can be said to regulate some technical aspects of the Internet, it is not a governmental body. ICANN formally disclaims any policy-making role, and

---

13 Bylaws for Internet Corporation for Assigned Names and Numbers (Web).
14 ICANN's Major Agreements and Related Reports (Web).
15 Eg, 'US to seek greater control over ICANN', ECT, 11 June 2002 (Web).

insists that it does no more than seek to build consensus on policy issues within the international Internet community. Its standards are circulated not as compulsory edicts but as part of the friendly sounding Requests For Comments (RFC) series.[16] Even for those who find this convincing (of whom there are no doubt a few), it opens up a legal challenge from the opposite direction: a mere private body with such great control over the international market in Internet services must tread carefully indeed if it is not to be accused of violating competition law, whether in the US, the EU or elsewhere. Of course, the lawful regulator of a particular market is not subject to competition law; but therein lies ICANN's legal dilemma. Can the same body be a private government contractor for the purposes of US administrative law, yet a regulatory body for the purposes of US antitrust and EU competition law? This is a fine line to walk, indeed.[17]

ICANN is run by a board of directors, which has 15 voting members.[18] These are the President, two members each from the three supporting organisations that do much of the day-to-day work (namely the Address Supporting Organization, the Country-Code Names Supporting Organization and the Generic Names Supporting Organization), and eight members appointed by the Nominating Committee. The Nominating Committee selects candidates from the wider Internet community, applying a set of broad and intimidating criteria marking out those suitable for the job. There are also six non-voting members.[19] (The Nominating Committee mechanism replaced an earlier system where eight 'At Large' directors were elected by Internet users generally;[20] one at least of the 'At Large' directors did not go quietly.[21]) The need for diversity is emphasised in ICANN's bylaws, and only three of the current voting members are from the US; nonetheless, complaints at pro-US bias are repeatedly made.

In all of this, the influence of the US Department of Commerce is undoubted, yet hard for outsiders to quantify. Ownership of the root remains with the Department: ICANN is merely a contractor looking after it on its behalf. Current relations between them are embodied in a Memorandum of Understanding, which requires departmental consent for several types of decision which ICANN might make. The Memorandum expires in September 2006 (or is terminable on 120 days' notice); the Department is under no sort of obligation to renew it.[22] Meanwhile, ICANN is obliged to keep the Department informed of every detail of its workings. It is hard to imagine that ICANN would do anything to which it knew the Department was opposed: ICANN has few enough friends, and it could not survive long with the Department as an enemy. What is not publicly known is how the Department uses

---

16 Internet RFC/STD/FYI/BCP Archives (Web).
17 Froomkin, M, 'Wrong turn in cyberspace: Using ICANN to route around the APA and the constitution', (2000) 17 Duke LJ 17 (Web); Blue, L, 'Internet and domain name governance: Antitrust litigation and ICANN', (2004) 19 BTLJ 387.
18 For current membership, see 'Board of Directors' (Web).
19 See 'Bylaws for Internet Corporation for Assigned Names and Numbers' (Web), especially Arts VI and VII.
20 'ICANN board adopts reform plan, ditches elections', Register, 1 July 2002 (Web).
21 See Karl Auerbach home page (Web); 'ICANN board member wins Ruling', Wired, 29 July 2002 (Web).
22 See the original Memorandum of Understanding (25 November 1998) and the successive amendments (up to No 6, 17 September 2003), all at 'ICANN's Major Agreements and Related Reports' (Web); 'We're stuck with ICANN: Official', Register, 17 September 2003 (Web).

this influence, if it does – it is not obvious that it would have any particular view on the more technical questions, and the more obvious its influence becomes, the more raucous is the international protest at current arrangements.

ICANN is therefore a weak body. Its legitimacy is openly doubted on all sides.[23] It is often accused of acting without accountability, though it is rarely explained what an accountable Internet government would be like, or indeed to whom it would be accountable. It is accused of being a bully whenever it does something new, and it is taunted with being ineffectual when it does nothing. Attempts to develop new technical standards that will command sufficient general support routinely bring both sets of accusations. Its relations with the larger registrars often degenerate into acrimonious contract renegotiations, and sometimes actual litigation[24] – which ICANN does not have the money to carry on at any great length. Money is a continual problem: the size of its budget is always a controversial question, and any attempt to increase it is seen as re-opening the question of what services it is supposed to provide. The very need to fight its corner in public, over the news media and in the courts, generates a need for hard cash, which it is finding hard to satisfy.[25]

The existing literature is overwhelmingly critical of ICANN. However, the question that usually gets lost in the heat of debate is of what would be a preferable mode of governing the Internet; without a clear answer to that question, much of the criticism of ICANN merely beats the air. ICANN's general constitutional position is entirely unsatisfactory, but the only obviously satisfactory arrangement would be a body established by international treaty; blame for failure to make such a treaty should presumably rest with the nations that should have negotiated it, rather than with ICANN itself. Any system for governing the Internet is bound to come under powerful pressure from governments, from corporate lobbyists and from the more powerful registrars; and with so much money at stake, negotiation of key contracts was never going to be anything other than acrimonious. The question is always, if ICANN is not to govern the Internet, then which body should? An obvious proposal would be the International Telecommunications Union (ITU), which already co-ordinates much international network activity. Whether that would be satisfactory to the major parties involved remains to be seen; involvement of the ITU has been opposed in the past by the US on the ground that the Internet should be managed by the private sector, not public bodies.[26]

While ICANN is undeniably weak, perhaps weak government is precisely what is wanted, and the best system is one where the governing body can act effectively only in areas where there is either an overwhelming technical necessity to act, or an international consensus on what should be done. The test of this is perhaps the one instance where ICANN acted well outside that area, and decisively changed the legal landscape by so doing: its imposition of a single set of rules on the major gTLDs for resolving disputes, the famous or infamous Uniform Dispute Resolution

---

23   Frankel, T, 'Accountability and oversight of ICANN', SSRN, September 2002 (Web); Komaitis, K, 'ICANN: Guilty as charged?', [2003] 1 JILT (Web).

24   See 'Litigation Documents' (Web).

25   See, eg, 'ICANN grows up at last', Register, 24 May 2004 (Web).

26   For discussion, see King, I, 'Internationalising Internet governance: Does ICANN have a role to play?', (2004) 13 ICTL 243; 'Internet governance: A grand collaboration', UN Conference, March 2004 (Web).

Policy (UDRP), considered below. Whether this was a bold, simple and ultimately successful solution to a recurrent problem, or a shameful betrayal of the interests of ordinary domain holders to the interests of the trade mark lobby, is a matter on which many people have opinions; as the most prominent issue where ICANN went beyond the technical and into the legal, it must be a major factor in determining the value of ICANN's contribution to the good of the Internet.

Current issues in Internet governance

Much of what ICANN does is of a purely technical character. This section points to a few selected issues that are either on-going or recently resolved: they are selected for intrinsic interest, constitutional significance or general relevance to legal rights.

Language and the DNS

As originally conceived, the DNS system assumed that domain names would be strings of (Roman) letters and (Arabic) numerals. It was never likely that this would be acceptable to the majority of the world, which uses different alphabets. The problems here have been technical rather than ideological – allowing non-Roman domain names is expected to increase use of the world wide web and hence boost the profits of all concerned – though inevitably some have ascribed the exceedingly slow progress on the problem to a pro-Western bias. The first non-Roman domain names were made available in March 2004; work is proceeding on a number of non-Roman alphabets.[27]

The ccTLDs

The list of ccTLDs is (loosely) based on the ISO-3166 list of two-letter English country codes; adopting this list (originally compiled for a quite different purpose) helped IANA to assign most country codes on a largely non-controversial basis.[28] As already noted above, there is little consistency in the way in which individual nations employ their codes. Individual nations have quite different attitudes to trading practices. There is no consistency as to whether registration should be handled by a public body or by a private body or bodies. There are also different national policies on whether applicants for registration need to demonstrate some genuine connection with the nation concerned; for example, in December 1999, Italy went from a policy of demanding some local connection to allowing open access to all, thus enabling foreign companies to buy domains such as sell.it and kick.it, without any Italian connection.

Renegotiation or clarification of relations between ICANN and individual national registrars has been necessary for various reasons. Regime change, such as in Afghanistan[29] and Iraq,[30] is merely the most spectacular reason for renegotiation. More common are routine requests to appoint a new national registrar

---

27 Wilson, C, 'Internationalised domain names: Problems and opportunities', [2004] CTLR 174; Wilson, C, 'Expanding the domain name system (DNS) with internationalised domain names (IDNs)', (BILETA, April 2005) (Web).
28 English country names and code elements, ISO-3166 (Web).
29 'Afghans plant flag in cyberspace', BBC News, 10 March 2003 (Web).
30 'This is what is happening to Iraq's Internet domain', Register, 30 June 2004 (Web).

('redelegation' of the domain, in the jargon), or simply to change technical arrangements or contact details for the existing registrar. This can sometimes involve prolonged negotiations, and difficult judgments as to who is the most appropriate person or body to act for particular nations.[31]

As a body, the ccTLD registrars have formed a rather vocal lobby.[32] Much of ICANN's funding has in the past come from them, and their occasional threats to withdraw from involvement with ICANN can be powerful, as this would underline ICANN's failure to date to achieve much by way of international consensus, or to be accepted as a representative world government of the Internet. Contract renegotiations have already proved difficult, as ICANN has often assumed that these are occasions for the imposition of new terms, which national registrars have resented, especially where the need for renegotiation has been purely technical or occasioned purely by a change of personnel.[33] A noticeable softening of ICANN's line has occurred since late 2003, which has enabled it to make some inroads into the backlog of unfinished ccTLD business that had built up. However, this has not noticeably reduced the dissatisfaction of the ccTLD registrars as a body. In particular, the Council of European National Top-Level Domain Registrars (CENTR) has openly insisted that ICANN is exceeding its proper functions, and has failed in achieving any international consensus.[34] (Contrary to what its name suggests, CENTR's members include some non-European registrars.) In principle, of course, there can be no defence of ICANN: there can be no good reason why a vital international communication network should be governed by a California corporation. But this argument is merely one tool in a wider political struggle.[35]

Plans for a .eu domain have been laid for quite a while, though this domain is only just becoming available at the time for writing.[36]

The gTLDs

When ICANN took over the administration of the Internet in 1998, there were three gTLDs available to all comers without restriction: .com, .net and .org. In addition to these 'unsponsored' domains, there were four 'sponsored' domains, where only a narrow class was eligible for domain ownership: .gov, .edu, .mil, and .int. A single company, Network Solutions Inc (NSI), administered the unsponsored domains; registration of new domains was charged by NSI at US$100 per domain. Rectifying this situation was rightly seen as a priority, and some of the most bitter battles in Internet administration have been between ICANN and NSI, and with VeriSign after it bought NSI in 2000.[37]

Competition was introduced into the market for domain names by the registration of subordinate registrars, who could sell domain names in competition

---

31 See 'IANA Reports about ccTLDs' (Web). For an overview, see Yu, P, 'The neverending ccTLD story', SSRN, 2003 (Web).

32 See, eg, 'Europe threatens to invade ICANN', Register, 10 February 2003 (Web).

33 See, eg, 'Net body accused of bullying tactics', BBC News, 7 July 2002 (Web).

34 See CENTR home page (Web); 'Europe sticks up two fingers at ICANN budget', Register, 28 May 2004 (Web); 'Global poker game for the Internet goes on', Register, 3 May 2005 (Web).

35 For discussion, see von Arx, K and Hagen, G, 'Sovereign domains: A declaration of independence of ccTLDs from foreign control', (2002) 9 RJOLT 4 (Web).

36 See especially Regulations 733/2002/EC and 874/2004/EC.

37 Kalosieh, D, 'Network Solutions and the alleged privitization of the domain name system', (2000) 5 WVJOLT 3 (Web); 'Dot.com registrar sold for $21bn', BBC News, 7 March 2000 (Web). See also 'VeriSign sells off NetSol', Register, 16 October 2003 (Web).

with VeriSign (though actual registration was effected through VeriSign itself). This competition drove down the price of new domains by a considerable amount. Nonetheless, VeriSign still held a dominant position. It was partly forced to relinquish it: registration of .org domains was redelegated in 2002 to the Internet Society,[38] and the registrarship for .net will go out for tenders generally when VeriSign's current contract expires in 2005, though (at the time of writing) VeriSign is a strong contender in that tendering process. Verisign's contract as registrar for .com expires in 2007; Controversially, ICANN have now renewed it to 2012, though that renewal is being challenged in federal proceedings.[39].

Relations between VeriSign and ICANN remain acrimonious. There are many complaints against VeriSign's business practices, including alleged abuses of the data it holds on .com domains, and the practice of 'domain slamming', under which misleading invoices are sent to domain name holders, apparently requiring immediate payment to retain the name, but in fact (for those who read the small print) selling optional services.[40] VeriSign denies that ICANN has any role as its regulator. Particular controversy currently attaches to services that VeriSign wishes to provide, but to which the subordinate registrars object. One is the 'Waiting List Service', under which applicants pay a fee for an option to buy a particular domain name should its current owner vacate it; ICANN has allowed this, over complaints by subordinate registrars that it is anti-competitive.[41] Another matter of controversy is VeriSign's 'Site Finder' service, by which attempts to access pages in non-existent domains (presumably through typographic or other errors) would result in redirection to VeriSign's search engine. ICANN was threatened with litigation by VeriSign if it refused to allow this, and with litigation by various other interested parties if it did; it chose to disappoint VeriSign, which immediately commenced antitrust proceedings in a federal court.[42] This action has now been thrown out, the trial judge finding no evidence of an alleged anti-competitive conspiracy by ICANN.[43] VeriSign has now commenced an action in a California court for breach of contract against ICANN over the same matter; ICANN is attempting to move this dispute to arbitration.[44] Various litigants are suing VeriSign over the matter.[45] A settlement has been negotiated between ICANN and VeriSign, but is being challenged by others.

Expansion in the number of gTLDs was also a priority when ICANN was established. Jon Postel famously proposed in 1996 that there should be 150 new gTLDs, to be managed by 50 new registrars. However, a powerful brake was established by lobbyists for major corporations, concerned that an increase in available domains implied greater freedom to create names that infringed their trade marks. Much debate ensued; 44 applicants, each of which paid a US$50,000 application fee, proposed more than 200 domains. In November 2000, ICANN created just seven new gTLDs, four

---

38   'Spurned bidders slam ICANN org redelegation', Register, 2 September 2002 (Web); 'ISOC wins org contract', Register, 15 October 2002 (Web).
39   'VeriSign and ICANN strike monster net deal', Register, 25 October 2005 (Web).
40   Eg, 'VeriSign ordered to stop domain slamming', OUT-LAW, 20 June 2002 (Web).
41   'Internet monopoly alert!', Register, 18 July 2002 (Web); 'ICANN board approves controversial domain name service', E-Week, 8 March 2004 (Web).
42   'VeriSign calls ICANN bluff in world's biggest game of poker', Register, 29 February 2004 (Web).
43   *VeriSign, Inc v ICANN* 2004 US Dist LEXIS 17330 (CD California, 26 August 2004); 'VeriSign antitrust claim against ICANN rebuffed', Register, 27 August 2004 (Web).
44   'ICANN, VeriSign, and the swamp', CircleID, 13 November 2004 (Web).
45   '3rd lawsuit against VeriSign; seeks class action status', CircleID, 29 September 2003 (Web).

unsponsored (.biz, .info, .name and .pro) and three sponsored (.aero, .coop and .museum).[46] Subsequently, they also created .jobs, .mobi and .travel. This restrictive approach, and apparent lack of judgment in making the selection, resulted in much opprobrium for ICANN, especially from US legislators. Dissatisfaction at the lack of choice available built up to the extent that there was considerable support for domain names unrecognised by ICANN, and new.net started to sell such unrecognised names to all comers, even though most Internet users were unable to access them.[47] Applications for further sponsored gTLDs are receiving consideration.[48]

Debate over new domains reveals wide differences of opinion over what the naming system is for, and the extent to which it should be used as an instrument of policy. Many feel that there is no role for any policy beyond making available as many names as possible, as efficiently as possible. From that point of view, a choice would have to be made of the best way of selecting registrars – whether, as at present, by selecting the best tender (for some value of 'best'), or a simple auction, or even a lottery.[49] Others seek to attain substantive policy goals through the system – for example, to control the selection of names that infringe trade marks. The problem is, of course, that any goal which is to be promoted through the naming system presupposes an enforcement machinery and an enforcement cost. For example, it is often suggested that pornographic sites should be restricted to a particular gTLD, to be called .sex or .xxx; but this cannot work unless all other sites are somehow policed to check that they have no such content.[50] Given ICANN's weak administrative machinery and lack of political legitimacy, it cannot practically be used for such a global policing role without major changes.

Disputes over allocation of particular domain names

Internet domain names are allocated on a 'first come, first served' basis. Yet even though names are in principle an infinite and inexhaustible resource, there have from the very first been disputes over who should own particular names, and whether the first person to apply for them truly deserves to keep them. The cybersquatter, who registers a particular name purely out of mischief or in the hope that a legitimate owner will buy it out, has long been a feature of Internet life.

In theory, the network administrators could have maintained 'first come, first served' as an absolute principle, refusing to become involved in who 'should' own particular names. The convenience of this approach, especially for bodies anxious to maintain the appearance of even-handedness, is obvious enough. This was not really an option, however, as NSI realised when a disappointed complainant against cybersquatting sued it for contributory trade mark infringement. While this action ultimately failed,[51] it made it clear that some sort of dispute resolution policy was

---

46 See Ciocchetti, C, 'The Internet opens its doors for biz-ness', [2001] DLTR 34 (Web); Cave-Browne-Cave, J, '.biz means business – fact or fiction?', (2002) 16 IRLCT 67.

47 'New.net cuts out ICANN', Wired, 8 April 2001 (Web).

48 'Public Comments for Proposed Sponsored Top-Level Domains', ICANN, 31 March 2004 (Web); 'ICANN goes domain crazy', Register, 14 December 2004 (Web).

49 Manheim, K and Solum, L, 'An economic analysis of domain name policy', (2004) 25 HCELJ 317 (Web).

50 For some of the difficulties, see Eastlake, D, '.sex considered dangerous', RFC 3675, February 2004 (Web).

51 *Lockheed Martin Corp v Network Solutions, Inc* 194 F 3d 980 (9th Ct, 25 October 1999) (Web).

called for. Further, that policy would have to recognise rights which bore at least some resemblance to rights recognised by the US courts, or registrars would forever be the target of actions by dissatisfied claimants. A dispute resolution policy was rapidly introduced by NSI, and as rapidly revised and re-revised; controversially, the policy attempted to channel serious disputes to the ordinary courts, by providing for domain names to be put on hold pending actual litigation. No one version of the policy was universally deemed satisfactory.

On the formation of ICANN, much debate took place on what should replace NSI's policy. The World Intellectual Property Organisation (WIPO) conducted an extensive consultation process, which (after much debate) led to a new Uniform Domain Name Dispute Resolution Policy (UDRP), which ICANN adopted in October 1999. It applies to all disputes over names in the .com, .org and .net domains, and has also been adopted for many of the national domains. Its merits are a matter of heated debate. If one of its objects was to allow ICANN and its registrars to administer the domain name system without being sued, then it is certainly a success: disputes are fast and vigorous, but the parties are directing their fire at one another rather than at the administrators. In other respects, the balance it strikes between the various policy objectives is controversial.[52]

In substantive terms, the rights created by the UDRP are *sui generis*. The UDRP allows an exception to the basic principle of 'first come, first served' only when three criteria are satisfied: (i) that the name 'is identical or confusingly similar to a trade mark or service mark in which the complainant has rights', (ii) that the current holder has 'no rights or legitimate interests' in the name, and (iii) that the name 'has been registered and is being used in bad faith'. There is considerable vagueness here, but also a considerable infusion of trade mark law; for some this is a welcome recognition of the basic rights of trade mark owners, for others it is an illegitimate extension of those rights. Other types of legal rights do not really feature; the framers' attitude was that those other rights varied so much within the different legal systems of the world that it would be a mistake for network administrators to try to enforce them.

Procedurally, the system relies on mandatory arbitration, with no system of appeals. There are no interim orders: the name cannot be suspended until the arbitration panel rules on the dispute. This certainly ensures that the system is quicker and cheaper than any conceivable court process. However, it unsurprisingly leads to the charge that the panels are unaccountable, even biased either in individual cases or in the sense of favouring certain classes of claimant. It also intensifies complaints about the vagueness of the policy itself.

Whether domain names can now properly be said to be 'property', or to be 'owned', is a matter of opinion. Academic discussion is just getting into gear to consider that question,[53] and related ones such as whether they can function as security for loans.[54] What is clear is that if they are property, they are not property of a sort with which the legal systems of the world can easily deal; any one name is subject to a variety of different legal jurisdictions, which might in principle say very

---

52 For the history of the UDRP and its predecessor policies, see Halpero, M and Mehrotra, A, 'From international treaties to Internet norms', (2000) 21 UPJIEL 523; Rains, C, 'A domain by any other name', (2000) 14 Emory ILJ 355.

53 Yee, K, 'location.location.location: A snapshot of Internet addresses as evolving property', [1997] 1 JILT (Web); Chander, A, 'The new, new property', (2003) 81 Tx LR 715.

54 Lipton, J, 'What's in a (domain) name? Web addresses as loan collateral', [1999] 2 JILT (Web).

different things about who is entitled to it. The following section considers the detail of the UDRP, and (in less detail) the policies of some national domains. The final section reviews the place of the ordinary courts in such disputes. As the registrars of the leading gTLDS are based in the US, in principle disputes relating to them may be referred to US courts; therefore, the rights of Europeans and others to names in .com or .org may turn on provisions of US law.

DOMAIN NAME OWNERSHIP DISPUTES: THE UDRP AND ANALOGOUS SYSTEMS

The resolution of disputes over domain names in the major gTLDs is provided for in the UDRP[55] and in its associated rules.[56] The bulk of both documents is concerned with setting the ground rules for disputes, and for immunising ICANN, its registrars, its dispute resolution providers and its decision-making panels from any legal proceedings. Both the Policy and the Rules make explicit provision for legal proceedings to be carried on before, during or after the attempt to invoke the Policy. The Policy and the Rules derive their force against the current holder of the name from being incorporated into the contract under which the domain name was originally registered; this contract also incorporates a warranty by holders as to their good faith, and an agreement to submit to the jurisdiction of a relevant court should a UDRP decision in their favour be challenged.[57] Both the Policy and the Rules may be amended by ICANN's fiat, though at the time of writing they have survived for over five years without change.

The purpose of the Policy is very narrow, and deliberately so. The dispute process relates only to the particular domain name or names in issue, and the only remedy under it is to 'cancel, transfer or otherwise make changes to domain name registrations' where the grounds stated in the Policy are made out.[58] The registrar 'will not cancel, transfer, activate, deactivate, or otherwise change the status of any domain name registration under this Policy' unless the Policy's grounds are established.[59] No other type of dispute can be pursued under the Policy: 'All other disputes between you [the registered owner] and any party other than [the registrar] regarding your domain name registration that are not brought pursuant to the mandatory administrative proceeding provisions … shall be resolved between you and such other party through any court, arbitration or other proceeding that may be available'.[60]

Procedure

A complaint under the UDRP is commenced by sending a copy of the complaint to an ICANN-approved dispute resolution provider, such as WIPO.[61] The Rules contain

---

55 Uniform Domain Name Dispute Resolution Policy (Web).
56 Rules for Uniform Domain Name Dispute Resolution Policy (Web).
57 Uniform Domain Name Dispute Resolution Policy (Web), para 2.
58 *Ibid*, para 3, and see para 4i.
59 *Ibid*, para 7.
60 *Ibid*, para 5.
61 'Approved providers for Uniform Domain-Name Dispute-Resolution Policy' (Web). On differences between dispute resolution providers, see Kesan, J and Gallo, A, 'The market for private dispute resolution services', SSRN, March 2005 (Web).

a checklist for what must be included in the complaint; as well as obvious matters such as contact details for the complainant and the respondent, it must describe the grounds of the complaint and the remedy sought, identifying any legal disputes over the same matter, waiving certain types of claim against the network administrators, and warranting the good faith of the claim.[62] The dispute resolution provider must check the complaint for compliance with the Rules, and if it seems satisfactory must forward it to the respondent within 3 days.[63] The respondent then has 20 days in which to send a response.[64] As soon as the identity of the panel that will decide the case is known, the dispute resolution provider must forward the entire file to it.[65] In normal cases, the panel should present its decision to the dispute resolution provider within 14 days.[66] The provider must then pass it on to interested parties within 3 days.[67]

Complaints are considered by panels drawn from lists of potential panellists maintained by the dispute-resolution service provider. The complaint will specify whether it is asking for a single panellist (chosen by the dispute-resolution service provider) or a three-member panel (one from a list of three specified by the complainant, one from a list of three specified by the respondent, and one chosen by the dispute-resolution service provider according to certain detailed criteria).[68] If the complainant asks for a single panellist, it is open to the respondent to demand a three-member panel, but if so the respondent must pay half the fees for the proceedings. In all other cases, the complainant pays all fees.[69] (At the time of writing, fees at WIPO are US$1,500 for a single-panellist case and US$4,000 for a three-panellist case.) Panellists must be impartial, and 'any circumstances giving rise to justifiable doubt as to the Panellist's impartiality or independence' must be disclosed.[70]

There is detailed provision on such matters as communication between all interested parties, and the language in which the dispute is to be conducted.[71] Each dispute resolution provider has its own supplementary rules. Compliance with the Rules must be strict, though there is provision for correcting non-compliant documents. Time limits are also strict: absent exceptional circumstances, non-compliance forces the panel to proceed to a decision. The panel is to draw 'such inferences ... as it considers appropriate' from any breach of the Policy or of the Rules.[72] Neither party is allowed to communicate with the panel without copying the message to the other party.[73] Transfer of the domain name before the dispute is resolved is subject to severe restrictions.[74]

---

62 Rules for Uniform Domain Name Dispute Resolution Policy (Web), rule 3.
63 *Ibid*, rule 4.
64 *Ibid*, rule 5.
65 *Ibid*, rule 9.
66 *Ibid*, rule 15(b).
67 *Ibid*, rule 16.
68 Uniform Domain Name Dispute Resolution Policy (Web), para 6.
69 *Ibid*, para 4g; Rules for Uniform Domain Name Dispute Resolution Policy (Web), rule 19.
70 Rules for Uniform Domain Name Dispute Resolution Policy (Web), rule 7.
71 *Ibid*, rules 2 and 11.
72 *Ibid*, rule 14.
73 *Ibid*, rule 8.
74 Uniform Domain Name Dispute Resolution Policy (Web), para 8.

Once the panel has been selected, it controls the resolution of the dispute. The panel is under a general duty to treat the parties equally and to give each party a fair opportunity to present its case, but has freedom of action within the Policy and the Rules. It has power to waive the precise application of the Rules and time limits in exceptional circumstances. It also has power to determine 'the admissibility, relevance, materiality and weight of the evidence'.[75] It may request additional statements or documents from the parties.[76] It is also empowered, 'in its sole discretion and as an exceptional matter', to order in-person hearings, including hearings by telephone conference, video conference, or web conference.[77]

The panel must produce a reasoned decision, 'on the basis of the statements and documents submitted and in accordance with the Policy, these Rules and any Rules and principles of law that it deems applicable'. Three-member panels may act by majority, in which case a dissenting opinion may also be produced.[78] The decision must be published in full on the Internet unless there are 'exceptional' circumstances to justify redaction (suppression) of portions of it.[79] A decision that the domain name in dispute be cancelled or transferred will be implemented 10 business days after the registrar is informed of the decision. If within that period the respondent notifies the registrar that legal proceedings have been started over the matter, the registration will be left in place to await the outcome of those proceedings.[80] If the panel forms the view that the complaint was made in bad faith ('for example in an attempt at Reverse Domain Name Hijacking or was brought primarily to harass the domain-name holder') then it must say so, though this ruling has no consequence within the dispute-resolution proceedings.[81]

There is no system of appeals within the Policy and Rules, and a decision in favour of the complainant cannot in practice be challenged except by going to the courts. It is not entirely clear whether a disappointed complainant can simply start a fresh set of proceedings under the Policy in the hope of finding a more favourably-disposed panel; this is not forbidden by the Policy and, as proceedings under it are not technically proceedings before a court, it is not obvious that any principle of issue estoppel would prevent it. No unanimous view has emerged from proceedings on re-filed complaints, some panels apparently being happy to reconsider the complaint, others viewing such complaints with suspicion, at least if there is no evidence that circumstances have changed since the original complaint.[82]

Assessment

The UDRP process is a popular one with complainants, and has processed in the order of 15,000 claims in its short life.[83] Even its worst critics agree that it is

---

75 Rules for Uniform Domain Name Dispute Resolution Policy (Web), rule 10.
76 *Ibid*, rule 12.
77 *Ibid*, rule 13.
78 *Ibid*, rule 15.
79 Uniform Domain Name Dispute Resolution Policy (Web), para 4j.
80 *Ibid*, para 4k.
81 Rules for Uniform Domain Name Dispute Resolution Policy (Web), rule 15(e).
82 Flint, D, 'If at first you don't succeed', [2001] Bus L Rev 293.
83 Statistical Summary of Proceedings under Uniform Domain Name Dispute Resolution Policy (Web).

considerably faster and much cheaper than any conceivable legal process to replace it; it also provides an effective remedy. The Rules are relatively simple, sufficiently so that they can for the most part be understood without technical legal training. Indeed, many urge them as a model for online dispute resolution that could well be copied for other sorts of disputes.[84]

Yet the speed, efficiency and finality of proceedings is bought at a high price; for many, much too high a price. The simplicity of the Rules ensures that many matters are not dealt with, and many ambiguities are created; and the resolution of these matters is largely left to the individual panellists, who of course do not all resolve them in precisely the same way. The usual methods for imposing consistency on judges – precise and detailed rules, and a rigorous system of appeals – are absent, and can only be introduced at considerable cost. Given this inevitable trade-off, the question is whether the right balance is struck.[85] Many points of view are apparent:

(a) For many, far too much freedom is given to panellists, who can exploit ambiguities to get their way, or indeed openly run roughshod over the Policy and the Rules in the knowledge that there is no appeal. Others are more muted in their criticisms, but nonetheless urge that clarificatory changes are necessary: burdens of proof should be more openly spelled out, the effect of non-compliance with the Rules should not be so absolutely in the discretion of the panel, and so on.[86]

(b) There is concern that it is *too* cheap and easy to bring a complaint, a failed complainant suffering no penalty beyond wasted fees and legal costs. It is argued that panellists should not merely be allowed to declare a claim abusive, but should be able to fine the complainant or inflict some other penalty.

(c) Charges of bias are regularly made. It is said that the complainant's ability to choose between dispute resolution providers imports a bias (as some providers have a better complainant success rate than others);[87] respondents have been accused of bias in their selection of panellists for three-member panels; the dispute resolution providers have been accused of favouring panellists who support the providers' preferences for the values to guide this area of law. The panellists too stand accused, in some cases of personal bias, in others of a general pro-complainant bias. A major study of the matter concludes that '... the panellist selection process is not random. Rather, it appears to be heavily biased toward ensuring that a majority of cases are steered toward complainant-friendly panellists'.[88] It is undeniable that complainants win most cases; in fact, in the order

---

84   For discussion, see Helfer, L, 'International dispute settlement at the trademark-domain name interface', (2001) 29 Pepp LR 87; Christie, A, 'The ICANN domain name dispute resolution system as a model for resolving other intellectual property disputes on the Internet', (2002) 5 JWIL (Web). On online dispute resolution generally, see below, p 260.

85   For contrasting approaches, see Thornburg, B, 'Fast, cheap and out of control: Lessons from the ICANN dispute resolution process', (2001) 7 JSEBL (Web); Froomkin, M, 'ICANN'S "Uniform Dispute Resolution Policy" – Causes and (partial) cures', (2002) 67 Brook LR 605 (Web); Chan, P 'The Uniform Domain Name Dispute Resolution Policy as an alternative to litigation', (2002) 9 E-Law (Web).

86   McCarthy, K, 'Why ICANN's domain dispute rules are flawed', Register, 11 July 2001 (Web).

87   See especially Mueller, M, 'Rough justice: An analysis of ICANN's Uniform Dispute Resolution Policy', November 2000 (Web).

88   Geist, M, 'Fair.com?: An examination of the allegations of systemic unfairness in the ICANN UDRP', (2002) 27 Brook LR 903, 935 (Web).

of 80% do so.[89] However, simple economics suggests that bias is not the only possible explanation for this; the investment involved in bringing a complaint is not entirely trivial, and so we would only expect complaints to be made if they already have a high chance of being accepted. Much of the charge of bias is really a charge that the grounds themselves are too broad, which is considered below.

(d) Others complain that the dispute resolution process usurps the role of the courts, allowing panellists to make arbitrary and unaccountable decisions on matters of legal rights. This criticism chimes well with the more general complaint that ICANN and all its works lack political legitimacy. To the extent that this is a complaint about procedures, it is a weak one, as either party is free to take matters to a court if it wishes. There are undoubtedly disputes for which the URDP is unsuited. It cannot deal effectively with cases where the essential facts are in dispute – no witnesses can be called, there is no discovery, and there is no guarantee that the panellist has any experience with resolving the kind of issue involved. Again, where there is a serious issue of competing legal rights, the panel will not always have the necessary expertise to deliver a reasonable and defensible verdict. But the charge of usurping the role of the courts has most bite when it comes to the substance of the grounds: much weight is placed on the rights of trade mark owners and little on matters limiting those rights, such as 'fair use' and constitutional rights to free speech.

It will be seen that many of these objections are not really to the procedure itself but to the grounds on which a respondent may lose its domain name. To these grounds I now turn.

Grounds

The single criterion for depriving the respondent of its domain name is stated quite briefly in the Policy, though some further guidance is given on two of the three elements of the test.

Applicable Disputes. You are required to submit to a mandatory administrative proceeding in the event that a third party (a 'complainant') asserts to the applicable Provider, in compliance with the Rules of Procedure, that

(i) your domain name is identical or confusingly similar to a trade mark or service mark in which the complainant has rights; and

(ii) you have no rights or legitimate interests in respect of the domain name; and

(iii) your domain name has been registered and is being used in bad faith.

In the administrative proceeding, the complainant must prove that each of these three elements are present.[90]

If the panel finds that the complaint was made in bad faith, was an attempt at 'reverse domain name hijacking', or that its primary aim was to harass the respondent, the panel should say so.[91] It is unclear whether this constitutes a ground

---

89 'Statistical Summary of Proceedings under Uniform Domain Name Dispute Resolution Policy' (Web).

90 Uniform Domain Name Dispute Resolution Policy (Web), para 4a. The case law is now considerable. For one overview, see 'WIPO overview of WIPO panel views on selected UDRP questions' (Web).

91 Rules for Uniform Domain Name Dispute Resolution Policy (Web), rule 15(e).

for rejecting the complaint even if the three elements are made out; neither the Policy nor the Rules say so expressly, but it would be strange if a panel which holds that the complaint 'constitutes an abuse of the administrative proceeding'[92] were nonetheless obliged to uphold it. Factors which have led panels to find bad faith have included a failure by the complainant to tell the panel the whole story,[93] and bringing complaints which the complainant must have known had no merit.[94]

The three elements of the test are now considered one by one.

Domain is identical or confusingly similar to a trade mark or service mark

There is very little in the Policy or the Rules to spell out the detail of this element of the test. Unsurprisingly, the lawyers involved in these disputes make frequent reference to legal principles of trade mark law, and (equally unsurprisingly) it has tended to be US federal trade mark law unless some other jurisdiction is plainly more relevant. (A 'service mark' is simply a trade mark in respect of services.)

In some respects the Policy is narrower than federal trade mark law: either identity or confusing similarity must be shown; the subtleties of 'trade mark dilution' are not mentioned, and not all panels would accept that they must be read in by implication. The Policy does not require proof that the respondent has infringed the complaint's trade mark or service mark; the question that is asked is similar but nonetheless distinct. In other respects it is broader: federal trade mark law bites on infringement of the mark only in the course of trade, whereas a domain name may offend against the Policy whether or not its registrant is engaged in trade, let alone whether it competes with the complainant's trade. (Indeed, a *failure* to use the domain in trade may be part of a case that it was not acquired for any legitimate reason.) In certain crucial respects the protection given to the US trade mark is simply irrelevant, because the UDRP process focuses on the characters used in the name (ignoring even capitalisation); graphic elements of a trade mark are entirely irrelevant. 'Nike loses its swish, Coca-Cola its distinctive typeface, Guinness its harp'.[95] The Policy's test is thus in several ways distinct from the requirements of federal trade mark law.[96]

Despite this, the pull of federal trade mark law is hard to deny. An obvious similarity to an existing registered trade mark is unlikely to be enough to justify a complaint if the claimant would have no remedy in trade mark law: this is particularly so if the trade mark is an entirely generic one such as 'shoes'[97] or 'les pages jaunes'.[98] Conversely, if the respondent has undeniably infringed the complainant's trade mark, some panellists would find it almost inconceivable that the respondent could have any legitimate interest in so doing, or could possibly be acting in good faith.

---

92   *Ibid*, rule 15(e).
93   Eg, *Re maggi.com* (WIPO case D2001-0916) (Web).
94   Eg, *Re dw.com* (WIPO case D2000-1202) (Web).
95   Quinn, G, 'Domain names II', (2000) 1 TELJ (3) 2.
96   On federal trade mark law, see below, p 192.
97   *Re shoes.biz* (WIPO case DBIZ2002-00245) (Web).
98   *Re les-pages-jaunes.com* (WIPO case D2000–0490) (Web). But contrast the very similar *Re londonyellowpages.com and 3 other domains* (WIPO case D2005-0091) (Web).

In the UK and Ireland, the trade mark regime is statutory and based entirely on registration, though there is some analogous common law protection under the tort of passing off. In the US, this more informal protection is often styled 'common law trade mark', and is seen as a useful supplement under state law for the federal system. So the 'trade mark' or 'service mark' referred to need not be registered, though the complainant will probably have to produce substantial evidence to justify its claim to the mark,[99] and can easily lose the case if the mark claimed is poorly defined.[100]

Whether a given domain name is 'confusingly similar to' a given trade mark is obviously a question with many borderline cases. It is relatively easy to satisfy the test when the domain name seems designed to divert those who were trying to get to the complainant's site, as by varying the complainant's trade name with common misspellings[101] or typing errors;[102] this 'typosquatting' is almost impossible to justify. Matters become more doubtful when the domain name is a parody of the complainant's trade mark. A broad view has been taken by some panels; abercrombieandfilth.com (a porn site) has been held to be confusingly similar to 'Abercrombie and Fitch',[103] and mcdonaldsspeakstojesus.com has been held confusingly similar to trade marks owned by McDonald's Corporation.[104] The latter ruling seems especially hard to justify, the panel declaring that:

> While Respondent contends it is 'not logical' to believe consumers would believe that the disputed domain names are affiliated with Complainant, the Policy does not require proof of affiliation or of a likelihood of confusion. Rather, the issue simply is whether the alphanumeric string constituting the domain name is sufficiently similar to the mark in issue.

But this test seems rather circular, absent some definition of 'sufficiently similar'; it also seems unsatisfactory to dismiss the question of a likelihood of confusion, since that is precisely the test that the Policy applies. Decisions along those lines have been subject to much criticism, partly because of what seems an impossibly broad reading of the Policy, and partly because no weight is given to the value of free speech.

Similarly controversial are cases where the name of the site has been chosen to criticise the products or management of the complainant. The Policy has been successfully invoked in relation to a number of such sites, including dixonssucks.com[105] and natwestsucks.com.[106] The panels in those cases stressed that the reference to the complainant is obvious and direct, whereas the significance of 'sucks' may not be. 'Some will treat the additional "sucks" as a pejorative exclamation and therefore dissociate it after all from the Complainant; but equally others may be unable to give it any very definite meaning and will be confused about the potential association with the Complainant'.[107] Other panels take a

---

99   Eg, *Re post-office.com* (NAF case FA0102000096761) (Web).
100 Eg, *Re manchesterairport.com* (WIPO case D2000-0638) (Web).
101 Eg, *Re harods.com* (WIPO case D2003-0504) (Web).
102 Eg, *Re microosoft.com* (WIPO case D2001-0362) (Web).
103 *Re abercrombieandfilth.com* (WIPO case D2001-0900) (Web).
104 *Re mcdonaldslovesbabies.com and 5 other domains* (NAF case FA0304000155458) (Web).
105 *Re dixonssucks.com* (WIPO case D2000-0584) (Web).
106 *Re natwestsucks.com* (WIPO case D2000-0636) (Web).
107 *Ibid, per* William Cornish (panellist).

different view; as one panel ruled, in rejecting an argument that asdasucks.net infringed the rights of Asda Group:

> [t]he Panel is unable to accept that 'a substantial number of people are likely to be confused about the potential association of the Domain Name with the Complainant ...' The Panel believes that by now the number of Internet users who do not appreciate the significance of the '-sucks' suffix must be so small as to be *de minimis* and not worthy of consideration. The Panel notes that the Complainant puts forward no evidence to substantiate that contention. The Panel believes that Internet users will be well aware that a domain name with a '-sucks' suffix does not have the approval of the relevant trade mark owner.[108]

The panel further noted, however, that Asda Group was UK-based and was unlikely to come to the attention of non-English-speaking audiences; different considerations might apply in more international cases.

While these 'sucks' cases seem at first sight to have worrying implications for free speech, there may in fact be less to them than meets the eye. The cases where the complaints have been successful do not seem to have involved suppression of dissenting views, but rather attempts to annoy the complainants into buying the domain from the respondent; panelists' views have been entirely supportive of free speech where that principle is relevant.[109] Someone who makes serious criticisms of a major company in such a public forum as the Internet is likely to have legal problems in plenty,[110] but it does not appear that the UDRP will contribute very much to them.

No rights or legitimate interests in respect of the domain

This second element is stated in vague terms, as it does not explain how a 'right' or a 'legitimate interest' in a name is to be established. It is also unpardonably vague as to the burden of proof: at one point the Policy says that it is for the complainant to prove absence of a right or interest,[111] but at another it talks of 'How to Demonstrate Your [the respondent's] Rights ... and Legitimate Interests ...', which suggests the reverse.[112] Some of the confusion as to substance (though not as to proof) is alleviated by a specification of three grounds, any one of which is sufficient to 'demonstrate your rights or legitimate interests to the domain name' and hence defeat the complaint:

(i) before any notice to you of the dispute, your use of, or demonstrable preparations to use, the domain name or a name corresponding to the domain name in connection with a bona fide offering of goods or services; or

(ii) you (as an individual, business, or other organization) have been commonly known by the domain name, even if you have acquired no trade mark or service mark rights; or

---

108 Re *asdasucks.net* (WIPO case D2002-0857) (Web). See also Re *guinness-beer-really-really-sucks.com and 10 other domains* (WIPO case D2000-0996) (Web); Re *lockheedmartinsucks.com and lockheedsucks.com* (WIPO case D2000-1015) (Web).

109 See, eg, Re *fullsailsucks.com* (WIPO case D2003–0502) (Web).

110 See especially, p 157.

111 Uniform Domain Name Dispute Resolution Policy (Web), para 4a, last sentence.

112 *Ibid*, para 4c.

(iii) you are making a legitimate non-commercial or fair use of the domain name, without intent for commercial gain to misleadingly divert consumers or to tarnish the trademark or service mark at issue.[113]

The common thread in all of these is that the respondent actually makes use of the name to identify itself or its product, or at least was making preparations to do so. The usage can be either on the Internet or elsewhere; it could be the respondent's own name, a name assumed for a particular purpose, or the name of some product or service it is selling. The wording tries to make it irrelevant whether the respondent would be able to protect the name in legal proceedings, though it also tries to exclude usage which is in some respect illegal (though, as many critics have pointed out, head (ii) does not quite do that). Obviously, the respondent's burden is easiest to satisfy if the domain name corresponds to the name it actually uses to describe itself or its business on a day-to-day basis.[114] But this cannot be an absolute principle. In a dispute over the domain oxford-university.com, the respondent claimed to have changed his name, so that he now was Mr Oxford University. The panel was dismissive. 'Even if DR Seagle has indeed made a change of name (no documentary proof of the claim was provided), the Panel would still conclude that the registrant has no rights or legitimate interests in respect of the domain name at issue'.[115]

In theory, there is no reason why 'rights or legitimate interests' should be limited to the three narrow specified grounds, as the Policy is quite explicit that they are not meant to limit the scope of the general words. In practice, litigants have not been very successful in articulating other sorts of 'rights or legitimate interests'. This is at first sight surprising, as it seems to discourage naming sites after the sort of information they contain. If someone wished to establish a web site about Communism, and (unsurprisingly) registered a domain containing the word 'communism' from which to do it, it would appear that they might have difficulty establishing a 'legitimate interest', even though they appear to have acted entirely reasonably. However, it would appear that this is rarely a problem: if even a *bona fide* registrant of that sort cannot establish a legitimate claim, then neither can anyone else. In practice, the domain will be secure.

One exception to this, however, is the fan site, where a fan creates a web site in some celebrity's honour, using the celebrity's name as part of the domain. It is hard to see what is 'illegitimate' about this, always assuming that any relevant intellectual property rights have been respected. Nonetheless, it seems clear that the domain can be claimed by the celebrity personally; the name is theirs. This has been established in a string of cases, some of the more famous of which concerned the domains jrrtolkien.com,[116] piercebrosnan.com,[117] juliaroberts.com,[118] madonna.com,[119] and jeanettewinterson.com.[120] (However, the pop singer Sting, real name Gordon Sumner, failed in his attempt to take sting.com from its registrant; he had neglected

---

113 Uniform Domain Name Dispute Resolution Policy (Web), para 4c.
114 Eg, *Re 4you.com* (NAF case FA0010000095847) (Web).
115 *Re oxford-university.com* (WIPO case D2000-0308) (Web).
116 *Re jrrtolkien.com* (WIPO case D2003-0837) (Web).
117 *Re piercebrosnan.com* (WIPO case D2003-0519) (Web).
118 *Re juliaroberts.com* (WIPO case D2000-0210) (Web).
119 *Re madonna.com* (WIPO case D2000-0847) (Web).
120 *Re jeanettewinterson.com and 2 other domains* (WIPO case D2000-0235) (Web).

to register a trade mark in his stage name, and failed to convince the panel that it was a mark protected at common law.[121]) These cases create a very strong presumption that the domain name must be its owner's name, and that it is not enough that the name fairly indicates the content of the site. It is true that none of these cases involved genuine fan sites, and that there were clear 'bad faith' grounds in each; unfortunately, the narrow approach adopted towards 'legitimate interests' seems to apply to real fan sites as well. Presumably, the same attitude will be taken to the names of fictitious celebrities, which would be claimed by the owner of the intellectual property rights in their stories; it would be a bold registrant who would claim to have a legitimate interest in (say) the domain mickeymouse.com in a claim by the Disney Corporation. Presumably, similar principles apply also to domain names for sites critical of the name's owner,[122] though the cases are not unanimous.[123]

Another difficult area is that of geographical names. If a domain name covers a particular geographical entity, can it be claimed by the legal government for that entity? Some of these claims have failed outright, the panel finding that the name is not protected by a trade mark registration, and refusing to apply any doctrine of common law marks. If the complainant can get over that hurdle, what next? Can a respondent plead a legitimate interest based on its connection with the geographical entity, or can the government insist that the name is theirs? While, of course, purely abusive registrations can be defeated,[124] there seems to be an assumption that a legitimate interest can consist of any plausible connection with the geographical entity, including *bona fide* provision of information relating to it. This has happened with stmoritz.com,[125] portofhelsinki.com,[126] newzealand.com[127] and mexico.com.[128] Indeed, the latter two complaints were both declared by the panels to be attempts at reverse domain name hijacking. Clearly these cases extend the notion of 'legitimate interests' quite a way; it remains to be seen whether this will develop into a more general doctrine. The case is, of course, quite different if the domain name denotes a political rather than a geographical entity: so the German government is entitled to federalrepublicofgermany.biz in circumstances where a claim to germany.biz would have been dubious.[129]

Bad faith registration and use of the domain

Bad faith is not defined in either the Policy or the Rules, and so is left very much in the hands of the panel. It is for the complainant to specify what the alleged bad faith consists of, and the complaint is likely to fail if this is not done.[130]

---

121 *Re sting.com* (WIPO case D2000-0596) (Web). On the celebrity cases generally, see Verna, A, 'WWW.WHATSINA.NAME', (2004) 14 SHJSL 153.
122 Eg, *Re montyroberts.net* (WIPO case D2000-0299) (Web).
123 *Re britanniabuildingsociety.org* (WIPO case D2001-0505) (Web).
124 *Re barcelona.com* (WIPO case D2000-0505) (Web). For subsequent litigation over this domain, see below, p 197.
125 *Re stmoritz.com* (WIPO case D2000-0617) (Web).
126 *Re portofhelsinki.com* (WIPO case D2001-0002) (Web).
127 *Re newzealand.com* (WIPO case D2002-0754) (Web).
128 *Re mexico.com* (WIPO case D2004-0242) (Web).
129 *Re federalrepublicofgermany.biz* (WIPO case D2004-0676) (Web).
130 Eg, *Re polo-style.com and ralph-lauren-polo.com* (WIPO case D2002-0148) (Web).

Technically speaking, there are two distinct requirements here – bad faith on registration and bad faith use – but as bad faith intent is usually inferred from a pattern of conduct over time, the same evidence can often be used to infer both. Nonetheless, the two requirements sometimes lead to surprising results. In particular, one panel has held that if the registrant is making no use of the domain at the time of the hearing, then the complaint must fail; even if the panel is convinced that any use would be in bad faith, nonetheless there can be no bad faith use if there is no use at all.[131] The point is a doubtful one, however, and other panels have been prepared to hold that inaction is 'use' for this purpose.[132]

Four sets of circumstances are stated to be 'in particular but without limitation … evidence of the registration and use of a domain name in bad faith'; a formulation which is presumably meant to guide the parties in presenting their arguments without tying the hands of the panel too tightly. These are stated as:

(i) circumstances indicating that you have registered or you have acquired the domain name primarily for the purpose of selling, renting, or otherwise transferring the domain name registration to the complainant who is the owner of the trademark or service mark or to a competitor of that complainant, for valuable consideration in excess of your documented out-of-pocket costs directly related to the domain name; or

(ii) you have registered the domain name in order to prevent the owner of the trademark or service mark from reflecting the mark in a corresponding domain name, provided that you have engaged in a pattern of such conduct; or

(iii) you have registered the domain name primarily for the purpose of disrupting the business of a competitor; or

(iv) by using the domain name, you have intentionally attempted to attract, for commercial gain, Internet users to your web site or other on-line location, by creating a likelihood of confusion with the complainant's mark as to the source, sponsorship, affiliation, or endorsement of your web site or location or of a product or service on your web site or location.

The classic instances of cybersquatting would involve (i) and (iv) and probably (ii) as well; however, any one of these alone is a sufficient basis for a panel to find that bad faith has been established. Typically, panels rely on a number of factors to bolster a finding of bad faith.[133]

The Policy is rather ambivalent on the matter of selling domains. Head (i) is unequivocal – what is objectionable is not selling a domain, but registering a domain *primarily* to sell it to the complainant. But it is far from obvious when an offer to sell will be treated as evidence of bad faith. Certainly, offers to sell the domain to the complainant have been treated as weighty indications of bad faith.[134] However, where the name is generic, much greater leniency is shown: where the name does not relate to the complainant particularly but to a particular product or service, it is far from obvious that the name should not be traded openly.[135] As currently worded,

---

131 *Re buyouarnetsunglasses.com* (WIPO case D2000-0265) (Web).
132 *Re telstra.org* (WIPO case D2000-0003) (Web); *Re crateandbarrel.org* (WIPO case D2000-1195) (Web).
133 Eg, *Re aerrianta.com* (WIPO case D2000-1165) (Web).
134 Eg, *Re worldwrestlingfederation.com* (WIPO case D1999-0001) (Web), which was the first case decided under the UDRP.
135 Eg, *Re cartoys.net* (NAF case FA0002000093682) (Web); *Re tombola.org* (eResolution case AF-0422) (Web).

the Policy inhibits settlement: a respondent will be reluctant to make a settlement offer if it can immediately be used as evidence of bad faith.[136]

The respondent's behaviour in relation to the domain and the dispute over it is always relevant and, if open to criticism, can be the basis of a finding of bad faith. If it is clear that the respondent knew of the complainant's trade mark, blatant infringement of it easily leads to an inference of bad faith.[137] Failure to provide proper contact details or to answer messages from the complainant will count against the respondent, as will evasiveness or obfuscation.[138] And conduct that seems calculated to annoy the complainant is likely to lead to an inference of bad faith, on the argument that it was an attempt to induce a sale of the domain.[139] More generally, evidence that the respondent has regularly engaged in cybersquatting will make it easy to infer that bad faith is present.[140]

Rules for other domains

The UDRP applies across all the gTLDs. The Policy and the Rules are supplemented by the procedural rules of each dispute resolution provider. Several of the domains are restricted in those who may own them, either in the sense that they are sponsored domains (such as .aero, .coop) or in that they are meant for a broad but not limitless category (such as .biz, .pro). For those domains, there are rules to resolve disputes over whether a particular registrant belongs in the category chosen. Note that while the most popular domains – .com, .org, .net, .info – are designed to look restricted, there is in fact no legal limitation; there is no mechanism for removing a .com domain on the ground that its registrant is not engaged in commerce.

The ccTLDs are more various, having freedom to specify their own dispute resolution policies. A number have simply adopted the UDRP; most have devised their own policies, which vary more or less from the UDRP model.[141] WIPO provides the dispute resolution service for a number of ccTLDs.[142]

Ireland

Disputes within the .ie domain are provided for by the IE Dispute Resolution Policy, in force July 2003.[143] The dispute resolution service is provided by WIPO, under rules[144] and supplementary rules[145] devised for the purpose. Both the Policy and the

136 Geissler, R, ' "For Sale" signs in cyberspace', [2002] IPTF 111801 (Web).
137 Eg, *Re nokiagirls.com* (WIPO case D2000-0102) (Web).
138 Eg, *Re telstra.org* (WIPO case D2000-0003) (Web).
139 Eg, *Re robbiewilliams.info* (WIPO case D2002-0588) (Web).
140 Eg, *Re nationalrentalcar.com* (WIPO case D2000-1803) (Web).
141 For a general survey, see Smith, G (ed), *Internet Law and Regulation*, 3rd edn, 2002, London: Sweet and Maxwell, pp 107–60.
142 'Domain Name Dispute Resolution Service for country code top-level domains (ccTLDs)' (Web).
143 IE Dispute Resolution Policy (Web).
144 WIPO Dispute Resolution Rules of Procedure for IE Domain Name Registrations (Web).
145 World Intellectual Property Organization Arbitration and Mediation Center Supplemental Rules for IE Domain Name Dispute Resolution Policy (Web).

Rules are in very similar terms to the UDRP. Fees are currently € 1,500 for a single panellist and € 4,000 for three panellists. The three elements necessary before action against a particular domain name can be taken are:

(a) that the domain name is identical or misleadingly similar to a 'protected identifier' in which the complainant has rights ('protected identifiers' can include trade marks, service marks, Irish geographical indications, and personal names with an Irish reputation); and

(b) the registrant has no rights in law or legitimate interests in respect of the domain name; and

(c) the domain name has been registered or is being used in bad faith. As with the UDRP, circumstances that can be evidence of bad faith are provided; unlike the UDRP, these include 'where the domain name is used in a way that is likely to dilute the reputation of a trade or service mark in which the complainant has rights'.

The Policy and Rules are an updated version of the UDRP; on both substantive and procedural points, they either incorporate points raised by UDRP case law or attempt to solve difficulties (such as how to deal with geographical indications) which have emerged in the course of those cases.

United Kingdom

The .uk domains have had a dispute resolution procedure since September 2001, though new versions of the Policy and the Rules are in force on 25 October 2004.[146] The dispute resolution service is provided by the registrar, Nominet, itself. Procedures are not dissimilar from those for the UDRP, though there are certain differences:

(a) The complainant must pay £ 750 (plus value added tax) to commence proceedings, payable once an expert has been appointed.

(b) In contested cases, Nominet will attempt informal mediation between the parties before any formal decision is made. The mediation is confidential, even from the expert who will decide the issue if the parties cannot be persuaded to settle; and '[n]either Party shall use any information gained during mediation for any ulterior or collateral purpose or include it in any submission likely to be seen by any expert, judge or arbitrator in this dispute or any later dispute or litigation'. If mediation does not resolve the complaint within 10 working days, an expert is appointed to decide the matter.

(c) There are strict word limits on submissions to the expert: complaints are limited to 2,000 words, though annexes may be attached; the response is similarly limited; the complainant may send in 2,000 words more in reply to the response. Over-lengthy submissions are returned to their authors; if they are not re-submitted, at the correct length, within three days, certain default procedures apply.

(d) An appeal lies from the decision of the expert to a panel of three experts; the appellant must pay a fee of £3,000 (plus value added tax). The appeal notice and response must each state its argument in 1,000 words (no annexes).

---

146 Dispute Resolution Service Policy (Web); Procedure for the conduct of proceedings under the Dispute Resolution Service (Web).

A domain name may be challenged by a complaint under this procedure only if (i) the complainant has rights in respect of a name or mark which is identical or similar to the domain name, and (ii) the registration was abusive. The rights in the name need not be ones enforceable in English law. However, a 'name or term which is wholly descriptive of the Complainant's business' cannot be the subject of a complaint.

An 'abusive registration' is a domain name which either 'was registered or otherwise acquired in a manner which, at the time when the registration or acquisition took place, took unfair advantage of or was unfairly detrimental to the Complainant's Rights', or 'has been used in a manner which took unfair advantage of or was unfairly detrimental to the Complainant's Rights'. In other words, the complainant needs to prove an abuse either in the way the respondent acquired the name, or in how it was used (but not both). There is a detailed, non-exhaustive list of factors, which may be evidence against the respondent, including:

(a) that registration was primarily with an eye to selling the domain to the complainant or a competitor of the complainant;

(b) that registration was primarily to disrupt the complainant's business;

(c) that the respondent has a history of cybersquatting;

(d) that '[i]t is independently verified that the [r]espondent has given false contact details' to Nominet;

(e) that the name 'was registered as a result of a relationship between the [c]omplainant and the [r]espondent' but has now been taken over by the respondent exclusively.

There is a similarly detailed, non-exhaustive list of factors which may be evidence pointing the other way, including:

(a) that the respondent made legitimate trade use of the name before the complaint came to its attention;

(b) that the respondent was commonly known by the name before the complaint came to its attention;

(c) that the name is 'generic or descriptive and the [r]espondent is making fair use of it'.

It is expressly declared that 'Fair use may include sites operated solely in tribute to or in criticism of a person or business'.

A respondent who has been found to have made abusive registrations in three or more cases in the two years preceding the complaint has to meet a reversed burden of proof: it will be presumed, in any new proceedings, that registration was abusive unless the respondent can prove otherwise.

DOMAIN NAMES IN DOMESTIC COURTS

As has already been hinted, domestic legal tribunals have a great deal to say on ownership of domain names. Indeed, from one point of view the UDRP's function is not so much to vindicate the rights of trade mark owners as to protect ICANN and its registrars from US trade mark litigation. While this text is written from the point of view of UK and Irish parties, nonetheless some understanding of the US position is necessary, partly to understand the workings of the system as a whole, and partly because European parties may very easily find themselves dragged into US litigation.

No legal system in the world has yet developed a comprehensive code to determine the ownership of domain names; and if informal arbitration of the UDRP sort is a long-term success, quite possibly none ever will. Most legal regulation of domain names is indirect: the court will not concern itself with who 'owns' the name, but a defendant who has used their domain name to commit a legal wrong may find that the court makes them give it up, either by issuing an injunction to that effect, or by attaching such dire consequences to retaining it that there is no alternative to abandoning it. This is the only way, at present, in which UK and Irish law can affect the ownership of a domain name. Direct regulation is possible, though rare: a legal system may explicitly state grounds on which a claimant may demand transfer of a domain name to them. This is now possible, in certain limited circumstances, in the US, under both a specific statute (the Anticybersquatting Consumer Protection Act 1999 or ACPA) and at common law. This direct claim – in effect, a claim to own the domain name – is of uncertain status, and it remains to be seen whether it will spread from the US to the rest of the world.

It is clear that how a claim to a particular domain name is resolved may depend on where the question is being asked. Each claim has to be looked on from the standpoint of the legal system that is being invoked. Jurisdictional questions are likely to involve asking whether there is some substantial link between the dispute and the relevant jurisdiction; this often means looking at how the domain name is being used, though occasionally the courts ask whether the domain can be said to be 'in' the jurisdiction, in the sense that its registrar is physically present there. Jurisdiction may also be acquired by prior agreement between the litigants – and, as noted above, participation in UDRP necessarily involves submission in advance to a mutually agreed jurisdiction for challenging the panel's ruling.[147] As to substantive law, differences between legal systems are inevitable. There are always national differences on relevant principles, mitigated or not by international treaty; and even when the law is similar, other differences will become apparent. Trade mark litigation, for example, will make it of paramount importance whether the mark is registered in *that country's* registry, and any claim based on interference with the claimant's business is likely to focus on interference in markets in *that country* alone.

US law – indirect claims to domain names

In the early days of the Internet, there was no express provision for ownership of domain names. Nonetheless, major corporations with substantial investments in branding themselves and their products were quick to look for legal remedies when 'their' names appeared on the Internet, and initially at least they used the legal doctrine most obviously suitable for protecting the use of names: federal trade mark law. Other doctrines can be invoked in principle, and these are considered immediately after. In applying these rules, no very noticeable deference is shown to UDRP proceedings, which are treated as even less significant than ordinary arbitration.[148]

---

147 Above, p 178.
148 See especially *Dluhos v Strasberg* 321 F 3d 365 (3rd Ct, 20 February 2003).

Trade mark

The earliest attempts to claim domain names were made through the medium of federal trade mark law, and judicial ire against cybersquatting resulted in some quite broad decisions. At the present time, however, a different attitude is apparent. Congress having introduced special provision for the standard case of cybersquatting (in the ACPA, considered below), there is much less for the general law of trade mark to do. Trade mark law is not really appropriate for the simple case of using another's US-registered trade mark as a domain name; more is required, both to show infringement of the mark and to point to the US as an appropriate forum for the dispute. This will become clearer when the basics of US federal trade mark law are briefly examined.

By the Federal Trade Mark Act 1946 (the Lanham Act), any commercial use of a registered mark, where 'such use is likely to cause confusion, or to cause mistake, or to deceive', is a breach of the mark owner's rights. Reproduction, copying or imitating the mark in the course of advertising or distributing goods or services, where 'such use is likely to cause confusion, or to cause mistake, or to deceive', is also a breach. The primary remedy is damages, though injunctions are also available.[149] Assessment of damages can take into account matters such as the plaintiff's loss and legal costs and any profits made by the defendant. The amount recovered depends on the court's assessment of the defendant's conduct and the equities of the case: up to three times the plaintiff's actual loss can be awarded as damages if the court thinks it appropriate. If the defendant has used a mark that can be stigmatised as a 'counterfeit' of the plaintiff's mark, the plaintiff automatically receives treble damages in the absence of extenuating circumstances; alternatively, the plaintiff can elect to receive statutory damages as the court thinks just, which are up to US$100,000 per mark per type of goods or services sold, or ten times that figure for wilful use of a counterfeit mark.[150]

Owners of famous and distinctive marks are further protected by the provisions on trade mark dilution. Various factors are listed for a court to consider in determining whether any particular mark is sufficiently famous and distinctive for this purpose. Assuming that the mark qualifies, the mark owner is entitled to remedies against 'dilution of the distinctive quality of the mark'. Dilution is defined as the 'lessening of the capacity of a famous mark to identify and distinguish goods or services'. This has been spelled out in case law as involving either 'blurring' (that is, weakening the association between the mark and the mark owner's products) or 'tarnishment' (that is, associating the mark with lower-quality products). Statute expressly states it to be irrelevant whether the dilutor is in competition with the mark owner, or whether there is any 'likelihood of confusion, mistake, or deception'. The primary remedy against trade mark dilution is an injunction, though damages and other remedies are available in addition where it can be shown that the defendant 'wilfully intended to trade on the owner's reputation or to cause dilution of the famous mark'. The anti-dilution provisions do not catch non-commercial activities, news reporting and news commentary, or fair use in comparative advertising.[151]

---

149 US Code Title 15 s 1114 (Web).
150 US Code Title 15 s 1117(c) (Web).
151 US Code Title 15 s 1125(c) (Web) and 1127 (Web) (definition of 'dilution'), inserted by Federal Trade Mark Dilution Act 1995.

There is now explicit protection for domain name registrars, who are given immunity from suit so long as they have acted in good faith, co-operate with the court, and comply with any court order. It is clearly envisaged that the registrar will take no independent action during the course of any dispute over a domain. Where the domain registrar receives a complaint of a trade mark violation and acts on it by transferring or cancelling the domain, the immunity does not apply, but the registrar is entitled to an indemnity from the complainant if the legitimacy of its action is challenged, if 'knowing and material misrepresentation' by the complainant can be established.[152]

Some cases on liability have taken a very pro-plaintiff line, at least in cases of blatant cybersquatting. In one case where the defendant registered the domain but made no use of it, he was nonetheless held to have made 'commercial use' of it for trade mark purposes, as his intention was to sell the domain to the plaintiff.[153] But even if that case is thought to have been correctly decided,[154] nonetheless in cases where the defendant's motives are more legitimate, more substantial evidence of commercial use is required, particularly if the plaintiff is relying on an alleged confusion between its business and that of the defendant.[155] Evidence of the extent of competition between the parties is highly relevant: are they selling similar products, to people in the same geographical area?[156] Various limits on trade mark law have proved inconvenient for plaintiffs, particularly the judicial reluctance to grant trade mark status to geographical designations or generic product descriptions.[157] A more nuanced line can be taken than in UDRP cases, especially as the court has more flexibility as to remedies – it can, for example, allow the defendant to retain the domain while issuing an injunction against infringing use.

'Sucks' sites initially got a rough ride from the federal courts. One defendant registered the domain jewsforjesus.com and used it to criticise the organisation 'Jews for Jesus'; another requested plannedparenthood.com and used it to criticise the practice of abortion. In both cases, the domain was removed from the defendant in trade mark proceedings; commercial use was established on rather minimal grounds (in the first case because the site was linked to commercial sites, in the second because the defendant used it to promote his own book on the issue); arguments based on free speech were given short shrift.[158] A more liberal attitude was apparent in the fuckgeneralmotors.com case, where the court refused to accept that mere criticism of a commercial entity was a commercial use, or that it amounted to

---

152 US Code Title 15 s 1114(2)(d)) (Web).

153 *Panavision International v Toeppen* 141 F 3d 1316 (9th Ct, 17 April 1998).

154 Cf the much more liberal decision in *Avery Dennison Corp v Sumpton* 189 F 3d 868 (9th Ct, 23 August 1999), on which see Margiano, R, [1999] 3 JILT (Web).

155 Eg, *First Jewellery Company of Canada v Internet Shopping Network* 2000 US Dist LEXIS 794 (SD NY, 1 February 2000).

156 Eg, *Brookfield Communications v West Coast Entertainment Corp* 174 F 3d 1036 (9th Ct, 22 April 1999); *Hasbro, Inc v Clue Computing Inc* 66 F Supp 2d 117 (D Mass, 2 September 1999).

157 For criticism see Akhtar, S and Cumbow, R, 'Why domain names are not generic: An analysis of why domain names incorporating generic terms are entitled to trademark protection', (1999) 1 CKJIP 226 (Web); Le, C, 'Genericness doctrine need not apply', (2004) 14 FIPMELJ 1093.

158 *Jews for Jesus v Brodsky* 993 F Supp 282 (D NJ, 6 March 1998); *Planned Parenthood v Bucci* 1997 US Dist LEXIS 3338 (SD NY, 24 March 1997).

tarnishment of the trade mark.[159] It now appears that 'sucks' sites will be safe from trade mark proceedings, so long as they can deal with any argument that their purpose is a commercial one.[160]

Jurisdiction in trade mark cases is rapidly evolving, at least from the perspective of a European domain name holder. Two early decisions seemed to hold that jurisdiction could be established merely because the web site was accessible from within the forum.[161] This was, however, quickly repudiated, the famous *Zippo* case demanding at least some evidence of interactivity with US customers before jurisdiction can be established.[162] It will be for the plaintiff to establish that the defendant purposely availed themselves of the benefits of the forum, though discovery may be available to help in this process – even discovery as to non-Internet activities of the defendant.[163]

Indirect claims to domain names may also sometimes be made on a variety of other grounds.

False descriptions

Quite apart from any matter of trade mark rights, federal law gives a right of civil action to those harmed by false or misleading representation of fact by a party engaged in commerce. This includes 'any word, term, name, symbol, or device, or any combination thereof'. The defendant's conduct must be 'likely to cause confusion, or to cause mistake, or to deceive as to the affiliation, connection, or association of such person with another person, or as to the origin, sponsorship, or approval of his or her goods, services, or commercial activities by another person'; or alternatively must misrepresent 'the nature, characteristics, qualities, or geographic origin of his or her or another person's goods, services, or commercial activities'. It is technically possible to found such a claim on the simple use of a misleading domain name, though in practice more is likely to be required to establish a cause of action.[164]

Unfair competition

Unfair use of a domain name may be the subject of proceedings for unfair competition, whether under the federal jurisdiction (enforced by the Federal Trade Commission), or under state law. Many state competition statutes contain explicit provision for business names; but the difficulties in establishing that any one defendant is subject to the jurisdiction of that state's courts may be considerable.

---

159 *Ford Motor Company v 2600 Enterprises* 177 F Supp 2d 661 (ED Mich, 20 December 2001).
160 *Bosley Medical Institute, Inc v Kremer* 403 F 3d 672 (9th Ct, 4 April 2005). See generally on this issue, Prince, D, 'Cyber-criticism and the Federal Trademark Dilution Act: Redefining the noncommercial use exemption', (2004) 9 VJOLT 12 (Web); Travis, P, 'The battle for mindshare', (2005) 10 VJOLT 3 (Web).
161 *Inset Systems, Inc v Instruction Set, Inc* 937 F Supp 161 (D Conn, 17 April 1996); *Maritz, Inc v CyberGold, Inc* 947 F Supp 1328 (E D Mo, 19 August 1996).
162 *Zippo Manufacturing Co v Zippo Dot Com, Inc* 952 F Supp 1119 (W D Pa, 16 January 1997); see above, p 61.
163 *Toys 'R' Us v Step Two SA* 318 F 3d 446 (3rd Ct, 27 January 2003).
164 US Code Title 15 s 1125(a) (Web), inserted by Federal Trade Mark Dilution Act 1995.

Publicity rights

Several states protect the rights of celebrities, and there is no reason why these laws should not be applied to domain name disputes. Their use in this way is uncertain, however, and of course there would also be substantial problems over jurisdiction.

Criminal forfeiture laws

Laws providing for forfeiture of criminal assets have sometimes been used against domains, in cases where the domain was used to market illegal goods, as often happens with drugs, pornography and copyright-circumvention technologies.[165]

US law – direct claims to domain names

The indirect remedies just examined are useful when the defendant has used the domain to harm another and/or to breach the criminal law. There are, as mentioned above, cases where merely registering a certain domain is enough to put the defendant into that category. But those legal procedures are elaborate tools at best. In a few cases, there is a simple, direct claim: that regardless of how the domain has been used, the current holder has no right to it, and should transfer it to the plaintiff forthwith.

Wrongful cancellation or transfer of a domain name: common law claims

In some limited circumstances, the former owner of a domain might claim that it was wrongly transferred or cancelled by the registrar; an action for breach of contract against the registrar might then be plausible. Presumably, there would be very few situations in which this could happen. Registrars have little incentive to expose themselves to litigation in this way, and the contract terms under which domain names are issued are carefully drafted to clarify their rather limited responsibilities and to minimise their exposure to hostile litigation. Nonetheless, cases occasionally crop up where a former registrant has a legitimate grievance, perhaps because a con artist used fraud to trick the registrar into transferring the name.[166]

The leading case involves the domain sex.com, which has considerable earning potential, and has been hard fought over accordingly. One Gary Kremen was allotted the domain in 1994, at a time when domain names were still being allotted merely on request, without payment being demanded by the registrar, or indeed production of any written contract. Then, in 1995, Steven Cohen claimed that the domain was his and, with the aid of forged documents, persuaded the registrar to transfer it to him. Kremen sued both Cohen and the registrar. He obtained a re-transfer of the name to himself, and judgment against Cohen for US$65m (though it is not clear that Cohen ever paid a cent[167]). His claim against the registrar failed insofar as it was based

---

165 See, eg, 'US crime-fighters seize web sites', ZDNet, 26 February 2003 (Web).
166 For discussion see McGillivray, R and Lieske, S, 'Webjacking', (2001) 27 WMLR 1661 (Web).
167 'Sex.com conman continues ludicrous legal fight', Register, 1 May 2003 (Web); 'Sex.com ruling upheld by Court of Appeals', Register, 5 April 2005 (Web).

on contract: as he had not paid for the domain, he could not enforce any agreement he had with the registrar, and he could not convince the court that he was a third party beneficiary of the contracts under which the registrar worked.[168] However, he was successful in his contention that the registrar had committed the tort of conversion against his domain, and the registrar was liable in damages accordingly;[169] the claim was ultimately settled for an undisclosed amount, believed to be in eight figures.[170]

The sex.com case is, in a sense, of historical interest only. As the Federal Court of Appeals noted, '[t]he facts date back to the Wild West days of domain name registration', and any such case today would be fought on the basis of the registrar's standard form contract, not the principles of tort. Nonetheless, the eventual result gives a fillip to the more general argument that a domain name can be treated as a physical object that the registrar is looking after for the current registrant – an argument of considerable general relevance, as it supports the use of an *in rem* jurisdiction.[171]

The most common situation today in which a plaintiff might lose their domain would be if it was taken from them through some other procedure, such as the UDRP. In that situation, statute expressly grants a right of action to determine whether the loss of the domain was lawful, and if not, '[t]he court may grant injunctive relief to the domain name registrant, including the reactivation of the domain name or transfer of the domain name'.[172] It is not at all clear what standards are to be applied in determining the lawfulness of the taking. In the leading case, the Federal Court of Appeals maintained that US federal law applied, and so asking whether the domain had rightly been taken from the plaintiff was the same as asking whether it could have been taken in proceedings under the ACPA. 'We would not lightly assume that Congress enacted the ACPA, but intended all domain name registrants to be governed by a different standard, administered by international dispute resolution panels, with no eventual recourse to whatever affirmative protections the US law might provide.'[173] The fact that one of the parties to the dispute was Brazilian was not considered relevant. Again, in a case where the registrar took away the defendant's domain name in compliance with a French ruling that it infringed a French company's trade mark, the Federal Court of Appeals held not only that it had jurisdiction to re-try the matter, but that the standard to be applied was whether the French company had rights in US trade mark law. The plaintiff's action to recover his domain name was an American action, to be determined by US law; the court's recognition of that fact 'does not imply any disrespect of any French court that may have taken jurisdiction of a related dispute in France'.[174] Whether it is a tenable position, that US trade mark law should govern the entire Internet merely because the registrars happen to live there, remains to be seen.

---

168 *Kremen v Cohen* 99 F Supp 2d 1168 (ND Ca, 8 May 2000).

169 *Kremen v Cohen* 314 F 3d 1127 (9th Ct, 3 January 2003), on which see Epstein, R, 'The Roman law of cyberconversion', [2005] MSLR 103.

170 'Sex.com epic battle finally ends', Register, 21 April 2004 (Web).

171 On which see below, p 199.

172 US Code Title 15 s 1114(2)(D)(v) (Web), inserted by the Anticybersquatting Consumer Protection Act 1999.

173 *Sallen v Corinthians Licenciamentos LTDA* 273 F 3d 14 (1st Ct, 5 December 2001).

174 *Hawes v Network Solutions, Inc* 337 F 3d 377 (4th Ct, 9 July 2003).

The Truth in Domain Names Act 2003

This highly specific legislation targets one very particular situation. Much typosquatting is used to trick people into visiting porn sites. So a porn site owner may register a name very similar to a famous name, relying on mistypings or misspellings to get potential customers. This legislation is an attempt to impose zoning on the net, by making it harder to access porn by accident. So an offence is committed by a defendant who registers a misleading domain name, with the intent to deceive persons into viewing obscene material. The penalty may include imprisonment for up to two years; this rises to four years if the domain name targets children.[175]

The Anticybersquatting Consumer Protection Act 1999 (ACPA)

The ACPA creates a right of action in favour of trade mark owners against those who have misused domain names; remedies can include cancellation or transfer of the domain name.[176] Non-US trade mark owners may invoke the Act, though there seems to be an outright refusal to recognise marks which would not be recognised under US law.[177] Liability is 'without regard to the goods or services of the parties', so that it is no defence that the domain's owner is not a competitor of the plaintiff. The remedies made available are expressly stated to be in addition to any other legal remedies available.[178]

The ACPA makes civil remedies available against a defendant who 'registers, traffics in, or uses' a domain, and has a 'bad faith intent to profit' from the mark; the domains against which the remedy lies are those which are identical or confusingly similar to the trade mark, or (in the case of 'famous' marks) dilutive of it. It appears that the possibilities for confusion are assessed by looking not merely at the name, but also at the way in which the domain has been used: so fan sites and 'sucks' sites may be saved by prominent disclaimers on their front pages, disavowing any connection with the person lauded or criticised.[179] It has recently been held that the legislation is not confined to cases where the site is being used commercially;[180] though since the plaintiff must still prove 'bad faith intent to profit', this may in practice not extend the law very much.

As will already be clear from this brief description, the ACPA is ambivalent over whether its primary aim is to allow seizure of offending names, or whether it is to impose liability on offending owners. The Act's most striking feature is the former, in that it allows the plaintiff to claim the name itself, even (as will be described below)

---

175 Clark, G, 'The Truth in Domain Names Act of 2003 and a preventative measure to combat typosquatting', (2004) 89 Corn LR 1476; Honig, M, 'The truth about the Truth in Domain Names Act: Why this recently enacted law is unconstitutional', (2004) 23 JMJCIL 141.

176 US Code Title 15 s 1125(d) (Web), inserted by Anticybersquatting Consumer Protection Act 1999.

177 See *Barcelona.com Inc v Excelentisimo Ayuntamiento de Barcelona* 330 F 3d 617 (4th Ct, 2 June 2003).

178 For an argument that the Act is unconstitutionally broad, see Snow, N, 'The Constitutional failing of the Anticybersquatting Act', (2005) 41 Will LR 1.

179 See, eg, *Taubman Co v Webfeats* 319 F 3d 770 (6th Ct, 7 February 2003).

180 *Bosley Medical Institute, Inc v Kremer* 403 F 3d 672 (9th Ct, 4 April 2005).

in a case where the name's owner cannot be located or is outside the federal jurisdiction. But the Act's remedies are not available unless there is a 'bad faith intent' on someone's part, albeit not always the owner's. None of these ambiguities matters in the straightforward case of a cybersquatter intent on using their domain name to divert custom to themselves, or to annoy the trade mark owner into buying the name itself; but the loose wording gives no clear answer when multiple parties are involved, or if the name has been sold on to other parties with no involvement in any illegality.

'Bad faith intent to profit' from the trade mark is not defined. It is expressly stated that the intent 'shall not be found in any case in which the court determines that the person believed and had reasonable grounds to believe that the use of the domain name was a fair use or otherwise lawful'. Various factors are mentioned which the court can take into account, though the list is not exhaustive.

(a) The extent of the plaintiff's rights must be borne in mind. In particular, the court can have regard to 'the extent to which the mark ... is or is not distinctive and famous ...' A defendant who knew, at the time of registering their domain, that there would be a conflict with the plaintiff's trade mark will find it hard to deny bad faith.[181]

(b) The defendant's own rights in the name are also relevant: the court can take into account 'the trademark or other intellectual property rights of the [defendant], if any, in the domain name' and 'the extent to which the domain name consists of the legal name of the person or a name that is otherwise commonly used to identify that person'. Does this mean that defendants without a trade mark of their own have evinced bad faith merely by virtue of that fact? Some US judges seem to think so;[182] but this lends weight to the claim that the entire regime is biased in favour of trade mark owners.

(c) The fact of *bona fide* use of the domain is also a factor, whether that use is 'in connection with the bona fide offering of any goods or services' or is 'bona fide noncommercial or fair use of the mark in a site accessible under the domain name'.

(d) Intent to divert consumers from the trade mark owner's web site is relevant, whether the motive is 'commercial gain or ... to tarnish or disparage the mark, by creating a likelihood of confusion ...'[183]

(e) Evasive defendants can expect to have their behaviour used as evidence against their case, whether this consists of their 'provision of material and misleading false contact information when applying for the registration of the domain name', their 'intentional failure to maintain accurate contact information', or 'prior conduct indicating a pattern of such conduct'.

(f) An offer to sell the name 'without having used, or having an intent to use, the domain name in the bona fide offering of any goods or services' is relevant; evidence that the defendant is a serial cybersquatter can also be taken into account.

While the factors are for the most part clear and precisely drafted, it remains the case that whether the defendant will lose their domain name will, in practice, turn on the

---

181 Eg, *Virtual Works, Inc v Volkswagen of America, Inc* 238 F 3d 264 (4th Ct, 22 January 2001).

182 Eg, *Sporty's Farm v Sportsman's Market, Inc* 202 F 3d 489 (2nd Ct, 2 February 2000).

183 For a case turning mainly on this point, see *Harrods Ltd v 60 Internet Domain Names* 302 F 3d 214 (4th Ct, 23 August 2002).

court's intuitive sense of whether bad faith is present, and of whether the defendant truly deserves to lose the name. As the Court of Appeals noted, in a case where the defendant had used the plaintiff's name for a web site narrating the poor treatment she had received from them, the judicial function

> is not simply to add factors and place them in particular categories, without making some sense of what motivates the conduct at issue. The factors are given to courts as a guide, not as a substitute for careful thinking about whether the conduct at issue is motivated by a bad faith intent to profit. Perhaps most important to our conclusion are [the defendant's] actions, which seem to have been undertaken in the spirit of informing fellow consumers about the practices of a landscaping company that she believed had performed inferior work on her yard. One of the ACPA's main objectives is the protection of consumers from slick internet peddlers who trade on the names and reputations of established brands. The practice of informing fellow consumers of one's experience with a particular service provider is surely not inconsistent with this ideal.[184]

Personal liability under the ACPA lies against anyone who 'registers, traffics in, or uses' the domain name with the requisite bad faith intent. The registrant is the obvious defendant; how far does the liability go beyond that? The notion of 'use' applies only to someone who 'is the domain name registrant or that registrant's authorized licensee'. However, no such careful drafting was used with 'traffics in', which is stated to refer to 'transactions that include, but are not limited to, sales, purchases, loans, pledges, licenses, exchanges of currency, and any other transfer for consideration or receipt in exchange for consideration'. The general defences for good faith intermediaries (including the domain registrar) apply.[185] Damages are available: if the ordinary measure (based on the plaintiff's loss and legal costs, and the defendant's profit) is not congenial, the plaintiff may elect for statutory damages of not less than US$1,000 and not more than US$100,000 per domain name, as the court considers just.[186] The plaintiff can also seek transfer, forfeiture or cancellation of the domain. It is not clear when a court may take a domain name from a registrant when the 'bad faith intent' was evinced by someone else; the literal wording of the ACPA permits this, but presumably the court would hesitate to do so if the registrant could plausibly deny complicity in the bad faith intent and conduct.

The legislation also contains some rather complex provisions relating to an *in rem* jurisdiction, which allows a plaintiff to file an action against the registrar of the domain name (if within the jurisdiction), if the registrant cannot be found (after following certain specified steps to search), or if the plaintiff 'is not able to obtain *in personam* jurisdiction over a person who would have been a defendant' in an ordinary action under ACPA.[187] The remedy under this provision is limited to forfeiture, cancellation or transfer of the domain name. The scope of these provisions is obscure, but an expansive view of them is being taken. The current view seems to be that they are not limited to actions under the ACPA for bad faith intent, but can be invoked by any plaintiff alleging trade mark infringement or dilution. Further, it seems to be irrelevant that the domain name's current owner is abroad, or that the

---

184 *Lucas Nursery and Landscaping, Inc v Grosse* 359 F 3d 806 (6th Ct, 5 March 2004).

185 US Code Title 15 s 1114(2)(d) (Web).

186 US Code Title 15 s 1117(d) (Web).

187 See Grotto, A, 'Due process and *in rem* jurisdiction under the Anticybersquatting Consumer Protection Act', (2001) 2 CSTLR 3 (Web).

reason why the plaintiff cannot obtain *in personam* jurisdiction is that the owner has no connection of any sort with the US.[188]

UK law

None of the UK jurisdictions has any specific legislation relating to ownership of domain names. For domains within .uk, the current terms under which Nominet grants names provide it with ample rights to remove the names on grounds of misbehaviour, such as supplying inaccurate contact details or failing to keep such details up to date, infringement of others' intellectual property rights, or under the dispute resolution procedure. Disputes over the application of these standard terms are a matter for the ordinary courts in any of the UK jurisdictions.[189]

The primacy of the 'first come, first served' principle has been maintained, notably in the first case to be litigated within the jurisdiction, which involved a comedy of errors concerning two firms with similar names (and a common ancestry). The domain pitman.co.uk was originally promised by Nominet to Pitman Publishing, though there was no formal registration. Then Pitman Training enquired after the name and Nominet, as the result of an administrative mistake, registered it to that company. When Nominet's blunder became apparent, it re-allocated the name to Pitman Publishing; Pitman Training commenced proceedings to reclaim it, and ultimately failed in its claim, being unable to demonstrate that any legal wrong had been committed.[190]

Proceedings by those aggrieved by another's choice of domain name have been urged on a variety of doctrinal bases, including conspiracy, inducing breach of contract, and abuse of process. It might also be possible to use other torts appropriate to the harm done in particular cases: so a name chosen to mock the claimant might result in proceedings for defamation. The most useful tools against cybersquatting have, unsurprisingly, turned out to be the actions for breach of trade mark and for passing off.

Trade mark

The basic principles of UK trade mark law were considered above.[191] Some basic principles need to be borne in mind. A domain name is not a trade mark: trade mark law is not about who 'owns' the domain name, but about whether the registrant's behaviour amounts to a breach of the claimant's trade mark rights. The single act of registering a name which resembles the trade mark has sometimes been held to amount to a breach of trade mark law in itself, but usually the enquiry is broader, looking at the totality of the defendant's conduct, including the way in which the domain has been used. Moreover, trade mark law does not confer rights to particular marks *simpliciter* – the rights are limited to particular markets, limited both territorially (a UK mark confers no rights in relation to French markets) and

---

188 See *Harrods Ltd v 60 Internet Domain Names* 302 F 3d 214 (4th Ct, 23 August 2002).
189 See Nominet Terms and Conditions (Web), especially cll 7 and 16–17.
190 *Pitman Training Ltd v Nominet UK* (Chancery Division, 22 May 1997) (Web).
191 Above, p 72; and see especially p 75 on jurisdiction.

by reference to types of goods (a mark relating to the supply of food has no relation to the market in software). Further, trade mark law regulates only trade use. If the registrant cannot be said to be using the mark as part of a business, then trade mark law cannot be a ground for taking the mark away or querying its use. This last requirement has proved no bar in suing cybersquatters – if the registrant seems intent on selling the name to the highest bidder, then legal intervention to prevent this is easy to justify – but in other cases this may prove a serious restriction on the use of the law in this area.

Liability can be established if the defendant uses a mark identical to that of the claimant in relation to identical goods; or if the defendant uses a similar mark in relation to similar goods if there is a likelihood of public confusion. This clearly catches a defendant who uses a competitor's name as a domain name to attract business that might otherwise have gone to the competitor.[192] Its application is not so obvious if the defendant is not a competitor, and/or has a plausible justification for its choice of name. In one case, Avnet, a company that sold goods by catalogue and over the Internet, had registered its name as a trade mark in relation to advertising and promotional services. The defendants, who were part of the aviation industry and went under the name 'Aviation Network', registered avnet.co.uk, and used it to sell space on the web to customers. Jacob J considered that, even though the web space sold would in many cases be used for advertisement and promotion, nonetheless Avnet and the defendants were each in a very different type of business, and Avnet's trade mark was not infringed.[193]

The ordinary provisions on breach of trade mark are of little use against cybersquatters, as the cybersquatter will not usually be selling identical or similar goods. More useful is the broader protection given to trade marks with a 'reputation', that is, a significant degree of public recognition. In relation to those marks, there is a breach by the use of an identical or similar mark which 'without due cause, takes unfair advantage of, or is detrimental to, the distinctive character or the repute' of the trade mark, even though what the defendant is selling is not similar to the mark owner's products. Where the cybersquatter deliberately registers a domain name similar to the claimant's famous mark, and it is clear that the motive is to make money by selling the domain name, then all the elements of the cause of action will be complete, as was held in the *One In A Million* case.[194] It would be a mistake, however, to assume that this approach will be taken with those who are not obviously trying to make money out of another's established trade mark.

From this, it can be seen that a wrong is unlikely to be established except in cases of blatant cybersquatting. Accordingly, the approach to remedies is strict. Damages are available in principle, though in practice it is exceedingly difficult to establish any particular figure that can be said to represent the claimant's loss or the defendant's gain. If the domain has been used in such a way as to damage the claimant's interests, then an injunction is the most obvious remedy, and use of the domain in breach of the injunction may result in prison.[195] Injunctions may

192 Eg, *Musical Fidelity Ltd v Vickers* [2002] EWHC 1000 Ch (Rimer J); [2002] EWCA Civ 1989 (CA); *International Business Machines Corp v Web-Sphere Ltd* [2004] EWHC 529 Ch (Web).
193 *Avnet Inc v Isoact Ltd* [1998] FSR 16.
194 *British Telecommunications plc v One In A Million Ltd* [1998] EWCA Civ 1272, [1999] 1 WLR 903 (Web).
195 Eg, *Marks and Spencer plc v Cottrell* (Chancery Division, 26 February 2001).

include prohibitions on using the domain, or similar ones, at all.[196] Cases where no use has been made of the domain are more problematic, especially if the remedy is being sought before the trial of the action, and so before the facts are clear: a court will be reluctant to restrain a defendant who appears to have an arguable defence to the action, though in those circumstances the defendant might be enjoined from disposing of the domain before trial.[197] However, if the only conceivable uses of the registered domain would involve infringement of the claimant's trade mark, then an injunction may be appropriate to prohibit use, or to order transfer of the domain to the claimant.[198]

Passing off

This tort, which was considered above,[199] protects the claimant's goodwill or general trade reputation. To establish the tort, injury to the claimant's interests within the jurisdiction must be shown. It is hard to see how mere registration of a domain name can do this, even if it is very similar to the claimant's name, but use of such a domain can easily do so. The tort is readily applied to the more blatant examples of cybersquatting. So the use of several well-known trade marks as domain names was within the tort.[200] And it is no defence that the domain was originally acquired honestly, if the defendant now plans to use it to damage the claimant's goodwill.[201]

However, if there is no clear evidence that the defendant meant to trade on the claimant's goodwill, the court will be reluctant to find liability established, as various cases on interim issues illustrate. In each of them, the court evidently regarded the underlying dispute to be very borderline were it ever pressed to a full trial.[202]

(a) An Internet consultant registered the domain fcuk.com, which he thought would attract potential clients. He pleaded ignorance of the use of 'fcuk' by the claimant, owner of a chain of clothing stores, and of the advertising campaign it was conducting based on the word. Rattee J found that there was insufficient evidence to justify an interim injunction, there being considerable doubt as to whether the claimant had any goodwill in the name or that the defendant's activities had injured it. 'I cannot help commenting that I find the case of both parties in this litigation unpalatable in the extreme …'[203]

(b) A London taxi firm registered the domain radiotaxis.com. The claimant, a rival company called Radio Taxi Cabs, complained of passing off. John Randall QC (sitting as deputy judge of the High Court) refused an interim injunction. The expression 'radio taxis' was entirely generic, and accurately described the

---

196 *Bonnier Media Ltd v Smith* 2002 SCLR 977.

197 Eg, *MBNA America Bank NA v Freeman* (Chancery Division, 17 July 2000).

198 *British Telecommunications plc v One In A Million Ltd* [1998] EWCA Civ 1272, [1999] 1 WLR 903 (Web).

199 Above, p 75.

200 *British Telecommunications plc v One In A Million Ltd* [1998] EWCA Civ 1272, [1999] 1 WLR 903 (Web).

201 *Metalrax Group plc v Vanci* [2002] EWCA Civ 609 (Web).

202 See also *Phones 4u Ltd v Phone4u.co.uk Internet Ltd* [2005] EWHC 334 Ch.

203 *French Connection Ltd v Sutton* (Chancery Division, 2 December 1999).

defendant's business; there was no sufficient evidence of public confusion between the defendant's business and that of the claimant; and the web site concerned, which did not allow ordinary members of the public to call cabs, did not appear to be damaging the claimant's business.[204]

(c) The defendant registered the domain vavavoom.co.uk with the intention, later abandoned, of using it for a fashion business. The claimant, Renault, who subsequently used the expression 'va va voom' extensively in relation to its Clio car, sought to buy the name. Negotiations went badly; the defendant raised its answering price considerably on realising that the buyer was Renault and, after a failure to agree a price, used the domain for links to other car manufacturers. Renault applied for summary judgment. Laddie J refused the application, holding that it was not inevitable that the defendant would lose: it was not obvious that Renault had goodwill in 'va va voom', as opposed to 'Renault' or 'Clio'; no member of the public was known to have been misled; and while some of the defendant's actions were ill-advised, there was no evidence of bad faith.[205]

These cases can be contrasted with the case where the defendant registered the domain easyrealestate.co.uk, using it to create an estate agency site, the design and colouring of which resembled that of the claimant. The claimant, which comprised easyJet, easyRentacar and associated businesses, did not own an estate agency business, but nonetheless claimed that the defendant was passing his business off as being connected to the claimant's business. An injunction was granted to the claimant by Bernard Livesey QC (sitting as a deputy judge of the High Court): the court was unimpressed by the defendant's *bona fides*: he had evidently known of the claimant all along, and had designed his site to match its site; he had no genuine interest in real estate agency, nor sufficient funds to establish a serious business in it; his conduct seemed calculated to force a substantial offer for the domain from the claimant. Judgment included an order for transfer of the name to the claimant.[206]

While damages are theoretically available if the tort is established, the claim in these cases is usually for an injunction, partly because damages would be difficult to calculate, but mostly because an injunction nips the problem in the bud. However, some care is needed if the defendant is caught before the domain has ever been activated or used in any way that might harm the claimant's goodwill: in those circumstances, no tort can yet have been committed. The key to this is the defendant's intent. If the court is convinced that the defendant means to use the domain to harm the claimant's goodwill, then an injunction to prevent the defendant from so doing can issue; threats to use it in just that way could provide a solid evidential basis for such an order. Or again, if the domain is such that *any* use of it is likely to injure the claimant's goodwill, this again can be the basis of an order. This is obviously most appropriate in the case of famous trade names, where the name is clearly connected with the claimant in the public mind. In those circumstances, the domain is an 'instrument of fraud', and the court is entitled both to disable

---

204 *Radio Taxicabs (London) Ltd v Owner Drivers Radio Taxi Services Ltd* (Chancery Division, 12 October 2001), discussed by Calleja, R, (2002) 12 C&L (6) 23.

205 *Renault UK Ltd v Derivatives Risk Evaluation and Management Ltd* (Chancery Division, 22 October 2000).

206 *Easyjet Airline Co Ltd v Dainty* [2002] FSLR 6.

the defendant from using it and to order the defendant to transfer it to the claimant.[207]

Irish law

The general structure of Irish law here is very similar to that of the UK. There are no legislative provisions governing ownership of domain names as such; a plaintiff seeking to remove a domain name from its current owner will probably have to rely on a combination of trade mark and passing off principles.

In one case, the plaintiff established a web site using the business names 'Local Ireland' and 'Localireland', which categorised and linked to other Irish web sites. It used the domain names localireland.com and local.ie. A few years later, the defendant started a similar operation, called 'Local Ireland-Online' using the domain localireland-online.com, though when litigation was threatened it agreed to rename itself as 'LocallyIrish' at locallyirishcom. On the plaintiff's application for an interlocutory injunction, Herbert J found that both parties had arguable cases, and noted that the parties were not content to treat the interlocutory hearing as settling the entire dispute. He applied the standard principles for interlocutory injunctions: the plaintiff having established that there was a *bona fide* question to be tried and that monetary compensation would not sufficiently compensate either side, the question was simply one of the balance of convenience – that is, which side would suffer the greater loss if it failed in the interlocutory hearing. He determined that the plaintiff, who had already made a substantial investment in its site, had more to lose than the defendant, who could pick a different name relatively easily. Accordingly, he granted the injunction, which included a provision prohibiting the defendant from 'possessing, holding, operating, managing or controlling an internet address or domain name under the name style or title "localireland-online.com" or "locallyirish.com" '.[208]

A similar approach was taken by Laffoy J in a case where rival companies each claimed to be entitled to hold fashion events which would select 'Miss Ireland'. Again, the balance of convenience was found to lie with the long-established business run by the plaintiff, and the injunction included a requirement that the defendant cancel the domain name it had been using.[209]

FURTHER READING

Caral, J, 'Lessons from ICANN: Is self-regulation of the Internet fundamentally flawed?', (2004) 12 IJLIT 1.

Crawford, S, 'The ICANN experiment', (2004) 12 CJICL 409.

Epstein, R, 'The Roman law of cyberconversion', [2005] MSLR 103.

---

207 See *British Telecommunications plc v One In A Million Ltd* [1998] EWCA Civ 1272, [1999] 1 WLR 903 (Web); *Britannia Building Society v Prangley* (Chancery Division, 12 June 2000).
208 *Local Ireland Ltd v Local Ireland-Online Ltd* [2000] IEHC 67, [2000] 4 IR 567 (Web).
209 *Miss World Ltd v Miss Ireland Beauty Pageant Ltd* [2004] IEHC 13 (Web).

Frankel, T, 'Governing by negotiation: The Internet naming system', (2004) 12 CJICL 449.

Froomkin, M, 'ICANN'S "Uniform Dispute Resolution Policy" – Causes and (partial) cures', (2002) 67 Brook LR 605 (Web).

Geist, M, 'Fair.com?: An examination of the allegations of systemic unfairness in the ICANN UDRP', (2002) 27 Brook JIL 903.

Hagen, G, 'Sovereign domains and property claims', (2003) 11 IJLIT 1.

Palfrey, J, 'The end of the experiment: How ICANN's foray into global internet democracy failed', (2004) 17 HJOLT 409 (Web).

Sherry, S, 'Haste makes waste: Congress and the common law in cyberspace', (2002) 55 Vand LR 309.

Struve, C, and Wagner, R, 'Realspace sovereigns in cyberspace: Problems with the Anticybersquatting Consumer Protection Act (ACPA)', (2002) 17 BTLJ (Web).

Thornburg, B, 'Fast, cheap and out of control: Lessons from the ICANN Dispute Resolution Process', (2001) 7 JSEBL (Web).

Weinberg, J, 'ICANN and the problem of legitimacy', (2000) 50 Duke LJ 187 (Web).

CHAPTER 8

SURFING THE NET

It is now appropriate to consider the rights and duties which arise during ordinary browsing of the Internet. The computer being used to surf the net (the 'client' computer) and the computer which supplies the pages for the client to read (the 'server') may exchange considerable quantities of data, and the users or controllers of those machines may considerably affect their legal rights and duties as a result. This chapter concentrates on the most common ways in which surfing the net alters the legal position of those engaged in the transaction. It concentrates on the civil law position.

Various legal principles are involved here. The first part of the chapter considers the general question of computer interaction. What legal rights are in issue when one computer sends data or instructions to another – what sort of conduct will amount to misbehaviour? Can a general legal theory be devised? This involves the question whether sending inappropriate messages or instructions to the other's computer can be regarded as a 'cybertrespass'. The next two parts of the chapter focus specifically on interactions using the web, and on the ordinary case where the client machine asks to see a particular page or run a particular program. The first asks how rights are protected on the server's side – what constitutes misbehaviour by the client, and to what extent is the server entitled to regulate precisely what the client can access. The second asks the converse question of how rights are protected on the client's side – what constitutes misbehaviour by the server. In both parts, issues of ownership of data are very much to the fore; a key issue is what each side may lawfully do with data obtained during interactions with other machines.

Search engines play a key role in surfing the net; indeed, without them the Internet would be a very different place – much less interesting, much harder to navigate, and significantly less transparent. Yet the law surrounding search engines is obscure. The final part of the chapter considers some of the issues that surround them, as well as the law on the related topic of advertising.

The material in this chapter is new, but it rests solidly on the foundation of material in the earlier chapters. In particular, the basic principles of unauthorised computer access,[1] intellectual property rights in data[2] and data protection[3] are relevant throughout.

PROTECTING RIGHTS: GENERAL

The Internet has been said to be a vast online library. The strength of the metaphor is obvious enough: people use client machines to 'browse' through written and pictorial material, in many cases receiving exactly the sort of data that could be

---

1   Above, Chapter 2.
2   Above, Chapter 3.
3   Above, Chapter 4.

expected from paper sources. And the application of much intellectual property law to the Internet is from this point of view unsurprising: consumers of copyright materials are bound by copyright law however they came across the work in question. But equally obviously the metaphor is misleading in many other ways. The 'library' is distributed across all machines connected by the Internet. The person does not actually visit any other location to read what is there, nor does the client machine; rather, it requests a copy of particular files, which it then assembles into a form that its human controller can read. For many purposes, consulting a particular Internet source is like taking a book off a shelf and reading it, but two features in particular ensure that the legal rights involved may be very different:

(a) Each of the computers involved – the client computer that requests data and the server which provides it – is a powerful calculating engine in its own right. It is possible for a client simply to request a particular file, which the server provides. But equally the client's request may trigger a particular program in the server, which then generates a new file precisely tailored to the client's needs. For example, a client may make a search request, which will set in motion a search program on the server machine; this program will generate a file stating the result of the search, which will be sent to the client. Again, in some circumstances the server may send a program of some sort to the client machine, which the client will then run.

(b) Transactions over the Internet generate significant amounts of data, and either or both of the computers involved may be programmed to store and make use of this data. Some of this is necessary if communication is to happen at all. Other uses of the data can improve the quality of communication considerably. A server which recognises a client as a previous visitor (through cookies or other methods) may be able to provide a better service for that client. But yet other uses may be unwelcome or even harmful, the more so because they are often completely invisible to the human operator. Equally, what the client does with data received is completely opaque to the server. If a copyright work is sent to the client, the server machine has no means of knowing whether it was read briefly and then forgotten, or saved permanently, or passed on to third parties in a clandestine manner.

From a legal point of view, the important point is to avoid thinking of the Internet as a technology which passively allows clients to 'see' what is happening elsewhere. It would be a fundamental mistake to treat the Internet as some sort of telescope, which relays an accurate picture of what is happening at a remote site. Rather, it is a channel of communication between two computers, each of which will react as programmed to whatever the other does. Each computer 'sees' what the other wants it to 'see'; which does not imply deception on either side, though it points to the *possibility* of deception. This exchange of data allows each side to give instructions to the other, including sending each other programs to run. This obviously gives great power to communication over the Internet, but also huge scope for abuse – especially as the human operators of the machines may not always appreciate everything that is going on within their machines.

This part of the chapter, then, discusses the general legal ground rules that limit the interactions between computers communicating via the Internet.

Criminal law

Wrongfully accessing or modifying other computers over the Internet may attract criminal penalties. The use of the criminal law here is simply an application of the law considered above. Wrongfully accessing data on another's computer, or detrimentally modifying its operations, are both generally illegal; this is simply a particular instance where the access or modification is done over the Internet.

Recall, first, that it is an offence under both Irish and UK law to access another's computer system in a wrongful manner.[4] So securing access to another's data, or starting up a program it holds, are potentially within this basic offence.

Recall, secondly, that there is also a more serious offence of 'unauthorised modification of the contents of any computer' in the UK and 'criminal damage to data' in Ireland. This covers modification of data already on the target system, or adding new data or a new program to it. As already discussed, the focus of the legislation is on data, not computer operations, and so it is by no means clear that running a program which has been insinuated into the target system breaches the legislation, unless the effects are destructive. But in most cases merely introducing the new program will be enough.[5]

It would therefore appear that many of the more serious abuses are caught by this basic legislation. Indeed, the UK government's refusal to legislate against spyware has been justified on the ground that it is already caught by existing offences.[6] This is probably right, and the legislation almost certainly covers any case where the access or damage is plainly unwelcome. But there is a substantial grey area, where consent may plausibly be pleaded.[7]

The use of cookies is at the forefront of this. When responding to requests from clients, some servers routinely send a small data file (a 'cookie'), recording the transaction. If the client ever revisits the server, the cookie may be retrieved and the client identified accordingly. Cookies may be used for a variety of purposes, some obviously legitimate and useful (to avoid the need for passwords), others more dubious (to build up a secret profile of how this particular client acts) and yet others downright illegal (spying on the client). Yet the criminal law seems too clumsy a tool to distinguish between these different uses: even though the cookie may not have been expressly consented to by the client (whose human operator may be completely unaware of it), nonetheless it seems unlikely that a court would find a breach of the criminal law.

The use of the criminal law here is therefore restricted; cases of obviously malicious behaviour aside, there is insufficient public consensus on appropriate behaviour between computer users to justify the infliction of criminal penalties. What of civil remedies?

Tort and 'cybertrespass'

If one computer communicates with another and, as a result, the second computer behaves in a way its operator does not care for, has the operator of the first computer

---

4   Above, p 17.
5   Above, p 26.
6   'Spyware', *Hansard* (Lords), 10 January 2005 (Web).
7   Above, p 20. For a prosecution which failed on grounds of consent, see 'Case prompts fears over web use', Irish Times, 14 August 1998.

committed a tort against the operator of the second? There is a persistent suggestion in the US that this is indeed so – that there is a tort of computer trespass or 'cybertrespass', which catches unwelcome intrusions against computer systems in much the same way as conventional trespass catches unwelcome intrusions against property or the person.

Some care is needed in defining this supposed tort, however, as various different arguments are at work here. Some are merely pointing out that a computer is personal property – a chattel or assemblage of chattels – and so the tort involved is simply trespass to goods (or some other tort protecting personal property). Others argue that the matter should be treated as a trespass to real property: interference with the operations of a computer on my land is a trespass, in the same way as any interference with the way I use my land is a trespass. (This argument is sometimes better stated as an argument based on nuisance, as nuisance traditionally involves interference with my land without any physical intrusion onto it[8]). Others still are making the argument that cyberspace should be treated as *analogous* to physical space: the 'cybertrespasser' is intruding onto a part of cyberspace that belongs to their victim, and must be penalised accordingly. This final argument, which assumes that legal references to a physical place should be read as including reference to cyberspace, has other implications if accepted; for example, it is often raised in the US in order to show that an Internet site is a 'place of public accommodation' and therefore within the anti-discrimination legislation.[9] Regrettably, these very different arguments are often run together.[10]

'Cybertrespass' is a very general notion. Some of its supporters can plausibly derive it from basic notions of respect for property.[11] It is a very broad legal tool for defining the legal boundaries between computer users who come into conflict with one another. Viewed from the point of view of the lawmaker, it provides a general common law solution that can be applied to regulate a variety of objectionable behaviours or technologies: spam, spyware, theft of data, viruses. In each instance, however, a case can be made that detailed statutory regulation is a preferable solution.[12] Much of the support for the tort of cybertrespass is expressly on the basis that it counters legislative gridlock; ultimately, the precise legal rights of computer users will be stated in a detailed legislative scheme, which may or may not include a notion of cybertrespass, and which will certainly be a good deal more precise than current arrangements. It follows that strong support for the existence of the tort may only be a temporary phenomenon. It also suggests that the powerful support the tort has gained in the US may be a symptom of gaps in its law: many of the US plaintiffs seem to be asking for remedies which within the EU would be granted under the data protection legislation,[13] or as an aspect of database right.[14] Put simply, there is

---

8   Cf Kam, S, '*Intel Corp v Hamidi*: Trespass to chattels and a doctrine of cyber-nuisance', (2004) 10 BTLJ 427.
9   See especially Cohen, R and Hiller, J, 'Towards a theory of CyberPlace: A proposal for a new legal framework', (2003) 10 RJOLT 1 (Web); 'The Internet: Place, property or thing?' (symposium transcript), (2004) 55 Mercer LR 867.
10   Epstein, R, 'Cybertrespass', (2003) 70 Chi LR 73.
11   Hardy, I, 'The ancient doctrine of trespass to web sites', [1996] JOL 7 (Web); Caffarelli, D, 'Crossing virtual lines: Trespass on the Internet', (1999) 5 BUJSTL 6 (Web).
12   Eg, Merrell, R, 'Trespass to chattels in the Age of the Internet', (2002) 80 WULQ 675 (Web).
13   Above, Chapter 4 .
14   Below, p 216.

much less for a tort of cybertrespass to do in the UK or Ireland than there is in the US, and this may go part of the way towards explaining why there is less support for it here.

In most states of the US, an action for trespass requires proof of damage. (Scots law also has this requirement, though Ireland and the other jurisdictions of the UK do not.) The US case law has therefore been dominated by the question of what sort of interferences with another's computer will constitute 'damage' for this purpose. Little unanimity has emerged. Some of the leading cases are:

(a) *Verizon Online Services, Inc v Ralsky*.[15] An Internet Service Provider (ISP) sued a notorious spammer, alleging that processing his spam had significantly slowed down its servers, leading to customer complaints. One ground relied on was trespass to chattels, as well as conspiracy and breaches of certain statutes. The District Court accepted that the defendant's behaviour constituted trespass.

(b) *eBay, Inc v Bidder's Edge, Inc*.[16] The defendant ran an auction aggregation site, which gathered data from a number of different Internet auction sites, so that its users would not have to visit each site separately. eBay, a major auction site, took issue with the defendant's behaviour: it did not object to searches made at the specific request of a consumer, but claimed that the defendant's regular automatic trawls for data were placing an unreasonable strain on its servers. The District Court granted an injunction against this 'trespass to chattels'. Judge Whyte argued that it did not matter whether the strain on the plaintiff's system was substantial or not: 'Even if, as BE argues, its searches use only a small amount of eBay's computer system capacity, BE has nonetheless deprived eBay of the ability to use that portion of its personal property for its own purposes.'[17]

(c) *Intel Corp v Hamidi*.[18] The defendant, formerly an engineer at Intel, sent e-mails to all of its current employees complaining of Intel's personnel practices. Intel claimed that the additional load on its server constituted a trespass. However, a majority of the Supreme Court of California denied this, insisting that trespass requires damage, and no quantifiable damage had been shown here. Spam cases such as *Verizon* were distinguished on the (not wholly convincing) ground that they turned on the sheer bulk of the spam, which threatened the effective running of the target system.

(d) *Ticketmaster Corp v Tickets.com, Inc*.[19] The plaintiff ran an online ticket agency; individual events for which it sold tickets had their own pages within the web site. The plaintiff objected to various other sites which created links leading directly to specific pages; its strong preference would have been for links to its home page, as much of its advertising was there, and so was not seen by those following a 'deep link' to a specific page. Threatened action against Microsoft for this deep linking resulted in a favourable settlement.[20] However, a similar complaint against the

---

15   203 F Supp 2d 601 (D E Virginia, 7 June 2002). See 'Verizon settles lawsuit against spammer', Comp Week, 31 October 2002 (Web). *Verizon* is only one of a number of cases to the same effect.
16   100 F Supp 2d 1058 (D N Ca, 24 May 2000). See 'eBay, Bidder's Edge end legal dispute', News.Com, 1 March 2001 (Web). See similarly *Register.com, Inc v Verio, Inc* 356 F 3d 393 (2nd Ct, 23 January 2004), discussed below, p 249.
17   100 F Supp 2d 1058, 1071.
18   30 Cal 4th 1342 (Ca Supreme Court, 30 June 2003) (Web).
19   2000 US Dist LEXIS 4553 (D C Ca, 27 March 2000); 2003 US Dist LEXIS 6483 (D C Ca, 7 March 2003).
20   'Ticketmaster and Microsoft settle linking dispute', NYT, 15 February 1999 (Web).

defendant was contested; a District Court refused to grant an injunction for cybertrespass, and ultimately struck out that head of claim. The tort was said to be inapplicable unless the plaintiff could show either physical injury to the server or that its use or utility was impaired; neither of which was proved to the court's satisfaction. If the plaintiff had a good claim, it would be in breach of copyright, not in trespass.

It is possible that the results of these cases can be reconciled with one another, though many of the *dicta* are directly contradictory. Of all of the cases, *Hamidi* is the most hostile to the notion of cybertrespass, one judge tartly commenting that the invocation of trespass involves 'colorful analogies' which 'tend to obscure the plain fact that this case involves communications equipment, used by defendant to communicate'.[21] However, even *Hamidi* is very far from rejecting the notion of cybertrespass entirely, and leaves courts with a great deal of flexibility in what they can treat as actionable 'damage'. The real objection to liability on those facts seems to be based on free speech. If Mr Hamidi had a right to communicate his message at all, there can be no real objection to the manner in which he chose to do so; and there was uncontradicted evidence that Intel employees who asked to receive no more e-mails from him found their wishes respected.[22] The result of the case is understandable, but it would probably be a mistake to see it as a rejection of the very concept of 'cybertrespass'.

Should this flexible approach be adopted in Ireland or in the UK? Academic commentary has stressed that there is an element of arbitrariness in which tort is supposed to be in issue: some support the use of trespass to chattels (which in England and Wales would now be conversion),[23] others prefer to rely on a general tort of deliberate harm.[24] The very tenuous type of 'harm' in these cases sits unhappily with traditional notions of trespass or even of nuisance. A deeper question is whether the law actually needs the cybertrespass tort: would it fulfil some useful function that is not already provided for? If there is an answer to this, it must be along the lines that the law is deficient in civil remedies here, and that leaving matters to the legislature encourages an unhealthy reliance on the criminal law for disputes which are better pursued in civil courts.[25]

Surfing the net as contract between host and client

An alternative approach, with similarly broad consequences, is that those who surf the net, and those who provide web sites to surf to, should be seen as engaged in consensual activity. Those who create web sites presumably do so in order for others to use them, in accordance with the technical standards associated with the net; those

---

21   30 Cal 4th 1342, 1362 *per* Werdegar J (Web).
22   For discussion of the US law after *Hamidi*, see 'Trespass to chattels and the Internet', (2003) 17 HJOLT 283 (Web); DeGaetano, P, '*Intel Corp v Hamidi*: Private Property, Keep Out', (2004) 40 CWLR 355; Fibbe, G, 'Screen-scraping and harmful cybertrespass after *Intel*', (2004) 55 Mercer LR 1011.
23   Walsh, K, 'Trespass to chattels – Ancient tort tackles the scourge of cyberspam', (2002) 14 ILT 219.
24   Usually associated with *Wilkinson v Downton* [1897] 2 QB 57. See Adams, J, 'Trespass in a digital environment', [2002] IPQ 1.
25   McLeod, D, 'Regulating damage on the Internet: A tortious approach?', (2001) 27 Monash ULR 344.

who visit web sites equally expect to find web sites constructed appropriately. It is only a short step beyond that, to the idea that viewing a page on the Internet involves some sort of agreement between the server's owner and the client's owner, and that a significant departure from what either might reasonably expect of the other could be a breach of that agreement. Accordingly, some argue that surfing the net is a contractual activity, based on the technical standards that both sides must necessarily respect, involving an implicit contract that neither of those involved will abuse the trust placed in it by the other.[26]

As a matter of pure contractual theory, there is nothing much to be said against this; in other contexts, contracts have been found on even more tenuous bases. However, for lawyers 'contract' tends to be a very individualised notion. In their daily lives, reasonable people reasonably expect others not to assault them; nonetheless, assailants are treated as criminals or as tortfeasors, not as contract breakers. 'Contract' tends to be kept for particular agreements between specified people. So while there is no doubt that contracts can be made over the Internet (a matter considered below[27]), nonetheless the courts are unlikely to find some general contract to behave decently to which all net users are party. It would be very hard to establish agreement to such a contract on ordinary criteria, and even harder to discern its terms.

PROTECTING RIGHTS: THE SERVER SIDE

The previous section covered general arguments that anyone connected to the Internet might make. This part concentrates on a more specific problem: arguments that might be raised by the owner of an Internet server to protect its legitimate interests against the behaviour of others who access the server. If the server makes data available to others, when and on what grounds can its owner restrict access to it, or seek to control the way in which the data is used? If the data represents a site on the web, can anyone visit this site, or may the owner discriminate?

In the early days of the web, there was a very strong ethos of free linking. The plain and obvious purpose of the web was to communicate data. It seemed downright perverse for anyone to make data available and then attempt to restrict access, in much the same way as it would be perverse to shout your opinions out loud and then claim that they were confidential. However, this view is deeply out of tune with modern intellectual property law – someone who still maintains this view (and there are many of them) is effectively arguing that copyright and associated rights should not be applied to the Internet.[28] A counter-view has rapidly developed, that web sites are the absolute property of their owners. On this view, owners of web sites are entitled to restrict access as they choose, and if they permit access they can impose whatever conditions they choose. Justification for this was found in the same sort of socio-economic arguments that are used to justify property generally: such as that socially optimal levels of investment in web sites will not be achieved unless

26   Feigin, E, 'Architecture of consent: Internet protocols and their legal implications', (2004) 56 Stan LR 901.

27   Below, Chapter 9.

28   Eg, Jones, G, 'Loose strands in the web: Meta sites, intellectual property and cyber-consumers', (2001) 8 E-Law (Web).

those sites are protected in law.[29] As will become clear below, this argument too is very hard to square with the modern law; while the law gives some protection to web sites, it is much less than this argument suggests. The current position appears to be somewhere between the two views: web sites are not protected in law in the same way as private property is; but nonetheless there are certain specific abuses which may be committed by linking to a site or visiting it, which the law will restrain.

It is important to realise that, from a technical point of view, the owner of an Internet site has absolute control over it. Files can be added to or removed from the site on a whim; the server can be instructed to allow some requests but deny others; and at any time the owner may simply switch it off or disable its connection to the net, thus denying access to all. For many, this strongly suggests that we are looking at a property right: to suggest that the site's owner can pick and chose who visits the site, and to control what they do when there, seems powerfully analogous to a home owner's right to chose who may visit, or to tell visitors to keep their shoes off the sofa. But for others, this simply shows the dangerous temptation that analogies can present. The web site owner's power to keep out visitors is not really much like the homeowner's right at all, because it cannot in practice be used in any very discriminating way. It is not usually possible to identify visitors to a web site without persuading them to reveal identifying details, which most will be unwilling to do without some *quid pro quo*. And control over what the visitors do is limited at best. To say that the web site owner has a property right in cyberspace is not simply to recognise the technical reality, but to go far beyond it, granting the web site owner legal powers which have no equivalent in real space. The question is, therefore, to what extent the law is prepared to augment the already considerable powers of the web site owner, by allowing rigorous control of who may visit it and what they may do once there.

The absolutist view: Internet sites as private property

On one view, therefore, any Internet site is the private property of its owner, who has the absolute right to decide who shall be permitted to visit it and on what terms. Anyone who visits an Internet site must respect the wishes of its owner, and can be denied access if they do not. This view has relatively little support in the cases – though a handful of the US cybertrespass cases assert it vigorously.[30] No court in the UK or Ireland has ever asserted such a doctrine. Nonetheless, it is often adhered to out of caution, as the safest advice that lawyers can give to web surfing clients is to respect any web site policies telling them how to use the site. Some, indeed, have urged site owners not to create any link to another site without a formal agreement with that other site's owner.[31] This school of thought became particularly fashionable after the decision in the *Shetland Times* case, which, while it avoided any detailed statement of the rights of web site owners, nonetheless strongly suggested that they could forbid any link to it of which they disapproved.

Shetland Times involved rival web sites. The pursuer owned a print newspaper, the *Shetland Times*. He established a web site for it at www.shetland-times.co.uk. The

---

29   Hardy, I, 'The ancient doctrine of trespass to web sites', [1996] JOL 7 (Web).
30   See above, p 211.
31   Eg, Brock, A, 'Website linking agreements', [2001] EBL 8.

home page included various headlines from the print edition; clicking on the headline activated a link to the full text of the relevant story. The home page also included advertisements. The defender, a former editor of the *Shetland Times*, established his own site at www.shetland-news.co.uk, an Internet-only newspaper. He copied headlines and links from the pursuer's site, so visitors to his site would click on a headline and be led to the full text story on the pursuer's site. The pursuer objected to this – apparently because the defender's site enabled readers to bypass the pursuer's home page, thus reducing his advertising revenue. An interim interdict was claimed for breach of copyright, and was granted by Lord Hamilton in October 1996. However, the parties settled the case before a full hearing on a permanent interdict could be conducted. Under the settlement, no damages or costs were payable, and the defender could continue to link to the pursuer's site as before. However, any such link was to be accompanied by the legend 'A *Shetland Times* story', and close to any such link would be the *Shetland Times* logo. Further, both the legend and the logo would be linked to the pursuer's home page.[32]

On what legal doctrine can such a result be based, and does it support the broad claims of ownership by web site owners?

Trespass

The notion of cybertrespass chimes well with the concept of web pages as private property, where visitors must comply with the owner's expressed wishes or be considered to have committed a tort. And *dicta* in some of the US cases certainly support that approach. But as has been explained above, the US cases are far from unanimous; the requirement of 'damage' is taken by most judges to require quite substantial misbehaviour by the defendant, and falls far short of treating every undesired link or every undesired visit as tortious. There is no sign that the Irish or UK courts will recognise such a tort at all; if they did, they would have to go far beyond the current US approach before they could be said to have recognised web sites as property.

Copyright

This variant of the argument is that web sites are indeed property, because they are the intellectual creation of their authors; in short, they are intellectual property. While the analogy between intellectual property and more tangible forms of property certainly can be over-emphasised, nonetheless it shares certain basic features with it: those with whom the owner does not wish to deal can be excluded; those licensed to use it can go no further than the licence permits. On this view, the rights of those who surf the web are wholly reliant on the implied permissions of those who own the sites to which they surf; there are many reasons why owners rarely revoke this permission, but if they do so, the law should respect their rights.[33]

---

32 *Shetland Times Ltd v Wills* [1997] FSR 604 (Web). For more detail on the case, see *Shetland Times v Shetland News* (Web); 'Shetland showdown' (Web). For commentary on the case, see O'Donnell, T, 'Law in the outer limits?', [1997] 3 WJCLI (Web); Connolly, J and Cameron, S, 'Fair dealing in webbed links of Shetland yarns', [1998] 2 JILT (Web).

33 On web sites and copyright, see generally Evans, M, 'Protection of data on the Internet', [2002] IPQ 50.

The weakness in the argument is that it seems to overstate the protection that copyright law gives to web sites. As was discussed above, it is not clear that web sites constitute copyright works; no doubt some of the individual design elements are protected by copyright, but that is a much lesser claim. (Analogously, there is a significant distinction between saying that I own a particular house, and saying that I own items of value within it.) Further, it is not established that mere web surfing is automatically breach of copyright subject only to the 'implied licence' defence. Other defences may be applicable, such as 'fair dealing'. And while visiting a page on the web undeniably involves copying the relevant files from the server to the client, it seems unlikely that this transient copying can be an infringement of the copyright owner's rights.[34] There is not the slightest doubt that breach of copyright *can* be committed while browsing the web, such as by making a permanent copy of files, contrary to the expressed wishes of the files' owner. But the picture of the web surfer as always one step away from breach of copyright, saved only by the owner's implied licence, does not seem to correspond to the legal realities.[35]

A variant on the copyright argument, which was accepted by Lord Hamilton in *Shetland Times*, was that the provision of web pages constituted a 'cable programme' service within the legislation, and so its content was by the express terms of the statute protected by copyright law. As noted above, the argument was not unreasonable given the terms of the statute. UK law has since been amended, by redefining 'cable programme' to exclude the Internet. But even in Ireland, it is not clear how good this argument is. It merely seems to provide a plaintiff with another route into copyright law; statute does not say that entirely unoriginal features of a cable service will be protected, nor does it expressly modify the definition of infringement. It is therefore not clear what, if anything, it adds to a simple argument that the web pages in question are protected by copyright.[36]

Database right

It can be argued that most web sites are 'databases' and as such are protected by *sui generis* database right. Database right is in many ways very similar to copyright, but was introduced by the EU to get over the lack of intellectual originality in many compilations; it was considered that the effort and resources involved in creating databases should receive legal protection even though their lack of originality would usually be obvious. This makes database right an obvious technique for protecting web sites; and some of the case law within Europe has indeed prohibited unwelcome deep links as an infringement of the site owner's rights.[37]

But again, those who argue that web sites are private property overstate the extent of liability. Databases are not protected against any and every extraction of data from them; only 'substantial' extraction results in liability. The law here remains to be worked out in detail, and some of the rulings to date are considered below; but

---

34   Above, pp 51 and 53–54.
35   Reed, C, 'Copyright in WWW pages – News from Shetland', (1997) 13 CLSR 167.
36   Above, p 51.
37   See above, p 62.

evidently we are very far from a position where web surfers have to rely on an implied licence by the site owner to render their web surfing legal.[38]

Owning the address itself

The final argument is that the very address of the site or of pages within it belong to its owner. So if the name www.megacorp.com belongs to MegaCorp, then use of that address by others may be said to be wrongful. As was noted above, these addresses can for some purposes be treated as embodying intellectual property.[39] So any attempt to access the page would necessarily involve the use of the site owner's property. This is a rather different sort of argument from the others. It is hard to find a real-world analogy for it – it is as if someone were to claim ownership of a locked room, not by showing that they owned the land on which it stood, but by showing that they owned all of the keys. But what would be the legal source of this 'ownership'?

Any attempt to invoke copyright law would involve showing that the address was an 'original literary work', which seems an unlikely thing to say: creation of such an address does not suggest any great ability. No such argument was made in *Shetland Times*, where the defendant had copied headlines from the pursuer's site to his own, and had linked those headlines to the full stories on the pursuer's site. Rather, the pursuer argued that the *headlines* were copyright. This was contested by the defendant, who pointed out that it was difficult to regard such gems as 'Bid to save centre after council funding "cock up" ' as original literary works. Nonetheless, he conceded that something as short as a headline *could* be copyright, and Lord Hamilton held that it was at least arguable that these headlines were – which was enough to justify the interdict asked for. But the case gives no support to the idea that the address of a site is protected by copyright.

An (as yet untried) argument is that an Internet address is protected as a trade mark. This might be plausible in some cases, as web addresses used by companies are often very similar to their trade marks.[40] So this argument could be used to assert a sort of ownership over the name of the domain, and hence a right to control the use of that name. But this would be a strange argument, as there is no very obvious reason why a site owner's right to control access to its site should depend on whether it has registered a particular trade mark. Most probably the argument would be rejected, at least if it were raised on its own, as the sole reason for objecting to the use of the link. It is, after all, the obvious way of referring to the site and, unless the site owner can give some other reason to justify limiting access, a claim for breach of trade mark seems inadequate.

Restricted sites: a special case?

Matters may be somewhat different if access to the site, or part of it, is deliberately restricted, for example by the use of a password system. Attempts to circumvent the password requirement might bring the case within the unlawful computer access offences; the civil law might protect the content of the site under the law of

---

38   Below, p 220.
39   Above, p 192.
40   On trade mark law generally, see above, p 72.

confidence. Of course, each case would require close analysis; and the matter may turn on how careful the site owner was in handing out passwords. But, in principle, it seems that protection should be available.

The leading US case is, however, not encouraging. Robert Konop, a pilot with Hawaiian Airlines, created a secure web site where he posted bulletins critical of his employers. Access to the site was by password. Konop created a list of those eligible to access the site, mostly fellow employees; a new user of the site would be asked by it to enter their name, and if the name was on Konop's list then a password would be generated. This process involved the user clicking on a button indicating acceptance of the site's terms and conditions, which included a term prohibiting the user from disclosing the content of the site. A vice-president of the company, who wished to view the site, asked one of his other pilots if he could use the pilot's name for this purpose; on obtaining agreement, he did so. On these facts, the Federal Court of Appeals held that Konop had no cause of action.[41] Viewed from the other side of the Atlantic, this seems a surprising result. An express undertaking of confidence was requested and was given; why should it not be enforced?[42] It is also unclear how the unlawful access offence can be avoided: the access here seems hard to distinguish from the ordinary case of using another's password, which is clearly criminal.[43]

Conclusion

It therefore appears very hard to argue that web sites are treated in law as their owners' private property, from which they can keep all others away. Nonetheless, there is no lack of those arguing that that is so. Indeed, there is a substantial risk of creeping copyright liability, as web site owners increasingly dress up indefensible copyright claims as claims that their servers are being wrongfully accessed.[44] It is to be hoped that such claims can be resisted.

As will have been apparent from the discussion above, while the various rights that a web site owner has do not seem to add up to 'ownership' of the site, nonetheless they are substantial, and allow an action for some of the more objectionable behaviour that web surfers may get up to. These actions for misbehaviour are now considered thematically.

Controlling links

Assuming, therefore, that there is no general right for a site owner to control who creates links to their site, nonetheless there are in UK and Irish law three sets of circumstances where legal action could be taken against an improper link.[45]

---

41   *Konop v Hawaiian Airlines Ltd* 302 F 3d 868 (9th Ct, 23 August 2002), cert denied 537 US 1193 (2003). For discussion, see Motooka, W, 'Can the eye be guilty of trespass? Protecting noncommercial restricted websites after *Konop v Hawaiian Airlines*', (2004) 37 UC Davis LR 869.

42   On the law of confidence, see above, pp 71 and 82.

43   Above, Chapter 2.

44   Galbraith, C, 'Access denied: Improper use of the Computer Fraud and Abuse Act to control information on publicly accessible Internet websites', (2004) 63 Md LR 320.

45   For the approach of other jurisdictions, see Fernández-Díez, I, 'Linking, framing and copyright: A comparative law approach', SSRN, August 2001 (Web); Volkmer, C, 'HyperLinks to and from commercial websites', (2002) 7 CLRTJ 65 (Web).

Links which encourage the commission of legal wrongs

If a link is established to the claimant's site with the clear intention of facilitating a wrong against the claimant, then the person who created that link will be complicit in any wrong committed. The most obvious application would be encouraging breach of copyright or of database right. So if my web site contains material in which I have copyright, then creating a link to my site which encourages others to take it will be a secondary infringement. Obviously enough, these cases have very little to do with the fact that intellectual property is being stolen *from its owner's web page* – a wrong would equally be committed if copyright material had found its way onto a third party's site, from which others are encouraged to take it. Nonetheless, these legal principles restrain those encouraging others to visit particular pages in order to commit legal wrongs against their owners.

Links which misrepresent the site linked to

A link to another's site may result in liability if it misrepresents the site linked to. The way in which the link appears is at the discretion of the party creating it, and so they are responsible for it. Many sorts of misrepresentation are possible, and the law of defamation might be relevant in some cases. However, the usual complaint is that the linker wrongly gives the impression that the link has been authorised by the owner of the linked site, or even that the site linked to is the work of the linker.

These complaints of misrepresentation have been made in various ways in different legal systems: copyright, trade mark, database right, unfair competition and cybertrespass have all been invoked, with varying degrees of success.[46] For the UK and Ireland, remedies are most likely to be available where there is some sort of misattribution or wrongful suggestion as to the ownership or authorship of the pages linked to. In that situation, remedies may be available under the rubrics of moral right, trade mark, or passing off.

It is sometimes suggested that links to others' sites may be *inherently* misleading – in other words, that web surfers are likely to assume that the material linked to is all part of the same site, and so a failure to warn when links go off-site amounts to a misattribution of identity. The more cautious lawyers have therefore advised against unauthorised links for that reason. However, while the courts will no doubt be quick to detect evidence of misattribution, they have yet to accept this concept of inherent misrepresentation; and as the general public becomes increasingly sophisticated in its use of the web, it seems unlikely that they will do so in the future. 'Spoofing' frauds aside, it is an easy matter to discern whether a link leads off-site or not, and it is hard to see that a mere failure to mention the matter is a legal wrong.

Links which infringe database right

As has already been noted, many if not most web sites constitute 'databases' within the meaning of the Database Directive. However, this does not protect the owner of

---

46 Spencer, C, 'To link or not to link', (2002) 1 IJECLP (4) 37; Deveci, H, 'Hyperlinks oscillating at the crossroads', [2004] CTLR 82; Links and Law home page (Web).

the database from every use of it that they find unwelcome. No actionable wrong is committed unless a 'substantial part' of the database is extracted or made available to the public.[47] Obviously, therefore, it is unlikely that a single link to a site can ever constitute breach of database right. The question is how many unwelcome links can be created before an infringement of the right will be found.

There is already a considerable European case law on this, though the UK and Ireland have yet to make much contribution to it; database right played no part in the *Shetland Times* dispute, though if similar facts arose today it seems certain to be mentioned. Various factors are relevant. The number of links, and the frequency with which links are made, is obviously of great importance; the absolute number is not as important as their bulk when put alongside the totality of the site linked to. Questions of fairness have also played a role. The business concept behind the claimant's site will be examined, and if the defendant's linking practices undermine this concept with resulting loss of revenue, that is a substantial point in the claimant's favour. However, the case law does not speak with one voice. Some of it concentrates on the question whether the linked site is a 'database' at all,[48] and cannot be said to deal well with the question whether there is actionable extraction. And the question whether there is any real interference with the claimant's business is often impossible to answer. Some courts are ready to assume interference; others are more sceptical, noting that the defendant's links very probably bring *more* custom to the claimant's site, albeit not quite in the way the claimant envisaged. The case law is therefore a very mixed bag.

Most of the cases have involved facts similar to those of *Shetland Times* concerning links to news stories, the litigation involving German, Danish or Dutch parties. Most of the German cases have gone in favour of the linker, the court arguing that merely copying headlines and allowing deep links is not substantial enough an extraction to amount to infringement.[49] A harsher attitude was taken in the *Mainpost* case, where breach was found,[50] but in the subsequent *Paperboy* case, the Bundesgerichtshof refused to find liability for an even more substantial extraction, consisting of headlines and short fragments of stories.[51] The precise terms of the German law have recently been changed, and so uncertainty is extreme.[52] In Denmark, the *Newsbooster* case result in one of the clearest statements against deep linking: in deciding against the linker, the court stressed the linker's systematic and repeated copying, the fact that it was running a pay service in competition with the site linked to, and that the deep links bypassed the advertisements on the site.[53] At the other extreme is the Dutch *Krantem.com* case, where the Rotterdam District Court refused to find liability. The decision itself is not particularly remarkable – only

---

47   Above, p 62.
48   Eg, *NVM v De Telegraaf* (Netherlands Hoge Raad, 22 March 2002), Judgment (Dutch) (Web).
49   Eg, *Elektronische Pressespiegel* (Landgericht München, 1 March 2002), Judgment (German) (Web).
50   *Mainpost v NewsClub.de* (Oberlandesgericht München, 12 July 2002, reversing Landgericht Berlin, 30 January 2001). See 'Deep linking takes another blow', Wired, 25 July 2002 (Web). The case was later settled: see *NewsClub-Prozess* (Web).
51   (Bundesgerichtshof, 17 July 2003) Judgment (German) (Web); summary at [2003] EBL (Nov) 13. See 'Deep links are legal in Germany – Official', Register, 20 July 2003 (Web).
52   'Germany: deep linking lunacy continues', Register, 13 August 2002 (Web).
53   *Dagblades Forening v Newsbooster* (Copenhagen Bailiff's Court, 5 July 2002), Judgment (English translation) (Web), summarised at [2002] EBL (Oct) 14. See 'Court cuts off deep linking', ZDNet UK, 9 July 2002 (Web).

headlines were taken, and the source of each was expressly acknowledged along side the link. It is unsurprising that a court would refuse to find liability for such minimal linking. However, the court went further, doubting that headlines were protected by database right at all, as they could not be said to represent substantial investments but were mere spin-offs from the ordinary process of story writing. The court also questioned the relevance of bypassing advertisements: the deep links brought more business to the linked site, and it would have been open to the site's owner to place advertisements on the pages linked to as well as on the front page.[54] Judgments generally have paid a certain amount of attention to the possibility of technical counter-measures by those who do not wish their pages to be linked to. However, courts have stopped short of declaring that those who use no protection have no legal complaint, or that those who do will have the law to help them.

Most of the remaining European case law has involved rival job sites, where one online job search engine holds deep links leading to details of jobs held by another. These cases have consistently gone against the deep linker; they include decisions of the Tribunal de Commerce de Paris,[55] the Tribunal de Grande Instance de Paris[56] and the Landgericht Köln.[57] In these cases, the courts have tended to stress that the parties are competitors, that considerable investment had been made in the databases, and that advertising banners had been circumvented by the deep links. In the one decision that stands out, from the Tribunal de Commerce de Nanterre, the court emphasised both that the amount of data taken was relatively small, that the site from which it was taken was expressly acknowledged, and that a link to its home page was provided.[58] The line drawn is therefore a fairly consistent one.

Controlling presentation of data: framing and inlining

There is a natural tendency, when looking at a web page, to assume that all the elements displayed on the screen come from the same site. However, this is not necessarily so. Many sites use a technique known as 'framing', under which two or more pages are displayed at once, each in its own window or 'frame'. There is no technical reason why all the frames should have come from the same site. Or, again, a page may include an image along with text rather than in a window of its own (an 'inline' image). Again, there is no reason why the image should come from the same site as the text. Using these methods and others, a web page may include material held on other servers and fully integrate them into the page; indeed, some sites ('metasites') consist almost entirely of such material.

---

54 *Alemeene Dagblad v Eureka Internetdiensten (Krantem.com)* (Rotterdam District Court, 22 August 2000), Judgment (Dutch) (Web), English translation (Web); summarised at (2001) 1 ECLR (2) 12.
55 *Havas et Cadres On Line v Keljob* (26 December 2000), Judgment (French) (Web), summarised at (2001) 1 ECLR (2) 16.
56 *Cadremploi v Keljob* (5 September 2001, reversing the decision of the Cour d'Appel de Paris, 25 May 2001), Judgment (French) (Web).
57 *StepStone v OFiR* (preliminary injunction 17 January 2001, judgment 28 February 2001), Judgment (German) (Web), summarised at [2001] EBL (Jun) 13. See further 'StepStone sets precedent with hyperlink ban', Register, 17 January 2001 (Web).
58 *StepStone France v OFiR France* (8 November 2000), Judgment (French) (Web).

While this may at first seem an obvious example of taking someone else's copyright material, matters are not so simple. The framer copies nothing, but simply includes in their page instructions to include the image from another site when the page is displayed on screen; at no point does the framer hold a copy of anyone else's materials. If there is a copy, it is constructed by the client machine, the controller of which will not usually have any reason to suspect any breach of the law. It could be construed that the owner of the client computer is making an unlawful copy and the framer is liable as having 'authorised' this, but it is certainly an unusual example of liability.[59]

The owner of the site whose material is being used in this way may feel aggrieved for a number of reasons, usually either that they are not receiving proper credit for their work, or that their advertising material is being bypassed. The specific complaint, that no proper acknowledgment is being made of the ownership of what is taken, can be made through actions for passing off, or breach of trade mark or of moral rights. These actions would be particularly appropriate if the framer or inliner expressly claimed credit for work which was not theirs. It is very often much simpler, however, just to make a general complaint at abuse of legally protected material, relying on copyright or database right.[60]

Very few disputes in this area have got as far even as a first-instance judge; there have been a number of highly publicised disputes, but nearly all have settled at an early stage.[61] One that reached the US Federal Court of Appeals involved a dispute over whether a page framing the plaintiff's copyright material could be said to be a work derivative of that copyright. The ruling was (in effect) that there were good arguments both ways, the plaintiff's claim for a preliminary injunction being rejected in the absence of evidence of harm.[62] European litigation is also rare, though more encouraging for plaintiffs: in one case, for example, the Landgericht Köln was prepared to find a breach of database right in the framing of various poems in an Internet archive. The degree of extraction was on the low side, but the court was influenced particularly by the defendant's circumvention of advertising banners.[63]

Objections to copying

Finally, there is the simple complaint that material available on the Internet by the defendant has been wrongfully copied. As was noted above, the US case law often discusses this as a trespass to the site from which the material was copied.[64] From the Irish or UK perspective, however, and absent some contract or other prior legal relationship between the parties, the arguments with the best chance of success will be based either on copyright or on database right.

---

59   On liability for copying, see above, p 52.
60   For a general review, see Chan, C, 'Internet framing: Complement or hijack?', (1999) 5 MTTLR 143 (Web).
61   Eg, *Washington Post v Total News*, on which see Tucker, R, 'Information Superhighway robbery: The tortious misuse of links, frames, metatags, and domain names', (1999) 4 VJOLT 8 (Web) paras 55–58. See also 'Settlement terms', 5 June 1997 (Web).
62   *Futuredontics, Inc v Applied Angramics, Inc* 1998 US App LEXIS 17012 (9th Ct, 23 July 1998), affirming 1998 US Dist LEXIS 2265 (D C Ca, 30 January 1998).
63   *Derpoet* (Landgericht Köln, 2 May 2001), Judgment (German) (Web). See also the *Medizinisches Lexicon* and *baumarkt* cases, discussed in 'The Database Right File' (Web).
64   Above, p 216.

Copyright liability has been discussed above.[65] As has been noted, it is probably a mistake to think of 'copyright in web pages', for which there is no statutory provision. Rather, text and other elements of the pages may well be protected. The plaintiff would have to establish that what was taken was something that copyright law protects, and will also have to be ready for any defence that may be raised, such as that a licence to copy had been granted. The law of implied licences is poorly defined in the UK and Ireland; in other contexts the courts have been very reluctant to infer their existence, but it is not impossible that making material available to all on the net will be taken as a strong indication that copying is not objected to. Much might depend on the purpose for which the material was made available, or would reasonably have been taken to be by visitors to the site.

Database right has also been discussed above.[66] While it is in many ways similar to copyright, the differences are important in this context. The right is broader in that many if not most web sites are protected by it; it is narrower in that a plaintiff must demonstrate a substantial extraction before remedies are available. While the defences available to a defendant are narrowly stated, the courts are to a certain extent making up for this by taking into account the fairness of the defendant's conduct in determining whether the extraction is 'substantial'.[67]

It is not necessary to make a formal assertion of either right. Nonetheless, where data held on the site is valuable, and litigation to protect it is a real possibility, thought should be given to a notice asserting copyright and database right, and spelling out the limits of any licence to use the data.

PROTECTING RIGHTS: THE CLIENT SIDE

This section concerns the other side of the equation: where a client machine has surfed to a particular site, when can its owner complain of the way in which its server behaves? The law here has been slower to develop. There has been a steady evolution both of the ways in which servers have acted, and in the social norms related to this. Often there is no clear consensus as to the acceptability of new programming techniques. Nonetheless, some of the ways in which the server may exploit the connection with the client are coming to be recognised as abuses.

Some cases are plain enough. If the server uses the channel of communication to the client in a destructive way, such as by sending a worm or virus, then there is a clear breach of the statutes forbidding wrongful computer access.[68] Using the web to inject a virus into a target system is no more acceptable that any other technique to achieve the same result. In other cases, where the harm is rather less, the law is not so clear. This section looks thematically at four distinct issues: control of how the client machine behaves; privacy; discriminatory practices by the server; and issues relating to the reliability of data received.

---

65 Above, p 215.
66 Above, p 216.
67 Above, p 220.
68 Above, p 26.

Control of the client

Some ways of programming the server temporarily remove control of the client from the person operating it; the server sends instructions which conflict with the probable wishes of the client's owner. At the very least, this might disrupt viewing of the web, and in some cases might perhaps even trap the client for a significant amount of time at locations where its controller has no interest in being. Programming practices of this sort include the creation of additional 'pop-up' windows, typically containing advertisements.[69] These windows sometimes appear on their victims' screens immediately, and are sometimes simply set running in such a way that they will be seen later ('pop-unders'). Sometimes software is installed on the client system which will create pop-ups on subsequent occasions, either according to a timetable or in response to particular events. There are also various techniques for 'mousetrapping' visitors, that is, making it difficult for them to leave particular web pages. These techniques include the creation of multiple pop-ups to distract the visitor, or reprogramming the client so that attempts to leave the page have unexpected results.

It is not obvious that any of this should be the concern of the legal system, so long as the effects on the client machine are merely annoying rather than destructive. Social norms for Internet advertising are not yet settled, and it may not be wise to set them until the pace of technological development has slowed. Software to block the more irritating advertising practices is becoming more generally available, and it is already an integral part of some web browsing programs. It may also be questioned whether advertising which annoys visitors does anything to promote the product being advertised. One reason why some advertisers produce multiple pop-up windows is because they are paid by the number of pop-ups. We can reasonably expect that, as one aspect of the development of e-commerce, more sophisticated advertising metrics will be used, which will encourage advertisers to maximise take-up of their products rather than maximise offence to potential customers.

Existing legal powers are minimal. These advertising practices are obviously similar to spam in that they are unrequested and unwelcome advertising, but anti-spam laws across the world are not usually drafted so as to catch them. If the advertising is misleading or has especially offensive content, it can be controlled under general powers relating to advertisements in any medium.[70] In the US, the Federal Trade Commission's general powers have sometimes been sufficient to act against the creators of pop-ups merely on the ground that they interfere with the running of the target computers, though this seems infrequent.[71] Another possible avenue likely to be confined to the US is the class action for cybertrespass.[72]

Some pop-ups have been specifically designed to attract business away from particular firms and towards their rivals. In one case, the defendant circulated

---

69 Bae, E, 'Pop-up advertising online: Slaying the hydra', (2003) 29 RCTLJ 139.

70 See, eg, *Federal Trade Commission v Zuccarini* 2002 US Dist LEXIS 13324 (D E Pa, 10 April 2002). See also *Shields v Zuccarini* 89 F Supp 2d 634 (D E Pa, 22 March 2002), on which see Williams, R, 'Trademark law on the Internet – Mousetrapped', (2002) 6 CLRTJ 329 (Web).

71 See, eg, *D Squared Solutions*, FTC, 9 August 2004 (Web), on which see 'FTC settles with pop-up ad "spammers"', InfoWorld, 9 August 2004 (Web). For a review of the US position, see Leon, M, 'Unauthorized pop-up advertising and the copyright and unfair competition implications', (2004) 32 Hof LR 953.

72 Wilson, G, 'Internet pop-up ads: Your days are numbered!', (2004) 24 Loy LR 567.

advertising software, by including it with free software, such as screensavers, requested by users. This adware worm monitored the user's behaviour on the web, and if the user showed any interest in certain classes of product, then a pop-up would appear with an advertisement relating to that product. The practical result was that when those infected by this adware visited certain commercial sites, a pop-up advertising a rival product immediately appeared, obscuring the site visited. Was this actionable by the sites affected? The matter has proved controversial in the US. Clearly, the adware contained a list of sites which would trigger pop-ups; as the addresses of sites often correspond to their owners' trade marks, actions for breach of trade mark could be considered. Various attempts to sue on this basis are reported, but none was successful.[73] It is doubtful that such an action would succeed in the UK or Ireland; the use of the mark did not confuse the products advertised on the web site with those of its rival, it merely attempted to generate an 'initial interest confusion', which is not unusually regarded as actionable.[74]

Privacy

Considerable quantities of data may be sent by the client machine while transacting with the server. Most of this is technical information relating to the machine itself, though some of it can sometimes be used to identify the person using it. Where a web site owner wants to find out more about those visiting their server, a number of techniques can be employed. Web bugs can be used to record each visit to the page, collecting data such as the IP address of visitors and the model of browser they used.[75] The visit may be recorded by means of a cookie, which is a small data file deposited by the server onto the client, and which may be retrieved later.[76] Alternatively, the server may insinuate spyware onto the client system, a program which may accumulate data on the client machine and then send it back to the server.[77] Most of these processes are invisible to the human user of the client machine, though the more knowledgeable users can do a certain amount to block them by appropriate security settings or through programs which serve as counter-measures. Last but not least, the visitors may themselves input significant amount of information in answer to questions asked by the server; but having given the information, the visitor will have no control over how it is used.

What is this information used for? There is a broad continuum of information practices, from the clearly legitimate to the clearly illegal, with much in between. At the legitimate end are cases where information is voluntarily given by users for stated purposes; most contracts require a certain amount of information to be exchanged and, so long as the data is not abused, there seems no reason to object.

---

73 *1–800 Contacts, Inc v WhenU.com, Inc* 414 F 3d 400 (2nd Ct, 27 June 2005); *U-Haul International, Inc v WhenU.com, Inc* 279 F Supp 2d 723 (D E Va, 5 September 2003) and *Wells Fargo and Co v WhenU.com, Inc* 293 F Supp 2d 734 (D E Mi, 19 November 2003). See also *Gator.com Corp v LL Bean, Inc* 398 F 3d 1125 (9th Ct, 15 February 2005). For discussion, see Chatterjee, N and Merriett, C, 'Pop-up advertising as "use in commerce" under the Lanham Act', (2004) 20 SCCHTJ 1113; Lerner, J, 'Trademark infringement and pop-up ads', (2005) 20 BTLJ 229.

74 On 'initial interest confusion', see below, p 237.

75 See 'Web beacon' (Web).

76 See 'How Internet cookies work' (Web).

77 See, eg, 'PCs "infested" with spy programs', BBC News, 16 April 2004 (Web).

Again, many of the uses to which cookies are put are perfectly legitimate: by placing an identifying cookie on a visiting machine, a frequent visitor to the site can be identified automatically, avoiding the need to re-enter identifying information or to use a password. At the other extreme are clearly illegal practices, such as the use of spyware to steal personal data such as credit cards numbers. The middle ground is more difficult. By building up a record of which web sites a client visits and the products in which its owner expresses an interest, a profile of the owner can be built up.[78] To what extent should this be regarded as illegal? And what warnings should be given for the benefit of those who find these practices particularly objectionable? There is as yet no consensus.

The present position is confused. The information practices of major web companies are often debated: witness the controversies that have surrounded the use of client data by Google's GMail[79] and the retailer Amazon.[80] Discussion is dominated by the US legal system, which (as discussed above[81]) has a somewhat patchwork system of specific laws on different aspects of consumer privacy.[82] The area is usually controversial. Particularly objectionable behaviour results in calls for further legislation, or enforcement action by the Federal Trade Commission, or a class action on behalf of its victims, or all three.[83] Legislation is always under discussion, though its detail is always vigorously debated; federal legislation against spyware seems likely to emerge soon, though in what form is obscure.

As to actual litigation, most famous is the *Doubleclick* case, where the Internet advertisers Doubleclick arranged for 1,500 busy sites to set cookies on client computers which visited them, recording the visit and certain information from the client. This data might be retrieved on subsequent visits, and used to select banner advertisements. So the advertisements that the visitor saw on later occasions would have been selected by reference to that user's profile built up from previous visits. Various actions were started in state and federal courts. The federal class action failed, Judge Buchwald noting that all the data in the cookies represented data given voluntarily, and that it had not been misused with criminal intent.[84] Action by the attorneys-general of 10 states continued, a settlement eventually being reached under which Doubleclick paid US$450,000 towards the cost of investigating the

---

78   Halstead, D and Ashman, H, 'Electronic profiling' (Web).

79   See, eg, 'Google's GMail sparks privacy row', BBC News, 5 April 2004 (Web); Burnes, C, 'Google Mail – Useful new service or frightening privacy invasion?', (2004) 4 PDP (6) 12; 'More on GMail and privacy' (Web); Goldberg, M, 'The googling of online privacy: GMail, search-engine histories and the new frontier of protecting private information on the web', (2005) 9 LCLR 249.

80   Eg, 'Privacy groups target Amazon again', News.Com, 8 October 2002 (Web).

81   Above, p 101. For discussion of the US position, see Siebecker, M, 'Cookies and the common law: Are Internet advertisers trespassing on our computers?', (2003) 76 So Calif LR 893; Hertzel, D, 'Don't talk to strangers: An analysis of government and industry efforts to protect a child's privacy online', (2000) 52 FCLJ 429 (Web); Zimmerman, R, 'The way the cookies crumble: Internet privacy and data protection in the twenty-first century', (2001) 4 LPP 439 (Web).

82   See generally White, J, 'The search for a viable cause of action against private individuals who use cookies to obtain personal information', (2005) 55 Syr LR 653.

83   For an unsuccessful class action, see *In re Northwest Airlines Privacy Litigation* 2004 US Dist LEXIS 10580 (D Minn, 6 June 2004).

84   *In re Doubleclick Inc Privacy Litigation* 154 F Supp 2d 497 (S D NY, 29 March 2001); for settlement of this action, see *In re Doubleclick Inc Privacy Litigation* 2002 US Dist LEXIS 27099 (S D NY, 24 May 2002). See 'Cookies remain intact while plaintiffs' claims crumble', Shaw Pittman, April 2001 (Web).

matter, and gave various undertakings. These included the posting of an online privacy policy to which Doubleclick would be legally committed, restrictions on the transfer of data to others, and the creation of a cookie viewer to enable consumers to see what data was held on them.[85]

As to the law in the UK and Ireland, various provisions are relevant. In principle, issues of human rights could be relevant, as the right to private life may be thought to be in issue. In practice, however, matters are likely to turn on more specific provisions.

The computer access offences

These offences have been considered above.[86] They are obviously useful in the case of destructive behaviour, or the more intrusive spyware, such as keylogging software or software which sniffs out credit card numbers. This approach is of less use for the more ordinary sorts of cookie, which only contain information given voluntarily. As noted above, there are difficulties in the way the legislation defines consent or authorisation for others to intrude onto a computer system, and prosecutions would accordingly be difficult in a case where it was plausible to allege consent.[87] If there is no intent to cause harm but merely an attempt to collect data, which was to be used only to target advertising more precisely, it is not obvious that the substantial penalties in the legislation are appropriate anyway.

Data confidentiality

In response to concerns about cookies, the Data Privacy Directive of 2002 included a specific provision on 'the use of electronic communications networks to store information or to gain access to information stored in the terminal equipment of a subscriber or user'. This wording seems broad enough to include not only cookies but also any form of spyware. This is only to be permitted 'on condition that the subscriber or user concerned is provided with clear and comprehensive information in accordance with Directive 95/46/EC, *inter alia* about the purposes of the processing, and is offered the right to refuse such processing by the data controller'. So the target of the information gathering must be told what is going on, and given the chance to opt out. Two exceptions are allowed: storage or access which is necessary for the sole purpose of transmitting a message over the network, or which is strictly necessary for the provision of an information society service explicitly requested.[88] This Directive has now been incorporated into UK[89]

---

85 For the settlement terms of 26 August 2002, see 'Agreement' (Web). See 'Doubleclick to open cookie jar', Wired, 27 August 2002 (Web); Zarksy, T, 'Cookie viewers and the undermining of data-mining: A critical review of the *Doubleclick* settlement', [2002] STLR P1 (Web).

86 Above, Chapter 2.

87 Above, p 209.

88 Directive 2002/58/EC on privacy and electronic communications, art 5(3). See King, I, 'On-line privacy in Europe – New regulation for cookies', (2003) 12 ICTL 225; Debussere, F, 'The EU E-Privacy Directive: A monstrous attempt to starve the cookie monster?', (2005) 13 IJLIT 70. For regulation of 'information society services', see above, p 133.

89 Privacy and Electronic Communications (EC Directive) Regulations 2003 (UK), SI 2003/2426, regs 6, 30 and 31.

and Irish[90] law. These national provisions allow for a civil action for loss suffered through breach, though there is a defence that all due care was used to avoid breach. Public enforcement is in the hands of the Information Commissioner/Data Protection Commissioner, on the same terms as for breaches of data protection law generally; the ultimate sanction is a fine.[91]

While the general aim of creating legislation that is technologically neutral is to be encouraged, nonetheless the broad style of drafting leaves difficulties. The precise information to be supplied is not absolutely clear; the statement that it should be 'in accordance with Directive 95/46/EC' seems to refer to provisions which themselves are vaguely stated.[92] And what steps must be taken before a court may conclude that this information has been 'provided' to the user? Presumably, this is not simply a requirement that it be made available, but that it be displayed with some prominence. Yet is this really desirable? Cookies are ubiquitous and convenient. Much of their convenience is lost if there is a legal requirement to call attention to their use. 'It is difficult to imagine the experience of using the Internet where consent to the use of cookies was required upon each visit to a new web site. "Tedious" is the word that springs to mind.'[93] There is as yet no case law to spell out the impact of the provision.

Data protection law generally

In addition, there is the possibility that the general law of data protection applies. However, various difficult issues arise simply in determining whether the legislation applies at all. Are cookies 'personal data' at all? Typically they will identify a particular computer, rather than a particular person. Home computers may be used by more than one family member, and there is no easy way for the server to detect whether this is so. It could therefore be suggested that cookies do not identify individuals at all, and so the legislation does not apply. National Data Commissioners are characteristically bullish about this; for example, the UK Information Commissioner has suggested that 'in the context of the on-line world' cookies function as personal identifiers and so are within the legislation.[94] Another difficult question is whether the legislation applies to a cookie set on a client machine within the EU by a server which is outside. The Article 29 Working Party has suggested that the storing of the cookie constitutes processing within the EU, and therefore data protection law protects all EU clients, wherever the server is located.[95] These points of view remain highly arguable.

---

90   European Communities (Electronic Communications Networks and Services) (Data Protection and Privacy) Regulations 2003 (IE), SI 2003/535, regs 5 and 16–19.

91   On enforcement of data protection law, see above, p 88.

92   The reference is to the main Data Protection Directive 1995/46/EC; presumably the precise reference is to Arts 10 and 11 on information to be given to data subjects on collection of data, on which see above, p 90.

93   Sharpe, A, 'The way the cookie crumbles', (2002) 2 PDP (6) 6.

94   See 'Compliance advice – Website frequently asked questions', 26 June 2001 (Web), para 6.

95   *Working Document on Determining the International Application of EU Data Protection Law to Personal Data Processing on the Internet by Non-EU Based Web Sites*, 5035/01/EN/Final, 30 May 2002 (Web).

On the assumption that data protection law applies, certain issues become relevant:[96]

(a) Processing will have to be justified on some statutory ground, such as consent; the difficulties with applying a requirement of consent in this context have already been noted. Consent must be consent to the actual processing envisaged: there is no scope in EU law for the argument that has so impressed US judges, that voluntarily giving the data amounts to consent to all lawful uses of it.

(b) The notification to the data subject must include the purpose for which the data is to be used. This must include not simply the immediate uses, but any subsequent ones, such as transferring it to third parties.

(c) Unlike the US, there is no specific legislation protecting children's financial interests online. No doubt, the Directive's requirements will be interpreted in an especially demanding fashion on this issue.

(d) No data can be sent back to the server except in accordance with the legislation. This may be particularly problematic if the server is outside the EU.

While none of the legislation provides expressly for it, the most obvious way of securing compliance with data protection requirements is by posting a privacy policy on the web site. The policy must include all particulars required to be brought to the attention of data subjects, in language they are likely to be able to understand. The policy (or at least a link to it) must be placed reasonably prominently. No doubt, the courts will apply the same presumption that they do in contract law generally, that consent to unusual or stringent terms must be demonstrated by stronger evidence than would be appropriate for usual terms.

Assessment

Enforcement of EU privacy law is abysmal. Failure of web sites to provide any kind of privacy policy is still apparently the norm.[97] Even cases where servers have accidentally revealed customer details to all comers are not uncommon.[98] Low levels of compliance with data protection law cannot be much of a surprise. Computer security is difficult and expensive even when the need for it is compelling. The legislation's requirements are open-ended; even in a simple case, it requires detailed legal advice to secure full compliance. And the consequences of breaking the law are minimal. Even if a clear breach is established, enforcement proceedings are unlikely. If the EU were serious about compliance with the law, it would have to be made much simpler, and enforcement would have to be treated as of much higher priority.

Would more effective enforcement be justified? Consumer attitudes to online privacy are confused. There is certainly anxiety about privacy, albeit poorly focused anxiety. But consumers have many anxieties, and the trade-offs have not yet been faced. People want privacy, but they also want to be able to move about the web easily; and personalisation is popular too. The truth is that breaches of privacy,

---

96 For a general review, see Grant, H and Brownsdon, E, 'Websites: New guidance from the Information Commissioner – part 1', (2001) 1 PDP (8) 8, and 'part 2', (2001) 2 PDP (2) 6.

97 'Top UK sites "fail privacy test" ', BBC News, 11 December 2003 (Web).

98 Eg, 'Which? under fire over security scare', BBC News, 22 June 2001 (Web); 'UK web shoppers' details exposed', ZDNet UK, 13 August 2002 (Web).

while they are widespread, have not actually done a great deal of harm. Some practices are obviously abuses: the slightest use of a credit card number without its owner's consent, for example. But most uses of private details are not objectionable. People are very willing to hand over personal details when given a reason to do – convenient access to their favourite sites, or notification of news or products of interest to them – and it is very hard to put this down completely to ignorance of the possibility of abuse.[99]

Is the problem not so much a legal one as a technical one? This is not clear yet. At the time of writing, anti-spyware software is in its infancy; the more technically adept users can obtain a measure of security, but most users do not. Cookies are a different matter: it is very easy indeed to configure a web browser to refuse all cookies, or at least to ask the user whether they wish to accept each one. But anyone who does so almost immediately discovers that the web has become a very unfriendly place. Much time is then taken deciding whether to accept particular cookies; the need to remember passwords is hugely increased; and many servers simply refuse entry unless they are allowed to place a cookie. It will be seen, therefore, that the problem is only partly technical. Rather, some sort of compromise is needed between the various legitimate interests involved.[100]

Discrimination against the blind and the partially sighted

In its origins, the Internet was very much a text medium. But as greater sophistication in web design has become the norm, more emphasis has been placed on the visual appearance of web pages; some of this conveys additional information, though most of it is mere 'eye candy', dressing up mundane information in attractive ways. This is all to the good if it makes the web a more interesting place to be; but it makes life harder for those whose sight is poor or non-existent.

Is this problem technical, social or legal? It is technical in that specially written software can alleviate it: text can be processed to produce synthesised speech or Braille.[101] However, even the best of such software will fail certain tests unless the web pages were written with this issue in mind. Graphics are wasted on the blind unless there is attached to them a verbal description of their content. The important text may be swamped by a large amount of coding to produce visual effects, making it hard to locate: much of the software developed to help the blind is quite limited, and text needs to be left where the program can find it. Economic pressures hinder more than they help: unless the web site is targeted especially at people with poor vision, the additional effort needed to make them accessible may seem excessive to the pages' creators. There are modifications to copyright law to make it easier for the visually impaired to read copyright material,[102] but this addresses only one aspect of the problem.

---

99   Hann, I, Hui, K, Lee, S and Png, I, 'The value of online information privacy: An empirical investigation', SSRN, 2003 (Web); Baumer, D, Earp, J, and Evers, P, 'Tit for tat in cyberspace: Consumer and website responses to anarchy in the market for personal information', (2003) 4 NCJOLT 217 (Web).
100 Borking, J and Raab, C, 'Laws, PETs and other technologies for privacy protection', [2001] 1 JILT (Web); Kenny, S and Borking, J, 'The value of privacy engineering', [2002] 1 JILT (Web).
101 'Text is best for website accessibility', Register, 4 August 2004 (Web).
102 Copyright (Visually Impaired Persons) Act 2002 (UK) (amended by SI 2003/115 and SI 2003/2500).

Legislation on disability discrimination does not focus on the Internet, but nonetheless applies to it. Both UK and Irish law make detailed provision in particular contexts (such as employment and education), but also have general provisions that appear to apply to all web sites within the jurisdiction, though the precise definition of 'discrimination' is not always helpful:

(a) The UK legislation prohibits discrimination in relation to the provision of services to members of the public, including free services. 'Services' are not defined, but include 'access to and use of information services'. The wording of the legislation is unhelpful in that it condemns only any 'practice, policy or procedure which makes it impossible or unreasonably difficult for disabled persons to make use of a service' and any 'physical feature' with the same effect. Neither of these applies neatly to web page design; though presumably a sympathetic court could say that a web designer's failure to consider the position of those with less than perfect vision amounts to a relevant policy or procedure. The duty imposed by the legislation is to take such steps as are reasonable to avoid discrimination; there is an additional duty to take reasonable steps to provide 'an auxiliary aid or service' to facilitate use of the service by the disabled. Enforcement is by ordinary civil action as for breach of statutory duty; an award of damages can include a sum for injured feelings.[103]

(b) The Irish legislation also prohibits discrimination in relation to the provision of services to members of the public, including free services. 'Services' are defined as 'a service or facility of any nature which is available to the public generally or a section of the public'. Again, the wording was not really drafted with the web in mind, but it seems broad enough: discrimination includes 'refusal or failure by the provider of a service to do all that is reasonable to accommodate the needs of a person with a disability by providing special treatment or facilities, if without such special treatment or facilities it would be impossible or unduly difficult for the person to avail himself or herself of the service'. Redress for breach of the legislation is provided by the Director of Equality Investigations; it can include an order for compensation, and a prohibition on continuing the discrimination.[104]

Authoritative guidelines on good practice have been laid down by the World Wide Web Consortium (W3C); these include a grading system to indicate how well a site makes provision for those with limited vision.[105] Litigation is rare. There has been some US litigation.[106] There is apparently no UK or Irish litigation yet, though a number of sites have improved their text-only provision following threats of litigation. The rate of non-compliance is very high.[107] The leading case internationally is an Australian decision on the accessibility of the Sydney Olympic Games site, where the Human Rights and Equal

---

103 Disability Discrimination Act 1995 (UK), ss 1, 19–21 and 25, as amended. For discussion, see Mason, S and Casserley, C, 'Web site design and the Disability Discrimination Act 1995', (2002) 12 C&L (5) 16.

104 Equal Status Act 2000 (IE), ss 1, 2, 4, 5, 21 and 27.

105 See 'Web Accessibility Initiative' (Web).

106 For the US position, see Mendelsohn, S and Gould, M, 'When the Americans with Disabilities Act goes online', (2004) 8 CLRTJ 173 (Web); Moberly, R, 'The Americans with Disabilities Act in cyberspace: Applying the "Nexus" approach to private Internet websites', (2004) 55 Mercer LR 963.

107 *The Web – Access and Inclusion for Disabled People*, Disability Rights Commission, 2004 (Web).

Opportunity Commission was prepared to order greater use of text, to label images and to index files.[108]

Reliability of data

An under-explored area is that of responsibility for harm suffered in reliance upon the contents of a web site. Many scenarios are imaginable.

(a) If information is supplied under a contract with the user of the client machine, action is certainly conceivable. Various US cases have involved Internet dating agencies, where one of the parties matched together turned out to have criminal designs on the other. If the injured party sues the dating agency, it is clear that the case calls for a careful investigation of precisely what services the agency was undertaking to provide.[109]

(b) False information which is relied upon may alternatively create an action in negligent misstatement. As a rule, it is very hard to found such an action on a statement made to persons generally, though if reliance upon it is obviously foreseeable, such an action is not impossible. Information which was in some way individualised seems a much better candidate for liability. Close attention would be needed both to the context in which the information was given and any warning notices that accompanied it.[110]

(c) It is sometimes suggested that incorrect data might be regarded as a defective product and so attract liability under the defective products legislation.[111] It seems unlikely that the idea of a 'product' can be pushed quite so far, though the idea is not impossible if it relates to a program or a discrete database.[112]

(d) Negligent dissemination of viruses would seem an obvious target for liability, though there does not appear to be any case law.

SEARCH ENGINES

In the early days of the web, it was often said that it resembled a huge international library, but one in which chaos reigned: books scattered all over the floor, the index either smashed or never written in the first place. Such an institution might, of course, be tremendous fun to browse in, but it would be of limited use for serious research or business. With the development of modern search engines, this point of view is much rarer. Some items are easier to locate than others, but as a generalisation it is no longer true that useful items are hard to locate.

---

108 *Maguire v Sydney Organising Committee for the Olympic Games* (Australian Human Rights and Equal Opportunity Commission, 24 August 2000) (Web). For discussion, see Russell, C, 'Access to technology for the disabled: The forgotten legacy of innovation?', (2003) 12 ICTL 237.

109 Compare *Fox v Encounters International* 318 F Supp 2d 279 (D N Maryland, 25 September 2002) with *Carafano v Metrosplash.com, Inc* 339 F 3d 1119 (9th Ct, 13 August 2003), on which see Lipschutz, J, 'Internet dating', (2004) 23 TELTJ 225.

110 Salt, J, 'Liability for information and the information society', (1997) 5 IJLIT 308.

111 Eg, Leadstrom, N, 'Internet web sites as products under strict products liability: A call for an expanded definition of product', (2001) 40 WLJ 532 (Web).

112 See Directive 1985/374/EC on defective products, especially Art 2 (definition of 'product').

The technical aspects of search engines are partly responsible for this: development of new techniques for searching, and the occasional intellectual property battles over who owns them, have been at the core of this.[113] But the economic aspects have been no less challenging. It is no mean feat to offer search facilities free to the entire world, and yet to generate sufficient revenues to pay for rapid and effective searching technology. Both the financial and the computing aspects of the major search engines attract considerable attention. Huge attention has focused on the recent flotation of Google, the current market leader in search engines, and on its increasing diversification into sales of personal search tools and of data generated through analysing search enquiries.[114] Rivals such as Yahoo! also attract considerable attention.[115]

The core economic problem of search engines is that users expect them to be free; pay services are available, but are usually only economically viable if they give access to content not available elsewhere. Web users expect useful, comprehensive and unbiased search results quickly and for nothing; whereas the money to run such a system can only be obtained from firms seeking to advertise their products. Evidently, these aims conflict. A variety of tools can be used to reconcile them. The owners of the search engine may require payment from those who want their sites included in the search database. They may also display advertisements, perhaps modifying the content of the advert to reflect the searcher's interests; so, for example, if a client uses the engine to search for 'cars', the results page will incorporate paid advertisements for particular makes of cars. This 'contextual advertising' is controversial, however, not least because its workings may not be transparent to the consumer. It is, however, in the creation of the search rankings that the pressures on search engine owners are most acute: advertisers want their products to come to the attention of searchers, whereas searchers want unbiased results. One common solution is to provide two sets of results to each search enquiry: one of which is an unbiased list, the other of which consists of 'sponsored links' to sites which have paid for this service. All of these techniques have legal difficulties, which are considered below.

Public concerns over search engines are widespread, but unfocused. As the wide array of information on the web becomes easier to access, there are concerns over possible invasions of privacy, particularly when search engines are used to find out about particular individuals. Search engines often find themselves blamed for the content of the sites they index, when it is perceived to be too easy to find sites whose owners have offensive views or illegal aims. And as search engines do more to profile their users and customise search results, issues of users' privacy come more to the fore.[116]

---

113 'How Google works', Economist, 16 September 2004 (Web); Brin, S and Page, L, 'The anatomy of a large-scale hypertextual web search engine', (Web).

114 'How good is Google?', Economist, 30 October 2003 (Web); 'The weakness of Google', Economist, 29 April 2004 (Web).

115 'Yahoo! and Google escalate portal wars', Register, 18 May 2004 (Web); 'Google's long-term dominance doubted', ZDNet UK, 26 May 2004 (Web).

116 Eg, 'Emergence in Europe of a new monopoly on dissemination of information via the Internet and worrying collection of personal data', OJ 2004/C33E/224 (Web). Cf 'Life beyond Google', BBC News, 6 April 2004 (Web).

This section, the final one of the chapter, covers the legal issues that have arisen in relation to search engines under three general themes: problems with the content searched; problems with the rankings produced; and problems with advertisements.

Content

A search engine executes search requests by comparing them with its own database of web sites, looking for matches. But where does this database come from? It must be compiled from the web, and updated as necessary; perhaps by using 'web spiders' to search the web for new links or to update the information on old ones. Or again the creators of the database may accept links from site owners who have asked to be added to it; the creators may or may not charge for this service. Or again the database's owners may seek content from elsewhere: as traditional publishing houses increasingly move towards electronic media, so there are more and more opportunities for search engines to acquire access to online content.[117]

In most cases, increasing the content of a search engine database is beneficial to all concerned. Nonetheless, in a few cases a legal objection may be made.

Sites whose owners object to inclusion

Which site owners do not wish to become part of search engine databases? Ironically, the major complainants here are database owners themselves, and especially the owners of search engines. To allow another search engine to catalogue the database, and reproduce parts of it on request, undermines the engine's business model, which almost certainly depends on would-be searchers coming to it directly, rather than going to its rivals.

How can a site owner make it clear that web spiders are unwelcome? No doubt this will be mentioned in the site's terms and conditions, if it has any. More useful in practice is a well-recognised convention whereby limits on the access permitted to spiders are listed in a file called robots.txt in the head directory of the site.[118] This allows the site owner to be explicit as to where spiders may go; and if it is thought desirable, the site owner can distinguish between different spiders which are to be subject to different limitations.[119] This convention appears to be well observed.

Legal action, if the spider exceeds the permitted limits, would presumably be for breach of copyright,[120] infringement of database right[121] or cybertrespass.[122]

---

117 For some of the issues, see Hanratty, E, 'Google library: Beyond fair use?', [2005] DLTR 10 (Web).
118 Eg, Google's (Web).
119 See 'Web Robots Pages' (Web).
120 Cruquenaire, A, 'Electronic agents as search engines: Copyright related aspects', (2001) 9 IJLIT 327. Cf *Nautical Solutions Marketing, Inc v Boats.com* 2004 US Dist LEXIS 6304 (D M Fla, 1 April 2004).
121 Ruse, H, 'Electronic agents and the legal protection of non-creative databases', (2001) 9 IJLIT 295; Groom, J, 'Are "agent" exclusion clauses a legitimate application of the EU Database Directive?', (2004) 1 SCRIPT-ed 1 (Web).
122 Rosenfeld, R, 'Spiders and crawlers and bots, Oh My', [2002] STLR 3 (Web).

As noted above, these wrongs are not ideally defined from the point of view of the owner of the data taken, although some judgments on database right seem to be groping towards an idea of which 'takings' really threaten legitimate interests and which do not.[123]

Objections to the nature of the link

The site owner may be complaining not that a link is made to the site, but as to precisely how this is being done. Some complaints of this sort take us back to the controversies over deep linking.[124] Another type of complaint relates particularly to image search engines, which often help searchers by providing small, low-resolution 'thumbnail' copies of the images. If the owner of the images objects to their use in this way, is the display of the thumbnail actionable? In *Kelly v Arriba Soft Corp*, the US Federal Court of Appeals held that while the entire process obviously involved a copying of the image, nonetheless if the thumbnail alone was kept and displayed to searchers, then there was fair use and, accordingly, no actionable wrong had taken place.[125] However, a similar result has been rejected in Germany, the Landgericht Hamburg noting that German copyright law has no such broad 'fair use' exception, and that it would be for the legislature not the courts to create such an exception, if appropriate.[126]

Linking to illegal content

Finally, a search engine may incur liability by cataloguing and linking to sites engaged in illegal conduct. This may be because the site holds data in breach of copyright.[127] Alternatively, the content linked to may be deemed criminally offensive. This can lead to considerable controversy, both amongst the immediate participants in the dispute, and amongst the wider community of net users, anxious to know how their search results are being manipulated, if they are.[128] One famous dispute, where Yahoo!'s auction site advertised Nazi memorabilia of various sorts, was considered above.[129] Equally controversial has been Google's difficulties with the Chinese government, which at some points led it to block access to Google entirely.[130] Access has now been restored. Google is regularly accused of censoring itself to suit the Chinese government; some of these accusations are admitted.[131]

---

123 Above, p 216.
124 Above, p 219.
125 336 F 3d 811 (9th Ct, 7 July 2003). This withdraws and replaces an earlier opinion, much commented on in legal circles (280 F 3d 934, 9th Ct, 6 February 2002).
126 Gierschmann, S, ' "Thumbnails" – No "fair use" exception in Germany', Bird and Bird, 12 May 2004 (Web).
127 Walker, W, 'Application of the DMCA safe harbor provisions to search engines', (2004) 9 VJOLT 2 (Web).
128 'Google's Ethics Committee revealed', Register, 17 May 2004 (Web).
129 Above, p 155.
130 'China blocking Google', BBC News, 2 September 2002 (Web).
131 'Google admits omitting Chinese news links', ZDNet UK, 27 September 2004 (Web).

Search ranking

When it receives a search request, how does a search engine produce a list of sites relevant to that request, with the most relevant sites at the top of that list? The details of the process are important trade secrets of search engine owners. But certain basic features of it are obvious enough. There are too many sites for evaluation of each one to involve human intervention: the process of determining what each is about must be mostly automatic, except where the site owner is prepared to pay for a fuller evaluation. The automatic evaluation will inevitably be based primarily on the text content of the site: sites which frequently mention woolly llamas will be high up the rankings when the search request is for 'woolly llamas'. Some features of the text will be treated by the search engine as more important than others for this purpose. Text which appears in headings will be treated by the search engine as especially pertinent, as indicating the topic of the text which follows it. Moreover, it is possible to include in a web page certain 'metatags', which are invisible when the page is displayed but which give information about the page itself: so the metatag *description* typically includes a short sentence summarising the page, and the metatag *keywords* lists search terms that are relevant to it. So the creators of the pages can also say what they are about, thus increasing the possibility that their pages will come to the attention of those searching for material of that sort.

However, the commercial pressure on businesses to bring their web sites to the attention of consumers is often intense. Indeed, the main business of some advertising firms is to push their clients' sites higher up the ranking list for common web search queries. It would be naïve to assume that these firms will confine themselves to literal descriptions of what these sites have to offer, if other means of attracting custom present themselves. A number of techniques have been used to push particular sites higher up the rankings, some of them deceptive. Sites may be 'cloaked' so that they are categorised by the search engine in a manner quite different from that which their content might suggest.[132] Sites may make liberal use of a competitor's trade mark to attract those searching for the rival's site. Some search engines give more prominence to sites which have many other sites linking to them, on the theory that this indicates their popularity; advertisers may exploit this by creating 'link farms' which link to their clients' sites in order to boost their popularity. (This and related activities are known as 'link spamming'.[133])

Relations between search engine owners and the 'rankings industry', which attempts to boost its clients' search rankings, can often be fraught. Each watches the other's activities closely, and modifies its practices to block any unwelcome development. Extreme measures have sometimes been taken: there is at least one case of a company hacking into a search engine to secure the results it wanted.[134] As to litigation, search engine owners are generally fairly safe from legal action by those who have attempted to increase their rankings; indeed, one US federal judge has been prepared to rule that search rankings are speech protected by the first amendment.[135] In general, relations between the two camps are utterly fluid and

---

132 See, eg, Edelman, B, 'WhenU spams Google, breaks Google "no cloaking" rules' (Web).
133 See, eg, 'Interview with a link spammer', Register, 31 January 2005 (Web).
134 'Spammer breaks into AOL search engine', ZDNet UK, 20 June 2002 (Web).
135 *Search King, Inc v Google Technology, Inc* (D W Okla, 27 May 2003) (Web).

relatively lawless, though some trade regulators have made it clear that they will not allow covert payments by companies to the search engine owners.[136]

But while those who try to increase their ranking have no legal protection if they fail, their rivals are in a stronger position. Those who see their rankings slipping for no apparent reason may ask whether any abuse of their trade mark or any passing off has occurred. It has even been suggested that a new metatag *trade mark* should be introduced, so that the legal rights involved will be clearer.[137] At present, the law is vague. It is no doubt possible for one firm to create a site which purports to be that of its rival, so that a site which appears to belong to Firm A in fact belongs to Firm B, and any orders placed at it would be fulfilled by Firm B. But this is so obviously and flagrantly illegal that few firms would dare. What is much more common is that Firm B seeks to divert custom from Firm A: Firm B's web site is clearly labelled as belonging to Firm B, but by the use of false metatags, sponsored links and other devices Firm B tries to ensure that those who search for Firm A will find Firm B's site prominently listed in their search results. So this is not so much an attempt to confuse B's products with A's, as an attempt to generate an 'initial interest confusion': an expression of interest in A will generate advertising for B. This is, however, slightly outside a traditional understanding of trade mark and passing off law, and it is currently an open question whether the law will be extended to cover this deceptive, but not plainly illegal, tactic.

Case law

No clear message emerges from the cases, except that the technology and the social practices connected with 'initial interest confusion' are rapidly evolving. There are three reasons why we cannot expect clear rules to emerge from the cases, in any jurisdiction. First, the notion of trade mark misuse is vague anyway. Secondly, each case can only be resolved by looking at the totality of the web site concerned: courts seem influenced not so much by particular dubious tactics but by whether, considered overall, the site can be regarded as deceptive. Thirdly, web sites can be, and often are, changed with great speed, and so there is a tendency for cases to get bogged down in the minutiae of what the defendant's site looked like at different times. This is not a context in which a common law system is likely to produce firm rulings on what is acceptable and what is not.

In the UK, two significant rulings have been laid down.[138] First, in the *Mandata* case, the parties were rival suppliers of logistics software for the road haulage industry. The claimant accused the defendant of unfairly diverting Internet business from the claimant – the facts are sparsely reported, but the method appears to have been, over a two month period, simply including the claimant's name and the name of its software in the defendant's own site's metatags. The claimant sued for breach of trade mark and for passing off; liability was disputed on procedural grounds only,

---

136 'Britain cracks down on paid search', News.Com, 16 June 2004 (Web); cf 'Search engines could face legal action for advertorial in results', [2001] EBL (Oct) 3; *ASA adjudication in respect of Freeserve plc*, 16 June 2004 (Web). See Sinclair, A, 'Regulation of paid listings in internet search engines: A proposal for FTC action', (2004) 10 BUJSTL 353.

137 McCuaig, D, 'Halve the baby: An obvious solution to the troubling use of trademarks as metatags', (2000) 18 JMJCIL 643.

138 For general principles of trade mark and passing-off, see above, p 72. See also Murray, A, 'The use of trade marks as meta tags: Defining the boundaries', (2000) 8 IJLIT 263.

and summary judgment was granted in favour of the claimant. As to damages, Master Bowman seemed particularly impressed by the significant amounts that the claimant had spent in creating its site and the defendant's attempts to exploit this: 'This was a deliberate, albeit unsophisticated appropriation of the claimant's rights for which some compensation ought undoubtedly to be paid.' However, he refused to assume in the claimant's favour that custom had been lost to the defendant, and that head of damage was excluded; £15,000 was awarded.[139]

The *Reed* case involved two well-established groups of companies with similar names. Reed Executive was a subsidiary of Reed Employment, a chain of employment agents who had registered the trade mark 'Reed' in relation to employment agency services; it established a web site at www.reed.co.uk. Reed Business Information was a subsidiary of the publisher, Reed Elsevier; it established a web site at www.totaljobs.com. While Reed Executive and Reed Business Information could plainly be regarded as competitors, nonetheless their businesses were not identical: Reed Executive was in essence about matching up job applicants to potential employers, whereas Reed Business Information was more about advising and training job seekers in interview techniques and CV writing. Reed Executive had three complaints about the totaljobs.com site, relying particularly on its trade mark:

(a) The metatags included the word 'Reed', in the phrase 'Reed Business Information'.

(b) The copyright notice referred to the site's owner as 'Reed Business Information Ltd'.

(c) The defendant had paid for inclusion of its site in an online directory of services, using the keyword 'Reed'.

Applying trade mark principles, it was held that the products of the two rivals firms could not be regarded as identical, nor could the defendant be said to have used a mark that was identical to that of the claimant. The question was therefore whether there was any likelihood of confusion between the rival marks. The Court of Appeal drew a distinction between trade mark principles and passing off principles: for passing off purposes, the courts were interested in whether there was confusion in fact; for trade mark purposes, the courts would assume that the claimant's registered mark had an existing reputation and ask about confusion on that basis. Differing from the trial judge, who had held that there was a real possibility of confusion, the Court of Appeal found the evidence to that effect rather flimsy, and dismissed the action. The court was clearly impressed by the lack of evidence that the defendant had engaged in any fraud or deliberate attempt to confuse.[140]

US cases have similarly turned on their own facts.[141] In the *Playboy* case, Terri Welles, a pornographic model, established her own site, in which she repeatedly

139 *Roadtech Computer Systems Ltd v Mandata (Management and Data Services) Ltd* (Chancery Division, 25 May 2000).

140 *Reed Executive plc v Reed Business Information Ltd* [2002] EWHC 2772 Ch (Pumfrey J) (Web); [2004] EWCA Civ 159 (CA) (Web). For commentary, see 'Court of Appeal – Trade marks', (2004) 27 IPD (6) 4; Colman, C and Wilson, C, '*Reed Executive v Reed Business Information*', (2004) 15 C&L (2) 10.

141 For general discussion, see Padawer, H, 'Google this: Search engine results weave a web for trademark infringement actions on the internet', (2003) 81 WULQ 1099 (Web); 'Confusion in cyberspace: Defending and recalibrating the initial interest confusion doctrine', (2004) 117 Harv LR 2387; Grynberg, M, 'The road not taken: Initial interest confusion, consumer search costs, and the challenge of the Internet', (2004) 28 SULR 97; Marra, J, 'Making confusion a requirement for online initial interest confusion', (2005) 20 BTLJ 209.

mentioned that she was a former 'Playmate of the Year'; the site's metatags also used this phrase's abbreviation, 'PMOY'. Playboy magazine, which had conferred the title, objected to its use in competition to their site. However, the Federal Court of Appeals accepted Welles' argument that the use of Playboy's mark was fair use, did not dilute it, and was not deceptive of the public. However, it remitted to a lower court the question whether 'PMOY' was entitled to trade mark protection in its own right.[142] Contrast the *JK Harris* case, where the defendant's site made repeated reference to the rival firm of JK Harris, with details of a federal investigation of the firm and of numerous complaints supposedly from former customers. The references to JK Harris were so numerous and so prominent that the site would rank highly in any search for 'JK Harris'. An injunction was issued, one ground being the risk of an 'initial interest confusion' which would lead those searching for JK Harris to the defendant's site.[143]

A general theme therefore seems to be emerging, that the courts will act against obviously deceptive practices, but otherwise will leave well alone. And it is not surprising that the courts are unwilling to be specific about which practices will attract legal consequences.

Advertising

The topic of advertising on the Internet is thoroughly intertwined with the topic of search engines. One reason for this is the large numbers of visits that these sites receive. Advertising on the net is overwhelmingly by search engines or for them. A second reason is that the most effective advertising on the net is contextual advertising – advertising targeted at those especially likely to be interested in it – and search engines are the best sites for this, as search requests are an excellent indication of what people are interested in. Two techniques are particularly prevalent: sponsored links, and targeted banner advertisements. So someone whose search enquiry includes the word 'chocolate' can expect to see sponsored links to chocolate manufacturers; they should also not be surprised to see banner advertisements at the top of the screen for particular brands of chocolate. These typical forms of paid-for advertising are increasingly the norm, a compromise between the wish to bring the advertisement to the consumer's attention and the wish to avoid unduly impeding the progress of those determined to ignore it.[144]

Contracts for this sort of advertising are typically pay-per-click: the advertiser expects to be paid a given amount by its client for every web surfer who clicks on the advertisement and is thus redirected to its client's site.[145] While in many ways this is a satisfactory arrangement – it certainly gives the advertiser an adequate incentive to maximise click-throughs to the site – it nonetheless has an inherent vulnerability to fraud. A fraudster may click on the advertisement multiple times to extract

---

142 *Playboy Enterprises, Inc v Welles* 279 F 3d 796 (9th Ct, 1 February 2002).

143 *JK Harris and Co v Kassel* 2002 US Dist LEXIS 7862 (D N Ca, 22 March 2002).

144 For general discussion, see 'Banner-ad blues', Economist, 22 February 2001 (Web); 'Google decides banner ads, skyscrapers are not evil', Register, 14 May 2004 (Web).

145 See generally 'Audience measurement metrics' (Web); Kang, J, 'Web affiliate arrangements', (2004) 12 ITLT (9) 8.

additional revenue;[146] or the threat to do so may be used as a tool of blackmail.[147] While this 'click fraud' is clearly illegal, this is difficult for the legal system to deal with, both for lack of proof and for the reluctance of the victim to complain publicly.[148]

Internet advertisers will have a number of legal bases to cover, some peculiar to this form of advertising, others common to all forms.

Keying

Contextual advertising, as currently practised, relies heavily on keying: banner advertisements and sponsored links are displayed in reaction to specific keywords entered by searchers. These keywords will have been purchased from the search engine's owners by organisations wanting publicity for their web sites. While the ethics of this are not entirely straightforward, trade regulators tend to allow it so long as there is no obvious deception or biasing of the search results. However, rival firms will object if the keywords used are their trade marks, and the search engine's owners may be sued for contributory trade mark infringement.

Surprisingly, no UK or Irish case law on this issue seems yet to have been reported. General principle suggests that trade mark rights would be infringed by use of another's mark or use of a similar mark in a confusing manner.[149] Other jurisdictions have been more lively, though with inconclusive results in many cases:

(a) In the US, various actions against search engines have been started, though with little success.[150] This may have encouraged Google's owners in their recent policy change (in respect of their US site) that they will no longer check for trade mark infringement except in response to a complaint. Whether this policy is sustainable in the long term is an open question. A major action against Google in respect of its keyword policy is proceeding.[151]

(b) A number of French rulings in quick succession have condemned the sale of keywords which are the trade marks of rival firms.[152] The rulings have been criticised, as they have included the sale of some entirely generic terms such as *vols* and *voyages* merely because they form part of a trade marked term.[153]

(c) A similar action has been brought in Germany, though without success.[154]

---

146 Eg, 'Google sues over "click fraud" ', MacNewsWorld, 9 December 2004 (Web); 'Exposing click fraud', ZDNet, 19 July 2004 (Web).

147 Eg, 'Man charged over Google blackmail attempt', Register, 25 June 2004 (Web).

148 See 'Click fraud: problem and paranoia', Wired, 10 March 2005 (Web); 'Exposing click fraud', News.Com, 19 July 2004 (Web).

149 For discussion, see Miller, N, 'Has your trademark been Googled?', (2004) 15 C&L (1) 36; Tyacke, N and Higgins, R, 'Searching for trouble – Keyword advertising and trade mark infringement', (2004) 20 CLSR 453.

150 For one action still ongoing, see *Playboy Enterprises, Inc v Netscape Communications Corp* 354 F 3d 1020 (9th Ct, 14 January 2004).

151 Brittin, J, '*Google v American Blind*: Trademark infringement litigation in the search engine world', Holland and Knight, April 2004 (Web); Abrahamson, T, 'Trademark owners keyed-up after latest Google move', Alameda County Bar Association, September 2004 (Web).

152 See, eg, 'Google back in court over Adwords', Register, 26 April 2004 (Web); 'French court says Non! to Google's Adwords', Register, 21 January 2005 (Web). For one ruling (in French), see *Google/Viaticum, Luteciel* (Cour d'Appel de Versailles, 10 March 2005) (Web).

153 'Is Google's Adwords search system legal', (2004) 12 ITLT (2) 7.

154 'Google Germany wins Adwords trademark fight', Register, 22 September 2004 (Web).

The cost to a search engine's owner of having to check whether a particular term is registered as a trade mark, is not trivial. No doubt, Google and others will continue to insist that they need not make this check unless the courts give them a very substantial reason to do otherwise.

General controls on advertisements

In addition, the general law on advertising in every relevant jurisdiction applies to Internet advertising. In particular, the following practices are either condemned or made subject to onerous restrictions in the UK, Ireland and many other jurisdictions:[155]

(a) Misleading claims as to products advertised are clearly illegal.[156]

(b) Laws on pornography and public decency apply to advertisements as to all Internet content.

(c) Rivals may complain of trade mark infringement or unjustified disparagement of their products.

In addition to these general controls, certain categories of goods and services (such as pharmaceuticals[157]) are subjected to additional restrictions, if indeed they can lawfully be sold at all.

FURTHER READING

Bellia, P, 'Defending cyberproperty', (2004) 79 NYULR 2164.

Dahm, A, 'Database protection v deep linking', (2004) 82 Tx LR 1053.

Dockins, M, 'Internet links: The good, the bad, the tortious, and a two-part test', (2005) 36 UTLR 367.

Dogan, S and Lemley, M, 'Trademarks and consumer search costs on the Internet', (2004) 41 Houston LR 777.

Fritch, D, 'Click here for lawsuit – Trespass to chattels in cyberspace', (2004) 9 JTLP (Web).

Lipton, J, 'Mixed metaphors in cyberspace: Property in information and information systems', (2004) 35 LUCLJ 235.

Reid, P, ' "Regulating" online data privacy', (2004) 1 SCRIPT-ed 3 (Web).

Rowland, R and Campbell, C, 'Content and access agreements: An analysis of some of the legal issues arising from linking and framing', (2002) 16 IRLCT 171.

---

155 See generally Morgan, S, 'Caught in the web', [2004] LSGI (Jan) 38; Thünken, A, 'Multi-state advertising over the Internet and the private international law of unfair competition', (2002) 51 ICLQ 909.

156 See especially Trade Descriptions Act 1968 (UK); Consumer Information Act 1978 (IE).

157 Clarke, S, 'E-commerce pharmacy law', (2001) 6 BR 357; Hörnle, J, 'Online pharmacies – At the borderline of legality?', [2004] EBL (Jul) 6.

Short, J, 'An economic analysis of the law surrounding data aggregation in cyberspace', (2004) 56 Maine LR 61.

Sloan, M, 'Web accessibility and the DDA', [2001] 2 JILT (Web).

Suh, J, 'Intellectual property law and competitive Internet advertising technologies: Why "legitimate" pop-up advertising practices should be protected', (2005) 79 SJLR 161.

Yung, J, 'Virtual spaces formed by literary works: Should copyright or property rights (or neither) protect the functional integrity and display of a web site?', (2004) 99 Nw ULR 495.

CHAPTER 9

CONTRACTS IN E-COMMERCE

Development of commerce over the Internet has been rapid. It has obvious advantages from a commercial point of view, both in the extent to which it can be automated and in the wide range of potential customers to which it gives easy access. Nonetheless, experience has quickly taught would-be Internet marketers that some products are much easier to market this way than are others. On the computing side, development of robust software for negotiating contracts was no easy task, and indeed some of the more effective methods involved have been the subject of litigation by those who claim to have discovered them first.[1] It has also become clear that consumers are not so impressed by the technology that they will forgive sloppy performance in other respects.[2] Competence in both computing and non-computing aspects is required.

Relevant markets have quickly reorganised. In the early years of the web, many commentators were struck by its ability to dispense with traditional market intermediaries: for example, airline tickets could be bought directly from the airline without the need for travel agents. 'Disintermediation' was the order of the day. This remains true in some market sectors, but overall it now seems clear that market intermediaries are not gone. Some traditional intermediaries have survived in new guises: while books can now often be bought directly from the publisher's web site, successful online bookshops have also sprung up. And other intermediaries with no clear counterparts outside the Internet have also appeared, such as price comparison sites and search engines. The re-alignment of the market is therefore properly seen not so much as disintermediation but as reintermediation: the development of a new network of intermediaries to meet consumer demand.[3]

Legal attitudes have also evolved rapidly, though with an increasing recognition that online contracts are not so very different from other sorts. The most important provision in the relevant legislation is the non-discrimination principle: that the laws applicable to contracts should 'neither create obstacles for the use of electronic contracts nor result in such contracts being deprived of legal effectiveness and validity on account of their having been made by electronic means'.[4] There are certainly peculiarities in the law of online contracts, though most have to do with the precise contract terms that parties are likely to think appropriate; general contract theory, which is largely indifferent to the way in which parties decide to communicate with each other, seems to need no fundamental change to accommodate the Internet. This is an area where there has been much international debate, and the UNCITRAL model law on e-commerce has been most influential, providing the starting point for many legal systems' laws on the issue.[5]

---

1   See especially *Amazon.com, Inc v BarnesandNoble.com, Inc* 239 F 3d 1343 (Fed Ct, 14 February 2001).
2   See, eg, 'E-shopping a "stress-filled chore" ', Register, 8 September 2003 (Web).
3   For some of the issues, see Collard, C and Roquilly, C, 'Electronic commerce and closed distribution networks: Proposals for solving legal problems', [2000] 2 JILT (Web).
4   Directive 2000/31/EC on electronic commerce, Art 9.
5   *UNCITRAL Model Law on Electronic Commerce*, 1996, amended in 1998 (Web). See Gabriel, H, 'The fear of the unknown: The need to provide special procedural protections in international electronic commerce', (2004) 50 Loy LR 307.

This chapter considers the legal issues raised by contracting online. It starts with general considerations that need to be borne in mind when designing an e-commerce site. It then considers how agreement is proved in this context, and how the terms of any Internet contract are determined. It then considers matters of legal form and methods of payment. It then reviews dispute settlement, considering first the jurisdictional and choice of law rules likely to apply, and then arbitration agreements. Finally, it considers two special cases: consumer contracts, and contracts made through intermediary sites such as eBay.

WEB SHOP DESIGN – LEGAL CONSIDERATIONS

As with any enhancement to a company's presence on the web, creation of an online shop will involve considerable planning, even if the core software is being bought off the shelf rather than designed specially for the job. Planning considerations that will be especially important from a legal point of view are:[6]

(a) *What jurisdictions are involved?* Where are potential clients likely to be located? If they end up in dispute with the web site's owners, in what forum are they likely to raise their complaints? And which tax authorities are likely to regard sales by the site as entitling them to a payment?[7]

(b) *How anonymous can customers be?* How much does the seller need to know about the buyers' identities? Might there be a need to contact them later and, if so, will an e-mail address be enough? Are there opportunities for fraud by customers and, if so, what level of knowledge is necessary to deter it?[8]

(c) *What level of security is appropriate?* What precautions should be taken against data thieves?[9] And if payment is to be by credit card number, what level of encryption is required?

It will also be necessary to consider which items of information should be passed on to customers. Quite apart from the need to describe what is being sold and to clarify contract terms, legislation may require that other specific details must be given: within the EU, particular attention must be given to the legislation on information society services[10] and on distance consumer contracts.[11]

It is for the most part assumed today that contracts made on the web will be on much the same terms for all customers. While that is likely to remain so for the foreseeable future, nonetheless the potential is there for differing terms, and it may well be exploited if the web site owner has enough information about the other party to make sensible choices. Dynamic pricing – that is, determining the price by reference to a decision algorithm in each instance – may certainly become a reality.[12] If it does, a number of legal controls may become relevant, particularly through

---

6   For a general survey of issues, see Mason, S, 'Approaching contract risk in E-commerce', (2002) 3 DDRM 15.
7   See, eg, 'Christmas shoppers must obey Customs on-line', OUT-LAW, 2 December 2004 (Web).
8   Grijpink, J and Prins, C, 'Digital anonymity on the Internet', (2001) 17 CLSR 379.
9   See, eg, 'Online stores come under attack', BBC News, 18 May 2005 (Web).
10   Above, p 133.
11   Below, p 262.
12   See Weiss, R and Mehrotra, A, 'Online dynamic pricing: Efficiency, equity and the future of e-commerce', (2001) 6 VJOLT 11 (Web).

competition law, anti-discrimination law, and the strictures of the data protection legislation against automated decision taking.[13]

AGREEMENT

Turning to the actual proof of agreement, we initially meet the question whether it is possible to form an agreement with a computer, or indeed whether two computers can agree with one another. Some writers have treated this as a philosophical question, asking whether computers can be regarded as responsible moral agents, or at least whether they should be so treated. But this seems to miss the (legal) point. If a contract is formed, it will be between real people responsible for their actions; computers do not fall into that category yet, and do not seem to be close to doing so. Equally, it is probably a misconception to say that computers can form contracts as agent for their owners, as lawyers tend to reserve the word 'agent' for legally responsible people or entities. If the owner or controller of a computer becomes party to a contract, it can only be because they have objectively signified their consent to it. Programmed action by a computer can amount to such objective signification; identifying it does not involve ascribing an 'intention' to the computer, any more than recognising a signature on a formal contract document involves ascribing an intention to the pen. Indeed, the courts seem to have had no difficulty in finding a contract formed even by very simple machinery, where it plainly manifested its owner's intent to contract.[14]

Agreement generally

Agreement is traditionally analysed as an offer of contractual terms, followed by an acceptance of those terms. While this traditional analysis is distinctly unsatisfactory in some contexts, it seems quite appropriate for the Internet, and we would expect agreement to be signified by a message assenting to terms communicated by an earlier message. As with communications in other contexts, it must be borne in mind that messages resembling offers and acceptances may nonetheless be nothing of the sort: they may merely be 'invitations to treat', which discuss possible contract terms but do not amount to assent to any particular terms. How a message should be treated is determined by the impression it gives to an objective recipient of the message. So a contract is formed when a message objectively saying 'I offer to contract on the following terms...' is replied to by a message objectively saying 'I accept your terms'.[15]

---

13   Above, p 96.
14   Eg, *Thornton v Shoe Lane Parking Ltd* [1971] 2 QB 163 (automatic car park machinery). For discussion, see Lerouge, J, 'The use of electronic agents questioned under contractual law', (1999) 18 JMJCIL 403; Allen, T and Widdison, R, 'Can computers make contracts?', (1996) 9 HJOLT 25 (Web); Weitzenboeck, E, 'Electronic agents and the formation of contracts', (2001) 9 IJLIT 204; Finocchiaro, G, 'The conclusion of the electronic contract through "software agents": A false legal problem?', (2003) 19 CLSR 20.
15   For a general survey of agreement issues from an English perspective, see Werner, J, 'E-commerce.co.uk – Local rules in a global net', (2001) 6 IJCLP (Web). For comparative approaches, see Winn, J and Haubold, J, 'Electronic promises: Contract law reform and e-commerce in a comparative perspective', (2002) 27 ELR 576; Poggi, C, 'Electronic commerce legislation: An analysis of European and American approaches to contract formation', (2000) 41 Va JIL 224; Gautrais, V, 'Les Principes d'UNIDROIT face au contrat électronique', (2002) 36 RJT 2 (Web).

Additional questions relate to the time and place of agreement. Sooner or later we can expect that the message saying 'I accept' will come to the attention of a responsible human being representing the offeror. But does formation of the contract wait until that happens? That seems to put a premium on sloth and inefficiency, as those who are slowest at attending to their work would be treated the most generously by the law of contract. The common law rule for other forms of communication is that messages are deemed to be accessed and considered with reasonable speed following their receipt; which usually means that messages received during working hours are deemed to be accessed and considered almost immediately.[16] Presumably the same rule applies to electronic communication in UK jurisdictions. The Irish legislation, drawing on the UNCITRAL model law, has detailed rules on when and where electronic communications are deemed to have been sent and received; they also allow for the sender of a message to require confirmation, providing in effect that a failure to confirm will result in the message being deemed never to have been sent.[17]

In relation to paper mail, a special rule (the 'postal rule' or 'mailbox rule') applies: acceptance of contractual terms is deemed complete on posting, so that the contract is considered to be formed when and where that posting took place – whether or not it was in the other side's jurisdiction, and whether or not the message ultimately arrived. Whether this rule applies to e-mail, or indeed to Internet communications generally, is a matter of some dispute; no statutory provision applies.[18] In determining whether the rule applies to novel forms of communication, the English courts have distinguished between 'instantaneous' communications (such as ordinary speech and conversations over the telephone) and 'non-instantaneous' communications (such as paper mail); the rule is said to apply to the latter only.[19] E-mail is definitely not instantaneous – but then, strictly speaking, no method is! The distinction is perhaps better summed up as being between 'synchronous' communication (which requires sender and recipient to act simultaneously) and 'asynchronous' communication (which does not). E-mail is definitely in the asynchronous category, which makes it similar to paper mail for this purpose. So if the distinction is taken seriously, perhaps e-mail should be subject to the postal rule. However, it is possible that the courts have fallen out of love with the postal rule. At the time it was laid down, in the middle to late 19th century, post was a fast and reliable service, to a far greater extent than it has ever been since that time; the rule has not recently been extended to cover other forms of communication. It is therefore possible that the courts will regard the rule as a legal fossil and refuse to extend it to e-mail *even if* paper mail seems the closest analogy. Meanwhile, furious academic argument for[20] and against[21] the application of the postal rule continues.

---

16 *The Brimnes* [1975] QB 929 and *The Pamela* [1995] 2 Ll 249 (both involving telex). Cf *UNCITRAL Model Law on Electronic Commerce*, 1996, amended in 1998 (Web), Art 15.

17 Electronic Commerce Act 2000 (IE), ss 20 and 21.

18 *Ibid*, s 19(2) plainly assumes that some electronic acceptances may be revoked after they have been sent, but says nothing about when that would be.

19 *Brinkibon Ltd v Stahag Stahl und Stahlwarenhandels GmbH* [1983] 2 AC 34.

20 Fasciano, P, 'Internet electronic mail: A last bastion for the mailbox rule', (1997) 25 Hof LR 971; Watnick, V, 'The electronic formation of contracts and the common law "mailbox rule"', (2004) 56 Baylor LR 175.

21 Rogers, K, 'Contract conclusion on the web: Untangling the weakest link', (2002) 36 Law Teach 220; Houghton, K and Vaughan-Neil, K, 'E-mail and the postal rule', (2002) 12 C&L (5) 31; Christensen, S, 'Formation of contracts by email – Is it just the same as the post?', (2001) 1 QUT LJJ 1 (Web).

Electronic communications made in error have yet to give rise to much litigation. The most prominent examples have been web site pricing errors, where goods have been offered at absurdly low prices due to clerical errors by the web site owner's staff.[22] In some cases, those who have spotted the errors immediately tell their friends, with the result that many have tried to buy at that price. While litigation has been threatened in some of these cases, few have got as far as judgment.[23] The basic contract law position is that there is no defence of mistake as such: if an offer meets with an acceptance, neither party is allowed to say that their agreement was the result of a slip of the pen or of the mouse. However, where a mistake is made by one side and is obvious as such to the other, then the courts have not allowed that other to snap up the 'offer'; there is no true agreement, and the supposed contract is void.[24] Of course, there is usually room for argument about whether the mistake was obvious; very low prices are sometimes offered for promotional reasons, and certainly a web store that boasted of its low prices might find it difficult to argue that certain prices were too low even for them. But, equally, consumers who evidently appreciated that a mistake had been made would have difficulty convincing a court that a genuine contract on the mistaken terms had been created.[25]

Turning to particular contexts in which contracts might be made over the Internet, the slightly strange terminology needs comment. Most of the scholarship here has its roots in pre-Internet computer contracts, and particularly the practice of enclosing software disks in clear shrinkwrap, with a notice warning that opening the packaging amounted to agreement to the manufacturer's terms. The validity of those contracts was much debated, and not unnaturally they came to be called 'shrinkwrap' contracts.[26] Confusingly, contracting on the web by clicking on an 'I accept' button was quickly styled 'clickwrap'; and there is a more diffuse notion that simply browsing to a particular page containing a contractual notice may amount to agreement to the notice – 'browsewrap'. This is clearly false etymology; nonetheless, this jargon is well established.

Agreement by e-mail

Contracts formed by e-mail are likely to raise much the same problems as contracts formed using the paper post.[27] These will include authority to contract, identity of parties, incorporation of terms, and interpretation. As discussed above, the applicability of the postal rule may be important, particularly in determining where the contract will be taken to have been made.

---

22 Eg, 'Comet red-faced over website blunders', BBC News, 27 September 2002 (Web); 'Aer Lingus incurs sky high costs after website error', Sunday Business Post, 12 October 2003.

23 For one case which led to a substantial settlement, see 'Keep-up pressure on Kodak, say campaigners', Register, 1 February 2002 (Web), discussed in Rogers, K, 'Snap! Internet "offers" under scrutiny again', [2002] Bus L Rev 70.

24 *Hartog v Colin and Shields* [1939] 3 All ER 566.

25 For discussion, see Leng, T, 'Website pricing errors – Who bears the risk of mistake?', (2004) 20 CLSR 396; Thompson, D, 'Contrasting and advertising over the Internet', (2000) 1 IJECLP (1) 53.

26 See especially Gingras, C, 'The validity of shrink-wrap licences', (1996) 4 IJLIT 77; Germanowski, G, 'Is the "shrinkwrap" licence worth the paper envelope it's printed on?', (1998) 6 IJLIT 313.

27 See, eg, *Thoresen and Co (Bangkok) Ltd v Fathom Marine Co* [2004] EWHC 167 Comm, [2004] 1 Ll 622 (Web).

Clickwrap

'Clickwrap' occurs when the operator of the client machine clicks on a link which says that it amounts to agreement – for example, clicking on text saying 'click *here* to show that you agree', or a prominent link icon with 'I AGREE' on it. From a legal point of view, use of clickwrap clarifies matters considerably. Presenting such a link to the other party is clearly a contractual offer. Given its existence, it will be very hard for customers to say that there was a contract before the link was clicked, and almost impossible to deny that there was a contract after that point. So a wide range of potentially difficult problems in identifying offers and distinguishing them from invitations to treat simply do not arise.[28] No doubt there can still be borderline situations – especially in cases of mistaken identity or incomplete communication – but the overwhelming mass of cases are standardised and straightforward. There is now a considerable bulk of US cases (mostly concerning forum selection clauses) holding clickwrap contracts *prima facie* valid,[29] and there seems little doubt that they are valid in Irish and UK law as well.[30]

It is another question, however, what the terms of that contract will be taken to be. The great advantage of clickwrap, from the point of view of the server's owners, is that it enables them to impose terms on their customer. It has been used to avoid problems of accidentally mispriced items, and it can be used to specify the forum in which any dispute will be litigated. However, this very freedom to impose terms may be a convenient point of legal attack by the other party. First, some US cases have refused to apply terms which are considered unconscionably biased against consumer interests.[31] While UK and Irish notions of 'unconscionability' do not stretch so far, nonetheless consumer protection legislation will in many cases lead to the same result.[32] Secondly, to say that all the terms have been 'agreed' in these circumstances seems to stretch notions of agreement to their limits. The US courts tend to hold that an *opportunity* to read is enough: if it is clear that the customer is being asked to agree to something and it is *possible* to see what those terms are, then clicking on 'I agree' amounts to a contract on those terms. They have not been sympathetic to arguments that the terms were not, in fact, read.[33] It may be, however, that UK and Irish courts will be more demanding as to proof of agreement; and in some (non-Internet) cases the courts have held that rather minimal notice may mean that the consumer agrees to the terms only in so far as they were usual and reasonable.[34] Questions that may be

---

28   See, eg, 'No legal recourse for buyers as Amazon rejects £7 iPaq pricing', Register, 19 March 2003 (Web).

29   The first clear ruling was *Hotmail Corp v Van Money Pie Inc* 1998 US Dist LEXIS 10729 (D N Ca, 16 April 1998). For a review of the US cases, see Condon, W, 'Electronic assent to online contracts: Do courts consistently enforce clickwrap agreements?', (2004) 16 RULR 433.

30   For discussion, see Gatt, A, 'The enforceability of click-wrap agreements', (2002) 18 CLSR 404.

31   Eg, *Comb v Paypal, Inc* 218 F Supp 2d 1165 (D N Ca, 30 August 2002); *AOL v Superior Court (Mendoza, real party in interest)* 90 Cal App 4th 1 (Ca Court of Appeals, 21 June 2001).

32   See below, p 261.

33   Eg, *Caspi v Microsoft Network LLC* 323 NJ Super 118 (NJ Superior Ct, 2 July 1999) (Web); *Forrest v Verizon Communications, Inc* 805 A 2d 1007 (DC Court of Appeals, 29 August 2002) (Web). For discussion of the US principles, see Budnitz, M, 'Consumers surfing for sales in cyberspace: What constitutes acceptance and what legal terms and conditions bind the consumer?', (2000) 16 GSULR 741. As to whether terms are actually read, see Hillman, R, 'On-line consumer standard-form contracting practices: A survey and discussion of legal implications', SSRN, March 2005 (Web).

34   See, eg, *Interfoto Picture Library Ltd v Stiletto Visual Programmes Ltd* [1989] QB 433.

asked by the court include: how prominently were the terms posted; whether it was possible to get to the 'I agree' button without seeing the terms, at least fleetingly; and whether unusual or particularly onerous terms were particularly brought to the consumer's attention.

Browsewrap

'Browsewrap' is agreement proved by the simple fact that one party browsed the other's site. The usual scenario is that the site owner puts up a prominent notice saying 'Browsing this site will be taken as agreement to the following terms: ...'; the argument is that continuing to browse in the face of the notice amounts to agreement.[35]

Some US case law has treated this argument with suspicion, though the more recent case law goes a long way towards accepting it:

(a) In *Pollstar v Gigmania Ltd*,[36] the plaintiff complained of appropriation of information on their site, contrary to the terms posted to it. However, while a link to those terms would certainly have appeared on the defendant's screen, it was obscure: small grey type on a grey background. It might not have been apparent to the defendant that it was a link. Nonetheless, the District Court thought it arguable that these terms could be taken to have been agreed.

(b) In *Specht v Netscape Communications Corp*,[37] the plaintiffs complained that free software they had downloaded from the defendants violated their privacy. The defendants sought to rely on a compulsory arbitration clause on the site from which the software had been downloaded. Applying the standard of the reasonably prudent offeree, the Federal Court of Appeals viewed the page where the plaintiffs had been invited to download the software; it noted that the link to the contractual terms was lower down that page. The defendants were not entitled to assume that the plaintiffs had read the entire page. Agreement was not established.

(c) In *Ticketmaster Corp v Tickets.com, Inc*,[38] the plaintiff also complained of appropriation of information from its site; the defendant regularly collected information from it using a spider. Terms limiting the user's rights to take this information were posted prominently and 'could not be missed', and it was clear to the District Court that the defendant knew of the terms. Agreement was established.

(d) In *Register.com, Inc v Verio, Inc*[39] the defendant made repeated automatic enquiries to a database of domain name owners, maintained by the plaintiff, which was a domain name registrar. Responses to such enquiries were in a standard format, reminding the enquirer that the data came subject to terms and conditions, which included a term prohibiting the use of the data for mass mailing purposes. Was this term enforceable? The defendant stressed that the terms were only brought to its

---

35   For discussion of some leading cases, see Case, D, 'Common mistakes made by licensors in administering click-wrap agreements', [2003] Syr ULTJ (Web).

36   170 F Supp 2d 974 (ED Ca, 17 October 2000).

37   306 F 3d 17 (2nd Ct, 1 October 2002).

38   2003 US Dist LEXIS 6483 (D C Ca, 7 March 2003). For discussion, see Zynda, T, '*Ticketmaster Corp v Tickets.com, Inc*: Preserving minimum requirements of contract on the Internet', (2004) 19 BTLJ 495.

39   356 F 3d 393 (2nd Ct, 23 January 2004).

attention *after* it made each enquiry. The Federal Court of Appeals said that this might be a convincing argument if the defendant's use of the service was sporadic, but in the circumstances its knowledge of the terms was clear.

A clear line is therefore emerging in the US law: the terms bind if the person browsing the site knew of the terms or ought reasonably to have known of them. Whether that line is properly drawn, and should be followed in Europe, is another matter. Some, at least, of the US judges evidently have their doubts. As Judge Hupp noted in the *Ticketmaster* case:

> For reasons dealing with the desirability of clear unmistakable evidence of assent to the conditions on trial of such issues, the court would prefer a rule that required an unmistakable assent to the conditions easily provided by requiring clicking on an icon which says 'I agree' or the equivalent. Such a rule would provide certainty in trial and make it clear that the user had called to his attention the conditions he or she accepted when using the web site ... However, the law has not developed this way.

While it is understandable that the US case law should have reached this position, it is not a happy state for the law to be in. This definition of 'agreement' is not merely artificial, but is actually perverse. Indeed, in the *Register.com* interpretation of it, the defendant's repeated denials that it agreed to the terms became evidence that it *did* agree, because these denials clearly established knowledge of the terms, which was all that was required. It is also striking that the court in *Register.com* relied on the fact that notice of the terms was sent many times, even though (as the court knew) few of these notices were seen by any human. This seems to stretch the idea of 'agreement' well past breaking point. While there may be good reasons for allowing web site owners to impose such terms, the attempt to say that these terms are *agreed* by those browsing the site is bizarre.

If such terms are to be imposed at all, a better justification must be found. The court in *Register.com* simply assumed that in these cases the web site owner is entitled to impose terms, and that those viewing the site were bound to accept the terms. 'Each [person browsing] was offered access to information subject to terms of which they were well aware. Their choice was either to accept the offer of contract, taking the information subject to the terms of the offer, or, if the terms were not acceptable, to decline to take the benefits.'[40] But this is to assume the very point in issue: does a web site owner have the right to impose this choice? This is really the 'cybertrespass' issue in a slightly different dress; the *Register.com* court is treating the site owner as the absolute owner of private property, who is entitled to deny entrance or impose conditions on entrants entirely as they see fit.[41] A court which is not inclined to recognise a tort of cybertrespass may find this argument less than compelling.

FORM

It is obvious enough that the new techniques for communication made possible by the Internet have considerable implications for the form in which people communicate and express their legal transactions. But the implications are not all

---

40   356 F 3d 393, 403 *per* Judge Leval.
41   Above, p 209.

straightforward, and the importance of the law is far from obvious. In many cases, form is adhered to out of habit rather than for straightforwardly rational reasons. Many of the reasons for existing forms have little to do with the law's requirements. And when actual legal requirements of form are looked at in detail, there usually turn out to be a number of different reasons for them. In asking how to apply existing requirements of form to Internet communications, and asking whether changes to the law are required, we need to bear in mind the very limited role of the law, and precisely what that role is.[42]

It is commonly said that legal form has three functions.[43] One is the evidentiary function – a requirement of form is often a requirement of satisfactory evidence before a transaction is recognised. There is no reason in principle why electronic communications cannot fulfil such a function; clearly they are superior to speech in this regard; forgery of electronic records is certainly possible, but no more so than with paper records. The second function is the cautionary function – by requiring a formality that takes some effort to arrange, the law deters people from entering into that type of transaction impulsively or frivolously. The Internet's general ethos of speedy and efficient communication runs quite counter to this, and this may limit the sort of transactions to which it should be relevant. Many might oppose a change to the law which would allow (for example) parties to marry by visiting a virtual chapel and each clicking on an 'I do' icon. The third function is the channelling function – facilitating legal regulation of certain types of transaction by making them all fit into the same mould. This is particularly relevant to taxing Internet transactions. But it is far from clear how much legal requirements of form are affected by tax considerations.

Clearly, therefore, the question of legal form and Internet transactions is a complex one. The main concern of legislators to date has been to prevent e-commerce being strangled at birth by outdated formal requirements.[44] The UNCITRAL model law includes a simple declaration that legal effect is not to be denied merely on the ground that electronic form has been used.[45] EU law similarly requires that:

> Member States shall ensure that their legal system allows contracts to be concluded by electronic means. Member States shall in particular ensure that the legal requirements applicable to the contractual process neither create obstacles for the use of electronic contracts nor result in such contracts being deprived of legal effectiveness and validity on account of their having been made by electronic means.[46]

One jurisdiction at least seems to have reached this conclusion, in advance of explicit legislation, through its national system of courts.[47] Ireland has taken the UNCITRAL route, enacting straightforwardly that 'Information ... shall not be denied legal effect, validity or enforceability solely on the grounds that it is wholly or partly in

---

42 For a detailed study, see Reed, C, *Digital Information Law – Electronic Documents and Requirements of Form*, 1996, London: Centre for Commercial Law Studies.

43 The classic statement is in Fuller, L, 'Consideration and form', (1941) 41 Col LR 799, 800–04.

44 For a comparison of electronic signature laws worldwide, see Mason, S, *Electronic Signatures in Law*, 2003, London: LexisNexis, Chapter 15.

45 *UNCITRAL Model Law on Electronic Commerce*, 1996, amended in 1998 (Web), Art 5.

46 Directive 2000/31/EC on electronic commerce, Art 9.

47 See Scannicchio, T, 'Important decision of the Italian Supreme Court of Cassazione in the matter of electronic documents', [2002] 2 JILT (Web).

electronic form, whether as an electronic communication or otherwise',[48] though certain exceptions are made.[49] The UK has made rather more minimal provision, merely permitting regulations to be made to modify requirements of form as required;[50] a survey by the Law Commission for England and Wales has suggested that relatively few changes will be necessary.[51]

Writing

Statute often requires writing, or gives particular significance to written terms.[52] Does this include terms communicated over the Internet?

Irish law now generally provides that requirements or permissions to give information in writing are to be read as permitting the use of electronic form, 'whether as an electronic communication or otherwise'. However, this general provision is limited: if the recipient of the information is a private body, then either it must be 'reasonable to expect that it would be readily accessible to the [recipient] for subsequent reference', or the recipient must consent to the use of electronic form. The accessibility requirement presumably entails that the communication must be capable of being saved as a file, and perhaps even that the sender should warn the recipient to save it for future reference.[53]

UK law has no such general provision, though there are now regulations covering certain specific situations.[54] The legislative assumption seems to be that this question can safely be left to the courts. Some individual statutes have their own definitions of 'writing'.[55] The most general proposition is in the Interpretation Act 1978, which says that, unless the context otherwise requires, 'writing' includes 'typing, printing, lithography, photography and other modes of representing or reproducing words in a visible form'.[56] Electronic impulses are, of course, not visible, and so the ambiguity in the statutory formulation becomes important – is the 'writing' itself required to be 'in visible form', or is it enough that it can be used to *reproduce* the written form? Traditionally, a broad view of 'writing' has been taken, and a narrow definition would seem to be incompatible with EU law; but it remains to be seen whether a broad view will be applied to electronic communications generally.[57]

---

48   Electronic Commerce Act 2000 (IE), s 9.
49   *Ibid*, ss 10 and 11.
50   Electronic Communications Act 2000 (UK), ss 8 and 9. See also Electronic Communications Act (Northern Ireland) 2001 (NI), ss 1 and 2.
51   *Electronic Commerce: Formal Requirements in Commercial Transactions*, Law Commission, December 2001 (Web). There is a list of regulations permitting electronic communications in Mason, S, *Electronic Signatures in Law, op cit* fn 44, Appendix 1.
52   See especially the regulation of 'written standard terms of business' in Unfair Contract Terms Act 1977 (UK), s 3, on which see Macdonald, E and Poyton, D, 'A particular problem for e-commerce: Section 3 of the Unfair Contract Terms Act 1977', [2000] 3 WJCLI (Web).
53   Electronic Commerce Act 2000 (IE), s 12.
54   See, eg, Consumer Credit Act 1974 (Electronic Communications) Order 2004 (UK), SI 2004/3236.
55   Eg, Copyright Designs and Patents Act 1988 (UK), s 178 (definition of 'writing').
56   Interpretation Act 1978 (UK), Sched 1 (definition of 'writing'). For another general (but in this context unhelpful) statute, see Requirements of Writing (Scotland) Act 1995 (Sc).
57   For discussion, see *Electronic Commerce: Formal Requirements in Commercial Transactions*, Law Commission, December 2001 (Web), Pt 3.

Signature

Some statutes require not only writing, but also that the writing be signed. There seems to be no intrinsic reason why these requirements should not be satisfied by appropriate electronic communications. Unfortunately, the issue has been confused by references to 'electronic signatures'. This technology (which was discussed in an earlier chapter[58]) uses cryptographic techniques to identify the sender of messages. Obviously enough, it fulfils many of the functions that a manuscript signature does, and it is natural that parallels have been drawn between the two. But talk of 'electronic signatures' is metaphorical, and metaphors are at their most dangerous when we forget what they are. 'Electronic signatures' provide a measure of security, and it would be surprising if they were not treated in law as at least as secure as manuscript signatures. But they have other functions as well: encrypting messages, for example. Additionally, there is always a danger in tying legal definitions to particular technologies, especially when those technologies are changing so rapidly.

So while it seems obvious that 'electronic signatures' should count as signatures for legal purposes, it may be a mistake to state this baldly in legislation, or to give them any special status. And it would certainly be a mistake to say that nothing less will do, that the *only* electronic means for satisfying a requirement of signature electronically would be an 'electronic signature'. This is particularly so given that there is no agreed definition of 'electronic signature', some writers confining this expression to cryptographic techniques, others using it for *any* electronic method of signifying consent or authorisation. In relation to any particular legal requirement of 'signature', it will be necessary to ask what sorts of electronic communication should suffice – a question which inevitably involves asking what function the legal requirement is meant to serve.

The problem is recognised, but not solved, by the UNCITRAL model law, which says that a data message sent by a particular method can amount to a 'signature' if 'that method is as reliable as was appropriate for the purpose for which the data message was generated or communicated, in the light of all the circumstances, including any relevant agreement'.[59] EU law similarly attempts to turn the 'signature' question into one of the reliability of the technique used. An electronic signature must be taken to satisfy national requirements of 'signature' if it is 'based on a qualified certificate and...created by a secure-signature-creation device' – roughly, in the current state of the technology, if it uses one of the more secure forms of encryption. In addition, no electronic signature can be refused legal effect merely on the ground that it is in electronic form, or is not based upon a qualified certificate, or is not created by a secure signature-creation device.[60] These two EU requirements together try to make Member States accept encryption as sufficient to constitute a 'signature', while leaving the door open for developing technology. However, this leaves a great deal of room for national initiatives here.

Irish law provides that an electronic signature can be used to satisfy a legal requirement of signature, provided that (in the case of signatures required from private individuals) the person to whom the signature is given consents.[61] An electronic

---

58   Above, p 105.
59   *UNCITRAL Model Law on Electronic Commerce*, 1996, amended in 1998 (Web), Art 7.
60   Directive 1999/93/EC on a Community framework for electronic signatures, Art 5.
61   Electronic Commerce Act 2000 (IE), s 13.

signature is defined for this purpose as 'data in electronic form attached to, incorporated in or logically associated with other electronic data and which serves as a method of authenticating the purported originator'.[62] This is vague, but certainly does not seem to be confined to cryptographic technology. Probably it covers agreement by clickwrap, and agreements where one or both sides send a graphic file showing what their manuscript signatures look like. Arguably it covers even a typed name at the foot of an e-mail, so long as consent by the addressee could be shown (and quite possibly consent could be inferred if the reply treated the arrangement as legally binding). This is certainly broad, and can cover some quite significant transactions, including transactions relating to land; it has been suggested that this was unwise.[63]

There is no similar legislation in the UK, where statute provides merely that an 'electronic signature' is admissible evidence as to that message's authenticity or integrity.[64] 'Electronic signature' is defined in very broad terms: it includes any part of an electronic message that purports to help to establish its authenticity or integrity.[65] This is of little help in applying legal requirements of 'signature'. The courts have in the past tended to take a broad view of 'signature' in relation to other technologies, so long as the intention to authenticate the document is clear; for example, a typed signature at the end of a telex message has been held to amount to a signature,[66] as has a fax of a signature.[67] Perhaps understandably, therefore, most commentators do not support wholesale change to the law, but rather detailed amendments to particular legal requirements of signature, each precisely tailored to the rationale for each requirement.[68] As noted above, however, EU law requires that secure encryption must be treated as fulfilling national requirements of signature[69] and, as it is not clear that that is the law, to that extent the UK may be in breach of its obligations to the EU.

Additional formalities

Even signed writing is not enough for some documents: additional formalities that may be required include witnesses to signatures, and sealing. There is no explicit provision for these cases in EU law.

In Irish law, electronic signatures can be witnessed electronically, so long as certain rigorous requirements are satisfied. The main document must indicate that a witness is required, and both the main signature and that of the witness must be 'an advanced electronic signature, based on a qualified certificate'.[70] In practice, this requires encryption, though there has been a deliberate attempt to define it in technology-neutral terms, which includes requirements that the parties use 'means

---

62 *Ibid*, s 2(1) (definition of 'electronic signature').
63 Brown, G, 'Trouble down the line', (2001) 95 LSGI 18.
64 Electronic Communications Act 2000 (UK), s 7(1).
65 *Ibid*, s 7(2).
66 *Good Challenger Navegante SA v Metalexportimport SA* [2003] EWCA Civ 1668 (Web).
67 *Re a Debtor (No 2022 of 1995), ex p IRC* [1996] 2 All ER 345.
68 Eg, Reed, C, 'What is a signature?', [2000] 3 JILT (Web).
69 Above, p 253.
70 Electronic Commerce Act 2000 (IE), s 14.

that are capable of being maintained by the signatory under his, her or its sole control', and that the signature is 'linked to the data to which it relates in such a manner that any subsequent change of the data is detectable'.[71] Deeds may similarly be created using an advanced electronic signature, based on a qualified certificate, provided that any other parties involved consent.[72]

No explicit provision for this problem is made in any of the UK jurisdictions, the problem being left to the courts and to possible secondary legislation. The legislation on deeds seems equivocal as to whether deeds may take electronic form.[73] Again, the UK may be in breach of EU law here to the extent that electronic commerce is impeded.

PAYMENT

Payment systems have yet to change as radically as have other market mechanisms involved with the Internet. The conservatism and apparent solidity of banking institutions militates against rapid adoption of new technologies. In fact, ICT is increasingly used in banking institutions, but much of it is in proprietary systems rather than part of the Internet, and we are a very long way from a point where payment over the net is a simple and secure process.[74] The risk of fraud is omnipresent.[75]

Traditional banking

Electronic elements in banking systems are of increasing relevance. Particular mention might be made of electronic clearing (using the CHAPS system) and electronic funds transfers;[76] of EFTPOS systems for authorising payments by credit cards and debit cards (such as Visa, MasterCard, SWITCH, Laser); and Internet access to one's own account details, often with powers to give instructions for payment. There is even a small market niche for 'Internet-only' banks, which expect their customers to contact them solely via the Internet, though the prospects of these ventures are uncertain.[77]

For most consumers, the most common method of making a payment over the Internet is by authorising the payment with a credit or debit card. The consumer sends their card number and other details to the supplier, typically over a connection using strong encryption, and the supplier confirms all details with the issuer of the card. Consumer trade over the Internet would have been very awkward without this device, and so it is tolerated despite the obvious and inherent risks of fraud. Neither

---

71 *Ibid*, s 2(1) (definition of 'advanced electronic signature').

72 *Ibid*, s 16.

73 See especially Law of Property (Miscellaneous Provisions) Act 1989 (E&W), s 1.

74 For possible future developments, see 'Internet forces British banking industry to modernise', Register, 24 May 2005 (Web).

75 For a general survey, see Bohm, N, Brown, I and Gladman, B, 'Electronic commerce: Who carries the risk of fraud?', [2000] 3 JILT (Web).

76 See, eg, Donnelly, M, 'Electronic funds transfers: Obligations and liabilities of participating institutions', [2003] Comm LP (Feb) 35.

77 For general reviews, see Azzouni, A, 'Internet banking and the law', [2003] JIBLR 351; Casanova, J, 'Establishing Internet credit card programmes in the United Kingdom', [2001] JIBL 70.

supplier nor issuer can be sure who sent the authorisation, and can in practice only check for anomalies in the authorisation, and for card numbers reported as stolen. And the consumer can only trust that revealing their financial details is not treated as an opportunity for fraud by an employee of the supplier or the issuer – if indeed the online site they are dealing with is not wholly fraudulent in intent. Many consumers are concerned about the possibility of fraud, and assume that the risks involved in disclosing their numbers are greater in Internet contexts than others.

Where fraud or other problems emerge, the UK law on payment cards is relatively pro-consumer:

(a) Consumers are not liable to the issuers for fraudulent unauthorised use of a card; it is for the card's issuer to prove authorisation if this is disputed. So if goods are paid for by a con artist who gives another's number, then when the consumer disputes the payment, the issuers will charge the loss back to the supplier.[78]

(b) Where consumer goods purchased with a credit card turn out to be defective or substandard, the card's issuer is liable to the consumer for any misrepresentation or breach of contract by the supplier; an issuer found liable in this way may attempt to recoup the loss from the supplier.[79] The jurisdictional limits of this provision are, however, quite unclear. It has recently been held that the provision does not apply where the contract was made wholly outside the UK and was governed by a foreign law, and the goods were supplied or despatched from outside the UK. Gloster J seemed especially struck by the breadth of the UK's domestic protection: '[i]f that protection were to be extended to use of credit cards anywhere in the world, UK consumers would be put at a massive advantage to holders of cards issued on the same networks in any other country'. She refused however to lay down definitively where the line between 'foreign' and 'UK' transactions was to be drawn for this purpose.[80]

The Irish position is comparable. There is a similar right to cancel fraudulent payments on distance contracts, though no burden of proof is specified.[81] There is, however, no direct equivalent to the UK right to pursue the credit card issuer for the supplier's poor service, except in the case where the card is only for use with that particular supplier – a card specific to a particular store or chain of stores – and even then the consumer must exhaust their remedies against the supplier first.[82]

E-money

The desirability of more flexible and simpler systems is obvious enough; and many have dreamed of the holy grail of e-banking – 'true' electronic cash that can be

---

78 Consumer Protection (Distance Selling) Regulations 2000 (UK), SI 2000/2334, reg 21. There are also similar, older provisions applying only to credit cards: Consumer Credit Act 1974 (UK), ss 83 and 84, as amended by various instruments, including Financial Services (Distance Marketing) Regulations 2004, SI 2004/2095.

79 Consumer Credit Act 1974 (UK), s 75. The price of the item concerned must be more than £100 and less than £30,000: s 75(3)(b).

80 *Office of Fair Trading v Lloyds TSB Bank plc* [2004] EWHC 2600 Comm (Web).

81 European Communities (Protection of Consumers in Respect of Contracts made by means of Distance Communication) Regulations 2001 (IE), SI 2001/207, reg 10.

82 Consumer Credit Act 1995 (IE), s 42(2).

transferred without reference to its issuer, much as coins and notes can be transferred without reference to the bank which issued them.[83] Progress in this direction has been slow, however,[84] perhaps because payment by more conventional means is not actually impossible, and so consumer demand is not as frantic as it might otherwise be. Banking is a highly regulated industry, and so it is perhaps not surprising that radical innovation has been slow. There have been repeated suggestions that the way forward is with 'micropayment' systems for relatively small amounts, but such systems as have emerged have not yet proved very popular.[85] The greatest success to date is PayPal, which allows for transfers between account holders by e-mail; this proved popular with users of the auction site eBay, and the bank was purchased by the owners of eBay in 2002.[86] A rather limited legal framework for 'true' electronic cash has been introduced by directive, which refers to it as 'an electronic surrogate for coins and banknotes'.[87]

DISPUTE RESOLUTION

If the parties to a contract fall out over its performance, which tribunal should resolve their dispute? Formal legal procedures are considered first, and then less formal methods. Only a relatively brief description is given of what are quite technical areas.

The jurisdictional matters considered here are now fairly well settled within Europe, though possible reforms are in the air.[88] The position of consumers has received much attention.[89] Matters are currently very different outside Europe.[90] Negotiations towards an international agreement on jurisdiction have been continuing for quite some time.

---

83 Cf Downey, C, 'The high price of a cashless society; Exchanging privacy rights for digital cash?', (1996) 14 JMJCIL 303.

84 See 'Survey of developments in electronic money and internet and mobile payments', Bank for International Settlements, March 2004 (Web).

85 For commentary, see Sifers, R, 'Regulating electronic money in small-value payment systems: Telecommunications law as a regulatory model', (1997) 49 FCLJ 702 (Web); Shirky, C, 'The case against micropayments', December 2000 (Web).

86 Gonzáles, A, 'PayPal: The legal status of C2C payment systems', (2004) 20 CLSR 293; 'Paying through the mouse', Economist, 22 May 2004 (Web).

87 Directive 2000/46/EC on the taking up, pursuit of and prudential supervision of the business of electronic money institutions; implemented by Electronic Money (Miscellaneous Amendments) Regulations 2002 (UK), SI 2002/765, and European Communities (Electronic Money) Regulations 2002 (IE), SI 2002/221. For commentary, see Chuah, J, 'The new EU directives to regulate electronic money institutions', [2000] JIBL 180; Bamodu, 'G, 'The regulation of electronic money institutions in the United Kingdom', [2003] 2 JILT (Web).

88 See, eg, Calliess, G, 'Coherence and consistency in European consumer contract law: A progress report', (2003) 4 German LJ 4 (Web); Riefa, C, 'Article 5 of the Rome Convention on the law applicable to contractual obligations of 19 June 1980 and consumer e-contracts: the need for reform', (2004) 13 ICTL 59.

89 See, eg, Gillies, L, 'A review of the new jurisdiction rules for electronic consumer contracts within the European Union', [2001] 1 JILT (Web); van der Hof, S, 'European conflict rules concerning international online consumer contracts', (2003) 12 ICTL 165.

90 Marlatt, R, 'The cyberspace showdown jurisdictional jurisprudence – The United States versus the European Union', (2000) 9 Currents 89; Meehan, A, 'Your place or mine? Jurisdiction over Internet sales', (2001) 1 UCDLR 92.

Jurisdiction and enforcement of judgments

As usual, a sharp distinction must be drawn between the position within Europe and the position where a non-European party is involved.

Disputes within the EU will be within the Brussels Regulation, and the nations of the EEA are drawn into the same regime by the Lugano Convention.[91] The basic regime is as follows:

(a) Parties to a contract may agree on the jurisdiction that will handle any dispute, and such an agreement is generally enforceable. Or when a dispute actually occurs, the parties may then agree to resolve it in a particular jurisdiction, and that agreement too is enforceable. The agreement must be in writing, or in accordance with international trade practice or the parties' own established practice; '[a]ny communication by electronic means which provides a durable record of the agreement shall be equivalent to "writing" '.[92]

(b) Where there was no agreement on jurisdiction, the basic rule is that defendants are amenable to the jurisdiction in which they are domiciled – in other words, claimants must follow defendants.[93] In addition, however, the courts of the jurisdiction where the contract was supposed to be performed have jurisdiction. For this purpose, and unless otherwise agreed, the place of performance of contracts for the sale of goods is the place of delivery, and the place of performance of contracts for services is the place of the provision of the services.[94]

(c) Consumers benefit from special exemptions when dealing with a business that has the same domicile as the consumer, or has a branch in that nation, or has made the contract as part of activities directed at the domicile (even if it is also directed at others).[95] Consumers may, at their option, sue in their own domicile or that of the defendant, and are liable to be sued only within their own domicile.[96] Consumers cannot contract out of these protections unless (i) all parties are domiciled in the same state and the agreement is to sue in that state; (ii) the agreement allows the consumer to sue in some state which the Regulation does not; or (iii) the agreement is made after the dispute has arisen.[97]

(d) All courts within EU nations must recognise the judgments of other EU courts. There are very few exceptions, notably 'if such recognition is manifestly contrary to public policy in the Member State in which recognition is sought' and 'if it is irreconcilable with a judgment given in a dispute between the same parties in the Member State in which recognition is sought'.[98] 'Under no circumstances may a foreign judgment be reviewed as to its substance.'[99] Procedures for enforcing a foreign judgment are specified in the Regulation.[100]

---

91 For general reviews, see Takahashi, K, 'Jurisdiction in matters relating to contract', (2002) 27 ELR 530; O'Hanrahan, A, 'Conflicts of law on the net: An Irish perspective', [2001] ULLR 27.

92 Regulation 44/2001/EC on jurisdiction and the recognition and enforcement of judgments in civil and commercial matters, Art 23.

93 *Ibid*, Art 2.

94 *Ibid*, Art 5.

95 *Ibid*, Art 15.

96 *Ibid*, Art 16.

97 *Ibid*, Art 17.

98 *Ibid*, Art 34.

99 *Ibid*, Art 36.

100 *Ibid*, Arts 38–52.

Where there is more than one defendant, or more than one issue to be resolved, the actions may be commenced together in the same jurisdiction – all that is necessary is that *one* of the actions could be started in the plaintiff's chosen forum under the above rules.[101]

Where the defendant is not domiciled within the EU, the traditional rules apply. The rules of England and Wales allow a claimant to serve proceedings on anyone present within the jurisdiction, or who has submitted to it. Permission to serve proceedings outside the jurisdiction can be sought on a number of grounds: that the defendant is domiciled within the jurisdiction; that the claim is in respect of a contract made within the jurisdiction; that the contract is governed by English law; that the contract contains a term that the English courts shall have jurisdiction; or that the claim is in respect of a breach of contract committed within the jurisdiction. In all of these cases, permission is at the court's discretion, and the claimant will have to show both that there is a serious issue to be tried and that England is the appropriate forum for the dispute.[102]

Choice of law

The question of which jurisdiction's laws are applied to the contract is settled by the Rome Convention.[103] If the parties agree on an applicable law (either in the contract, or later) then that law governs, subject to any mandatory rules of the forum which cannot be derogated from by contract. The parties' agreement is usually express; arguments based on implied agreements must be 'demonstrated with reasonable certainty by the terms of the contract or the circumstances of the case'.[104] If there is no agreement, then the contract is governed by the law of the country with which it is most closely connected. The presumption is (though it may be displaced by evidence to the contrary) that the contract is most closely connected with the jurisdiction in which the party who is to render 'characteristic performance' resides or has their head office.[105] (Very roughly, the 'characteristic performance' means whatever is being bought, as opposed to the payment for it.) There are various special cases: the Convention does not apply to contracts of carriage, and employment contracts have their own rules.

Consumers of goods or services are entitled to special protection, as long as the other party received the order in that jurisdiction, or had advertised in that jurisdiction, or specifically invited the order. If there was no agreement on which

---

101 *Ibid*, Art 6.

102 See Civil Procedure Rules (E&W) r 6.20 (Web). Asking 'where' the contract was made may entail consideration of the postal rule, above, p 246. See, eg, *Apple Corps Ltd v Apple Computer Inc* [2004] EWHC 768 Ch (Web). On possible reforms, see Elacqua, B, 'The Hague runs into B2B: Why restructuring the Hague Convention on Foreign Judgments in Civil and Commercial Matters to deal with B2B contracts is long overdue', (2004) 3 JHTL 93 (Web).

103 The Convention is part of UK law by virtue of the Contracts (Applicable Law) Act 1990 (UK), and part of Irish law by virtue of the Contractual Obligations (Applicable Law) Act 1991 (IE). See generally O'Brian, W, 'Choice of law under the Rome Convention: The dancer or the dance', [2004] Lloyd's MCLQ 375; Hill, J, 'Choice of law in contract under the Rome Convention: The approach of the UK courts', (2004) 53 ICLQ 325.

104 Art 3.

105 *Ibid*, Art 4.

jurisdiction applies, then the laws of the consumer's own jurisdiction apply; even if there was agreement, consumers are still entitled to the benefit of mandatory rules in their favour in their home jurisdiction. However, none of this protection applies where the contract was for the supply of goods or services outside the consumer's home jurisdiction.[106]

Alternative dispute resolution

The expense and formality of legal processes provide a powerful incentive to avoid them if any suitable alternative presents itself. Sometimes it does not: if one party to a dispute will not co-operate at all, then the other has no alternative to either invoking compulsory legal processes or abandoning the dispute. But those cases apart, there are advantages for both sides in resolving the dispute by less formal methods. For these and other reasons, there are powerful pressures today towards alternative dispute resolution.[107]

Very roughly, there are three methods of alternative dispute resolution: the parties can negotiate with one another alone; they can arrange for a mediator, whose role is to assist them in negotiating; or they can appoint an arbitrator to decide the dispute for them. Any or all of these can be done purely online; 'online dispute resolution' (ODR) is not a term of art. The practical ease of communicating solely by e-mail is obvious; whether it satisfies the needs of the parties is a harder and more complex question. Communication between all parties can be more precisely regimented, as required.[108]

Practical experience of ODR is very mixed. Various dispute resolution services exist, and their continued existence suggests that some market actors at least consider that they give value for money. The UDRP system for resolving disputes over domain names is very unpopular in some circles, but (as already discussed) there are many reasons for that, few of which amount to criticism of the dispute resolution process *per se*.[109] Least satisfactory of all are the compulsory arbitration services provided by some major net traders for their customers, which several times have had their rulings quashed because the arbitration clause was not truly agreed to, or amounted to an unconscionable contract.[110]

Debates over ODR continue to rage, one side pointing to the speed and cheapness made available, the other suggesting that a serious and unsettling sacrifice of legal values is being made.[111]

---

106 *Ibid*, Art 5.
107 Wahab, M, 'Globalisation and ODR: Dynamics of change in e-commerce', (2004) 12 IJLIT 123; Moeves, A and Moeves, S, 'Two roads diverged: A tale of technology and Alternative Dispute Resolution', (2004) 12 WMBRJ 843.
108 Krause, W, 'Do you want to step outside? An overview of Online Alternative Dispute Resolution', (2001) 19 JMCIL 457; Ferriter, C, 'E-commerce and international arbitration', (2001) 1 UCDLR 51.
109 Above, p 180.
110 Eg, *Specht v Netscape Communications Corp* 306 F 3d 17 (2nd Ct, 1 October 2002) (Web).
111 For discussion, see Hörnle, J, 'Disputes solved in cyberspace and the rule of law', [2001] 2 JILT (Web); Caplin, L, 'Resolving consumer disputes online: A review of consumer ODR', [2003] Comm LP 207.

CONSUMER PROTECTION

Concern about consumer protection on the Internet has been stimulated by two interrelated concerns. The first is that the considerable volume of consumer law will turn out to be inapplicable or inappropriate for transactions over the Internet. The second is that consumer confidence in relation to Internet transactions will suffer if proper legislation is not put in place. While the evidence for both of these propositions is weak (particularly so in the latter case), nonetheless concern at the state of consumer law has been manifest.[112]

This section briefly reviews consumer protection in law, and then focuses on the special protection given to Internet transactions by the Distance Contracts Directive. Also, of particular relevance to Internet transactions, is the provision of information society services, that is, services provided (whether to consumers or others) over the Internet. These were considered above.[113]

General consumer law

The amount of general consumer law is considerable; some of it has already been encountered in earlier chapters, particularly the various controls on consumer advertisements.[114] There is much legislation regulating the terms of particular types of transactions – both very general types such as contracts for goods and services, and more specific provisions for package holidays, consumer credit and other financial services. And there is legislation preventing unreasonable modification or exclusion of terms. Perhaps, surprisingly, there is very little legislation specifically protecting the rights of children: the general assumption is that the general run of consumers are powerless in these matters unless aided by legislation, and so the case of children does not particularly stand out.[115]

Enforcement of these norms is left largely to the civil law: disappointed consumers may sue, and business attempts to enforce unpaid debts against consumers would give those consumers an opportunity to complain of poor service. Increasingly, however, the emphasis is moving to enforcement by trading standards officers and to the possibilities of internal co-operation between such officers.[116] The influence of trade bodies in increasing standards is very far from clear.[117]

---

112 See, eg, Prins, J, 'Consumers, liability, and the online world', (2003) 12 ICTL 143; Scott, C, 'Regulatory innovation and the online consumer', (2004) 26 L&P 477.

113 Above, p 133. For application of those provisions in the context of financial services see Tym, R, 'One click and you're home? Implementation of the Electronic Commerce Directive', [2002] JIBFL 285.

114 Above, p 241.

115 See Bynoe, R, 'Minors, mobiles and the law', (2005) 15 C&L (3) 24, and reply (2005) 16 C&L (1) 12; Angel, H, and Hörnle, J, 'Kid spenders – How to tap into the children market?', [2004] EBL (Dec) 6; Angel, H, and Hörnle, J, 'Kid spenders – How to find out about them?', [2005] EBL (Jan) 10.

116 See especially Regulation 2006/2004/EC on co-operation between national authorities responsible for the enforcement of consumer protection laws; Cox, N, 'The extraterritorial enforcement of consumer legislation and the challenge of the Internet', (2004) 8 Edin LR 60.

117 See, eg, European Distance Selling Trade Association (EMOTA) home page (Web).

The Distance Contracts Directive

The Directive has now been implemented into national legal systems, with relatively little elaboration in Ireland's case, and with rather more in respect of the UK.[118]

The Directive applies only in favour of consumers (natural persons acting outside a business) and against suppliers (persons acting in a commercial or professional capacity). It applies only to 'distance contracts', which means contracts which (a) relate to good or services, (b) are made under the supplier's organised distance provision scheme and (c) are made making exclusive use of one or more means of distance communication up to the point at which the contracts are made. 'Distance communication' means any method for making contracts without the simultaneous physical presence of both parties; this certainly seems wide enough to include nearly all contracts made over the Internet. A non-exhaustive list of means of distance communication is given: it includes 'Videotex (microcomputer and television screen) with keyboard or touch screen' and 'Electronic mail', though it does not otherwise refer to the Internet.[119]

Various contracts are wholly excluded from the effect of the Directive. It does not apply to financial services, which have their own (in many ways similar) Directive.[120] There are various miscellaneous exemptions in relation to, for example, contracts involving real property rights (other than leases), transport[121] and contracts concluded at auction. Application of some of the Directive's provisions are withheld for specific types of contract, including contracts for food supplied to the consumer's home, or provision of accommodation, transport, leisure or catering services on a specific date or within a specified period.[122]

Assuming that the Directive applies, certain rights are guaranteed to the consumer, which cannot be refused even if the consumer earlier agreed to waive them. Enforcement of these rights is diverse: in some instances, the right is stated to form part of the contract and so can be enforced in a civil action; in others, the supplier commits an offence by violating the right; and in yet others, an injunction can be sought by local trading standards officers to compel compliance.[123]

---

118 Directive 1997/7/EC on the protection of consumers in respect of distance contracts, enacted as Consumer Protection (Distance Selling) Regulations 2000 (UK), SI 2000/2334 (as amended by SI 2005/689), and as European Communities (Protection of Consumers in Respect of Contracts made by means of Distance Communication) Regulations 2001 (IE), SI 2001/207. See generally Bradgate, R, 'The EU Directive on Distance Selling', [1997] 4 WJCLI (Web); Henderson, K and Poulter, A, 'The Distance Selling Directive: Points for future revision', (2002) 16 IRLCT 289.

119 Directive 1997/7/EC, Art 2 and Annexes; Consumer Protection (Distance Selling) Regulations 2000 (UK), SI 2000/2334, reg 4 and Scheds; European Communities (Protection of Consumers in Respect of Contracts made by means of Distance Communication) Regulations, 2001 (IE), SI 2001/207, reg 3 and Scheds 1 and 2.

120 Directive 2002/65/EC concerning the distance marketing of consumer financial services, enacted as Financial Services (Distance Marketing) Regulations 2004 (UK), SI 2004/2095, and as European Communities (Distance Marketing of Consumer Financial Services) Regulations 2004 (IE), SI 2004/853.

121 On the scope of the transport exception, see *easyCar (UK) Ltd v Office of Fair Trading* (Case C-336/03) (Web), discussed at (2005) 16 C&L (1) 24.

122 Directive 1997/7/EC, Art 3; UK SI 2000/2334, regs 5 and 6; IE SI 2001/207, reg 3.

123 Directive 1997/7/EC, Arts 11 and 12; UK SI 2000/2334, regs 25–28; IE SI 2001/207, regs 13–18.

Prior information

The Directive requires that certain details be supplied to the consumer 'in good time' before the contract is made. There is no particular requirement as to form, but the commercial purpose of the communication must be made clear, the provision must be 'in a clear and comprehensible manner' and 'appropriate to the means of distance communication used'. Due regard must be had to principles of good faith in commercial transactions, and to the protection of minors and others unable to give consent. The details required are:

(a) the identity (and, if payment in advance is required, the address) of the supplier;
(b) the main characteristics of the goods or services;
(c) the price, including all taxes;
(d) delivery costs, where appropriate;
(e) the arrangements for payment, delivery or performance;
(f) the existence of a right of cancellation (where the Directive gives one);
(g) the cost of using the means of distance communication (if not the basic rate);
(h) the period for which the offer or the price remains valid; and
(i) (where appropriate) the minimum duration of the contract in the case of contracts for the supply of products or services to be performed permanently or recurrently.[124]

Confirmation of information

There is also a requirement that certain information be provided in writing 'or in another durable medium'. This must be provided either before the contract is made, or 'in good time' after it; in the case of contracts for services, this must be at latest during performance, and in the case of goods to be supplied to the consumer, this must be at latest at the time of delivery. 'Durable medium' is not defined; presumably, some sorts of electronic media are durable, but it is not clear that a mere file which the consumer can store is enough. The required information overlaps somewhat with the list of information required prior to the contract; it is evidently envisaged that both requirements may be satisfied by producing one (rather detailed) single document. The information is to include the first six items of the prior information (above), and also:

(a) conditions and procedures for exercising the right of cancellation (the UK version of the Regulation is particularly detailed and specific here);
(b) the supplier's (geographical) address, to which the consumer may address any complaints;
(c) information in relation to any after-sales services and guarantee; and
(d) any conditions for cancelling the contract, where the contract is of unspecified duration or has a duration exceeding one year.

This requirement does not apply if the contract is for services, which are supplied on only one occasion and through the means of distance communication, and are

---

124 Directive 1997/7/EC, Art 4; UK SI 2000/2334, reg 7; IE SI 2001/207, reg 4 and Sched 3.

invoiced by the operator of the means of distance communication; though in that case the supplier must take all necessary steps to ensure that the consumer can obtain the supplier's (geographical) address.[125]

Cancellation

The consumer has a right to withdraw from the contract 'without penalty and without giving any reason'. The consumer must be reimbursed as soon as possible, and certainly within 30 days; if the price was covered by credit, there is provision for cancelling that credit. In the case of goods, the consumer may be charged for exercising this right, up to a maximum of the direct cost of returning the goods. (The UK provisions have considerable detail both as to the method of cancellation and its precise effect.) The provisions on the duration of the right are tied to the question of whether the supplier satisfied its obligation to provide confirming information (which includes information on the right to cancel):

(a) In the case of goods, the consumer has seven days in which to cancel, the period starting to run when the contract was made, or (if later) when the confirming information was received. If no such information was sent, the consumer has three months in which to cancel, starting from the day on which the goods were received.

(b) In the case of services, the consumer has seven days in which to cancel, the period starting to run when the contract was made, or (if later) when the confirming information was received, to a maximum of three months from the date of contract. If no such information was sent, the consumer has three months from the date of the contract. However, subject to contrary agreement by the parties, the right is cancel is gone as soon as the supplier begins to perform with the consumer's consent.[126]

Certain goods and services are excluded from this right: where the price turns on financial market fluctuations not under the supplier's control; goods which are personalised or made to the consumer's specifications; goods which are inherently impossible to return, or liable to deteriorate or expire rapidly; recordings or software which the consumer has unsealed; newspapers, periodicals and magazines; and gaming or lottery services.[127]

Time of performance

The supplier must execute the consumer's order within 30 days from the date on which the consumer originally forwarded the order and, if the goods or services are not available, then as soon as possible. At all events within the 30 day period, the consumer must be informed, and must be able to obtain a refund.

---

125 Directive 1997/7/EC, Art 5; UK SI 2000/2334, regs 8 and 9; IE SI 2001/207, reg 5.

126 For a recent modification to the UK rules on services, see Consumer Protection (Distance Selling) (Amendment) Regulations 2005 (UK), SI 2005/689.

127 Directive 1997/7/EC, Art 6; UK SI 2000/2334, regs 10–18; IE SI 2001/207, regs 6–8. There is an overlap here with the right of cancellation under Directive 1985/557/EC (contracts negotiated away from business premises).

It is expressly stated that this right is subject to contrary agreement, though (as is left implicit) that agreement may be scrutinised for unfairness under general consumer legislation. It is also provided that the supplier may supply alternative goods of equivalent quality and price, as long as certain additional requirements are met: that the consumer was informed of this possibility prior to the contract or in the contract itself; that this information was clear and comprehensible; and that if in these circumstances the consumer exercises their right of cancellation, the supplier will bear the cost of return.[128]

Credit cards

The Directive also contains a provision protecting consumers against fraudulent use of their credit card; this was considered above.[129]

AUCTION AND OTHER INTERMEDIARY SITES

Sites which put buyers and sellers in contact with one another, and perhaps provide opportunities for bargaining, are growing in popularity. Such sites are usually classified by the nature of the interested parties as sites where business sells to other businesses (B2B), or where business sells to consumers (B2C) or consumers sell to one another (C2C). The legal issues affecting such sites are many and various.[130] It is sometimes difficult to fit the workings of these sites into any existing legal category: they have affinities with auction houses or commercial exchanges, and usually have elements of agency as well. Commercial (B2B) sites are not considered in detail here;[131] the competition law issues are considerable.[132]

The section concentrates on eBay, by any measure the most important consumer intermediary site. First operating in 1995, it was in its origins a C2C operation; but with broadening appeal it increasingly became an outlet for professional sellers – indeed, there is a large and querulous lobby group for professional sellers[133] – and so must today be regarded as combining C2C with B2C. The service it provides is unique, and hard to categorise. In many ways it is like an online auction house; but eBay itself denies that it is running auctions,[134] and (as will be noted below) some courts seem to agree.[135] Sellers advertise their goods on eBay, and potential buyers make bids according to eBay's idiosyncratic rules; once the winning bid is identified, eBay largely drops out of the picture, though it encourages participants to give their

---

128 Directive 1997/7/EC, Art 7; UK SI 2000/2334, regs 19 and 20; IE SI 2001/207, reg 9.

129 Above, p 256; Directive 1997/7/EC, Art 8; UK SI 2000/2334, reg 21; IE SI 2001/207, reg 10.

130 For a general review, see Ramberg, C, *Internet Marketplaces – The Law of Auctions and Exchanges Online*, 2002, Oxford: OUP.

131 See generally 'B2B exchanges – Time to rebuild', Economist, 19 May 2001 (Web).

132 Foy, A, 'The regulation of B2B Internet exchanges – A European perspective', [2000] JIBFL 312; Levine, G, 'B2Bs, e-commerce and the all-or-nothing deal', (2002) 28 RCTLJ 383.

133 Professional eBay Sellers' Alliance (PESA) home page (Web). See, eg, ' "Integrity of eBay marketplace" at risk – Sellers' group', Register, 24 January 2005 (Web).

134 See, eg, 'Your user agreement', eBay UK (Web).

135 On the nature of the eBay process, see Mitchell, J, 'Internet auctions, agency and consumer rights', (2003) 14 C&L (4) 31; Reynolds, A, 'E-auctions: Who will protect the consumer?', (2002) 18 J Contract L 75.

opinion of how the other party has conducted themselves – data which is then made freely available to inform future users of the site.

Various legal issues have emerged in the practical operation of this system.

Security, privacy and reputation

The eBay system relies entirely on control of data: insisting on revelation of certain details but keeping others confidential. Attacks of various sorts have been mounted on this, to steal customer details or credit card numbers.[136] Publication of comments by buyers and sellers about each other is obviously capable of attracting libel actions, but so far eBay has successfully fought off attempts to make it secondarily liable for these.[137]

Misleading or fraudulent offers

Some limited control can be exercised on the content of offers to sell. In particular, eBay has rules against over-use of brand names in sellers' descriptions of what they are selling ('key word spamming').[138] However, attempts to make eBay act on the assumption that certain types of goods are inherently likely to be stolen or counterfeit have so far had little success.[139]

The bidding process

Various frauds have been uncovered, by which groups of sellers make fraudulent bids to drive up the price.[140] eBay's managers have themselves been accused of a similar fraud, under which some bidders were treated as increasing their bid even though they did not intend to do so; the sums involved in each instance are trivial, but a class action has been commenced on behalf of the considerable numbers of buyers affected.[141]

Sale

While European users of eBay are subject to tax,[142] eBay is otherwise little involved in the legal consequences of sale. Sellers of non-existent goods have sometimes been traced and prosecuted for fraud.[143] Attempts to blame eBay's managers in those circumstances have achieved little success.[144]

---

136 Eg, 'eBay provides backdoor for phishers', Register, 28 February 2005 (Web).
137 See especially *Grace v eBay, Inc* 120 Cal App 4th 984 (California Court of Appeal, 22 July 2004).
138 'Search manipulation and keyword spamming', eBay (Web).
139 See, eg, 'eBay faces Tiffany's Wrath', Motley Fool, 23 June 2004 (Web). See also Elfenbein, D, 'Do anti-ticket scalping laws make a difference online? Evidence from Internet sales of NFL tickets', SSRN, September 2004 (Web).
140 Eg, 'Eight fined in eBay auction scam', Register, 8 November 2004 (Web).
141 'EBay charged with shilling', Internet News, 23 February 2005 (Web).
142 'EBay users hit by sales tax', BBC News, 6 June 2003 (Web).
143 Eg, 'Boy's eBay con nets £45,000', BBC News, 12 October 2004 (Web).
144 Eg, *Gentry v eBay, Inc* 99 Cal App 4th 816 (California Court of Appeal, 26 June 2002) (Web). For discussion, see González, Á, 'eBay law: the legal implications of the C2C electronic commerce model', (2003) 19 CLSR 468.

Civil actions between buyer and seller certainly are possible. However, much of the special protection given to buyers by consumer law may be inapplicable. First, the seller may not be demonstrably in business. (No doubt, in appropriate cases a court would draw inferences from the volume of the seller's other dealings on eBay to establish whether the seller was in business.) Secondly, much consumer law is inapplicable to sales at auction, and while eBay's site denies that it runs auctions, it is not clear whether a court would agree. A live question is whether eBay-mediated sales are sales at auction within the meaning of the distance contracts legislation (above); the German Bundesgerichtshof has recently held that they are not, seemingly on the ground that an 'auction' requires a physical auction house and auctioneer.[145] The point has yet to be resolved in the UK and Ireland.

Policing the marketplace

As will be apparent, control of eBay and its users takes a number of different forms, not all of which are compatible with one another. The criminal law certainly applies, and has been used to great effect when the defendants turn out to be local. Civil law may be similarly useful in disputes between users, though eBay's ability to draft terms with which users will be taken to agree has allowed its managers to minimise their liability. And its carefully crafted reputation system, which makes it difficult to elicit consumer trust without an existing list of satisfied customers, continues to attract both praise and criticism.[146] The merits of this amalgam of controls are a matter of intense debate.[147]

FURTHER READING

Condon, W, 'Electronic assent to online contracts: Do courts consistently enforce clickwrap agreements?', (2004) 16 RULR 433.

Cordera, M, 'E-consumer protection: A comparative analysis of EU and US consumer protection on the Internet', (2001) 27 RCTLJ 231.

Donnelly, M and White, F, 'The Distance Selling Directives – A time for review', (2005) 56 NILQ 200.

Hillman, R and Rachlinski, J, 'Standard-form contracting in the electronic age', (2002) 77 NYULR 429.

Hörnle, J, 'Online Dispute Resolution in business to consumer e-commerce transactions', [2002] 2 JILT (Web).

---

145 See 'Germany's Federal Supreme Court grants a right to revocation regarding eBay-auctions', heise online, 3 November 2004 (Web); Spindler, G, 'Internet-auctions versus consumer protection: The case of the Distant Selling Directive', (2005) 6 German LJ 3 (Web). For an earlier German decision, see 'Contracting in the Internet: German contract law and Internet auctions', (2001) 2 German LJ 7 (Web).

146 For discussion, see Calkins, M, 'My reputation always had more fun than me: The failure of eBay's feedback model to effectively prevent online auction fraud', (2001) 7 RJOLT 4 (Web); Gillette, C, 'Reputation and intermediaries in electronic commerce', (2002) 62 LLR 1165.

147 Reich, E, 'Fair cop', [2004] NS (3 July) 26; Snyder, J, 'Online auction fraud: Are the auction houses doing all they should or could to stop online fraud?', (2000) 52 FCLJ 453 (Web).

Rabinovich-Einy, O, 'Going public: Diminishing privacy in dispute resolution in the Internet age', (2002) 7 VJOLT 4 (Web).

Reisch, L, 'Potentials, pitfalls, and policy implications of electronic consumption', (2003) 12 ICTL 93.

Reynolds, A, 'E-auctions: Who will protect the consumer?', (2002) 18 J Contract L 75.

Savirimuthu, J, 'Online contract formation: Taking technological infrastructure seriously', SSRN, May 2004 (Web).

Schiavetta, S, 'The relationship between e-ADR and Article 6 of the European Convention on Human Rights pursuant to the case law of the European Court of Human Rights', [2004] 1 JILT (Web).

St Oren, J, 'International jurisdiction over consumer contracts In e-Europe', (2003) 52 ICLQ 665.

Watnick, V, 'The electronic formation of contracts and the common law "mailbox rule" ', (2004) 56 Baylor LR 175.

GLOSSARY OF COMPUTING AND E-COMMERCE TERMS FOR LAWYERS

Italicised terms have their own definition.

Adware A *program* which displays an advertisement.

Algorithm A procedure or formula for carrying out a particular task.

Application A *program* which performs tasks for its users (as opposed to system software, which helps to maintain the computing system so that it can run applications as required).

Bandwidth Technically, the rate at which *data* can be sent down a particular channel; the more bandwidth available, the more data can be sent in a given time. Informally, the word is used to indicate the resources used by transferring data; so a message which should not have been sent might be described as 'a waste of bandwidth'.

Banner advertisement A graphic on a web page which serves as an advertisement; consumers who click on the graphic are redirected to the advertised site. Typically, these are short but broad images stretching across the user's screen without occupying very much of it.

Biometric identification A form of identification which relies on the physical characteristics of the person whose identity is in question: examples would be identification based on fingerprints, on appearance, on what their voice sounds like, or on their signature. This is to be contrasted with identification which relies on what the person knows, whether that is personal information (mother's unmarried name, for example) or some password or key.

Business to Business (B2B) Trade between business concerns. Contrast *B2C* and *C2C*.

Business to Consumer (B2C) Trade between business concerns and those not in business (that is, consumers). Contrast *B2B* and *C2C*.

Blog Short for 'web log'. Any regularly updated web site. Typically, the author of a blog (a 'blogger') is attempting to attract a regular audience who will revisit the blog periodically.

Cache A temporary store for data. Caches are much used by *Internet service providers*, for situations where many clients request the same file from elsewhere; rather than fetching it each time it is asked for, a copy is kept in the cache. Again, while surfing the web, most browsers retain a copy of pages visited, to save time and *bandwidth* if the user reverts to a page they have previously seen.

Certification Service Provider (CSP) An organisation which produces certificates as to the existence of some fact or state of affairs. A typical example is of organisations which certify the *public key* of named individuals: see *public key infrastructure*.

Chat room A site which enables multiple users to chat in real time (that is, as if they were face-to-face).

Click fraud Most internet advertising is 'pay-per-click', so that an advertisement for a given site is paid for at a fixed rate every time the advertisement is clicked on, redirecting the person who did so to the advertised site (see *banner advertisement*). 'Click fraud' is the name for a variety of frauds attempting to exploit this, either by generating large numbers of false clicks, or by threatening to do so for blackmail purposes.

Client A computer requesting something from another computer (the *server* or *host*).

Cloaking A general term for presenting a false appearance. For example, a site advertising product A may be 'cloaked' so that it will appear to a *search engine* to be advertising the rival product B, with the result that those searching for product B may find themselves diverted to the product A site.

Code Instructions for a computer. A discrete set of instructions is usually referred to as a *program*.

Compilation Conversion of a *program* from a high-level language to a low-level language. See *computer language*.

Computer language A grammar and syntax for writing *code*. Computer languages differ greatly in their complexity and their ease of comprehension to humans. At the lowest end, 'machine code' is simply a string of 0s and 1s. The high-level languages, while not much like human languages, are nonetheless relatively easy for programmers to understand. Programmers typically write in a high-level language; this *source code* is then converted into a lower level *object code* (the process is called *'compilation'*), which is then executed by the computer. The process of *compilation* involves a certain amount of simplification and compression. Accordingly, while it is certainly possible to reverse the process (*'decompilation'*), the high-level code which results may be very different from the original *source code*, though it will have the same effect. This has important implications for attempts to protect *code* through copyright law.

Consumer to Consumer (C2C)   Trade between parties, none of whom is in business. Contrast *B2B* and *B2C*.

Contextual advertising   Advertising, the content of which varies with the circumstances. For example, a site which has a number of advertisements to show to visitors may use data about the visitor's interests to decide which advertisement to show.

Cookie   Data sent by a *web server* to a *web browser*, which is then stored and may later be accessed by the same server. A distinction is often made between 'session cookies', which are merely used to identify a visitor as he or she explores a site, and 'persistent cookies', which are retained for a long period to recognise a visitor even if their last visit was some time ago.

Country-Code Top-Level Domain (ccTLD)   A *top-level domain* which suggests a nationality, such as .ie (suggesting an Irish site) or .uk (suggesting a site in the UK). Contrast *Generic Top-Level Domain (gTLD)*.

Cracker   An alternative word for a *hacker*.

Cryptography   Concealment of data by *encryption*.

Cyberspace   Alternative term for the *Internet*. The term is particularly associated with William Gibson's influential science fiction novel *Neuromancer* (1984).

Cybersquatting   Holding a *domain name* without any plausible justification. The term is used variously and vaguely, though always pejoratively. The core case would be that of someone who acquires a name which is nothing like their own, and which they have no intention of using, motivated either by malice against a more legitimate holder or by a plan to sell the name at a profit.

Data   Information in a form accessible to a computer. Sometimes the word is used to designate all such information. Computer professionals, however, tend to use it in a more specialised sense, under which *programs* are not regarded as *data* but rather as instructions for processing data. The line between programs and data (in the second sense), while useful enough to professionals, is often confusing to others. So, for example, a word-processed document is usually thought of as mere data, whereas (if the word-processing format is of any sophistication at all) it is clearly a program.

Data matching   Comparison of *data* with a view to identifying common themes; for example, comparing two sets of personal *data* to see if they relate to the same individual.

Data mining   Establishing facts or making predictions from a database, typically by identifying particularly significant data items or patterns in the *data*.

Decompilation   Conversion of a *program* from a low-level language to a higher level language. See *computer language*.

Decryption   The process of recovering data which has been subjected to *encryption*.

Deep link   A *hyperlink* which goes directly to a document deep within a *web site*, rather than to the site's *home page*. From a technical point of view, a deep link is much the same as any other link, though there is a greater risk that it will become obsolete (as where the target site is revised or re-arranged). From a commercial point of view, many web site owners prefer those who view their site to start at the *home page*, and they resent deep links accordingly.

Denial of Service (DoS) attack   An attack on a *web server*, preventing it from fulfilling its function. Typically, the attack consists of overwhelming the *web server* with bogus requests to see pages. Sometimes the attack comes from several machines acting in a co-ordinated fashion; this is called a distributed denial of service (DDoS) attack. Computers conducting DDoS attacks are very probably *zombies*.

Digital Rights Management (DRM)   Control of *data* files with a view to protecting intellectual property rights in them. A typical DRM system might recognise when a CD contains copyright material, and prevent unlawful copying accordingly. An example of *trusted computing*.

Digital signature   An alternative term for an *electronic signature*.

Domain name   The name of a computer attached to the Internet. These names are arranged in a hierarchical fashion: so www.ucc.ie denotes the machine called 'www' (actually, a *web server*) within the second-level domain 'ucc' (which belongs to University College Cork) within the top-level domain 'ie' (Ireland). Domain names are essentially a human convenience: actual communication at the electronic level involves replacing the domain name with the corresponding *IP number*, through the *domain name system*.

Domain Name System (DNS)   The system for matching *domain names* with *IP numbers*. The DNS is a distributed system: if a particular domain name is searched for in a particular registry, that registry will return the appropriate number if it holds that information, but otherwise may refer the request to another registry better able to give an authoritative answer. The network of DNS registries is held together by a root server, which authoritatively designates top-level domains and the registries which can authoritatively designate sub-domains within them. This root server is controlled by the *Internet Assigned Numbers Authority (IANA)*.

Domain slamming   A blanket term for certain unfair business practices by domain name registrars. A typical example is this: the registrar sends its customer an invoice; the customer assumes that this is for some rental or fee necessary for retaining the domain, and pays without question; in fact, the invoice relates to additional and unnecessary services, as would have been obvious had the customer read the small print.

Download   To receive a *program* or *data* from another's computer. Contrast *upload*.

Electronic signature   Any electronic technique for authenticating electronic documents or identifying their author. The more secure methods available today involve the use of *encryption*, though methods involving the use of *biometric identification* are under development. The outer edges of the concept are vague. Some writers are happy to include any electronic indication of authorship (even a simple typed name at the end of an e-mail), others exclude all but the more secure methods. Also known as a *digital signature*.

Encryption   The process of making *data* secret by using a specified procedure (an 'encryption *algorithm*') to hide its meaning. *Data* encrypted in this way can usually only be made intelligible by someone who knows the key, which is a number used as part of the encryption and *decryption* processes. This key may be a *private key* or a *public key*.

Extensible Mark-up Language (XML)   See *XML*.

Framing   A technique for laying out web pages, in which two or more pages appear as distinct frames (or panes) within the same browser window.

Generic Top-Level Domain (gTLD)   A *top-level domain* which hints at a certain generic type of site, such as .com (suggesting a commercial site) or .org (suggesting a site belonging to a not-for-profit organisation). Contrast *Country-Code Top-Level Domain (ccTLD)*.

Hacker   A person who breaks into computer systems. Originally, the term merely denoted an expert in computing, and it only slowly came to denote those who put that expertise to bad uses. Those who prefer the original meaning usually refer to one who attacks others' computing systems as a *cracker*.

Hoax virus   A deception by which computer users are tricked into damaging their own systems, in the false belief that they are removing or disabling a *virus*.

Home page   The introductory page of a *web site*. For various reasons, the owner of a site may prefer that those visiting the site should come to this page, rather than being led immediately to another page within the site by a *deep link*.

Host   A computer which answers a request from, or provides a service to, another computer (the *client*). A computer the main function of which is to act as a host is called a *server*, and in practice the terms are often interchangeable.

Hyperlink   A link or means of access from one online document to another. Hyperlinks are an essential and popular feature of the *world wide web*, where they are (typically but not inevitably) presented to the user as bright blue underlined text, and activated by pointing at the text and clicking once.

Hypertext Mark-up Language (HTML)   The *computer language* for writing web pages. A typical page of HTML consists of text to appear on a web page, surrounded by angle bracket tags controlling its appearance; so 'Look at **this**!' is coded as 'Look at <B>this</B>!'. The original version of HTML, published in 1989, was relatively simple, stressing purely logical aspects of mark-up. So, for example, the tag <H1> denoted merely 'top-level heading', leaving it to each model of *web browser* to define how that would look, and encouraging competition in modes of expression. Later coders demanded more control over appearance, and so later versions of HTML are more elaborate, allowing greater control of details and the ability to incorporate diverse kinds of *data*. Further pressures for diversity have led to the development of *XML (eXtensible Mark-up Language)*, which allows individuals or groups to develop their own set of HTML-like tags for specialist use.

Information and Communications Technology (ICT)   Technology for processing, storing and communicating *data*. Logically this expression should include all means for doing this (including paper, pens and carrier pigeons), but in practice the term is reserved for electronic means such as computers and telecommunications.

Inline image   An image included as part of a web page, rather than in its own window.

Internet   A world-wide network of computers. Any computer which can itself communicate using the *Internet Protocol*, and is linked to others which do the same, can be said to be part of the Internet. Sometimes called simply 'the net'.

Internet Assigned Numbers Authority (IANA)   A body which performs various clerical and housekeeping functions involved in running the *Internet*, the most important of which is maintaining the DNS root, that is, the authoritative list of *top-level domains*. At the time of writing, IANA operates under the control of the *Internet Corporation for Assigned Names and Numbers (ICANN)*.

Internet Corporation for Assigned Names and Numbers (ICANN)   A body with certain important functions in governing the Internet, as described in the text. These include control of the *Internet Assigned Numbers Authority (IANA)* and defining the *Uniform Dispute Resolution Policy (UDRP)*.

Internet Protocol (IP)   An internationally recognised *protocol* enabling computers to communicate with one another as part of a wide area network. The wide use of this protocol gives rise to the *Internet*.

Internet Service Provider (ISP)   A person or organisation which provides others with access to the *Internet*. A commercial ISP may also supply other related services for its clients, such as providing them with e-mail accounts or access to discussion forums.

IP Number   The numerical code designating each computer attached to the Internet. Most connected machines have their own code permanently assigned to them, though where there is a shortage of address space, it is possible to assign a number temporarily ('dynamically'). Most Internet traffic currently runs under IPv4, which allows for addresses running from 0:0:0:0 to 255:255:255:255. The need for more address space and for certain technical improvements is forcing a gradual migration to IPv6, which allows for many more numbers. IP numbers and *domain names* are matched to one another through the *domain name system (DNS)*.

Keying Programming a computer to react to specific keywords. For example, a *search engine* may be programmed to react to a search enquiry for 'pizza' by displaying an advertisement from a particular pizza supplier, who has paid for this service.

Key-logging Recording the keys typed on a computer (with or without the operator's knowledge).

Link farm See *link spamming*.

Link spamming Many *search engines* give more prominence to sites to which many other sites have linked, on the theory that they must be more popular or useful. Some advertisers exploit this by the creation of multiple links to their clients' sites, a practice known (pejoratively) as 'link spamming'. A site which exists primarily to establish links of this sort is called a *link farm*.

Logic bomb A destructive *program* which is triggered by the occurrence of a specific event.

Malware A *program* designed to cause harm, such as a *virus*.

Metadata *Data* which describes other *data*. For example, Word document files typically include *data* specifying how long it took to compose them, and indicating revisions or earlier versions of the document. This *data* typically does not appear on screen or in a printed version unless the computer is specifically instructed to do so. Accordingly, from the perspective of relatively unsophisticated users, the metadata is secret.

Metasite A *web site* the content of which consists largely of references to material held at other sites, or links to such material. A *search engine* is a typical example.

Metatag An *HTML* tag which gives information about the entire document in which it is contained. For example, the metatag 'description' typically includes a short sentence summarising the page. The system of metatags is essential for the operation of *search engines*.

Moderated Subjected to prior editorial control. For example, a discussion forum may be set up so that all contributions to the discussion are vetted by an editor (or 'moderator') before other participants can see them. Contrast *unmoderated*.

Mousetrapping A blanket term for techniques to make it difficult to leave a web page. Methods include the creation of multiple *pop-ups* to distract the user, or reprogramming the browser so that the buttons normally used to leave have a quite different effect.

Netiquette Proper behaviour while on the *Internet*.

Object code A *program* in the form in which the computer will run it, as opposed to the *source code* in which it was written by the programmer. See *computer language*.

Online Dispute Resolution (ODR) Any method of resolving disputes principally using the *Internet*; such as arbitration or mediation where the parties communicate solely by e-mail.

Operating system A *program* which performs the most basic functions of a computer, and thus allows it to run other *programs*. An operating system must at the very least recognise input, send output to its appropriate destination, keep track of files and directories on the hard disk, and control peripheral devices such as disk drives and printers. It must also provide security, and prevent conflict between different *programs* and different authorised users. Common operating systems (each of which exists in various versions) are Unix, Linux, Windows, Windows NT, and the Mac OS.

Packet sniffing Intercepting *data* while it is in transit between computers, to search it for items of interest. The data is at that point divided into small chunks or 'packets', hence the name.

Peer to Peer (P2P) network A network which has no central server, individual members communicating directly with other members. The absence of a central server makes the network difficult for others to control.

Phishing   Tricking a victim out of important *data*, such as passwords or bank account details. The con artist typically poses as a bank employee conducting an identity check via e-mail, or establishes an apparently respectable *web site* requiring such details.

Pop-under   A *pop-up* which is launched behind the currently active window.

Pop-up   An additional browser window, typically one opening without any request from the person browsing.

Private key   A key for *decryption* which is kept secret. Under a system of *encryption* based solely on a private key, messages are encrypted using the key, and then can only be decrypted by those who possess the same key. Contrast *public key.*

Program   A set of instructions for a computer. Also referred to as 'software', to distinguish it from the computer which performs the instructions (the 'hardware') and the various human beings involved (the 'wetware').

Protocol   A set of rules for the transmission of *data* between computers. Use of similar protocols by sender and recipient is a precondition of effective communication. (The word 'language' would be more obvious, but computing specialists use *computer language* to mean the way that humans talk to computers, rather than the way computers talk to one another.)

Public key   A key for *decryption* which is not kept secret. Under a public key *encryption* system, two keys are produced, one public and one private. The two keys are related mathematically, so that a message encrypted using the public key can only be decrypted using the private key, and vice versa. Therefore the owner of the keys may encrypt messages using their private key: these messages can only be decrypted using the public key, thus providing evidence of their authenticity. Further, anyone may send a reply encrypted using the public key: this may only be decrypted using the private key, thus providing a measure of security.

Public Key Infrastructure (PKI)   The procedures of *encryption* by *public key* in practice create the need for various intermediaries; these intermediaries, their businesses, and the laws and procedures under which they work, are collectively referred to as *public key infrastructure.* Tasks performed include supplying the software for *encryption* and *decryption,* and publicly certifying the *public keys* of individuals.

Radio Frequency IDentification (RFID)   A technology by which a tiny chip can identify the object it is attached to. The chip is a transponder: it is normally silent, but it responds to radio transmission on a particular frequency. This (relatively new) technology is mainly used in stock control, but has considerable potential for identifying and locating other items, and people.

Random Access Memory (RAM)   The fastest type of memory available to any particular computer; it is several orders of magnitude faster than writing to a disk. From the computer user's point of view, RAM can be thought of as a temporary pad on which the computer can record interim computations or *data*. The amount of RAM available to a particular computer is one of the major factors determining its speed of performance.

Reverse domain name hijacking   Wrongly attempting to deprive another of a *domain name*, by pursuing a bogus complaint against them through a dispute resolution procedure or through the courts.

Script kiddy   A junior or inexperienced *hacker*; an individual who uses, or attempts to use, *code* without any adequate understanding of its function.

Search engine   A *program* which allows search of a database. In *Internet* contexts, this usually refers to an online engine which searches an index of *web sites* and their contents.

Server   A computer which provides services to other computers, for example by giving them copies of requested files, or access to a printer.

Source code   A *program* as originally written by the programmer, in a high-level language. It is then converted into *object code* in a lower level language before it is executed. See *computer language.*

Spam   Unrequested e-mail, typically sent in bulk.

Spider   A *program* which automatically surfs the web. Typically, such programs are collecting *data* on web links, perhaps so that they can be added to the database of an online *search engine*.

Sponsored Domain   A *top-level domain* which is restricted to a relatively small and cohesive group. For example, *domain names* within .aero can only be held by members of the air transport industry. Compare *unsponsored domain*.

Spoofing   Assuming a false identity.

Spyware   A *program* which spies on the computer on which it is running: for example, by copying files, monitoring the user's activities, or recording which keys are pressed (*'keylogging'*).

Standard   A definition or specification of a particular technology, which has been widely published to allow others to copy it, or at least to conform to it. A standard for a particular piece of hardware might specify what inputs it would require and what outputs can be expected; this allows others to incorporate into their own machines, or to design replacements to achieve the same result. Sometimes also called an 'open standard', to stress the distinction between it and a 'proprietary technology', the specifications of which may be deliberately concealed by its creators.

Technologically neutral   (of a legal rule or definition) Avoiding distinctions based on particular technologies. For example, general legal rules on gambling may be technologically neutral, but would cease to be so if they singled out *Internet* gambling for special treatment. Technological neutrality is generally seen as desirable, both in order to avoid awkward borderline situations, and to lessen the risk that the law might discourage new and innovative technologies.

Thumbnail   A small, low-resolution copy of an image.

Top-Level Domain (TLD)   The highest level within the *domain name system*; for example ucc.ie is within the TLD .ie (=Ireland). TLDs are usually divided into *generic TLDs (gTLDs)* and *country-code TLDs (ccTLDs)*, though the proposed new TLDs .eu and .asia threaten the neatness of this distinction.

Traffic data   *Metadata* relating to the transmission of communications. So traffic *data* relating to browsing a particular page on the web would include the location of the browser and the address of the page browsed, as well as the time at which this occurred. The precise significance of the term varies, but it would almost always be understood to exclude the *data* actually transmitted (in the example, the content of the web page itself).

Trojan horse or **Trojan**   An apparently benevolent, but actually malevolent, *program*. Trojans are typically spread by deliberate and deceptive human action, and are thus distinguished from *viruses* which typically propagate themselves.

Trusted computing   Computing which adheres to (human) laws: for example, processing of music files in such a way that copyright music is identified, and illegal use or copying prevented.

Typosquatting   A variant of *cybersquatting*, by acquiring a *domain name* which is readily typed by accident by those trying to get to a famous domain. The typosquatter may be relying on users' accidentally hitting the wrong keys (for example, mictosoft.com, yahooo.com) or not being able to spell the domain they really want (for example, hewlitpackard.com, googel.com).

Uniform Dispute Resolution Policy (UDRP)   A set of rules for resolving disputes over *domain names*, adopted for the .com, .org and .net domains and many national domains. More fully, the basic principles are set out in the Uniform Domain Name Dispute Resolution Policy, and the detailed rules to be followed are in the associated Rules for Uniform Domain Name Dispute Resolution Policy.

Uniform Resource Locator (URL)   A string of characters defining the place of a particular item of data or other resource on the *world wide web*.

Unmoderated   Not subject to prior editorial control. For example, in an unmoderated discussion forum, all postings are automatically and immediately available to other participants. Contrast *moderated*.

Upload   To transfer a *program* or *data* to anothers computer. Contrast *download*.

Unsponsored domain   A *top-level domain* which is open to a wide variety of people. For example, anyone is entitled to register a name in .com. Some domains are restricted, but not to such a degree as to make them sponsored; for example, only businesses may register names within .biz, but that is such a broad criterion that .biz is still regarded as unsponsored. Contrast *sponsored domain*.

Virus   A *program* added to a computer without the knowledge of its user. Viruses are typically malevolent in intention (they are *malware*), and typically they take steps to replicate themselves and spread to other systems. *Worm* is usually just a synonym for *virus*, though used more precisely *worm* suggests a file which stands alone, whereas *virus* suggests a file which attaches itself to other files.

Voice over IP (VoIP)   Use of the *Internet* to send voice communications, whether one-way or two-way. In non-technical contexts, 'Internet telephony' is synonymous.

Web browser   A *program* used for viewing the *world wide web*. Common web browsers are Internet Explorer, Netscape, Firefox and Opera.

Web bug   An insignificant element of a web page, employed to keep track of visitors to the page.

Web master   The owner or controller of a *web site*.

Web server   A *server* that provides information to those who request it via the *world wide web*.

Web site   A distinct location on the *world wide web*. A site may consist of a single page, or a collection of pages forming a coherent entity.

White hat hacker   A *hacker* who seeks out vulnerabilities in computer systems with a view to warning their users about them.

Wi-fi   Short for 'wireless fidelity'. A set of *standards* for *Internet* communication using radio frequencies rather than wires.

World wide web   A network of computers using a particular *protocol* for communication over the *Internet*. Publicly introduced in 1991, it quickly proved very popular, not least because of the ease with which it could integrate text, graphics and other *data* into a format easily understandable by the recipients.

Worm   See *virus*.

XML (eXtensible Mark-up Language)   A way of defining customised versions of *HTML*, to write web pages for specialised communities.

Zombie   A computer which follows orders received from another computer, usually without the knowledge of its user. Illegally turning other computers into zombies is a common tactic of *hackers*, partly to cover their traces, and partly to increase the computing power at their disposal.

INDEX